GALLANTRY
AND
DISCIPLINE

The Duke of Wellington has desired Colonel Ponsonby to express to the Regiment his approbation of their appearance this day, His Grace is happy at having again under his Orders a Regiment which was distinguished for its gallantry and discipline, he has no doubt if occasion offer they will continue to deserve his good approbation as on the former and he hopes every Man will feel a pride in endeavouring to support the credit of the Regiment in the latter.

Regimental Orders, 20 April 1815

GALLANTRY AND DISCIPLINE

The 12th Light Dragoons
at War with Wellington

Andrew Bamford

Foreword by
HRH The Duke of York

Frontline Books
London

Gallantry and Discipline
This edition published in 2014 by Frontline Books,
an imprint of Pen & Sword Books Ltd,
47 Church Street, Barnsley, S. Yorkshire, S70 2AS
www.frontline-books.com

ISBN: 978-1-84832-743-6

For more information on our books, please visit
www.frontline-books.com, email info@frontline-books.com
or write to us at the above address.

Printed and bound by CPI Group (UK) Ltd, Croydon CR0 4YY

Typeset in 10.5/14.6 pt Adobe Caslon Pro

Contents

In gratitude for the support and assistance provided by the
Regiment, Regimental Trustees and Regimental Museum,
this work is dedicated to all members, serving and retired, of the
9th/12th Royal Lancers (Prince of Wales's).

Plates

Colour plates

Black and white plates

Maps and Charts

Foreword

by HRH Prince Andrew, Duke of York

As the 9th/12th Royal Lancers look toward amalgamation in 2015 I welcome this book which keeps alive our interest in earlier campaigns.

For the 12th Light Dragoons (as they were then) the Peninsula and Waterloo represent one of the earliest of many highpoints in their long and illustrious service and it rightly deserves our attention.

Leadership, teamwork and training are the key to success in this story and I know from my own service the importance of all three in creating an effective fighting force.

Amalgamation will bring change for the 9th/12th Lancers, but this is not a new challenge, in many ways the challenges will be similar to those faced by the 12th Light Dragoons shortly after these campaigns as they converted to the lance.

This book, as well as providing a wealth of detail about an illustrious period of a soon-to-be shared history, reminds us of the attributes of soldiering that will, I am sure, continue to endure and on which a tradition of loyal and distinguished service is founded.

Introduction

IN JUNE 1814, WITH THE LONG WARS against Revolutionary and Napoleonic France at last seemingly at a successful conclusion following Napoleon's first abdication and consequent exile to Elba, General Sir James Steuart looked forward to the return of peace and the resulting opportunity to restore to good order the regiment of which he was colonel. After three years of distinguished service in the Peninsular War, the 12th, or Prince of Wales's, Regiment of Light Dragoons was in need of a spell of home service to refill and remount its ranks. Steuart was only too aware, having held the colonelcy throughout the past two decades of conflict, that this service under Wellington was but the most recent of a series of deployments stretching back into the 1790s, and he therefore sought to obtain the aid of the Quartermaster General at Horse Guards, Major General James Willoughby Gordon, to make sure that the 12th got the respite that they had earned:

> Sir, as the British troops now in France may reasonably be expected soon to be ordered home, I take the liberty, as Colonel of the Prince of Wales's Regiment of Light Dragoons, earnestly to solicit you in their favour, that they may on their arrival be assembled together in one quarter in order to make arrangements for the establishment of uniformity, discipline, and field movements, under the command of Lt. Col. Ponsonby who has not yet had an opportunity of seeing the Regiment together, and it being also my wish to spend some part of next spring with my Regiment, to observe their system and progress. I know that when last in England the Regiment was particularly difficult in field movements therefore if Dorchester could be allotted as their Quarter it would be particularly agreeable to me. I beg to remind you that the 12th Lt. Dragoons have been little at home since the year 1793 having served in Italy, Corsica, three times in Portugal,

once in Egypt, in Spain, in Holland, and in France. During which period they have also taken their turn of Ireland.[1]

The letter tells us a lot about both the man who wrote it and the regiment at whose nominal head he stood. Although there had once been a time when a regimental colonel had been directly responsible to the monarch for the regiment that bore his name, and which he had likely raised and led in person, by the time of the Napoleonic Wars a colonelcy was largely a sinecure; a post that promised prestige and the chance of modest enrichment, to be awarded to a senior officer whose actual rank was very rarely below that of major general. Steuart, indeed, was a full general, and had been since 1803. For the most part, general officers appointed to regimental colonelcies troubled themselves little with the regiments bestowed upon them, unless perhaps to intervene when there was an opportunity to bestow a vacant commission upon someone who had done some useful service, or whose family might subsequently do one in return. Even the rump of the financial element, concerned largely with the annual supply of clothing and accoutrements – for which a lump-sum allowance was still provided by Horse Guards – and the purchase of horses, could largely be left to the person of the regimental agent. Steuart, though, was different. In his seventieth year when he penned his letter to Gordon, and a serving officer since the Seven Years War, Sir James came from an age when a regimental colonelcy had been a duty rather than a perk, and he retained that outlook unchanged into the new century.

That he troubled to intervene with the Quartermaster General, that he planned to personally observe and appraise the performance of his regiment, and that he took such an interest in matters of 'uniformity, discipline, and field movements' that truly fell within the remit of the regiment's commanding officer – at that time Lieutenant Colonel the Honourable Frederick Cavendish Ponsonby – were all symptoms of a dedication to his duty as he saw it. The results of this dedication served, at times, to exasperate both the officers of the regiment and the staff at Horse Guards alike, but Steuart's single-minded pursuit of regimental excellence, and the stream of correspondence that it generated, give us a wonderful insight into the internal workings of a cavalry regiment at war. In conjunction with the official reports, records, and returns now in the National Archives, and the private letters and memoirs of some of the regiment's officers, they allow the story to be told not just of great deeds on the battlefield, but of the forgotten labour behind the scenes, the recruits and remounts, drills and discipline, without which the 12th Light Dragoons would never have seen the battlefields of the Peninsula, let alone the final epic clash at Waterloo that – unknown to Steuart as he relished the return of peace – was only a year around the corner.

That I came to be in a position to tell this story arose from a series of happy coincidences, beginning when I moved to Derby in 2008 in consequence of my wife Lucy being appointed Keeper of Art for the city's Museums Service. Thanks to a twentieth-century decision to assign a regional home to each of the British Army's remaining cavalry regiments, Derby's Central Museum also plays host to the Regimental Museum of what was at the time of writing the local cavalry regiment for the East Midlands, the 9th/12th Royal Lancers. Through Lucy I became acquainted with the museum's then curator, Mike Galer, and I subsequently became one of its volunteer staff spending half a day a week answering enquiries – anything from the provenance of a nineteenth-century sword, to what someone's grandfather might have got up to during the First World War – whilst spending the rest of my time working to complete a doctoral thesis on the British Army's regimental system during the Napoleonic Wars. Within that thesis, now published by the University of Oklahoma Press under the title *Sickness, Suffering, and the Sword*,[2] I put forward a series of broad ideas concerning the advantages and disadvantages inherent in the internal organization of the British Army in the wars against Napoleonic France, but at the same time I was acutely aware that the sheer scope of that project prevented my focusing on the experiences of a single unit. Thus, the concept had already begun to form in my mind of testing my ideas by making just such a study of a single regiment during the course of the twelve years between the Peace of Amiens and the Battle of Waterloo, and so as my volunteering introduced me to the substantial body of archival material held by the museum it made increasing sense that the regiment on which I should focus ought to be the 12th Light Dragoons.

Of course, since the Derby museum is for the combined 9th/12th Royal Lancers – the ancestor regiments having both converted to the lance during the years immediately after Waterloo, and amalgamated in 1960 – this does rather beg the question of why study the one and not the other. A number of reasons, however, dictated the choice of the 12th. For one thing, although I deliberately wanted to avoid a focus on a regiment considered as a particularly famous or elite unit, the story of the unfortunate 9th Light Dragoons during the Napoleonic era is one composed almost entirely of hard service and bad luck that would have taken any study altogether too far in the opposite direction. In many ways their story demonstrates what could happen if things did not go well for a cavalry regiment, but it was not the typical experience that I was looking for.

Nor, alas, was it a particularly well-documented story, whereas the museum's archival holdings for the 12th during the Napoleonic era proved far more substantial. In particular, I was delighted to find the hefty leather-bound tome whose contents underpin much of this work. Bearing a weighty plaque commemorating its gift to the 12th Lancers in 1925 by their then Colonel, Field Marshal Sir William Birdwood, it contains Sir James Steuart's regimental correspondence as Colonel of the 12th Light Dragoons between the years 1806 and 1815. Another similar volume – a note on the inside cover telling the remarkable tale of its salvage from an Irish junk shop by a Victorian subaltern – contains Steuart's standing orders for the regiment. Further ledgers contain details of orders received, regimental postings, and details of rank and file service. These latter documents, alas, all begin part-way through the period of this study, so that there are omissions for much of the regiment's earlier service. However, it is possible to supplement the records held by the regiment with those in The National Archives at Kew. Monthly returns and reports from the twice-yearly regimental inspections provide essential details to this story, and enable us to see the regiment as it was viewed from outside as well as from within. Lastly, the human side of the story has not been forgotten, and the memoirs of Lieutenant William Hay and the letters of Lieutenant John Vandeleur and of Lieutenant Colonel Ponsonby shed considerable light on how things appeared to the men on the spot at the time. I am pleased to say that, as an offshoot of this project, a revised and expanded version of Vandeleur's letters, with historical commentary and the addition of various other relevant primary documents, is shortly to be published by Frontline Books under the title *With Wellington's Outposts*.

As is reflected by the fact that some original documents that might ideally have been included here will instead be reproduced as part of *With Wellington's Outposts*, a certain selectiveness has necessarily been enforced by the need to get this work down to a manageable length. Some elements of doctrine on the one hand, and equine care on the other, have deliberately been summarized as I am aware of forthcoming books by David Blackmore and Paul L. Dawson respectively that will address these subjects in more detail. I have also had to be selective with the number of maps included in this work, concentrating on those that are most essential to support the narrative. In particular, since the 12th were engaged on a far flank at both Salamanca and Vitoria, I have not included maps of those battlefields. Readers desirous of additional cartographical references are directed to the Napoleon Series Map Archives at http://www. napoleon-series.org/military/c_maps.html.

It is also necessary to add a few brief notes on terminology and spellings. Original spellings and punctuation have been retained in quoted matter, without [*sic*] or any similar comment. For commonality's sake, I have also employed the archaic spelling of serjeant throughout this narrative, since this is used almost without exception in all primary sources quoted. It should also be explained that the word 'trooper' is used as synonymous with rank and file, as distinct from its modern usage as the lowest military rank in a mounted unit. In the era covered by this book, the rank of private was used by infantry and cavalry alike, but trooper as a colloquial expression for a cavalryman dates back at least to the eighteenth century.[3] Lastly, unless in a direct quote, I have used modern spellings for all place names with the exception of those such as Lisbon and Brussels where a British corruption of the local name is in widespread use.

Finally, it is my pleasant duty to thank those who have aided in the completion of this project. As well as Mike Galer at the regimental museum I have had the consistent support of the regimental trustees and home head-quarters, and must in particular thank Richard Charrington, Christopher Glynn-Jones, Martyn Pocock and Philip Watson. My wife Lucy has again cooperated with David Beckford to produce the maps and graphs for this title. Lucy, along with my father, Mick Bamford, has also helped proof-read the manuscript: for this I am extremely grateful, although the responsibility for any mistakes remains mine. Michael Leventhal and Stephen Chumbley at Frontline Books and freelance editor Donald Sommerville have been consistently helpful and supportive, as have Adrian Philpott and Lisa Stanhope of the 12th Light Dragoons re-enactment group. In addition, I must also name the following who have offered their help, advice, and encouragement during the course of the project: José Luis Arcon, David Blackmore, Dave Brown, Danielle Coombs, Paul L. Dawson, Carole Divall, Gareth Glover, Raul Gomez, Alexandre Heroy, Oscar Lopez, Ron McGuigan, Bryan McMillan, Frank McReynolds, Rafael Pardo, Ian Robertson, John Rumsby, Steven H. Smith, Richard Tailby, Dominique Timmermans and Rob Yuill. Many of the above are contributors to the Napoleon Series discussion forum, which remains the centre of an excellent web of knowledge on this era. Last of all, I must thank the Colonel-in-Chief of the 9th/12th Royal Lancers, HRH the Duke of York, for furnishing this work with a Foreword on behalf of the regiment.

Chapter I

The Colonel and his Regiment

THE REGIMENT THAT WOULD ULTIMATELY become the 12th Light Dragoons began life almost a hundred years before the era that forms the subject of this book. In July 1715, with the recent succession of George I threatened by a Jacobite uprising, Brigadier Phineas Bowles, a veteran of Marlborough's campaigns, was given a commission to raise a new regiment of dragoons to help put down the rebellion. The rising had been crushed before Bowles's Dragoons could take to the field, and escorting prisoners from Preston to London would turn out to be the closest that the regiment would come to active service for over three-quarters of a century.[1] Whilst the great wars of the eighteenth century spread across the globe, and other units won renown on the battlefields of three continents, the 12th Dragoons – as they officially became in 1751 when the British Army numbered its cavalry regiments – remained on garrison duty in Ireland. Initially deployed in 1718, the regiment stayed there until 1793, a total of no less than seventy-five years. Throughout this time, other regiments saw service in the war of the Austrian Succession, the 'Forty-Five' Rebellion, the Seven Years War and the various struggles in North America, whilst the 12th remained in garrison, frequently cut back to not much more than cadre strength. Duties were minimal, and the officers in particular spent the bulk of their time on non-military business. In contrast to Steuart's papers, an earlier letter book also held by the regimental museum – the correspondence of Lieutenant Colonels William Burton and William Pitt, successive commanding officers between 1767 and 1772 – is almost entirely filled with civil and political affairs. Judging by this correspondence, Burton's main concerns for much of 1768 were first the appointment of a curate to the living of Stackallen, which he hoped to secure for a clergyman connected to his family, and then the succession of the post of Prothonotary of the City of Londonderry, concerning which he had been repeatedly petitioned to exert his influence with the Lord Lieutenant, Lieutenant General Lord Townshend.[2]

Notwithstanding this apparent neglect of military duties, however, it was also at Burton's instigation that the 12th was converted, also in 1768, into a regiment of light dragoons. In conjunction with this change came the adoption of the connection with the Prince of Wales, bringing with it the three-feathered badge and the 'Ich Dien' motto which have been retained by the regiment and its successors. Burton – as his correspondence with Townshend reveals – was an astute player of the political patronage game, as was the regiment's then colonel, General Benjamin Carpenter, and obtaining a royal distinction for their regiment was an undoubted coup in this regard. In practical terms, however, it would be some years before the change of designation to light cavalry made any real difference to the regiment, although it did see them exchange cocked hats for a succession of helmet designs, and, in 1784, swap their red jackets for the dark blue that would distinguish British light cavalry throughout the Napoleonic era and beyond. This change also saw the regiment's black facings changed for yellow, so as to stand out more readily on the new jackets; this facing colour would be retained throughout the regiment's Napoleonic service.

Unsurprisingly, the military efficiency of the cavalry regiments stationed in Ireland – and there were plenty of them, for the savings obtained in posting a unit there during peacetime were considerable – was not good. Trouble was also set up for the future by the fact that the regiments perforce recruited their strength almost entirely from Irishmen, which would ultimately cause difficulties during the 1798 Rebellion and eventually lead to the disbandment of the 5th Dragoons amidst accusations of disloyalty. The 12th escaped this ignominy, but the fact that a 1767 inspection found 150 Irishmen out of an all-ranks strength of 153 shows both how shrunken the regiments on the Irish establishment had become, and how focused their recruiting base in terms of both officers and men.[3] One of the young Irish-born officers towards the end of this period was a certain Lieutenant the Honourable Arthur Wesley, who spent eighteen months on the strength of the 12th between June 1789 and January 1791 as he leapfrogged his way up the promotion ladder. The future Duke of Wellington spent little time on regimental duties, however, serving as an aide to the Lord Lieutenant and devoting much of his remaining attention to Irish politics.[4]

It was perhaps a good thing for young Arthur that he left the regiment shortly before Sir James Steuart obtained the colonelcy, for Steuart had marked views on officers who purchased their way from regiment to regiment, and who spent time away from their military duties. Steuart was appointed to the 12th on 9 November 1791, in succession to the late Lieutenant General the Hon.

George Lane Parker, and the appointment would prove a timely one for it came only a little over a year prior to Britain's entry into the war against Revolutionary France. Unlike the previous conflicts of the eighteenth century, this new war would finally pull the 12th Light Dragoons out of their Irish rustication and thrust them into the heat of battle for the first time. The change would require a wholesale reform of the regiment, but in Steuart they had found just the man to oversee it. Shaking the 12th out of its Irish stagnation, Steuart swiftly issued a series of detailed Standing Orders which, with minor modifications, remained in force throughout his colonelcy and which were expressly intended to establish the 'Fixed Rules and Directions for the Conduct of every Individual' that Steuart deemed 'necessary and essential, for the good Order and Discipline of the Regiment'.[5]

Steuart was born in August 1744, son and heir of Sir James Steuart, a Scots baronet who had trained in law.[6] His father was the son of Sir James Steuart, one-time Solicitor General of Scotland, and he in turn the son of Sir James Steuart, a former Lord Advocate for whom the baronetcy of Goodtrees had been created. Evidently, originality in Christian names was not a family trait. Later, the Goodtrees baronetcy would merge with the older Steuart baronetcy of Coltness, whilst in 1776 the family also inherited the estate of Westfield from the extinct line of the Denham baronets, requiring, in theory at least, that the surname be given as Steuart-Denham, or, confusingly, as Steuart in Scotland but Denham in England. The third Goodtrees baronet, father of the future colonel of the 12th, was possessed of strong Jacobite sympathies, which suddenly brought him to the forefront of events a year after the birth of his son, when the exiled Stuart dynasty made its last and most dramatic play for the British crown. Having already had contact with the Jacobite court-in-exile, Steuart senior was quick to pay homage to Prince Charles Edward Stuart upon the Young Pretender establishing himself at Holyrood House in September 1745, but did not take an active role in the rebellion and thus escaped the worst of the immediate crackdown that followed Charles's disastrous defeat at Culloden. Nevertheless, his known sympathies and attendance at the rebel court were enough to mark him as an active Jacobite, and he accordingly betook himself to the safety of a continental exile where he remained for the next quarter of a century. The infant James was initially left with relatives in Scotland, but later joined his parents on the continent and was educated there, with a focus on the military arts, first at Angoulême and then, after the outbreak of the Seven Years War forced the family to relocate to Germany, at the University of Tübingen which he attended between 1757 and 1761.

Steuart senior was already attempting to obtain a formal reconciliation with the British establishment – something that he would eventually achieve in 1771, although he had been able to return to Scotland some years prior to that – and certainly the one-time sympathies of the father did not prevent the son obtaining King George's commission, without purchase, as a cornet in the 1st Royal Dragoons effective as of 17 March 1761. As a teenage subaltern, Steuart saw service in the closing Seven Years War campaigns of Ferdinand of Brunswick's allied army in western Germany before obtaining, in January 1763, a captaincy in the 105th Regiment of Foot, the Queen's Royal Highlanders. This was a short-lived corps, raised for the war and soon to be disbanded, and thus the young Steuart spent the years from 1764 to 1766 on half-pay, making use of the freedom thereby obtained to travel extensively on the continent and complete his military education by observing the armies – and particularly the cavalry – of the European powers. Notwithstanding his accepting a posting to a marching regiment as a price worth paying for a captaincy, Steuart was already a died-in-the-wool cavalry soldier, and would remain so for the rest of his military career.

Resuming that career in June 1766 on the completion of his travels, Steuart purchased a captaincy in the 5th Dragoons, and then in 1772 moved across to the 13th Dragoons in which he purchased his majority. Both of these regiments were, like the 12th, on the Irish Establishment, and for a large part of his time with the 5th Steuart in fact served as ADC to Lord Townshend. After three years with the 13th, Steuart was transferred to the 1st Irish Horse – later retitled the 4th Dragoon Guards – but then in the following year returned to the 13th Light Dragoons as commanding officer with the rank of lieutenant colonel. Although he was obliged to purchase this step in his promotion, Steuart had been expressly recommended for the post, which required him to oversee the transformation of the newly retitled regiment into the light cavalry role. Steuart remained as lieutenant colonel in command of the 13th for the next fifteen years, although he obtained a brevet promotion to full colonel in 1782. In 1788, in response to a growing perception that the standards of the cavalry regiments stationed in Ireland were not what they ought be, Steuart was tasked with forming 'an improved system of interior discipline, economy, and field move-ments',[7] to which end he was given command of a large detachment totalling sixteen troops of horse – equivalent in size to a brigade command – and in the resulting manoeuvres was able to establish many of the systems subsequently enshrined in the manuals and drill books of Sir David Dundas.[8]

By this time he had inherited the family titles, his father having died in 1780, although he seems rarely if ever to have used the English Denham title, always signing himself as Sir James Steuart.[9] He was also by this stage a married man, having in 1772 wed Alicia Blacker, daughter of William Blacker of Carrick, County Armagh, although the marriage would remain a childless one.[10] However, whilst Steuart's marriage strengthened his links with Ireland, his inheritance of the family titles and the estate at Coltness in Lanarkshire also drew him back to Scotland, and to the commitments expected of a member of the landowning gentry. Notwithstanding close family connections with the Erskine dynasty, who were prominent Whigs, Steuart entered into the political scene as a supporter of Pitt the Younger's Tory administration, having been elected MP for Lanarkshire in 1784 with the support of the local magnate, the 8th Duke of Hamilton. Steuart retained this seat until 1802, when, the Duke having died, his successor wished the seat to go his own second son obliging Steuart to stand aside. There is no record of Steuart ever having spoken in Parliament, but he was a part of the political machine by which Henry Dundas – 'The Uncrowned King of Scotland' – controlled Scottish politics in Pitt's interests. It was in no small part down to these political connections that Steuart was able to obtain the colonelcy of the 12th, after repeatedly badgering the Duke of Hamilton to use his influence to obtain him such an appointment. However, the fact that he got a cavalry colonelcy, which would normally have gone to a more senior officer, rather the infantry colonelcy he had asked for and expected, may well reflect recognition of his successful record as a trainer of light cavalry. Certainly, the fact that he bagged such a high-status regiment at a relatively early stage in his career helps explain why he then held it for so long, as his rank and seniority eventually caught up with the prestige of his appointment.

A little under two years after Steuart's appointment, and with Britain at war with Revolutionary France, the 12th were ordered to join the British forces in the Mediterranean. At the time of the regiment's dispatch, Toulon was in allied hands and a campaign on the European mainland seemed a possibility, but by the time they arrived in the theatre the port had fallen. Allied attentions had now shifted to Corsica, where a squadron of the 12th was present at the taking of Bastia. Later the whole regiment was united at Civita Vecchia on the Italian mainland, where their good conduct obtained for them the unique distinction of a gold medal, awarded to the officers by Pope Pius VI. Three of the recipients, Captain Robert Browne, whom we shall meet again later, Captain-Lieutenant Michael Head, and Lieutenant the Hon. Pierce Butler, visited Rome in person and were granted an audience at which the officers received, along with a papal blessing, three hymn tunes which were subsequently adopted by the regiment to be played at each watch setting – a tradition which continued well into the twentieth century.[11]

When the 12th sailed for the Mediterranean they did so under the command of Lieutenant Colonel Sir James St Clair Erskine, one of the Whig Erskines alluded to above, and better remembered as the 2nd Earl of Rosslyn, to which title he succeeded in 1805. Steuart also prepared to accompany his regiment on active service – the only time in his colonelcy that he did so – but this was to enable him to take up a post as a brigadier general with the forces at Toulon, rather than to act in any regimental capacity. This possibility was, however, blocked by Steuart's promotion to major general in October 1793 for there was no vacancy in his new rank on the Mediterranean staff. Instead, he was slated for a cavalry command with the forces serving in Flanders, but this appointment was also overtaken by events and his political connections in Scotland saw him appointed to the staff there instead, with responsibility for overseeing the training of Fencible Cavalry.[12] Steuart served in this post for the next three years, although he initially sought to avoid it, citing a 'depression of spirits', which he attributed to rheumatism. After three years of summer training camps in Scotland, Steuart returned to Ireland where he was appointed to command the Southern District, in effect the Province of Munster. This appointment, in late 1797, brought with it the local rank of lieutenant general and coincided with the outbreak of the great Irish Rebellion, which would be Steuart's first – and only – test as a commander of troops on active service. The 12th Light Dragoons did not take part in these operations, having by this stage returned to the Mediterranean, but it is worth examining Steuart's involvement in them since doing so sheds considerable light on his character, which in turn helps illuminate the nature of his subsequent relations with the regiment.

The worst of the initial rebellion was concentrated in County Wexford, to the immediate north-east of Steuart's jurisdiction, whilst the later heavy fighting that followed the landing of French reinforcements took place further north, in Connaught. Therefore, much of Steuart's duties were of a supporting nature, first quelling the rebellion in his own jurisdiction, and then sending aid to his colleagues elsewhere. Steuart's conduct during this time came in for some criticism, most notably from Brigadier General John Moore, the future victor of Corunna, whom Steuart dispatched to aid in the pacification of Wexford once Munster had been rendered secure. Moore complained that Steuart had needlessly delayed this operation through detaining troops in Munster contrary to orders, due to fears for the security of the province.[13] He also described Steuart as being afflicted by 'a return of his nervous complaint', suggesting that the general's predisposition to melancholy was a deep-seated character trait, recognized by those who knew him. Moore, indeed, quoted Steuart as stating himself 'ever subject' to it. Moore further asserted that Steuart even went so far as to question his own fitness for the command that he had been given, leaving Moore, for his part, uncertain whether it was wise to encourage him to retain it.[14] Coming from an officer of Moore's calibre this is all pretty damning stuff, but Steuart's writings from the time, and his own later account of his service in Ireland – which eventually came to a close with his resignation from command of the Southern District in 1799 – paint a rather more complex picture.

Steuart's initial response to the rebellion, which he initially characterized as 'disturbances', was to rely on roving patrols of Yeomanry cavalry. These, he was keen to stress, were to be 'always accompanied by a civil magistrate or constable', and 'never to violate the law; to protect innocence, and never offend it; to be severe, where severity is unavoidably necessary; but to discriminate, as far as possible, the innocent from the guilty'.[15] This proposal met with the approbation of both the commander-in-chief in Ireland, Lieutenant General Sir Ralph Abercrombie, and at least some of Steuart's own subordinates, although it was certainly at odds with the rather more punitive measures subsequently adopted by Abercrombie's successor, Lieutenant General Gerard Lake. It is true that Steuart left the conduct of operations in the field to others, but it may be fairly pointed out that most of the active service took place outside the geographical remit of his command and that his sense of duty may well have acted against the option of his leaving it. However, whilst attitudes elsewhere hardened as the rebellion flared up again with the arrival of French support, Steuart retained confidence in his understanding of the circumstances that had led to the rebellion and, as result, continued to advocate conciliatory measures rather than repression. Writing in 1814, Steuart made it clear that he had definite political differences with the establishment and their approach to the Irish problem:

> I can only say that if the upper and the lower classes of the people in Ireland could be reconciled to each other, and the latter rendered industrious by the means of the former, Ireland would soon become a most happy and flourishing country. Those means are simple, let the residing proprietors of Estate employ the lower classes of the people in improving the soil, and the country in general as much as possible by piece work, the labourer would then work according to his industry and to his wants. On the present system almost all that is done is by Day Labour, so the most industrious labourer can not gain more than 10d per day to

maintain himself or his family, he must steal it or have recourse to more violent means, and thus war and retaliation is commenced between the labourer and his employer and or neighbour. In such a state of Society it is not difficult for ill designing men to work upon the minds of the wretched and dissatisfied, whose condition can hardly be rendered worse. Could a favourable change be appreciated in the condition of the lower classes they might be grateful to those who furnished them the means of subsistence. The residing proprietors would find themselves Secure, and absentees would return to their Estates, which they have quitted for want of comfort and Security at home. My great endeavour when in the command of the Southern District was as much as possible to reconcile the inhabitants to each other, but that is a work of time, as there are faults on all sides.[16]

This was an unusually balanced view, even allowing for the fact that Steuart was writing a decade and a half after the events it concerned, and in fact has far more in common with the views that Moore had expressed at the time than the latter ever realized. The problem that it emphasizes, though, is one that comes through time and time again in Steuart's dealings whilst colonel of the 12th Light Dragoons: he always knew best. Never mind that Lake, as commander-in-chief, intended to put down the rebellion by means of vigorous military action; Steuart in his district would do it by conciliation instead, even if it took far longer, and meant retaining troops that were needed elsewhere. Increasingly at odds with his commander, his subordinates and the local ascendancy, it is little wonder that Steuart suffered from nervous strain and depression. That he brought it on himself there is little doubt, but he retained his convictions unchanged. Exactly the same attitude would characterize his colonelcy of the 12th, and is evident throughout his correspondence covering that period.

Whilst their colonel was courting controversy in Ireland, the 12th Light Dragoons were also again on active service, making their first acquaintance with the climate of Portugal. They had returned from their first Mediterranean posting in 1795, mercifully too late for them to be dragged into the disastrous campaigns in Flanders which were then being brought to a conclusion. For the next two years they remained in Britain, posted first to Croydon and then to York, before the re-entry of Spain into the war as an ally of the French required the presence of a British force at Lisbon in order to assist Britain's oldest ally in the event of a Spanish invasion. Bearing in mind the depleted state of the British Army at this juncture, worn down by campaigns in the West Indies and

Flanders, any aid that could be sent would inevitably be rather tokenistic, and Lieutenant General Charles Stuart was given only three battalions of British foot, plus a mixed bag of Swiss and émigré Frenchmen – the debris of the evacuated Mediterranean garrisons – and a small force of cavalry. None of these units, the 12th included, were at anything like their full strength, whilst the Portuguese forces were ill-prepared and their commanders at loggerheads. Under the circumstances, it is perhaps a good thing that the Spanish made no effort to mount a campaign against Portugal, but the long dull years spent patrolling along the Tagus did at least enable the officers and men of the 12th to make good the deficiencies in their training, and become acclimatized to service in a warm climate, so that in 1800 Lieutenant General Simon Fraser could report that, 'No Corps can be fitter for service, no Dragoons more masters of their Horses.'[17] This was all well and good, for by this date the 12th's long stint in Portugal was approaching an end, and they were about to embark on an altogether more serious campaign, which would prove to be the regiment's first real test in combat.[18]

By the beginning of the nineteenth century, the British Army was at last beginning to regain some semblance of its past capabilities, but after the disastrous Helder campaign of 1799 it had yet to prove itself in the field. The opportunity finally to do so came because the Royal Navy had been able, in the years following Nelson's triumph at the Nile, to regain control of the Mediterranean, and with the Army now able to provide the troops it was therefore possible to send a force to evict the French from Egypt. Command of the British troops was given to Lieutenant General Sir Ralph Abercrombie, Steuart's former chief in Ireland, and the 12th Light Dragoons received orders to embark and join the expedition being assembled at Marmaris Bay on the coast of Turkey. Unfortunately for the British, and particularly for Abercrombie's cavalry force, Turkish promises to supply horses for their allies proved deceptive. By the time draught animals had been set aside for the artillery, there were barely enough to mount a third of the cavalry, and that on animals scarcely larger than ponies. Even with these local remounts, the 12th had only 128 horses for an all-ranks strength of 550 when it reached Egypt.[19] Since the French had a considerable force of cavalry available, this could well have been a major handicap but, in the event, the French commander, Menou, was slow to react and the British were able to land at Aboukir Bay and establish themselves on shore. Nevertheless, their limited numbers meant that the British cavalry took no part in the fighting at Mandara on 13 March, their work being largely confined to scouting, patrolling and raids against French supply convoys.

Not all these operations were successful, and the 12th met with disaster on 18 March when eighty men under the regiment's new commanding officer, Lieutenant Colonel Mervyn Archdall, who had replaced Erskine when the latter was appointed a brigadier general on the staff in Portugal, ran into a large French reconnaissance force. Although outnumbered, Archdall elected to attack. The 12th broke the French infantry but they then set off in pursuit of some fleeing hussars, only for the failure of this move to leave the troopers dispersed and their horses blown. It was a classic example of the sort of action that would lead Wellington a decade later to bemoan 'the trick our officers of cavalry have acquired of galloping at every thing, and their galloping back as fast as they gallop on the enemy'.[20] The extent of Archdall's misjudgement was brought home when his retiring command found that the French infantry had regrouped in their rear and they were now cut off. Nearly half the British force became casualties, with Archdall himself losing an arm and two officers and seven men being taken prisoner. As for the rest of the British army, the Egyptian campaign was a tough and sometimes bloody learning experience for the 12th Light Dragoons.

During Abercrombie's victory at Alexandria on 21 March the 12th – now under Lieutenant Colonel Robert Browne, whom we last encountered as a captain receiving the papal blessing – were only lightly engaged, but the regiment soon saw more serious action in the operations that followed, forming part of the contingent sent overland towards Cairo. By May 1801 there was a sizeable force operating in the desert, with Browne commanding a mixed cavalry contingent drawn from the 26th Light Dragoons and Hompesch's Mounted Rifles as well as his own regiment. This combined body was deployed to good effect on 17 May when Browne was able to force the surrender of a 600-strong enemy force composed of infantry, dragoons and a part of the French Corps de Dromadaires. Once Cairo eventually fell in June, the desert operations largely came to an end and the focus of the reinforced British army was concentrated on securing the capitulation of Alexandria. By September 1801 the campaign was brought to a conclusion and the French compelled to surrender, but the arduous campaign had worn the regiment down. Although the men were largely fit – only forty-nine sick out of 456 rank and file on 1 November 1801 – their equipment was worn, the men tired and the army still lacked sufficient horses.[21] Accordingly, the 12th received their orders for home, but only after they had turned over all their horses to other regiments.

Having returned from Egypt dismounted and depleted, the 12th Light Dragoons were posted to Ireland to rebuild their strength, and remained there through the Peace of Amiens and during the first three years of the renewed struggle that broke out in 1803. In late March 1806, shortly after the regiment finally returned to Britain, Major General Henry Grey carried out a detailed inspection of the regiment, as was required by the Army's *General Regulations.*[22] Since the 12th was at the time dispersed between Eastbourne, Hastings and Blatchington Barracks, the task took him three days and although he began on 19 March it was not until the 21st that he was able to compose his report. Grey began by listing the established strength of the regiment and comparing it with the numbers actually on the regimental books, and his listing provides an excellent introduction to the structure and organization of the regiment during the Napoleonic era. Although the actual numbers on the strength might frequently be lower, every regiment of cavalry in the British Army had a fixed establishment of officers, men and horses which represented its theoretical organization. This was set annually and based on what the government could afford to pay for. Thus, in times of peace, the numbers would drop, whilst in wartime they would rise. This could be achieved either by increasing or decreasing the number of troops in a regiment, by increasing or decreasing the numbers of officers and men in a troop, and, in the case of the horses, by leaving a portion of each troop dismounted.[23]

Grey began by listing the field officers of the regiment, all of whom were present. There was one colonel – Steuart himself – two lieutenant colonels, and two majors. That there were two lieutenant colonels on the strength was recognition of the fact that men promoted to be general officers also retained their regimental rank – indeed, were only paid in that capacity, unless specifically employed on the staff in their higher rank – and such was the case here. Mervyn Archdall had been promoted major general the previous year, and so whilst he was the senior of the two lieutenant colonels on the strength of the 12th, the function of regimental commanding officer was filled by the junior man, Robert Browne. After the field officers came the ten captains, of which the 12th had its full complement at the time of Grey's inspection and each of whom commanded one of the regiment's ten component troops, assisted by two or three subaltern officers. In the case of the 12th, which had a fairly large established strength at this time, these comprised two lieutenants and one cornet per troop which represented the largest officer establishment allocated during the period – units at a lower established strength might drop to only one lieutenant per troop. Here, however, Grey's inspection saw the 12th below its establishment for the first time, for there were only fifteen lieutenants on the strength out of the theoretical twenty, and seven cornets from a theoretical ten.

Next in Grey's listing came the regimental staff officers, the paymaster, adjutant, veterinary surgeon, and the surgeon and his two assistants. All these posts were filled at the time of the inspection. With the obvious exception of there being provision for a veterinarian to look after the horses, the structure of the regimental staff tallies closely with what one might expect on the staff of an infantry battalion of the period. However, whilst an infantry battalion would have a single quartermaster as part of the battalion staff, no such post existed in the cavalry at this time. Instead, as Grey's report notes, there were no less than ten quartermasters serving with the 12th when he inspected them, which was the regiment's full established strength. However, these troop quartermasters – which is what they were, it being no coincidence that ten posts equated to one per troop – were by no means a direct analogue, in function or status, to their infantry counterparts. The exact status of the role is hard to pin down. On the one hand, the 1795 *Rules and Regulations for the Cavalry* defined the quartermaster as 'the principal Non-commissioned Officer of the Troop', but the position carried rather more weight than that and, indeed, ranked senior not only to troop NCOs but to the regiment's serjeant major as well.[24] Furthermore, promotion to the rank of quartermaster was by warrant signed by the regimental colonel, and indeed Steuart's correspondence explicitly uses the term Warrant Officer in relation to the post, which is perhaps the best way of understanding the rank's intermediate status, although the post was by no means a complete equivalent of its twentieth-century namesake.[25] Although their duties were far wider, quartermasters did have responsibility for 'the Care of Necessaries and Appointments' belonging to the men in their troops,[26] which largely explained why there was no need for a quartermaster as part of the regimental staff. Quartermasters were promoted from the ranks, and the post served as a reward for deserving NCOs and, potentially, as a springboard from which a lucky few might make the further leap to full commissioned status.

Quartermasters being paid considerably more than serjeants, the post was also an expense, and not all those appointed to the rank were considered by their superiors to display the qualities necessary to set themselves fully apart from the rank and file from which they had risen. In 1808, therefore, colonels of cavalry regiments were canvassed for their opinions on how the establishment might be modified in order to resolve these concerns. Steuart, whilst seeing the merits of the system as it stood, was for once in step with his superiors at Horse Guards, and agreed 'that the Establishment of Troop Quarter Masters might be abolish'd with advantage to the Service' and that a single 'Quarter Master to each Regiment might be appointed, who should be a person of known integrity, knowledge, & activity, and who should be honoured with his Majesty's Commission' – this, in effect, would bring cavalry regiments into line with infantry battalions, and centralize matters of supply at a regimental level. In order to fill the vacancy for a senior troop NCO that would result from this change, Steuart proposed that 'one Serjeant to each Troop might annually be appointed by Letter of Service from the Colonel to do the duty of Quarter Master under the appilation of Quarter Master Serjeant, with two Shillings per day in addition to Serjeant's pay'.[27] This, by and large, is what was eventually implemented in December 1809, although the new NCO rank was instituted not as Steuart's proposed 'Quarter Master Serjeant' but as troop serjeant major.[28] However, this did not mean the immediate end of the old system, for whilst Quartermaster Abel Hammon made the jump to commissioned status as the new regimental quartermaster, his fellows remained in their posts until removed either by death or discharge, and troop serjeant majors were only appointed on a one-for-one basis as the number of troop quartermasters still on the strength dwindled away. Each troop therefore had, after December 1809, either a troop quartermaster or a troop serjeant major, but never both, and even at the war's end in 1815 there was still a single troop that retained its quartermaster.

Unlike the quartermasters they replaced, the new troop serjeant majors ranked beneath the serjeant major. Now indisputably the regiment's senior non-commissioned officer, this latter individual was specifically tasked by the *Rules and Regulations* with acting as 'an assistant to the Adjutant'.[29] Interestingly, the serjeant major is not specifically mentioned in Grey's inspection report, which simply states an establishment of fifty-four serjeants, all of which posts were filled. However, this figure rather nicely breaks down to give the five serjeants belonging to each of the ten troops, plus the four non-commissioned posts on the regimental staff: the serjeant major, paymaster serjeant, saddler serjeant and armourer serjeant, all of whom can be found counted individually in the regiment's monthly returns. To these posts there was added in 1810 the post of trumpet major, ranking as a serjeant but listed, after some indecision, as a trumpeter in the monthly returns – a clerical fudge which in turn required listing one of the trumpeters as an ordinary private in order to prevent the regimental establishment being exceeded.[30] The establishment of ten trumpeters equated, of course, to one per troop.

That each troop had an establishment of five serjeants was directly linked to the fact that, at the time of Grey's inspection, the regimental establishment was set at a rather hefty 1,000 rank and file, or 100 men per troop. Grey's figures do not break this lump sum down into corporals and privates, but the standard formula gave a regiment one of the former to every nineteen of the latter, with the resulting twenty-man building blocks forming the basis for increments or reductions in troop establishments over the years. This in turn was directly linked to the establishment of serjeants, there being the same number of serjeants as corporals allocated to each troop.[31] It is worth noting that there was no establishment provision for junior non-commissioned officers below the rank of corporal, but standard practice across the Army was reflected in Steuart's provision in the regiment's Standing Orders that 'one Lance Corporal will be appointed to each Troop . . . those Lance Corporals must be distinguished by some particular Mark on their Dress, which will be appointed according to the Fancy of the Commanding Officer'.[32] When Steuart composed these orders in the early 1790s, the regiment was still on a very low peace-time establishment, with only one serjeant and two corporals per troop, and it may be reasonably inferred that by the following decade the number of lance corporals per troop would have risen in proportion to the establishment number of non-commissioned officers.

If any evidence were needed that an establishment of a thousand rank and file was rather over-optimistic, it might be found in Grey's figures, which showed that the 12th was short of that total by 300 men. Furthermore, although the establishment provided a mount for all serjeants, trumpeters and rank and file, for a grand total of 1,064 troop horses, the regiment was not only unable to meet that figure but could not, in fact, even mount all the men that it had on strength. With only 650 troop horses, over a hundred men were perforce left dismounted. In recognition of the fact that its cavalry regiments were pegged at too high an establishment figure, the Army was already in the process of standardizing on a reduced establishment based on ten troops of eighty rank and file apiece – indeed, this had in theory taken effect in December 1805, so should have been in force for the 12th when Grey inspected them the following March. In all events, it was soon implemented, leaving the 12th still a little short of its establishment but with far greater likelihood of building up to it.[33]

For the remainder of the war, this structure continued without too many changes, although between December 1809 and December 1811 a portion of each troop was left dismounted during such time as the regiment was serving in the British Isles. Until 1814, the establishment included neither farriers nor boy soldiers: thereafter, provision for one of each was made in every troop. It is, however, clear from Steuart's Standing Orders that farriers were maintained on this same establishment, no doubt hidden amongst the private men, long before the post was made official, and that a farrier major to oversee them formed part of the regiment's non-commissioned staff.[34]

One final word is needed on the one organizational echelon that was completely missed out by the official establishments, namely the squadron. Formed by pairing two troops, the cavalry squadron had been the basic battlefield tactical unit since Marlborough's day, but had no permanent organizational existence within the regimental structure of the British Army's cavalry regiments at the time of the Napoleonic Wars. Instead, when a regiment deployed for active service it did so in multiples of two troops, which were then formed into squadrons for campaign service. With no permanently appointed squadron commanders, this role typically fell to the senior of the two troop captains, which in turn meant that half the regiment's troops were likely to be commanded by their senior lieutenant. Whilst some regiments posted a junior field officer as commander of at least one of their squadrons, leaving both component troops under their captains, the 12th in the Peninsula and during the Hundred Days rarely did so, largely because it was rare to find two of its field officers on active service with the regiment at the same time.[35]

Due to the sheer length of time for which he held the colonelcy of the 12th Light Dragoons, Sir James Steuart is, by default, one of the key figures in this narrative: a constant and querulous fixture who remained in place whilst others came and went. Indeed, as he pointed out in 1815, he had by then become the longest-serving soldier in the regiment, all those then in its ranks having joined since his appointment as colonel, and had earlier been quick to require that a tradesman who sought to take liberties with the officer in acting command of the regimental depot be reminded 'that the temporary command of ye 12th Regt. may fluctuate but that I am permanent as long as I live'.[36] Yet, as has already been shown with reference to his time in Ireland, his character was a complex and sometimes contradictory one, and is hard to pin down from his writing. The nervous strain that Moore identified in 1798 is certainly present throughout, and his letters descend on occasion almost into self-pity, as when he grumbled that 'I never can make myself properly understood about my Cudjeling System' following a lengthy correspondence in which he had tried and failed to do just that, or when he was obliged to complain to the Adjutant General at Horse Guards, requesting him 'to inform me where my Regiment is stationed and by whom it is Commanded not having heard any thing of them since they left France'.[37] On this occasion being subsequently informed that the 12th were at Dorchester, where he had himself requested they be sent, he further complained that he had 'been overlooked as Colonel contrary to the rules of the Service and of Discipline' and stated himself 'much hurt at being the Object of a neglect which my attention to the interests of my Regt. and my anxiety for its good and its discipline should not have subjected me to'.[38]

Steuart was a stickler for things being done fairly and by the book – and by his book at that – but was also on occasion quite prepared to bend the rules to a degree if he could oblige a person of wealth or influence in doing so; the more so if wealth and influence were accompanied by a noble title. In 1808, for example, he sought a promotion for Lieutenant George Erskine, related both to Steuart himself and to the 12th's former commanding officer, now Lieutenant General the Earl of Rosslyn. Not only did Steuart send in an official recommendation for young Erskine's promotion, he also wrote specially to the Military Secretary to the Commander-in-Chief, requesting that he be prepared to intervene on Steuart's behalf with the Duke of York, should any objection be raised:

> Should his short standing as a Lieut. appear to ye Commander in Chief any objection to Lieut. Erskine being allowed to Purchase a Troop may I flatter myself with the hope that his being a very near relation of his Colonel & a Young Officer in whose Promotion I very much Interest myself will give him some additional Claim to the favour of his Royal Highness to whom I have ever been most firmly attached as well as to his Majesty's Service too much indeed to recommend as I do at present any Officer who I did not think qualified for Promotion – and I request of you to lay this my Personal application before His Royal Highness with my earnest solicitation in favour of Lieut. Erskine.[39]

Evidently, Steuart was not above making use of the authority that came with a colonelcy in order to extend his patronage to those he wished to oblige, although in this case he was able to assert honestly that Erskine was a competent officer who deserved promotion based on merit as well as connections.

In his attitude to patronage, as in the close and personal attention that he paid to his role as colonel, Steuart was very much a creature of the eighteenth century. With the modernization of the British Army that had begun with the appointment of the Duke of York as Commander-in-Chief in 1795, the great days of the old-style colonel-proprietor had begun to fade, with the need for standardization across the Army as a whole cutting back on the amount of individuality that a regimental colonel could get away with. Yet to Steuart this was very much his regiment, and his letters read quite as if the 12th Light Dragoons were his in every sense of the word. In this stance, which to the man himself was simply a proper and necessary part of his duty, having been entrusted with a regiment by his Sovereign, Steuart probably made life harder for himself than he needed to. Indeed, it is telling that whilst his agents had assured him that he might expect to make in excess of £2,000 per annum as profit on his regimental accounts, Steuart instead frequently found himself at a substantial loss.[40]

Throughout the nine-year span covered by his surviving letterbook, which may be considered a good representation of his colonelcy as a whole, Steuart continued to take a deep and personal interest in every aspect of the 12th. Addressing his subordinates, he spoke confidently and with authority on topics ranging from the relative merits of plain and running snaffles during the training of a troop horse to the value of a properly structured officers' mess, and was as convinced that he knew the best ways of turning a recruit into a proficient cavalryman as he was of his ability to select the best mounts for them.[41] After all, as he reminded his officers more than once, had he not commanded a regiment of light dragoons himself? Thus, in 1811, he would brook no excuses from Portugal about the wear and tear of campaign service on regimental accoutrements, reminding Major George Wyndham, then in acting command of the 12th, that 'I have had the honor of being on Service my self in the Cavalry & was 20 years Lt. Col. to a Regt. of Lt. Drag's not now deficient in reputation'.[42] In other words, if Wyndham hoped to excuse matters by stressing that things were different when a regiment was on campaign, he would have to think again as Steuart had done it all before and, of course, knew better.

It is readily apparent that Steuart saw himself very much as a father figure to his regiment, and indeed he chose to make this explicit in his farewell letter upon leaving the 12th in January 1815 to assume the colonelcy of the 2nd Dragoons, writing that he parted from them 'with Sentiments truly paternal'.[43] These sentiments expressed themselves most obviously when he felt it within his power to do some small favour for a subordinate whom he considered worthy. He thought particularly highly of the regimental Riding Master, Lieutenant Joseph Philips, whose services were most diligent but whose personal means, as an ex-ranker, Steuart knew to be limited. Thus, when Philips was obliged to travel from Weymouth to Newcastle in order to inspect a consignment of horses, a trip for which he would receive a mileage allowance from the

Army, Steuart was keen to remind the depot commander that 'Lieut. Philips is anxious to be allowed a short time to see his friends in the neighbourhood of Durham, and I hope that you will find it in your power to accommodate him in that wish.'[44] In other words, Philips was to be allowed a brief holiday at the Army's expense.

This paternalistic attitude extended right down into the ranks of the regiment, particularly those who hailed, like their colonel, from Scotland. In one of his last letters before he left the regiment, Steuart wrote to its commanding officer to inform him that

> Archd. Macdougal who deserted from my Regiment in the Month of June 1813 surrendered himself to me a few days ago, and I granted him his pardon, and a pass to join the Regiment at Dorchester by the tenth of January next. The unfortunate fellow has a wife and a large and young family of children, and is most anxious for his discharge. I doubt if ever he will be a satisfied Soldier and if he could obtain his discharge on any reasonable terms I think it might be as well for the Regiment, and I should be glad of it.[45]

These were small matters, perhaps, but it is evident that Steuart saw them as part of his duty as colonel.

As well as his role as leader and guide to his command, Steuart also took extremely seriously the financial element of his colonelcy. Indeed, well he might, for the sums involved were by no means insignificant: in December 1808, Steuart noted that the debits in his regimental clothing account for the past three years alone amounted to 'no less than £1049, and the Tradesmens Bills unpaid chargeable to the same period amount to £3989' – these sums equate to £62,500 and £238,000 respectively when converted into modern currency.[46] Therein, however, lay the heart of one of the problems that would blight Steuart personally for much of the last decade of his colonelcy, and would in turn begin to have a baleful influence on the men under his command. The problem related to the aftermath of the Egyptian Campaign, when the regiment returned home after having disposed of its horses and much of its equipment to other regiments; to make matters worse, the 12th had then been issued with a consignment of worn and substandard ammunition pouches obtained second-hand from the 28th Light Dragoons. Steuart, naturally, began to re-equip the regiment out of his own pocket – trusting for recompense to the regulations by which items lost or destroyed on active service were for the government to pay for – whilst bemoaning the fact that doing so cost him some £4,000.[47] Unfortunately, the bureaucratic wheels ground painfully slowly, and Steuart was still waiting for his money in 1813. He was understandably keen to resolve the issue, and his correspondence is littered throughout with mention of this quest, at turns optimistic that a breakthrough is on the point of being made, only to revert to disappointment and anger as yet more layers of red tape again hold things up and deny him his compensation. The fact that he had accepted the substandard pouches from the 28th Light Dragoons of course complicated matters, since this gave an excuse for not compensating Steuart for the good ones lost in Egypt, and even the submission of a raft of paperwork, including detailed information from General Miles Staveley, colonel of the now-disbanded 28th, failed to bring things to a close, notwithstanding Steuart's belief that it would take only a few hours of the Board of Claims' time to resolve things in his favour.[48]

Since the sums involved were substantial, Steuart was not without reason in pressing his argument with such assiduity, but the case served also to instil a mindset of 'once bitten, twice shy' so far as regimental expenditure was concerned, and all the more so if that expenditure were to be incurred on campaign. Certainly, Steuart was a man who was careful of his money, such that even his accounts from the years when the 12th were at home see his ordering the exact bare minimum necessary to equip the effective strength of the regiment only – with precision down to the level of, for example, an 1811 order for '63½ Pairs Stirrup Leathers'.[49] In like fashion, he was keen to stress that he would only pay for those items that he was obliged to replace as Colonel; anything else, and anything lost or damaged through the fault of the user, was none of his concern. Thus, Standing Orders specified that 'When any Appointment which the Colonel is liable to provide becomes wanting, the Officers Commanding Troops will on those Occasions make a Return to the Commanding Officer of what is wanting, accounting in a distinct Manner by what Means each article became deficient.'[50] Without such an explanation, Steuart had no inclination to supply the deficiency, but whilst this stance was all very well on a regulated home-service establishment it began, as we shall see, to cause problems when the 12th were deployed to the Peninsula, and would ultimately land Steuart with a deal of explaining to do at Horse Guards.

If Steuart was grown canny when it came to expending his money on his regiment, he was by no means as sparing of his time and effort. Despite his advancing years which, if Richard Dighton's 1837 portrait of him is anything to go by, had added a few inches to his waistline even if they had done little to sap his energy, Steuart spent a large part of his time travelling, and a significant proportion of that time was devoted to journeys across northern England and the border country in search of fresh mounts for his regiment. Naturally, Steuart expected that the War Office provide appropriate recompense for these trips, and bemoaned the fact that the standard rate was insufficient, noting that,

> I make it my business with very few exceptions to purchase all the Horses for my Regt. and travel many Hundred Mile for that purpose, and I can not help observing that the present allowance for travelling charges is too low, poasting being now at 21d per Mile, which with trumpiters and Postilions brings it to full 2/ and the allowance is but 1s 6d.[51]

The sums soon mounted up, too, for the distances involved were by no means inconsiderable. In the same letter, Steuart noted that 'From the Month of March 1812 to March 1813 I travelled upwards of 1200 Mile for the purchase of Troop Horses', and had earlier recorded individual trips of 150 and 200 miles apiece, with the longest journey claimed for being 406 miles from Hamilton to Northallerton and back in February 1813, although this was actually only the mileage claimed for and not the complete journey, since Steuart carried on from Northallerton to London, conducted further private and regimental business there, and finally returned home via a second appointment with a horse dealer at Durham.[52]

Notwithstanding such exertions, and even for a Colonel as confident as Steuart that he possessed the secret to running a light cavalry regiment, it was clearly impossible for one man to manage the whole show, particularly by remote control. Firmly believing that good order and discipline were best established from the top down, Steuart sought to manage the regiment through the men serving in the key subordinate positions. For the most part, this meant the field officers and particularly the commanding officer, but once the 12th deployed its fighting strength to the Peninsula in 1811 much of Steuart's day-to-day correspondence was with the officer commanding the regimental depot, a post typically filled by one of the senior captains. It is clear from the tone of his letters to and about these various officers that Steuart had a mixed opinion of them, but it is testament to the man that he rarely descended into out-and-out condemnation of any individual. Officers whom he clearly thought well of he was quite happy to leave to it, although he was clearly annoyed when he felt that Ponsonby had gone over his head to Horse Guards, as much, one suspects, because of the implicit breach of their mutual trust as for the fact that his doing so had helped land Steuart in trouble. At the other end of the scale, as with the unfortunate Major Wyndham, rather than simply criticising, Steuart took the time to explain how and why an erring officer had failed in his duty, and sought to instil sufficient of his own accumulated wisdom to ensure that the offender would mend his ways.

Steuart's other major source of support in his duties were the regimental agents, Greenwood, Cox and Company of Craig's Court, London. There were several firms of army agents operating at the time, and every regimental colonel did his business via one or another of them. However, Greenwood, Cox & Co. – with various changes of name as the makeup of the controlling partnership changed – were the largest of these firms, and Steuart also enjoyed a friendly relationship with Charles Greenwood, the senior partner from 1803 onwards. Whilst routine matters were addressed to the company as a whole, anything of a more delicate nature was sent direct to Greenwood for his personal attention and it is evident from the personal and private requests made of him that Steuart trusted both his judgement and his discretion. Indeed, on one occasion when Steuart found himself with no candidate at hand for a vacant cornetcy, he was quite prepared for Greenwood to recommend in his name 'any Young Friend of good family and Education with some fortune' that he might wish to oblige.[53]

The full remit of the agents' duties was considerable, as is reflected by the fact that of 278 out-letters copied into Steuart's regimental letterbook, sixty-five of them – just under a quarter – are either to the firm or to Charles Greenwood in person. Greenwood, Cox & Co. served as a conduit for paperwork between Steuart, the regiment, Horse Guards, and the War Office, passing back and forth all manner of official documents. They worked with the agents of other regiments if a transfer of officers was being mooted, or, as was frequently the case due to the large numbers of colonels they served, acted for both regiments. They served as a post office for anything larger than a letter being sent between Steuart and the regiment.[54] They served as bankers to Steuart in his regimental capacity, and as such dealt with the various regimental tradesmen – an 1813 order, for example, required the firm to arrange for the purchase and delivery of '150 Cloaks, 50 Carabine Buckets, 50 Sets of Baggage Straps, 50 Sets of Cloak Straps, 50 long and short carriages and 20 Swords' for an impending reinforcement about to leave for the Peninsula, and 'a complete set of Chacoes and feathers, for the complete Effectives of the Regiment'[55] – as well as managing the details of Steuart's on-going claims for indemnification over his Egyptian losses. In short, there was little that went on within the regiment that did not in some way entail the input of Greenwood, Cox & Co. at some point in the proceedings.

Chapter II

Officers and Gentlemen

IT IS IMPOSSIBLE TO TRY to understand the lives and careers of Napoleonic-era officers without appreciating the nature of what it meant to be both an officer and a gentleman in the early nineteenth century. Concepts of military service as a profession bore only a limited relation to those of today, but unfortunately attempts by modern authors to judge the men of 200 years ago by modern standards have produced some mistaken assumptions and unfair judgements. Perhaps the best explanation is that furnished by the late David Howarth, attempting to convey a feeling of Wellington's officer corps at Waterloo to a general audience. Howarth drew a direct comparison between the officers of the British Army and the country gentry and lesser nobility from which many of them came, suggesting that the officer from this background,

> had an inborn habit of authority, and a very strict sense of what was fair. He had ridden a horse and handled a gun since he could walk. He had a sporting disregard for danger, which he cultivated on the hunting field. He was used to comfort at home, and so could treat the passing discomfort of active service as a picnic. He could be eccentric, occasionally angry, but he always treated his subordinates as men.[1]

Howarth's summary is perhaps a little generalistic if applied to the officer corps as a whole, which by 1815 was rather broader in composition and background than his version might suggest, but it comes rather closer to the truth when applied to that smaller and rather less diverse group of men who provided the officers of Britain's cavalry regiments.

Yet, because this conception of what it was to be an officer is so removed from a modern understanding, a perception lingers of nineteenth-century cavalry officers as men who owed their rank to their status and wealth, who cared little for their profession, and whose primary attributes were social and sartorial rather than military. Of course, such generalizations are by no means universal, and several authors have sought to rehabilitate the reputation of the men who led Britain's mounted troops. Ian Fletcher's *Galloping at Everything* does a fair and thorough job of reinvestigating the perception of battlefield performance from which it takes its title, whilst the growing number of recent Peninsular battle studies have done much to place cavalry warfare within the wider context of the combined-arms battle. Yet American historian Edward Coss still goes so far as to state – though largely accepting Fletcher's rehabilitation of Britain's cavalry – that 'command inexperience, regulations, training limitations, and leadership expectations' created cavalry officers who lacked the familiarity and skill essential for battlefield command, whilst asserting that Wellington's officer corps as a whole was institutionally lacking in a professional interest in, or duty of care towards, the men under their command.[2] Evidently, then, our understanding of these men is still marred by modern misconceptions.

Certainly, any characterization of cavalry officers as unprofessional was far removed from the standards laid down by Steuart, whose expectations for the commissioned ranks of the 12th Light Dragoons were, inevitably, far higher. The section in his Standing Orders dealing with the various duties of officers began with a series of articles that made clear that a thorough grasp of the profession of arms, as well as first-class leadership skills, were essential to the effective performance of an officer's duty:

> It is the Example of the Officers that will always Regulate and determine the Behaviour of Soldiers.
>
> In Quarters a Knowledge of every Circumstance relative to the Soldier and his Conduct, a Constant and unremitting attention to prevent and alleviate his wants or Difficulties, a thorough care of Horse, Arms, Appointments, and Œconomy, is what will ensure to Officers of Troops, that Chearful, regular, and easy Obedience, which the Soldier Committed to his Charge is happy in.
>
> In the field he must be Capable of disciplining, exercising, and instructing his Troop or Squadron, otherwise he would be unfit in Time of Service to Conduct and lead it to the Enemy. He could not be possessed of that Coolness and Clearness so essential in time of Danger; he could not profit of Circumstance, from an inability to direct others – the Fate of many might depend on his ill or well acquitting himself of this Duty.

It is not sufficient to advance with Bravery; - it is requisite to have that Degree of Intelligence which should distinguish every Officer in his Station. The exertion of Soldiers will always be in proportion to the Reliance they have on the Capacity of those that Conduct them.[3]

Steuart was certainly fully aware that the reality could fall rather short of the ideal at times, and was not afraid to point out any failings, but for the most part he was by no means unhappy with the calibre of officers serving in his regiment. If the men who filled the commissioned ranks of the 12th Light Dragoons were not hard-boiled professionals to the last man, nor yet were they a collection of uniformed dandies with little understanding of their military duties. In this, the mess of the 12th may be safely put forward as entirely representative of regiments of its type across the British Army.

Within the officer corps, three main distinctions in role existed, namely field, troop and regimental staff officers. The first two groups formed what we may think of as the typical officer career path, which we have already seen followed in the previous chapter as the young James Steuart worked his way up the ranks. In this scheme of things, little-changed since Steuart's days as a subaltern a half-century earlier, the young officer entered the regiment as a cornet, and rose first to lieutenant and then to a captaincy and the command of his own troop. The captain who achieved the next step and obtained his majority became one of the regiment's field officers, the term covering this rank and that of lieutenant colonel. Having obtained the latter rank, an officer now became eligible by the inexorable march of seniority for further promotion that could – as with Steuart – take him all the way to full general. Such ranks, however, were held in the Army as a whole, not in the regiment, something that we have already seen in the case of Mervyn Archdall at the time of the 1806 annual inspection being simultaneously a major general in the Army and a lieutenant colonel in the 12th Light Dragoons. Only if an officer was given a regimental colonelcy of his own would he cease to be a member of the regiment in which he held his lieutenant colonelcy.

Almost without exception, this career progression took the rising officer nowhere near any of the commissioned posts on the regimental staff. In the case of the surgeon, his assistants, and the veterinary surgeon, the posts required specialist skills and entailed a separate career path in which further promotion took the officer outside the regiment.[4] To an extent, the same might also be said for the paymaster, although here the qualifications were more financial than professional, including the provision of financial sureties.[5] For the adjutant meanwhile, as for the regimental quartermaster once that post came into being in 1809, the specialist skills were best acquired by service in the ranks, and the men filling these posts were perforce former non-commissioned officers. So too was the regimental riding master, although the semi-official nature of this post meant that this officer held a regular subaltern's commission but exercised his staff function to the exclusion of any troop duties.

The Field Return accompanying the autumn 1809 inspection provides an interesting breakdown of the ages, experience, and background of the officers then on the strength of the 12th Light Dragoons.[6] Ignoring Archdall, who was still on the books but serving as a major general in Ireland, there were thirty-six men listed – three field, seven staff, and twenty-six troop officers. Eight cornets were wanted to complete the regiment up to establishment, but all other posts were filled. Fifteen officers were English by birth, three Scots, seventeen Irish and one had not yet joined the regiment and confirmed his place of birth. The oldest officer was the surgeon, Benjamin Robinson, who was forty-two, and the youngest was Lieutenant Robert Carew, aged only nineteen and actually younger than both of the serving cornets. As was the case with a number of the subalterns, Carew had completed only a year's service, whilst at the other end of the scale Lieutenant Colonel Browne had served for twenty-five years, Major Blunden for twenty-two, Paymaster Robbins for nineteen and Major Spicer and Surgeon Robinson each for fourteen. Leaving aside Captain Vernon and Assistant Surgeon Lea, neither of whom had actually yet reported for duty with the regiment and for whom data was unavailable, average ages and experience for each grade are shown in Table 1.

Table 1: **Officer Ages and Experience, 1809**

	Age			Length of Service		
	Minimum	*Maximum*	*Average*	*Minimum*	*Maximum*	*Average*
Field Officers (3)	37	39	38	14	25	20
Captains (9)	20	31	24	4	9	6
Lieutenants (14)	19	30	24	1	11	5
Cornets (2)	22	23	22.5	1	2	1.5
Regt. Staff (7)	27	42	36	0	19	7

Particularly telling are the almost identical age and service profiles for captains and lieutenants, particularly when compared with the vastly greater service of the three field officers. This was partly because several senior captains had lately been promoted out of the regiment – most recently Henry Westenra, already a major by brevet, who bought himself a permanent promotion to that rank in the 8th Light Dragoons in 1808.[7] As a result the vast majority of those serving as captains and lieutenants in 1809 were relatively young men who had joined the Army since the Peace of Amiens, only three in each grade having service prior to 1803. This relative lack of experience at troop level may explain why the regiment would later need to look outside its own ranks when it came to replacing its field officers – it would not be until 1813 that even the most senior captain on the 1809 list obtained his majority, by which time three field officers had joined the regiment from other units. However, these three – Lieutenant Colonel Ponsonby and Majors Wyndham and Lord Waldegrave – were far closer in age and service to the captains and lieutenants than to the field officers they replaced, and their arrival marked the completion of something akin to a generational change as the regiment lost its Egyptian veterans and saw them replaced with the younger men who would lead it in the Peninsula and at Waterloo. This shift was nowhere more apparent than in the 1811 change of commanding officers.

After Steuart as regimental colonel, the regiment's commanding officer was the key man in the structure of the 12th, the man responsible for the day-to-day running of the regiment. Whilst lacking Steuart's permanency, the commanding officer was able to exert a far greater day-to-day influence, and – most importantly – was the man who would lead the regiment into battle. Regulations laid out that he was 'responsible for the Conduct of the Officers, Non-commissioned Officers, and Soldiers; in short, for the whole management of the Regiment'.[8] The commanding officer was, however, still obliged to follow regimental standing orders – in the case of the 12th Light Dragoons, this meant the hefty tome issued by Steuart – and not to deviate from established regimental custom.

Indeed, in the conception of the regulations, the security provided by rigorous orders such as those promulgated by Steuart in fact made the commanding officer's job easier, it being asserted that,

> The Commanding Officer can now have no difficulty whatever in keeping up the exact discipline of the Regiment, for if he sees an Officer deviating from it in the least degree, he has only to desire him to refer to the Standing Orders. Which being once issued as such, if the Officer commanding for the time being allows any body to deviate from them, he is negligent in the highest degree of his own duty: but it is not conceived possible, that when a code of Standing Orders are given to the Regiment, the Officers can want watching to make them adhere to them.[9]

Steuart no doubt would have agreed, but the repeated and plaintive references to the regularity with which his own Standing Orders were ignored by the officers of the 12th renders it abundantly clear that there was rather more to the commanding officer's job than slavishly enacting the dictates of an absent colonel.

Discounting short temporary appointments when the permanent incumbent was absent on leave or recovering from wounds, there were only two commanding officers during the years with which this book is concerned: Robert Browne and the Hon. Frederick Ponsonby. Both men were experienced cavalry officers and Steuart evidently valued that experience, and the different skills the two men brought to the role. Nevertheless, the way in which the two men were treated by their colonel, and their relations with him in return, differed considerably. Browne, who eventually left regimental duty in June 1811 upon promotion to major general, seems very much to have been the loyal and dutiful subordinate, a man who could readily be entrusted with matters of day-to-day detail and who excelled as a regimental administrator and organizer. Even after Browne's promotion deprived him of all but a tangential connection to the 12th, Steuart continued to use his services with respect to matters of regimental dress and accoutrements, employing Browne as his man-on-the-spot in London when the re-uniforming of the cavalry was being mooted in 1811, and expecting Ponsonby to defer to the senior man's expertise.[10] Ponsonby, for his part, was a rather different character, and more inclined to make his own mark. It would be wrong to see him as a rival to Steuart, who remained his acknowledged military superior, but Ponsonby certainly knew his own mind and, as the man who led the 12th through most of their active service under Wellington's command, he stands second only to his colonel as the major figure of interest in this narrative.

By the time that he joined the 12th Light Dragoons at the age of twenty-seven, Frederick Ponsonby was already an experienced light cavalry officer.[11] The second son of the 3rd Earl of Bessborough, he was born into a family whose extended connections made it a cornerstone of aristocratic Whig society. Frederick's mother, Harriet, Countess of Bessborough, was one of the great society hostesses of the age, somewhat eclipsing her husband the Earl, and it was through these connections that Frederick was able to get his foot securely onto the military ladder once he had settled upon soldiering as a career. With the Prince of Wales then still firmly espousing the Whig politics that he was obliged to abandon upon becoming Regent, and serving as colonel of the 10th Light Dragoons, it was understandable enough that his aid was sought in finding a place in that regiment for the young Frederick, who was accordingly gazetted cornet in January 1800. The 10th were described by the Prince as both a crack regiment and one whose 'Corps of Officers is entirely composed of men of Fashion and Gentlemen',[12] and it may be inferred that this pairing of ideals was something that Ponsonby kept with him for the remainder of his career, and which influenced his conduct once he became commanding officer of a regiment himself.

For the first six years of his career, Ponsonby rose through the ranks of the 10th, before moving briefly to the 60th Foot and then to the 23rd Light Dragoons as a major. As a result of this move, he would miss the Corunna campaign of 1808 in which the 10th served with some distinction, but the 23rd would soon find itself in the Peninsula as well, joining Sir Arthur Wellesley's little army in time for the Talavera campaign of 1809. At Talavera, the 23rd under Lieutenant Colonel Henry Seymour formed a brigade under Brigadier General George Anson along with the 1st King's German Legion (KGL) Hussars. Ordered to charge French infantry threatening the allied left flank, Anson's Brigade ran into serious trouble thanks to the unsuspected presence of a dry watercourse directly in its path. The KGL Hussars avoided the worst of it, but the 23rd were badly disordered and, although Seymour rallied about half the regiment and led them on, these troops were cut off and near-annihilated by a French counterattack. A rueful Ponsonby, left to collect the remainder of the broken regiment, mused that it was perhaps less of a given than he had supposed that the French would run at the mere sight of British cavalrymen.[13]

So badly were the 23rd broken by their misadventures at Talavera that the regiment was ordered home to be rebuilt, but Major Ponsonby did not go with it, instead remaining in the Peninsula as a staff officer. As such he saw action at Bussaco before being posted to join the British forces at Cadiz under the command of Sir Thomas Graham. Ponsonby served as Graham's assistant adjutant general, but when the Anglo-Spanish garrison launched a major sortie against the French besiegers, leading to Graham's British contingent fighting and defeating two French divisions at Barossa on 5 March 1811, Ponsonby played a rather more active role. By now a lieutenant colonel, he was the most senior cavalryman on the field and, although Graham's mounted forces consisted only of two squadrons of the 2nd KGL Hussars, Ponsonby threw himself into action, leading what Graham described as 'a brilliant and most successful charge against a squadron of French dragoons, who were entirely routed'.[14] Thus, when Ponsonby obtained the lieutenant colonelcy of the 12th Light Dragoons three months after Barossa, he had already seen two years of active duty in the

Peninsula, taken part in three major actions, and learnt – sometimes the hard way – exactly what could and could not be achieved by light cavalry on the battlefield.

Whereas Steuart's voluminous correspondence allows the historian to obtain a good feeling of the man's character, there is rather less of a written record for Ponsonby. However, many of the letters that he sent home to his mother from the Peninsula and from Flanders are included in the two hefty tomes making up the collected private correspondence of Lord Granville Leveson Gower, who was briefly Secretary at War for a few months in 1809 and, rather more permanently, Lady Bessborough's lover.[15] Furthermore, the fact that we have Steuart's letters to Ponsonby means that, even with those from Ponsonby to Steuart missing, it is possible to establish those issues that Ponsonby considered sufficiently weighty to raise with his colonel. Taken together, these two sources – along with the opinions expressed by his subordinates – enable us to grasp something of the measure of the man.

Certainly, as befitted one coming from a family so steeped in Whig politics, Ponsonby was – by the standards of the day, at least – liberal in his views. As a commanding officer he promoted the care of the men in his charge, and was strongly opposed to the institution of corporal punishment which was then a near-inescapable part of life in the British Army. Ponsonby even went so far as to seek to abolish completely the use of the lash in the 12th Light Dragoons, at a time when even the reforming Duke of York sought only to limit its use, although the consequences of this well-meaning initiative were not always as positive as might have been hoped.[16] William Hay, from his first meeting with Ponsonby when both officers were in Lisbon on their way to join the regiment, entertained the highest opinion of both his talents and the care and interest he took in his command. On their first meeting, realizing that Hay was ill with a fever, Ponsonby had positively forbade the young subaltern from continuing on active service, and had sent him home to recover; yet, as Hay later recorded, when Ponsonby was himself struck down by a fever during the Vitoria campaign, he sought to conceal it from his men and remain with the regiment, leading Hay to conclude 'what a fine, noble, unselfish fellow our colonel was'.[17] Then again, it is perhaps not to be wondered at that Ponsonby was so popular with his junior officers, since he was a man of the same generation. Comparing his age and service profile with those recorded for the officer corps at the time of the 1807 inspection, Ponsonby had only marginally more service – albeit more of it active – than some of his senior captains. This, in turn, renders it no surprise that Ponsonby, the young man of fashion schooled in the way of the

10th Hussars, wished to make the 12th a regiment in the same mould. During wartime, other concerns naturally took priority – beau he may have been, but Frederick Ponsonby was also a professional soldier – but once matters were apparently settled in 1814, peace allowed him a freer rein.

In many ways, Steuart and Ponsonby represented the old and the new respectively. Steuart was a creature of the eighteenth century, from a society steeped in hierarchy and governed by patronage. Ponsonby, by contrast, was a man of the coming century, more liberal in outlook, certainly, but also more personally ambitious, one of a class who saw military service not as an end in itself but as part of a career trajectory that might well go on to other, greater things. Looking back to the title of this work, it is tempting to see each man as personifying one of the two attributes picked out by Wellington in his description of the 12th Light Dragoons – Ponsonby as gallantry, and Steuart as discipline. Just as it was essential to strike the right balance between the two factors within the unit as a whole, so too was it necessary for colonel and commanding officer to strike a healthy balance in their own working relationship.

Majors Blunden and Spicer were the last of what might be termed the older generation of field officers – men who had joined in the 1790s and served through the Egyptian campaign – and their continued presence with the regiment, and Ponsonby's appointment from outside it, served to some extent as a block on promotions from within. Only when Spicer began to think of retirement was there a chance for movement, and even then some dextrous use of patronage meant that the resulting vacancy would initially be filled from outside, to the detriment of the senior captains of the 12th. Spicer's replacement was George Wyndham, who arrived in the 12th as a major in April 1811, having held that rank in the 78th Highlanders only since January of the same year. Wyndham's career had seen him jump from regiment to regiment, and although Steuart agreed to the exchange with Spicer as a result of the intercession of Wyndham's father, the Earl of Egremont, he felt obliged to inform the Earl,

> that the situation of ye 12th Lt Drag's requires the attendance of as many field officers as can possibly be provided, the first Lt. Colonel [Archdall] being employed as Major General, and the second [Browne] having the [brevet] rank of Colonel may possibly be appointed to serve as a Brigadier.

Major Spicer is an active and good Officer and before I can agree to his exchange I shall require the most positive assurances from his proposed Successor that he shall on no account accept any Staff Situation so as to deprive the Regt. of his attendance, and active[ly] discharge his duty as a Regimental Field Officer.[18]

This chance to command the regiment may, indeed, have been what attracted Wyndham to the 12th, but Browne's promotion and the consequent arrival of Ponsonby as the new lieutenant colonel – combined with Steuart's rapid disillusionment with Wyndham's abilities – meant that any hopes the latter might have entertained of obtaining distinction in the acting command of the 12th swiftly evaporated. Thus, whatever assurances the new major may have given of his commitment to regimental service with the 12th, Wyndham had by February 1812 left it to go on leave, and in the following month departed for good to assume a lieutenant colonelcy in the Regiment de Meuron, an émigré infantry regiment in British service, from which he shortly afterwards exchanged into the 20th Light Dragoons.[19]

Spicer's willingness to exchange out of the regiment made perfect sense in financial terms since he was already on the point of retiring; by exchanging into the 78th he obtained the difference between an infantry and a cavalry majority – £1,282 10s 0d at the official rate – and would subsequently sell his majority in the 78th in order to recoup the remainder of his investment in a commission.[20] Wyndham, for his part, was self-evidently one of the well-connected officers who used money and patronage to climb the promotion ladder without any feelings of regimental loyalty, and it may be inferred that it was only Steuart's ingrained inability to resist a request whose bearer sported a coronet that blinded him to this tendency. For an officer unwilling or unable to move out of the regimental circle, however, matters could be more frustrating. Spicer, and Wyndham after him, had been the junior of the regiment's two majors, the senior man – holding that rank since August 1799 – being Overington Blunden. From a Kilkenny landowning family, with a father who was a baronet and former MP, Blunden's career stagnated after he obtained his majority, and, not-withstanding the conferment of a brevet lieutenant colonelcy in January 1805 he seems to have felt himself passed over, particularly following Ponsonby's appointment. Having taken the regiment to the Peninsula in 1811, he quickly surrendered the command and returned home – his arrival in Britain taking Steuart somewhat by surprise – and began to agitate for the promotion that he considered his due.

Getting wind of what Blunden was up to, Steuart wrote to Colonel Henry Torrens, Military Secretary at Horse Guards, noting in his usual slightly querulous tone that,

> I have been told that [Brevet] Lt. Col. Blunden first Major of ye 12th Lt. Drag has returned to England from Portugal and has not reported himself accordingly to me his Colonel which I judge not to be consistent with the attention which is due to me, if I am mistaken and require too much I beg to be set right by the Commander in Chief.
>
> I am also informed that he is using influence to make an exchange into an other Regiment evidently to the prejudice of the Captains of ye 12th Lt Dragns. if so which I hope is not the case I earnestly request of His Royal Highness the Commander in Chief that it may not be permitted, the Captains having laid in their claims for Purchase.[21]

With the 12th's senior captain – James Bridger, of whom Steuart seems to have entertained a high opinion – already pleading his own case for preferment, believing himself slighted by the appointment of Wyndham, this would not do, and Steuart was therefore happy to forward Blunden's eventual application for promotion to a lieutenant colonelcy outside of the 12th. If Blunden exchanged into a different regiment as a major, as Steuart initially feared he intended, the 12th would get a new major in return and Bridger would be again passed over; however if Blunden were promoted, Bridger could move up into the vacancy.

Nevertheless, although he passed Blunden's claim on to Horse Guards, Steuart had little belief in its likelihood of success, knowing that the vacancies that Blunden was eyeing had in fact already been filled, and was soon obliged to inform the major that his application had been turned down.[22] Blunden thus remained a regimental major for the rest of the war, although he obtained a brevet to full colonel as of June 1813, setting him on course to rise to major general by seniority in 1819. By this date, however, his military career was effectively over and much of his time after 1812 was taken up with parliamentary duties, he having become member for Kilkenny in the election of that year. This caused a serious problem for the regiment, since Blunden was supposed to be serving as commander of the regimental depot and his frequent absences on parliamentary duty meant that it suffered under a series of interim commanders, to the detriment of its training function.[23] Sadly for Blunden, his efforts to make a parliamentary career at the expense of his military one were to no avail: he lost his seat only two years later and failed in a subsequent attempt to obtain a knighthood in return for his services, being advised that he had better return to soldiering instead.[24]

Bridger, meanwhile, finally got his majority in December 1812 in conse-quence of Wyndham's departure, although the commission passed briefly first to Major the Earl of Waldegrave, who transferred in from the 15th Hussars when Wyndham was promoted, but then left after only eight months – a mere three of them on active service – upon purchasing the lieutenant colonelcy of the 54th Foot. Steuart's letters contain no mention of Waldegrave's appoint-ment or his views on it, but it may be inferred that his weakness for a title may have been behind his allowing Bridger to be passed over: if that is indeed the case, he did at least in part make up for it by giving that officer a healthy endorsement to succeed Waldegrave.[25] Handing his depot command over to Blunden, Bridger served as Ponsonby's second-in-command in the later stages of the Peninsular War, and again during the Hundred Days.

Until Bridger went out to the Peninsula as a major in February 1813, the post of second-in-command had been a rather nebulous one, it being rare that the active portion of the regiment had more than one field officer present. Under these circumstances, it might be more fairly said that the commanding officer's right-hand man – or, as the *Rules and Regulations* had it, the 'Aid de Camp to the Commanding Officer'[26] – was the regiment's adjutant. That passage of Steuart's Standing Orders covering the duties of the post began by noting that 'The Duty of the Adjutant is too Comprehensive to be Contained in these orders in a few Words,' although this did not stop him trying to do so and the next two passages do in fact capture the essence of the role:

> His Duty is to attend to the Discipline of the Regiment in General, to regulate and Conduct all Drills, particularly those on Foot; those on Horseback he ought to be perfectly acquainted with, he ought to write a Clear and distinct hand, in Order to Keep Regimental Books in good order and make out his Returns neatly, he ought to fortify himself in Accounts as he may Occasionally be Called on to act for the Paymaster in his Absence.
>
> He is to Regulate all Rosters and Keep them with Exactness; in short he is to be active and persevering, never taking for Granted that any thing is Right, but Constantly seeing that it is so, & that the Orders of the Regiment are punctually Complied with, informing the Commanding Officer when he finds Neglect or Irregularities, which are not in his Power to Correct; the Dress and Appearance of Soldiers on and off Duty is particularly attended to by him.[27]

The *Rules and Regulations* went into rather more detail about the amount of paperwork that an adjutant was expected to deal with, giving a list of returns to be kept and blithely asserting that:

> It is very easy to keep up those books, &c. in perfect order, with method and attention; and if there is any defect in them, it will be laid to his charge. Above all things, he must take care never to put off entries, but to enter every thing up at once; and he must be very particular in the entries of all transfers of men and horses.[28]

Altogether, it was quite a task, although Steuart noted that the adjutant was to 'Keep no other Roster either for Officers, Non Commissioned Officers, or Private Men,' whilst the *Rules and Regulations* did helpfully remind its readers that 'He has the Serjeant Major and Regimental Clerk as his assistants.'[29]

At the time of the 1806 inspection upon the regiment's return from Ireland, the post of adjutant was held by John Gitterick who had been in that role since November 1804. Commissioned from the ranks via a quartermaster's warrant, Gitterick initially held dual rank as cornet and adjutant, rising to lieutenant and adjutant on Steuart's recommendation in December 1808 – unique to the post of adjutant, this double commission served as a means of increasing the pay for this essential position.[30] Interestingly, an 1812 inspection report on the 12th noted that although 'a zealous active officer', Gitterick 'has not all the necessary qualifications for an adjutant'.[31] The nature of these failings was not specified, however, and whatever they were they did nothing to prevent his promotion to a captaincy the following year, a promotion that took him out of the regiment. In order to replace Gitterick, Steuart's thoughts turned naturally enough to the man whom the *Rules and Regulations* named as his primary assistant, and he therefore wrote to Horse Guards recommending that the vacancy created by Gitterick's promotion 'may be allowed to remain so until Lieut. Colonel Ponsonby shall be able to judge whither Serjeant Major Griffith now at the Depot is fit for the situation in which case I shall take the liberty of recommending him'.[32] Ponsonby's approval being forthcoming, Griffith was duly commissioned as cornet and adjutant in July 1813.[33]

Notwithstanding the social and financial attributes expected of potential officers, it was by no means impossible to be commissioned from the ranks into a cavalry regiment, and Gitterick and Griffith were amongst several officers in the 12th who successfully made that transition. Five cornetcies were awarded to ex-rankers between 1803 and 1815, but it cannot be denied that these men remained a minority within the regiment and those who flourished did so only because Steuart was able to extend his patronage to them and keep an eye on their progress. Furthermore, almost without exception these ex-ranker officers spent their remaining careers on the regimental staff rather than as troop officers. By no stretch of the imagination was it easy for an ex-ranker to serve as an officer, particularly due to the financial pressures of a cavalry commission, as even a frugal man could be caught out by the Army's inability to reimburse officers for expenses they had occurred. Such was the fate of John Conolly, Gitterick's predecessor as adjutant, who was commissioned from the ranks in 1796. Three years later, Steuart purchased a lieutenancy for him, and he served as adjutant throughout the regiment's service in Portugal and Egypt. Conolly finally resigned the adjutancy in 1804, leaving the way open for Gitterick's appointment, and served thereafter as a troop officer. By 1807, however, claims made on his troop accounts – which had been poorly kept, leading to the onus of payment falling onto Conolly's own shoulders – forced him to sell his commission in order to meet his debts. Steuart generously allowed him the value of his lieutenancy even though he, Steuart, had paid for it, and also sought without avail to obtain him permission to sell his cornetcy despite Conolly having obtained it without purchase.[34]

Such an ignominious end to a career was not unique to Conolly, or indeed to men commissioned from the ranks. Bartholomew Ware joined the 12th as a cornet in May 1808, but two years later was returned absent without leave. Investigation established that Ware had been unable to re-join the regiment for the very good reason that he was a prisoner in Maidstone Gaol, where he was incarcerated for debt. Ware's only way of paying off his creditors and obtaining his release was to sell his cornetcy, but the wretched man spent nearly a year locked up before a purchaser could be found.[35] Slightly more fortunate was Cornet W. St John, arrested for debt in November 1815 within less than a year of his having been gazetted into the 12th. Unlike Ware, St John was able to obtain funds to clear his debts and obtain his release, but was understandably obliged thereafter to seek leave in order to put his affairs in order.[36] Finally, Cornet St George Barry managed to land himself in financial difficulty simply through the act of joining the regiment. Having purchased Lieutenant William Dowdall's commission as cornet before the latter had obtained permission to sell, he found himself liable, in theory at least, for Dowdall's regimental debts. Dowdall was the real villain of the piece, having sold out with unseemly haste for reasons that are not entirely clear but might well have been connected to his extensive money problems, but Barry had certainly acted imprudently by purchasing a commission without going through the official system, and the matter took some considerable time and correspondence to sort out.[37] All this suggests that it was therefore less a case of having birth or background on one's side, as having the ability to conduct one's affairs – financial and otherwise – with good sense. Consequently, one of the major responsibilities of regimental colonels, and one which Steuart took very seriously, was the vetting of potential officers.

As with regiments across the Army, the typical potential officer was the 'young gentleman' in his late teens seeking a first commission to set him on the ladder to military fame and fortune. Whilst in theory one could apply directly to the Adjutant General at Horse Guards if recommended by an officer of field rank or higher, Charles James's 1811 *Regimental Companion*, offering advice to those seeking King George's commission, noted that 'a letter to the Colonel of the regiment, through whom the recommendation is supposed to pass to the Commander in Chief, is more acceptable'.[38] Steuart, as was his wont, took this responsibility extremely seriously, seeing it as part of his duty as colonel to ensure in the first instance that the right sort of men were commissioned, and secondly that their careers progressed in the manner best suited both to themselves and to the regiment. It was for the latter reason that Steuart entertained such distaste for exchanges between officers of different regiments, preferring that, for troop officers at least, promotion remained within the 12th.

In no small part, Steuart's heavy focus on officer appointments and training was due to the fact that Britain's military system included few other checks to ensure that commissions were bestowed on suitable candidates and that officers received a thorough professional training. In particular the purchase system has come in for considerable modern criticism for its supposedly baleful effects. It is important to understand, however, that purchase served a combination of purposes, and was by no means intended as a way for wealth to trump ability although there is no denying that this was on occasion its result. It is also important to understand the roots of the system back in the turbulent seventeenth century, when having officers tied to their posts by a strong financial interest was an additional means of securing their loyalty. Such concerns were largely defunct in the more settled times of the late Georgian era, but purchase was nevertheless still considered important – by Wellington, for one – as a means of ensuring that the officer class had a direct connection to the fortunes of the nation. On a more prosaic level, purchase was also extremely economical for the Army, since the fact that a retiring officer could sell his commission meant that there was no need to make provision for pensions. Furthermore, the need to purchase, in conjunction with low pay, in theory ensured an officer corps prepared to serve for motives of duty and patriotism, not for wages. Finally, it should also be understood that the limitations and failings of the purchase system were understood at the time, and that one of the reforms instituted by the Duke of York on his becoming Commander-in-Chief of the Army was to set a minimum age of sixteen for first commissions – thus preventing the purchase of commissions for children who did not serve but nevertheless accrued seniority without leaving the schoolroom – and setting a minimum time to be served in each grade so as to prevent a recurrence of the crop of teenaged lieutenant colonels found at the head of regiments during the Flanders campaigns of the 1790s.[39]

But if the purchase of commissions was a product of the age and, at the same time, as regulated as the Duke of York could make it, it nevertheless remains a demonstrated fact that purchase in the cavalry was far more prevalent than in any other arm of service. The historian Michael Glover, from a sample of promotions across the Army as a whole covering the period 1810–13, has shown that 45.1 per cent of all officer promotions in the cavalry were through purchase as opposed to 17.7 per cent in the infantry.[40] Glover draws no conclusions from this data, but others have made the leap of linking high levels of purchase with a lack of professionalism. Thus, in an extreme case, we have Edward Coss using Glover's figures to assert that 'the cavalry was led by men with far less professional training than their infantry counterparts'.[41] However, this negative correlation between purchase and professionalism is hardly one that can be sustained: not the least of its failings being its inability to characterize accurately the sizeable group of officers who purchased some but not all of their promotions – it can hardly be assumed that an incompetent who had bought his way up to lieutenant would be transformed into a paragon of military virtue upon succeeding to a captaincy without purchase, nor that the reverse would hold good.

Looking at the period from 1803 to 1815, the figure for purchased promotions in the 12th comes out at 48.3 per cent, broadly in line with Glover's figures, but the figure for initial purchases of cornetcies – for which Glover offers no comparative figures – is only 33.3 per cent.[42] Whilst the number of free cornetcies represent a better proportion of free commissions than do the figures for officer promotions, the case of the 12th does corroborate Glover's contention of a high incidence of purchased promotion in the cavalry. There are, however, several good reasons for this, and they lie primarily with the infantry rather than the cavalry – that is to say, the question ought not be why there was so much purchase in the cavalry during wartime, but rather why there was so little in the infantry. To begin with, there is the question of supply and demand: the number of cavalry regiments actually dropped during the Napoleonic Wars, whereas the infantry establishment was vastly increased: naturally, with a sudden need for more infantry officers, free commissions became available in bulk whereas in peacetime nearly all infantry promotions, like those in the cavalry, were by purchase. Consider, too, that there would be little point in granting a free commission in a cavalry regiment to an impecunious but deserving individual, who would almost inevitably be unable to maintain himself in that role. This restriction also prevented the extension to cavalry regiments of the practice common in the infantry whereby a man of good family but inadequate means would serve in the ranks as a gentleman volunteer in the hope of distinguishing himself sufficiently to be awarded a free ensigncy – although the 12th did benefit indirectly from this practice, with a cornetcy made vacant by casualties at Waterloo being filled by one William Maxwell, who had fought in that battle as a gentleman volunteer in the 33rd Foot.

Cavalry officers required an income considerably larger than their counter-parts of the infantry, for purchase in the first place but subsequently to equip and maintain themselves on campaign and in the mess – although in the latter case it should be noted that inspection reports on the 12th regularly noted that the mess was run in an economical manner that permitted all officers to belong to it. Nevertheless, there is no denying that it was not a cheap business, and the cases of Cornets Ware and St John indicate what might happen to a young man who sought to live a life beyond his means. That this led, throughout the Napoleonic era and well beyond it, to a financial bar on the sort of men who might serve as cavalry officers is an unfortunate reflection of the social mores of the time. However, to assume that the men who could afford to buy their commissions and sustain the life of a cavalry officer also automatically lacked any sense of professionalism is to make a leap of faith which cannot be grounded on any evidence.

In any case, although suitable financial support was indeed one of the things that Steuart looked for when weighing up a prospective officer, it was by no means the only thing. Certainly, any potential cornet need have 'an allowance of £150 at least a year besides his pay', but Steuart made it clear that he would 'not approve of any purchaser for the Cornetcy who is not Highly recommended as a man of good family and good education'.[43] The means by which candidates for cornetcies were obtained were varied: for the most part they were either known to Steuart or had been recommended to him. By the standards of the time, these were the only ways in which Steuart and his fellow colonels could judge the potential officer-like qualities of anyone seeking a commission. Possession of any prior military education was unlikely, for although Britain had recently joined the continental powers in providing a military academy for aspiring officers in the shape of the Junior Department of the Royal Military College, established at Marlow in 1802 for boys aged thirteen to fifteen, places were extremely limited and fees substantial – barring free places for sons of dead or crippled officers, and discounts for sons of those serving. This kept the number of gentlemen cadets, and thus the number of graduates, small.[44] Only one gentleman cadet was appointed directly to a commission in the 12th during this period, this being Thomas Reed who was gazetted a cornet in August 1813 whilst still completing his studies, eventually joining the regiment in September the following year. Reed was not the first graduate to serve in the 12th, however, William Hay having passed out from Marlow in 1810 as an ensign in the 52nd Light Infantry before being promoted into the 12th in July 1811.[45] John Vandeleur, who served in the 71st Highland Light Infantry before transferring into the 12th as a lieutenant, was also a Marlow graduate. Steuart, having had one himself, certainly seems to have seen the value of a military education, and one of the last favours he was able to do for the retiring Lieutenant Conolly was to try and obtain a place at Marlow for that officer's son.[46]

Because of the lack of training for officers prior to their taking up a regimental appointment, it necessarily fell to the regiments to make up for this deficiency. Indeed, this was explicitly catered for in *General Regulations*, which noted that, 'It is expected that every Officer, who has been two years in the service, shall be capable of commanding a Troop or Company in every situation, and shall be perfectly acquainted with its interior Management, Œconomy, and Discipline.' By the same regulations, the regimental commanding officer was expressly tasked with 'the Instruction and Improvement of Officers under their command'.[47] Accordingly, Steuart's Standing Orders required that 'Every new Officer on joining the Regiment will pay Three Guineas to the Riding Master for himself and horse, and half a Guinea to the Rough Riders. Also one Guinea to the Serjeant, who is directed to Teach him the Carabine Exercise.'[48]

However, it was not just enough that an officer become personally competent in the drills and exercises: he also had to be sufficiently versed in them as to be able to instruct others. An 1811 report showed the system working as it should, noting that,

[T]he Captains are reported to have assisted the Commanding Officer in the Instruction & making the Subaltern Officers acquainted with their duties, who in their several situations are represented to be desirous of acquiring that Knowledge necessary for them to be qualified to be able to perform their duty with exactness.[49]

However, this required proper supervision, and when Blunden's absences to attend Parliament left the depot without a regular commander to oversee the training this led to a tailing-off in standards, causing Major General Oliver Jones to note that 'the subalterns are intelligent they are improved in the knowledge of their duty and I think greater progress would have been made had they been commanded by a more experienced officer', and recommend that the command be invested in 'a steady officer likely not to be removed'.[50]

Until his promotion and consequent departure for the Peninsula, the depot had had exactly that, in the shape of James Bridger. As depot commander for the bulk of the period from June 1811 to December 1812, the task of overseeing training fell to him, and Steuart laid down the advantages to be obtained for all concerned if the junior officers at the depot could assist:

On the Instruction of Officers I repeat it all depends and in order that they may be able to instruct they must be instructed no body can be above it & the study of Horsemanship is one of the greatest points. The Field Officers & Captains should ride with the Riding Master at a private hour and the Subalterns at an other, both should be able to instruct the soldier.[51]

In theory, at least, Steuart preferred it to be the case that no cornet should be sent on active service, or be considered as eligible for promotion, until fully conversant with his duties. The former restriction was a matter of common sense, for an untrained officer in the field would be a hindrance to his fellows and no use to the regiment – although an 1812 inspection report noting that 'The Subalterns are willing and anxious to learn their Duty, and appear active and Intelligent'[52] makes it clear that even lieutenants on active service were still considered to an extent to be under training – whilst the latter restriction served as an incentive for any man who might assume that a military career could be addressed in a half-hearted manner.

The amount of time considered necessary for an officer to become fit for service, and the amount of time typically spent as a cornet, seem in general to have roughly coincided. Certainly, it was rare for the regiment's cornets to be serving with the active troops overseas, with only one officer of that rank going out to Portugal in 1811, and only two to Flanders in 1815.[53] In order to formalize the process, Steuart instituted a system of classes by which the abilities of officers under training could be assessed. Unfortunately, as an unofficial regimental measure, this could not lawfully prevent a promotion taking place, and the situation in this regard in 1813 had a disappointed Steuart calling upon the temporary depot commander to shake his officers out of their complacency:

> Sir, I have received the State you sent me of the Depot Squadrons of my Regt. which is in general perfectly satisfactory except so far as it relates to the officers, I observe with pain that Lieut. Lane after having received unexpected promotion and having been a year in the Regt. is not yet sufficiently advanced in Discipline as to be fit for Service and what is more that Lieut. Hawkesley and Cort. [blank] should only be in ye 2d Class and Cort. Bennett in the 3d. If I do not very shortly see a different Report and a more favourable one of the state of discipline of these Gentlemen I shall report them to the Commander in Chief, and I positively declare that in future I shall not only not recommend any officer for promotion before he is reported fit for Service but that I will actually set my face against and oppose every such promotion, which you will be pleased to make known to the Officers serving under your Command.[54]

Of course, the poor progress that had angered Steuart was a direct consequence of the lack of an experienced officer to oversee training, with the letter's recipient, Captain William Coles, being one of the officers temporarily filling in for the absent Blunden and characterized as 'anxious to do well' but lacking in experience and without 'sufficient authority to manage the Young Officers'.[55]

The following year, Steuart put his new resolve to the test. Deeming none of the cornets then with the regiment sufficiently advanced in their training to qualify for a vacant lieutenancy, he had sought to obtain it for Cornet Goldsmid of the 19th Light Dragoons whose brother Albert was a well-thought-of lieutenant in the 12th. Being informed by Horse Guards that this could not be permitted as the younger Goldsmid was junior to several cornets of the 12th, Steuart therefore asked instead that the Duke of York,

> allow the Lieutenancy in the 12th Lt Drags to remain vacant for a very short time, until Cort. Newsome shall be reported to be fit for Service, as I recommend no Officer for promotion until they are sufficiently instructed as to be properly fit for Service, this I expect will immediately be the case respecting Cort. Newsome who is reported to me as extremely

attentive and has been for some time past in the first Class of exercise. I find this arrangement to be a great Spur to emulation and to the forming of Officers which I have all my life time considered as the great Pillar and Support of Discipline, I therefore hope that this will only be a delay and not a disappointment to the promotion of Cort. Newsome.[56]

Newsome, being confirmed as fit for service a month later, received his promotion and joined the regiment in the south of France just in time for the closing shots of the Peninsular War.

Nevertheless, Steuart was not completely inflexible and, as with the appointments of Majors Wyndham and Waldegrave, a request for preferential treatment from someone with the right connections would not go unheard. The Hon. Augustus Stanhope, youngest son of General the Earl of Harrington, was gazetted a cornet in the 12th in May 1812, but only nine months later, and still under instruction at the depot, he was offered a post as ADC to Lieutenant General Sir Stapleton Cotton, commanding the cavalry in the Peninsula. Perhaps recognizing that an officer with Stanhope's connections was unlikely ever to spend long on regimental duty, Steuart informed him that,

> it is with reluctance I should object to any young officer being placed in so advantageous a situation, as that offered to you by Sir Stapleton Cotton, at the same time I do think that it would have been full as well and more to your advantage, had you previously been better acquainted with the duty of a regimental officer, which you have not yet had a full opportunity of learning. My consent to your accepting the situation now offered to you must however depend on the sentiments of the Commanding Officer of my Regiment at the Depot, to whom I shall immediately write on the subject, and to whom I at the same time beg leave to refer you.[57]

Steuart accordingly instructed Blunden, commanding the depot, that he wished 'Cornet Stanhope to be indulged on the present occasion, if you have no particular objection,' which was as good as telling the major to approve the request.[58] Sure enough, Stanhope joined Cotton's staff later that year, having obtained his lieutenancy in the interim; in fairness, during this time he had also impressed his seniors with his attention to his duties and his training.[59]

Once a cornet had completed his training, and before then if he could get away with it, he could look to obtaining his lieutenancy. More so than the initial obtaining of a cornetcy, this step showed up the complex interplay between free and purchasable commissions. Just because an individual had purchased his cornetcy, there was no reason why he could not expect to receive a free promotion to lieutenant if his seniority put him in the right place at the right time; equally, having obtained a cornetcy without purchase did not prevent the bearer paying for a later promotion. Promotions became available for free generally because of the death of a serving officer, in which case all officers junior to the deceased moved up one place in regimental seniority, so that the death of a captain made the senior lieutenant a captain and the senior cornet a lieutenant, both gratis, whilst opening up a free vacancy for the appointment of a new cornet. An increase in the regimental establishment could also open up vacancies, as happened in the 12th when the number of troops was increased from eight to ten in the 1790s, although these vacancies took some time filling and the two vacant cornetcies stemming from this augmentation were never filled, Horse Guards having shown no inclination to put candidates forward.[60]

The fact that an officer may have obtained different steps in different ways set up some complicated arrangements when it came to selling on a commission, for unless special leave was granted – and it rarely was – a commission that had not been bought could not be sold. In 1806, for example, Captain Richard Bird chose to sell his commission and retire: his captaincy and lieutenancy he had bought, but he had obtained his first commission as cornet without purchase. Lieutenant Thomas Dickinson purchased the captaincy, which in turn meant there was a lieutenancy up for sale. Writing to Browne, Steuart noted that:

> You mention no Cort. in succession to Lieut. Dickinson, but I will not delay the matter longer in order to hear from you again, but on receiving this send in the name of the Cort. you recommend in succession to Lieut. Dickinson to the Agent and I will desire him to give it in . . . as Capt. Bird's Cornetcy is not allow'd him it will of course be filled up by the Commander in Chief.[61]

When a commission was put up for sale, the etiquette required that the man next in seniority be given first refusal. If he had the funds to purchase, all well and good; if not, the offer would pass to the next in line, and so forth. Of course, if there was a chance that a non-purchase vacancy might also be in the offing, the senior man would naturally wish to obtain promotion that way if at all possible, leading to some byzantine juggling of respective claims, exemplified by this 1812 letter from Steuart to the agents:

> My Application to the Commander in Chief for a Lieutenancy without Purchase for Cornet Calderwood has been strongly backed by an other from his Uncle, M[ajor] Genl. Durham which I hope will prove successful.

Should that not be the case you will be pleased to recommend Cornet Calderwood for the Lieutenancy by Purchase in succession to Lieut. Carew and I will be answerable to you for his proportion of the Purchase, that is to say the regulated difference.

Should Cornet Calderwood succeed without Purchase in that case, I beg of you in my name to recommend Cornet Seaford on money matters being settled to your satisfaction. Lieutenant Isherwood having also sent in his Resignation must in the above case be succeeded by Purchase by the next Cornet in succession whom I suppose to be Stacey.

Observe that the above is on the supposition that Calderwood has succeeded without purchase but if it is otherwise he must be recommended in succession to Carew and Penfold in succession to Isherwood.[62]

Steuart, it will be noted, was prepared personally to advance the funds necessary for Calderwood's promotion – as he had done in the past for another protégé, John Conolly – although in the event it was not required as Calderwood succeeded to the free vacancy.

As well as promotion – by seniority or purchase – it was also possible to advance one's career through judicious use of exchanges between regiments. Steuart himself had done this as a young officer, but his desire to watch over the 12th, and maintain the professionalism of its officer corps, meant that he was loath to see it take place in his own regiment. Certainly, for an exchange to take place, he had to be strongly convinced of its justification, and of the merits of the officer who would be joining the regiment. Since exchanges between regiments at least nominally required approval of both colonels, or at the very least the regimental commanding officers, this was an area over which Steuart was able to exercise rather more control than the matter of promotions, although the number of times that officers went over his head eventually caused him to issue an additional standing order requiring all potential promotions or exchanges be cleared with him first.[63] In this, he quite clearly had the interests of the regiment at heart, as evidenced in the enquiries he required Browne to make with respect to a potential exchange of 1810:

Sir, I have this moment received your Letter of ye 30th respecting the exchange between Captain Stamer and Capt. Wallace of ye 91st Regt, but you know the general reluctance I have to exchanges. I have at the same time the highest opinion of Captain Stamer as an Officer, therefore before I will even think of the proposed exchange I must have a detailed account of Capt. Wallace's Character, as an Officer also of his family, and

Education, and of his private Character and conduct, and I must also have a very strong recommendation from the Colonel of his present regiment, and also from the Lieut. Colonel of the Battalion in which he is now serving, having been satisfied in all these points I shall then take it into consideration whither I will or will not agree to the exchange. I beg also to know if Capt. Wallace ever served in the Cavalry, before he went into the Infantry, and in what Regt.[64]

Quite evidently, the character and experience of a potential new captain had to be investigated and, if anything, to an even greater degree than those of a potential new cornet: on this occasion, the results were positive and the exchange accordingly took place.

Under other circumstances, however, an exchange could be a positive thing for all concerned. Thus, in 1807, Steuart had written to inform the agents that:

I have this day received a Letter from Capt. Hawker. I know that he has a complaint very unfavourable to a cavalry officer & as his object is not really to quit the Service altogether that he has served very long in the 12th, is a very good man & an attentive officer I am not inclined to object to the exchange he proposes to make it with Capt. Morgan now of ye 15th Infantry & lately a Lieutenant in the 21st Dragoons who he represents to be a young man highly eligible & can be recommended to me in the strongest manner. If so you can find no difficulty in procuring them from ye 21st Drag's to which Regt. you are Agent. If they can be so procured have the goodness to forward the recommendations in my name having however previously obtained the concurrence of Lt. Col. Brown and the usual Certificate that all Regimental Accounts & Claims are settled & cleared. One circumstance however I must not omit & that is that if there is any Lieut. in the 12th Lt. Dragn's willing to purchase a Company of Infantry & then exchange with Capt. Hawker provided the transaction can be accomplished in any moderate time that arrangement must have the preference as was the case formerly with Capt. Amier.[65]

This last expedient was reflective of a fairly common practice, intended to create a promotion vacancy within the regiment rather than bring in an outsider, and could also be applied when an officer wished to sell out and retire. On this occasion no purchaser from within the regiment was forthcoming – or, if there was, no infantry company could be purchased in time – and Morgan completed the exchange and joined the 12th.[66] On other occasions, however, the practice had been used to good advantage, as when Joseph Philips, having obtained his lieutenancy in the 14th Light Dragoons, was then able to exchange back into the 12th in his new rank to resume his role as the regiment's Riding Master whilst Lieutenant Theobald Shiel, who had rather blotted his copybook in the 12th, joined the 14th to get a fresh start in a new regiment.[67]

Whilst it was of course vital for the regiment that the officers of the 12th Light Dragoons were able to perform their duties effectively, it was also essential to their individual and collective sense of honour that they did so in a manner conformable to the standards expected of a gentleman. This dual requirement set up something of a tension, since there were occasions when the two demands were incompatible. There were also, alas, occasions when behaviour fell short of the standards to be expected on both counts. In this the 12th was by no means unique, since these problems affected the British Army as a whole. Indeed, it may even be contended that the officer corps of the 12th was better able than most to combine successfully the twin requirements of officer and gentleman, since transgressions – or, at least, transgressions serious enough to make it onto the official record – were few and far between. For the most part it proved possible, thanks in no small way to some tactful handling on Steuart's part, to contain these matters within the regiment, and it is a consistent and recurring theme in inspection reports on the regiment for the inspecting officer to comment upon the harmony and accord within the officers' mess.

In particular, the 12th was free throughout this period from the curse of duelling, which, though by no means endemic in the Army as a whole, was sufficiently widespread as to promote official and unofficial campaigns against it. The last duel in the 12th was fought in the aftermath of the regiment's involvement in the Egyptian campaign, but the officer involved was not some reckless subaltern but the rather unlikely figure of Overington Blunden. His adversary was a former officer of the 12th, George Madden, who had been at the centre of a series of quarrels arising from the regiment's time in Egypt. Madden had been permitted to sell his commission to avoid being dismissed from the service after being found guilty of unofficerlike conduct stemming from his having accused Lieutenant Colonel Browne of perjury, but Blunden picked up the quarrel and the two men met with pistols in 1805. Madden, who would later serve with distinction in the Portuguese Army during the Peninsular War and ultimately regain his British commission as a result, missed with his shot, whereupon Blunden fired into the air.[68] Steuart's letters from the time of the duel have not survived, so quite what he made of the affair can only be guessed at. Certainly, it can have done little to improve Blunden's standing in Steuart's eyes, and the duel may well help explain the low regard in which Blunden was held by his colonel.

One important point to recognize in all this is that, although the officers of the 12th, in common with their counterparts across the Army, saw themselves as gentlemen, they were nevertheless at a considerable remove from the Regency bucks, beaux and rakes who might be deemed their civilian counterparts. Historian Anthony Clayton in his survey of the British officer corps rightly asserts that 'personal self-respect, above all not to be found lacking in personal honour in the eyes of fellow officers', was what transformed a 'louche young man about town' into an effective officer, but then goes on to suggest that much of an officer's time and money when at home was absorbed by 'women of various sorts and dubious relationships', and that this was not deemed a moral failing.[69] It is hardly remarkable that a group of for the most part unmarried young men sought female company when it was available, and the example of Wellington himself makes it clear that even a married officer could conduct amours if he did so with discretion. Discretion is the key word, however, and an officer who flaunted an unsuitable paramour would swiftly find that he had crossed the line between what was socially acceptable and what was not.

Such was the fate of Alexander Barton, whose career was almost destroyed due to an indiscreet liaison as a lieutenant. Barton's failing was not that he had taken an unsuitable mistress, but that he brought her with him to the station of the regiment. She being shunned by his fellows, Barton in turn spurned their company and withdrew himself from regimental society. Browne as commanding officer, and Steuart as Colonel, both intervened and eventually were able to secure a promise that he would 'terminate the improper connection he had formed and return to the society of his Brother Officers'. As Browne subsequently informed Steuart, Barton 'obtained leave of absence for that purpose which I had the honour to write to you, but in a short time afterwards he brought the person in question back to the Regt and secluded himself as before'.[70] This was particularly unfortunate timing on Barton's part, since there was a promotion vacancy on the cards for which Barton was in line through seniority but for which Browne felt himself unable to recommend him as a result of his conduct. Browne therefore told Steuart that he felt he had no choice but to recommend the next officer in seniority, Lieutenant James Clarke. Steuart, however, refused to forward either recommendation, instead telling Browne that he had granted Barton 'time to go to the Regt and represent matters to you before I finally recommend Lieut. Clark[e] in case he should be able to give you a more favourable impression of his past conduct and future amendment'.[71]

It rather seems as though Browne was not entirely happy with having to make the final step and choose one officer's claim over the other's, and that he hoped Steuart would make the decision for him. In giving Barton a further chance to repair his position with his fellows, however, Steuart had thrown the decision back to the regiment, and he followed this up with a request that Browne resolve matters once and for all, requiring 'that you should positively recommend to me such Officer in succession as you consider first entitled to promotion', and that 'without a system of this sort I could not support either your authority or my own'. Steuart then got to the crux of the matter surrounding Barton's case. The issue was now not, it should be noted, Barton's lady friend, but the fact that he had broken a promise to his fellow officers and thus transgressed the moral boundaries of what was expected of him as both an officer and a gentleman. Browne was told that:

> If you find that Lieut. Barton by his former breach of promise to you has forfeited his claim to the promotion which now offers, far be it from me to recommend him contrary to your Sentiments. On the other hand, if from his present appearances you feel reason to believe that he is really sensible of his error and will correct it, and that in other respects his conduct has been that of an Officer deserving of promotion, I shall be glad to send up his name in succession to Capt. Dickinson but all must rest with yourself in this first instance.
>
> I can not receive a promise from Lieut. Barton as satisfactory to me which you are inclined to regret. I am at the same time free to say that in my private opinion, if Lieut. Barton has given his word of honour to you that he will not in future bring the Woman in question to any place where the Regt. is quartered and that in other respects his conduct as an Officer has been unexceptional he may without impropriety be recommended passing over for once his late misconduct, but as I said before that must rest with you alone.[72]

Thus, Steuart was in fact more inclined to be understanding of a young man's failings – Barton was, after all, only twenty-four – than were the lieutenant's fellows. In all events, Browne took the hint and recommended Barton for the promotion. Steuart's confidence was rewarded by subsequent good service on the part of the new-made captain, who served with distinction thereafter. What is interesting in the context of standards of behaviour amongst the regiment's officers is that this is the only occasion where an 'improper connection' of a female nature so got in the way of military duties as to make it onto the official record, and that it did so primarily because of the social judgements passed on Barton by his fellow officers.

If the officers of the 12th were, if not a collection of plaster saints, at least careful to be discreet in their romantic entanglements, difficulties did on occasion arise through their fondness for cards and dice. This was something that Steuart was thoroughly set against, and upon the first of two occasions in which gambling amongst officers led to disciplinary problems, he characterized it as a vice that he had no wish to see become established in his regiment, and informed Browne 'that he would set my face against the promotion of any one who shall succour or encourage it'.[73] One might be inclined to doubt the strict honesty of Browne's assurance to Steuart that such games of chance were not usual pastimes amongst his officers, and indeed the problem was not gambling per se, but the combination of gambling and alcohol. On two occasions, a situation arose where wagers made – and lost – while an officer was in his cups were repudiated in the cold and sober light of the following day. This naturally created a situation where one of the two parties had to be at fault, although this then called for a judgement as to whether the guilty party was the loser, for attempting to avoid his debt, or the winner for accepting a wager from someone palpably unfit through drink to make it.

On the first occasion that this situation arose, Steuart took the latter course, asserting that Assistant Surgeon Wardroper had erred in attempting to collect the winnings he claimed from Lieutenant Theobald Shiel. An assistant surgeon had, in any case, fairly borderline status as a gentleman, and Steuart was firm in stating that Wardroper was entirely wrong 'in considering the debt he claims from Lieut. Shiel as a debt of Honour; the sum of £270 it appears was won in private which in no case is considered as a debt of Honour but much less so when won from a Brother Officer not sober at the time'. Indeed, Steuart went so far as to assert that Wardroper ought really to resign, 'but should he not be inclined to do so from a sense of the rectitude of his Conduct the case now before me must become one of a publick enquiry or Court Martial'.[74] Nevertheless, when Wardroper failed to do the decent thing and Steuart was obliged to turn the sorry matter over to the Adjutant General he did make it clear that whilst he considered Wardroper's conduct 'highly reprehensible' he by no means considered Shiel free from blame, and the eventual court of enquiry found the two men equally responsible.[75] Shiel, as we have seen, quickly exchanged out of the regiment whilst Wardroper, whom Steuart told the Adjutant General he wished gone from the 12th if it could be managed without a court martial, was superseded on 9 June 1810.[76]

For the next few years, the regiment and its officers had rather more serious things to occupy their minds, but the year after Waterloo saw a re-run of the Wardroper–Shiel scenario with rather larger sums at stake and a court martial at the end of the process. However, there was also a rather more sinister edge to this case, since the accusation made against Lieutenant the Hon. Augustus Stanhope was not only that he had taken advantage of the youth and drunkenness of the sixteen-year-old Viscount Beauchamp to win some £8,000 from him but that he acted 'in concert and conspiracy' with an unnamed third party – alleged to have won in excess of £7,000 – to bring this situation about deliberately. Stanhope, away from regimental duty serving as ADC to Stapleton Cotton, now Lord Combermere, invited Beauchamp to his quarters in Paris for dinner of Sunday 17 March 1816, first plying the youth with wine and then persuading him to play cards for high stakes. Stanhope kept the account of the game, and at its conclusion obtained from Beauchamp 'two several promissory notes or engagements to pay, at the end of three years the said several sums of money so claimed to have been won of him'. Beauchamp was the son and heir of Tory politician the Marquess of Hertford, but if Stanhope had counted on this connection to ensure that the debt was paid he was sadly mistaken. Beauchamp took his case straight to Wellington and in September 1816 a General Court Martial had no difficulty in finding Stanhope guilty and ordering his dismissal from the service.[77] Stanhope subsequently attempted first to persuade and then to force Hertford either to pay the money owed, or else secure him the return of his commission, but his increasingly violent and threatening behaviour ultimately saw him face further legal action.[78] Whilst on the face of it there are marked similarities with the Wardroper–Shiel case, the circumstances surrounding Stanhope's fall from grace are rather different. Not only did the whole affair take place outside the regimental environment, but the wronged party was not even a serving officer at the time – although he was later commissioned into the 10th Hussars – whilst if the court's findings are to be taken at face value then there was an element of pre-planning in the whole case that is far more suggestive of criminal intent. The role, and unknown identity, of the third party in the case also adds an air of mystery to the proceedings, but certainly this was more than just a drunken indiscretion on Stanhope's part.

The disgraceful termination of Lieutenant Stanhope's military career, after a certain amount of initial promise, is not a particularly positive or creditable end to this survey of the officers of the 12th Light Dragoons. Yet the fact that the case was the first public scandal to affect the 12th since the Blunden–Madden duel over a decade before is in many ways testimony to the fact that such behaviour was by no means the norm amongst the regiment's officers. The various cases discussed in this chapter represent the only occasions in which officers of the 12th transgressed the bounds of acceptable behaviour to a degree sufficient to make it onto the official record. By contrast, inspection reports consistently speak highly of the standards of officer training within the regiment and of the good relations characterizing the conduct of its commissioned ranks. When one considers that there were other regiments – infantry as well as cavalry – where dissent within the officer corps destroyed their effectiveness as military units, this represents a laudable record.

Whilst purchase was not in itself the evil that it has sometimes been made out to be, it undoubtedly contributed to an uneven system of promotions. The ease with which purchase or transfer permitted movement between regiments served to dilute the level of experience within regiments, reflected in the case of the 12th by the disappearance of a number of senior captains in the years prior to 1809, and the eventual influx of a mixed bag of new field officers from outside the regiment. However, whilst that influx included the dubious asset of George Wyndham, it also included the far more inspiring one of Frederick Ponsonby. Furthermore, retaining officers within the regiment was by no means always a good thing as the case of Overington Blunden makes abundantly clear. Yet whilst it is easy to fault Blunden for neglecting his military duties in favour of his parliamentary ones after 1812, there was nothing in the system as it then stood either to prevent his absences or to provide a replacement to cover them. In so obviously neglecting his military duties, Blunden is one of the few officers whose conduct might give some credence to modern accusations of lack of professionalism amongst British officers of the Napoleonic era, but men such as Blunden are very much the exception to test the rule, and to treat such behaviour as typical is as erroneous as to judge all medical officers by Assistant Surgeon Wardroper, or all subalterns by Lieutenant Stanhope. There is nothing in the historical record to suggest that the majority of the officers who served in the 12th Light Dragoons during the struggle against Napoleonic France were anything but men who did their duty to the best of their ability.

Chapter III

Rank and File

JUST AS THERE ARE MISCONCEPTIONS about the officers who led the regiments that fought in the Peninsula and at Waterloo, so too are there misconceptions concerning the men who followed them. Wellington did his rank and file a great disservice when he referred to them as 'the scum of the earth', but historians since have done them an even greater one by failing to repeat his qualification that the Army had made them into 'fine fellows'. At the same time, we have to be able to avoid extending too far the assumptions inherent in David Howarth's conception of the officer corps with which we began the last chapter. Cavalry officers may well have retained a strong connection with the landed gentry from which many of them came, but to assume that the cavalry rank and file were composed in like fashion of loyal tenants is rather to miss the point. The main reason that the cavalry officer corps retained much of its pre-war character was because there was only a very limited increase in the number of cavalry officers in wartime. Conversely, the fact that many cavalry regiments were at near cadre strength at the beginning of the 1790s meant that there was a far greater influx of rank and file recruits in order to bring the regiments up to fighting strength. The established strength of the 12th Light Dragoons increased fivefold during the 1790s, and even the more realistic establishment post-1805 represented a considerable increase on the peacetime strength. Because of the need to build up Britain's cavalry during the French Revolutionary Wars, and then maintain the regiments at strength throughout the subsequent struggle against Napoleon, cavalry regiments were, like their infantry counterparts, obliged to take what they could get so far as recruits were concerned.

Unsurprisingly, none of these concerns did anything to lower the standards or expectations of Sir James Steuart, who had his own firmly held ideas on the recruiting and training of his regiment's manpower. Steuart's standards for what he ultimately expected for the 12th Light Dragoons were set out in his Standing Orders:

> A good Soldier is obedient to his Officers, regular in his quarters, attentive to the Care and Cleanliness of his Horse, Arms, and all his appointments, and alert and exact in the Discharge of every Duty. It is Honour and Principle, and not Compulsion, that should prompt him to have an observance of all these Articles.[1]

This, then, was the ideal, but only with regards to the finished product – Wellington's 'fine fellows' – and not the raw material. Nevertheless, although the process of training could do much to turn even the most unpromising recruit into something fit for service, it was clearly to everyone's advantage if the men enlisted were of the best possible calibre to begin with. Thus, as with the selection of the regiment's officers, recruiting was something with which Steuart showed a continued concern throughout the period. Working on the premise that once the regiment was engaged in a prolonged campaign overseas a minimum of 100 recruits per year would be needed to maintain its effective strength, Steuart kept a close check on the activities of the regiment's recruiting parties, requiring the recall of those he considered unprofitable and suggesting the dispatch of others to areas that might usefully be tapped for fresh manpower.[2]

Because recruiting was a regimental responsibility, these were matters over which Steuart as colonel could exert considerable control. Although the Napoleonic Wars saw a growing tendency on the part of Horse Guards to intervene more directly in the recruitment process, many of the resulting initiatives were intended to fill the growing shortfall in infantry manpower, leaving the cavalry regiments untouched to a far greater degree. Certainly, except for supplementary measures taken during the Hundred Days when men were needed in a hurry, the practice of raising recruits did not significantly change during the course of the war. In basic terms, a recruiting party operated under the remit of a Beating Order issued by Horse Guards, which permitted a regiment to beat for recruits – literally by drum-beat in the case of the infantry – and entitled a recruiting party to billets whilst away from their parent unit. After 1796, the British Isles were divided into recruiting districts each under the supervision of an Inspecting Field Officer, but the duties of these individuals were largely supervisory and although the remit of their role was extended as time went on they were not permitted to interfere in internal regimental matters. Until 1812, therefore, regimental officers were detached from their regiments to undertake recruiting duties, and nearly every party maintained by the 12th prior to this date had an officer in charge of it, assisted by a serjeant and three or four privates. Thereafter, a greater degree of centralization meant that regimental officers were recalled from recruiting service and their parties were placed directly under the Inspecting Field Officer in whose district they were operating, with the day-to-day operations delegated to the serjeant commanding the party.[3]

The logic behind this was that too many officers were using recruiting duty as a means of obtaining a leave of absence, which was perhaps not an unreasonable concern given the views expressed by Steuart in a letter of 1806 when he noted that since he was informed that there were 'particular existing circumstances' that necessitated Captain John Pringle spending some time in Scotland, Lieutenant Colonel Browne ought to 'apply to have him stationed at Kelso on the Recruiting Service along with such a Party as you may think suitable'. This request may, however, have been tempered by the fact that Steuart was also assured by Pringle's brother-in-law that the family's connections in the area would result in 'his being able to assist him in getting some good recruits'.[4] On the other hand, when Captain George Erskine was on leave in Edinburgh three years later and Steuart was given to understand that good recruits might be got there, he informed Browne that,

> I think it advisable to apply for a beating order for Capt. Erskine now on leave of absence in Edn. & he may as well be employ'd in that way as being idle, at the end of his leave of absence you can either recall him and send a subaltern to succeed him in the recruiting service according to the success the recruiting Service is likely to meet with.[5]

Steuart was even prepared to grant a furlough to Serjeant Turner and Private Shedding – the latter having already produced one recruit from the area, thus alerting Steuart to the possibility – so that they could join Erskine and begin recruiting in advance of the beating order being issued.

These two cases represent extremes of the system, and both are unusual as well for the seniority of the officer involved. The norm was for subalterns to be employed on the recruiting service, and in making his suggestion to Browne with regards to Erskine, Steuart was quick to point out that 'I do not approve of Captains having Recruiting Partys' and that Erskine should be relieved by a subaltern as soon as practical.[6] Indeed, it was more typical for an officer to be detached on recruiting duty for a lengthy period, so that, for example, Lieutenant Simon Pepper left the regimental headquarters on this duty in November 1805 and remained detached until July 1807. The rank and file of a recruiting party also served lengthy stints, and so needed to be selected with care. To this end, Steuart required that men on recruiting duty 'are at all Times to appear Remarkably Clean and Regimentally dressed, as nothing Contributes more to Engage the Attention of the Country People than a regular good Conduct – and never engaging in Quarrels, is the sure Path to Cultivate a Friendship and Ensure Success'.[7] Not only were these men walking advertisements for the regiment – for which reason, no sick or wounded man could be employed on such duty – they were also the ones who had to use their persuasive talents to talk men into enlisting. For this reason, it was an asset to have a man in the party – like Private Shedding in Edinburgh – who could exploit a connection with the station to which the party was posted. Conversely, married men were thought to be less effective as recruiters and were eventually prohibited from the duty completely since it was felt that the presence of a wife could only serve as a diversion of their attention from the task at hand.

The popular conception of military recruiting during the horse and musket era owes much to Farquhar's comedy *The Recruiting Officer*, with the antics of Captain Plume and Serjeant Kite leading to a picture of bawdy irregularity that does not entirely fit the reality. Certainly, alcohol could be a great aid to enlistment, and recruiting parties were instructed as a matter of policy to attend fairs, wakes and any other such public gathering within a twenty-five mile radius of their station.[8] However, there was a stringent series of financial and other protocols to be observed, and the legal process that turned a man into a soldier had, by the beginning of the nineteenth century, acquired a range of checks and balances designed to prevent the enlistment of unfit persons, and to ensure that no one was enlisted who was not willing to serve. In the first instance, therefore, a recruit who had accepted the initial 'King's Shilling' bounty was given a cooling-off period of at least twenty-four hours before being formally attested before a magistrate. At this stage, the recruit could either repay the shilling along with a further twenty to defray expenses – this making up the Guinea of so-called 'Smart Money' – and depart, or go forward to face a medical examination.[9] If he passed the medical, he formally became a member of the regiment, and subject to military discipline. However, only a portion of the full bounty was paid over at this point, with the remainder only being issued once the recruit had been accepted at the regimental headquarters – or, if the regiment was overseas, the regimental depot. If a man were rejected at this stage, this would be at the cost of the officer who had recruited him, Steuart's Standing Orders requiring recruiting officers to guard against the eventuality by taking care 'that all Recruits are examined by a Knowing Surgeon or Apothecary of

Established Reputation – for any man who is troubled with Fits, or has the appearance of a Rupture, broken Bones, Sore Legs, Scald Head, Ulcers, or Running Sores on any part of his Body, will not be approved, but will be discharged at your Loss'.[10] Officers were also cautioned about enlisting apprentices, 'as they Cannot dispose of themselves': any man subsequently proven to be tied by articles of apprenticeship – an event usually caused by their being reclaimed by an irate master – was entitled to a discharge.[11]

Even after having joined the regiment, it was not impossible for a new recruit who had had second thoughts to extricate himself from service. The monthly return for December 1814 notes the discharge of one man, there 'Having been a misunderstanding in his Agreement',[12] although it is perhaps telling that this was during the lull of peace before the Hundred Days and it may be doubted if such understanding would have been shown in wartime. Similarly, whilst that same peacetime return shows that two men obtained their discharge upon providing a substitute willing to serve, in wartime it was necessary to provide two such substitutes. This could be an expensive undertaking, and the records show only five instances in the 12th during their wartime service. One of the men who did leave the regiment by this means was Robert Bell, whose father Steuart sent to the regimental depot – then at Weymouth – with the following letter for its commanding officer:

> Sir, the bearer Wm. Bell is going with two recruits to replace his son Robt. Bell, and I hope that the Recruits will be approved of, if so Mr Bell wishes much to bring his son home with him, if you find that this object can be accomplished with safety and propriety I should be glad he could be accommodated. Mr Bell is willing to account to you for the full Bounty of the two recruits and to give you satisfactory assurances that should either or both recruits desert before the end of the month, he will replace them without cost. If you approve of this Robt. Bell might properly be accommodated with a pass to return to Scotland with his father and not receive his discharge until the Substitutes have been finally approved of. Mr Bell is a man of respectable character.[13]

Presumably Robert had enlisted in an act of rebellion, and been pursued by his father whose pockets were evidently deep enough to make the substantial investment needed to reclaim his son. Whether Robert succeeded in making his point remains a matter of speculation.

In order to prevent as far as possible situations of this nature arising, or recruits not being accepted by the regiment, Steuart had his own standards, which were enshrined in Standing Orders along with a warning against the pitfalls that an unwary recruiter might fall into:

> You are to Enlist no man under the age of 17 or more than 21 years – no man under the Size of 5 feet 6 inches, or more than 5 feet 7½ inches high without their shoes. They must be light and Straight made (by no Means gummy) broad Shoulders, long Thighs, a good face, and in every Particular well made – no man to be Enlisted who Cannot wear his Hair, or who has the least Defect. You will endeavour to get Men bred and born in the Neighbourhood of the Country you are Recruiting in.[14]

The requirements in terms of physical characteristics largely speak for themselves, although it should be recalled that Steuart first framed these orders during peacetime and that wartime expediency required at least a modicum of compromise. As for the requirement that men be local to the place that they were recruited, this no doubt helped ensure that some account might be had of a man's character – although again, wartime requirements surely overrode this – but also helped protect against the minority of recruits who enlisted with the deliberate intent of absconding with as much of their bounty money as they could obtain. It was also to guard against such men that Steuart's orders went on to caution recruiting officers that they should 'endeavour to give the Recruits as little of their Bounty money as possible until they Join the Regiment'.[15]

Restricting the recruitment to men hailing from the locality in which the party was based also permitted Steuart to exercise closer control over the origins of the men who would serve in his regiment, and at various times he expressed both a strong partiality towards Leicestershire and Scotland as sources of suitable manpower, along with a distaste for recruitment in Ireland as the war went on. This latter was an unusual, and possibly counter-productive stance, since for the most part Ireland produced a disproportionately large amount of the British Army's manpower at this time and had initially supplied large numbers of men for the 12th Light Dragoons. However, the 10th Hussars at this time also adopted a similar policy on the grounds that Irishmen were considered prone to desertion, which may represent Steuart's thinking as well. Any suggestion of simple prejudice sits ill with his views on the 1798 rebellion, or with his standing order that 'No Reflection is ever to be cast on any Soldier on Account of his Country, those who do their Duty best, are ever to be most Esteemed'.[16] Nevertheless, after a series of suggestions that Irish recruiting parties be withdrawn, Steuart eventually informed Blunden that, 'If the Commanding Officer of the Depot can point out any place within Great Britain where Recruits are likely to be procured I have no objection to a Recruiting Party being sent, but I do not approve of sending any Recruiting Party to Ireland.'[17]

In total, the 12th maintained recruiting parties at a total of seventeen locations between 1808 and 1815.[18] Of these, the most significant were Leicester – which had a party continually throughout the period – Clones and Lisburn in Ireland, Castle Cary in Somerset, and Glasgow. Conversely, the party at Kilmarnock remained there for only two months, and those sent to Retford and Glastonbury only for three. In absolute numbers of recruits, the most productive stations were for the most part those that were maintained for a decent length of time, with Leicester alone bringing in nearly a third of all recruits. The most productive station in terms of monthly recruiting yield was Hamilton, which only played host to a party between June 1811 and August 1812 but from where thirty-seven men were recruited; an average yield of 2.5 recruits per month. At the opposite end of the scale, parties at Kilmarnock, Glastonbury, Bolton and Newark all failed to recruit a single man. The extremely good results for the party at Clones – ninety-eight recruits over fifty-eight months – make it particularly unfortunate that Steuart set his face so firmly against recruiting in Ireland, although it is only fair to note that recruiting levels for this station tailed off markedly in the eighteen months prior to the withdrawal of the party, which may have influenced Steuart's decision to drop it.

For the most part, like all regiments, the 12th had to rely on its own exertions to maintain its manpower strength. However, in the rush to get the Army back up to strength for the Hundred Days, the depots of cavalry regiments serving in the Indies were ordered to send out parties to recruit for other regiments. As part of this system, the 12th benefitted from the efforts of a party from the 25th Light Dragoons based in London as well as parties from the 8th Light Dragoons based in Dublin and Belfast. However, the first of these parties was not in place until June 1815, and it was not until the autumn, with the crisis over, that they began to send recruits to the depot. Only the Dublin party achieved a worthwhile return – fifteen recruits – with a further two from Belfast but none at all from the 25th's London-based party.[19] Steuart having now left the regiment, this period also saw the 12th send its own recruiting parties back to Ireland for the first time since 1813, with parties again stationed at Clones and Lisburn. Finally, in addition to recruits brought in by recruiting parties, it was also possible for men to enlist by presenting themselves at regimental headquarters or at the regimental depot, and a steady trickle continued to do so throughout the war.

As well as adult individuals who might present themselves, the depot was also the source of another form of recruits in the shape of boy soldiers. For the most part, this was a case of the regiment perpetuating itself by enlisting the sons of serving or former soldiers. Thus, in April 1813, Steuart was able to inform the officer commanding at the depot that he had obtained 'a sanction re-enlisting Mr Robt. Key Son of the late Serjeant Major to which you will be pleased to attend accordingly'.[20] However, only two months later a General Order opened up the enlistment of boys across the Army as a whole, causing Steuart to require that matters for recruiting boys within the 12th be put on a more formal footing:

> The Boys taken ought to be of well known good disposition, Soldiers' Sons in the Regiment to be preferred, I would not leave the selection of the subjects to Recruiting Parties, but would prefer inlisting them with the Regiment. As the system to be established should be a permanent one, and not fluctuating, I wish it to be established under my authority, as Colonel, so that no alterations shall take place, without my sanction.[21]

Captain Coles, then commanding the depot, proposed that, at the very least, any recruiting party within a reasonable distance of the depot might send potential boy recruits there to be approved, to which Steuart was happy to agree providing that it was understood that 'until Government make other arrangements no Boys shall be approved of or inlisted except by the Commanding Officer of the Regt. abroad or at the depot or by myself'.[22]

Having laid down the law on the matter of boy soldiers, Steuart was, however, soon to be disabused of his assumption that this was a matter to which he could attend in person, or even through a regimental proxy, since he was informed – and accordingly informed the depot – 'that the Recruiting of Boys, can not be taken out of the hands of Inspecting Field Officers'.[23] Whilst continuing to believe that Horse Guards had erred in taking the matter of choosing boy recruits away from the regimental officers, Steuart was more amenable to a proposal by Major General Oliver Jones, under whose command the depot of the 12th then came, that such boy recruits as were obtained should be trained as apprentices to regimental craftsmen. However, Steuart was concerned that this should not prevent them acquiring a good grounding in military training and discipline, 'particularly in the essential branch of Horsemanship which is best acquired when Young & before the Body become stiff'.[24] Steuart's preference for regimental recruiting of boys in the stated interest of 'procuring good subjects so as by degree to render the Service as respectable as possible',[25] was, whilst laudable, rather out of step with a national concern now focussed on quantity rather than quality when it came to military manpower. In the event, however, it hardly made a difference either way since the regiment obtained a grand total of three boy soldiers between the introduction of the new policy and the end of the war, and this not until the hasty recruiting of the Hundred Days.[26] One of these, furthermore, seems to have been a child of the regiment – fifteen-year-old Arthur Neale, listed as born with the army in Portugal – who would in all likelihood have been enlisted anyway.[27]

Boy soldiers aside, most recruits were in their late teens and early twenties, which fits with Steuart's preference for recruits aged seventeen to twenty-one. As of May 1838, a register of services was kept by what was now the 12th Royal Lancers, which contains the details of several men who had enlisted during the Napoleonic Wars and who were still serving at that date. However, the first page has been torn out, leaving information only for men who enlisted between 1809 and 1815.[28] This is a fairly limited sample, since less than thirty Napoleonic veterans were still serving by this time, but it is possible to supplement it by a second listing which has been bound up as part of the regimental Order Book.[29] Allowing for some duplications, and ignoring men who initially enlisted into other regiments and only joined the 12th later in their careers, these sources give information for a total of fifty-eight individuals. Of these, six were boys under the age of sixteen which leaves a sample of fifty-two typical adult recruits, although it should be noted that, since the regiment's own returns indicated no boys recruited before mid-1815, five of the six boys were actually enlisted as adults. The oldest man in the main sample was aged twenty-nine on enlistment and the youngest sixteen, whilst the average age of enlistment works out as nineteen years. This would suggest that although Steuart's target enlistment bracket of seventeen to twenty-one was not being slavishly followed to the letter – and it should be remembered that Steuart laid out his ideal when Britain was still at peace and the need for manpower much less pressing – it was certainly providing at least a guideline to recruiting parties. Just under three-quarters of this sample of recruits fell within Steuart's age range, and the bulk of those who did not were youths of sixteen who would soon grow into it. These figures, incidentally, put the age of the average recruit for the 12th Light Dragoons rather below the average for the Army as a whole, which was twenty-two years of age.[30]

With the bulk of men having enlisted for life, the average age of the regiment's rank and file rose slightly over the period of the Napoleonic Wars. This reflects the effect of a large influx of recruits in 1806, who, as they grew older as a body, raised the average age of the regiment. By the time of the Peninsular and Waterloo campaigns, these 1806 recruits – along with those enlisted in the years immediately either side – were mature men in the prime of life, and bore the brunt of the regiment's active service.[31] The shifting age profile is shown in Table 2.

Table 2: **Age Profiles, 1808–1815**[32]

| | 1809 | | 1812 | | 1815 | |
	Number	*% of total*	*Number*	*% of total*	*Number*	*% of total*
55 & up	1	0.1	1	0.1	0	0.0
46–50	0	0.0	10	1.4	2	0.5
41–45	4	0.5	17	2.4	5	1.3
36–40	14	1.7	54	7.6	11	2.8
31–35	83	9.9	94	13.3	59	15.3
26–30	149	17.8	132	18.6	85	22.0
21–25	230	27.4	153	21.6	143	37.0
19–20	233	27.8	109	15.4	64	16.6
18	100	11.9	81	11.4	15	3.9
17 & under	24	2.9	58	8.2	2	0.5

It is telling that the 1815 figures, which cover only that part of the regiment on active service, and not the depot as well as is the case for 1809 and 1812, show hardly any men under twenty. With an average recruitment age of nineteen, and many enlisted below that age, this emphasizes the amount of time it took to render a recruit fit for active service. This in turn helps explain why it was important to recruit men at a fairly young age, and why Steuart was so keen that his regiment do so.

If the recruiting parties of the 12th Light Dragoons ensured that their colonel's standards for age of recruits were largely met, rather more flexibility had to be shown with respect to Steuart's instruction that no man be enlisted outside of the rather restrictive height bracket of 5 ft 6 in. to 5 ft 7½ in. Instead, data for the regiment shows a far wider range of heights, with the regiment's tallest soldiers being over six feet and the smallest 5 ft 5 in. and under. However, the majority – a little under 86 per cent at the time of the 1809 inspection – were between 5 ft 5 in. and 5 ft 9 in. and the greatest concentration of heights did fall within Steuart's desired criteria.[33] As with the matter of the ideal age for recruits, Steuart's preference for specific heights was based on rather more than just a whim or fancy. Light dragoons were so-called for a reason: the men were expected to be mounted on lighter, faster horses than their counterparts in the heavy cavalry regiments, and this in turn influenced the requirements for manpower in terms of size and weight. Since troop horses were generally bought in job lots, as we shall see in the next chapter, it was also simply not possible to match troopers to their mounts in any meaningful way. In short, if the horses had to be standardized as far as possible, so too did their riders.

In one area, however, Steuart's recruiting instructions could be seen as indicative of rather less logical motivations. Yet despite Steuart's dislike of recruiting in Ireland, and likewise despite his attempts to boost recruiting from his native Scotland, the composition of the regiment in terms of where the men in the ranks came from changed little over the period of the Napoleonic Wars. 1809 saw the regiment just over half full of Irishmen, with the bulk of the remainder English and only 10 per cent Scots: a large portion of the last were men who had transferred from the Lanarkshire Fencible Cavalry when that force was disbanded during the Peace of Amiens. By 1815, the figure for Scotsmen had increased to 16 per cent, and the remaining manpower was now evenly distributed between Irish and English. Any Welshmen were counted as English, and none of the returns indicate the presence of any foreign-born soldier in the ranks of the 12th.[34] Whilst there was a change in the make-up of the regiment as a result of Steuart's attempts to direct the focus of its recruiting, it was therefore only a slight one. In a similar vein, the 1806 attempt by the 'Ministry of all the Talents' to increase the national recruiting yield by offering men the option of a short-term enlistment rather than service for life does not seem to have had a significant impact upon the 12th Light Dragoons. The proportion of men who had enlisted for the seven-year limited-service option peaked at 13 per cent at the end of 1808, and after remaining at a similar level for a year began to decline steadily towards the region of 8 per cent by the end of the war.[35]

Yet this indication of a relatively poor take-up of the short-service scheme, and the cavalry's inability to benefit from the replacement concept of inducing militiamen to volunteer for the line, does not seem to have adversely affected the strength of the 12th. Although Steuart was complaining by January 1814 that 'the Recruiting of the Regiment goes on too slow',[36] total regimental manpower declined only slightly in the last twelve months prior to Napoleon's first abdication. Nor did the strength of that part of the 12th serving overseas suffer – indeed it reached its high point in May 1814 just as the Peninsular War had ended – but this was achieved by stripping the depot of just about every man and horse fit for service. Had the war gone on much longer this would no doubt have caused problems but, in the event, it was peacetime reductions that really cut the regiment back, with a drop in strength that even the hurried recruiting initiatives of the Hundred Days could not solve in time for it to make a difference on the battlefield.

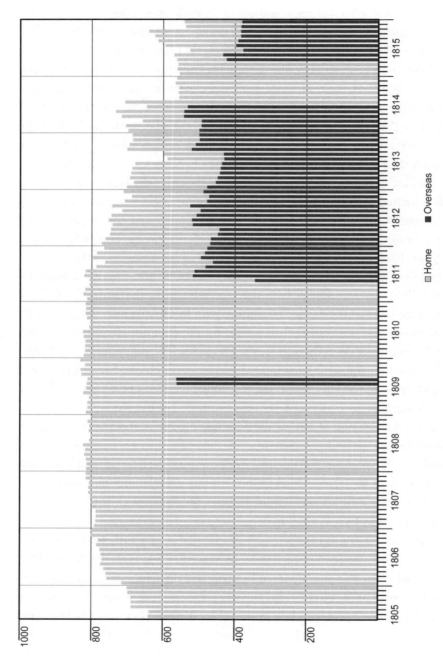

Chart 1: Rank and File Strength, 1805–1815

Once a man had been enlisted into the 12th, as with any unit, responsibility shifted from the recruiting parties to the regiment itself. The process now began of turning a recruit into a soldier, and the first requirement was that the man must look the part and possess the necessary equipment and accoutrements. The bulk of the trooper's uniform was provided by Steuart as regimental colonel, he in turn receiving an annual allowance to cover the costs. However, certain small items were deemed as 'Necessaries' and paid for by the individual soldier. The Standing Orders listed these as follows:

> Four good shirts, four pair of white Stockings and an old pair of Boots, two pair of good Shoes, two pair of Gaiters, Eight false Collars of linen about two Shillings p[er] yard, the Shirts to be made without Collars to turn down, and the men at all times will wear the false Collars as nothing Contributes more to the Clean and Soldierlike appearance of the Regiment, and is a Considerable Saving in the Article of Washing, as no man will be required to put on above two Shirts a week, however frequently ordered for Duty.[37]

For most new soldiers joining the regiment, purchase of regimental necessaries ate up most of what remained from the recruit's enlistment bounty, with the improvident few who had already squandered their down-payment finding themselves in debt to the regiment as soon as they joined it. Because necessaries that were lost or destroyed had to be replaced out of a soldier's own pocket, the potential existed for a cycle of losses, thefts and illicit purchases to develop, involving civilian clothes traders as well as soldiers, which, if soldiers were detected in it, could lead to severe punishments. Standing Orders noted that 'Should any Man be found guilty or even suspected of dispensing with any of his Necessaries, Arms, or Accoutrements whatsoever, or putting them in Pawn on any Pretence, such Man shall without Fail be brought to a Court Martial, and punished in an Exemplary Manner if found Guilty'.[38]

The combination of practicality and concern for appearance encompassed by Steuart's instructions regarding false collars was typical of his approach to the regiment's dress. In truth, though, and even without special care to ensure the cleanliness of the men's linen, the light dragoon uniform as worn at the outbreak of the Napoleonic Wars was already one of the most elegant and striking worn by Britain's cavalry.[39] Outlined in a General Order of 27 July 1796, this uniform comprised a tight-fitting dark blue jacket with collar and cuffs in the regimental facing colour – pale yellow for the 12th Light Dragoons – and decorated with braid for the rank and file and lace for the officers. In the case of the 12th, this was silver and arranged so as to form twenty horizontal bars across the front of the jacket. The jacket was worn with leather breeches and tall boots or, for dismounted duty, with shoes and gaiters. However, in 1807 Steuart resolved to put the whole regiment into Hessian boots, intending that this change should be complete by the following year's annual clothing issue. Hessians were better suited to mounted duty, with the heel sitting nicely on the stirrup, but since they were generally cut shorter than the previous issue they required that the breeches be replaced by pantaloons.[40] Headgear was the black leather helmet known as the Tarleton after the officer of that name who had introduced it during the American Revolution. After it had undergone various changes in design, it was established that the helmet should have a peak and a decorative bearskin crest. Regiments permitted to wear a distinctive badge – as was the case for the 12th with their Prince of Wales' Feathers – displayed this on the right-hand side of the helmet.

For daily work, an undress jacket was also issued, along with a black leather watering cap. The latter, if the drawing included with Steuart's letterbook is a fair representation, was rather ornate, fashioned along similar lines to the mirliton caps worn by some continental hussar regiments in the second half of the preceding century, and decorated with feathers in the same manner as the Tarleton.[41] This being rather impractical, it seems to have been replaced – at least in daily use – by a simple cloth forage cap, although there is no official mention of this in Steuart's letters or in inspection reports and returns. Standing Orders do, however, indicate the issue of a 'Stable Frock & Apron' to protect the uniform during dirty work, and, at the other end of the scale, gloves for mounted duty.[42] To protect against inclement weather a cloak was issued, ordered from 1796 to be made with sleeves, although Steuart's letters also note the provision of greatcoats, and flannel vests were also provided for added warmth when required.[43] Once the regiment was in the Peninsula, provision was made for the issue of overalls instead of leather breeches, and this was subsequently extended – by an order from Lieutenant Colonel Ponsonby of 4 November 1811 – to men serving at home.[44]

By this time, however, officialdom had also recognized the need for changes, and 1811 saw the beginning of a move towards a new-style uniform which was finally formalized in a warrant of 12 March 1812. Some of the changes, such as the adoption of overalls for all but review order, reflected a formalization of what the regiments were already doing, but other changes were less obvious in their justification. Certainly, the new uniform jacket and headgear were simpler and of a more modern cut, but whilst the former attribute could be justified on grounds of economy the latter was more indicative of a desire to ape continental fashions. The jacket remained dark blue, but the facings were now a full yellow and were far more obviously displayed, being sported on wide lapels as well as on the collar and cuffs. The lapels, however, were to be worn buttoned across when in marching order, thus showing a blue front, whilst officers when on campaign generally wore a double-breasted pelisse, undecorated apart from having the collar and cuffs in the facing colour. Piping on the jackets was also yellow but, by contrast, most of the silver braid had disappeared, being now largely restricted to epaulettes. The headgear for all ranks was now a shako, wider at the top than the bottom, and bound at the top with white braid for the troopers and silver for the officers.[45]

The process of redesigning the uniform was a lengthy one, causing delays and frustrations to those concerned. Steuart had no intention of spending money until it had been officially decided exactly what it should be spent on, and in January 1812 was complaining that 'I have as yet received no Official information respecting the alterations in the Appointments until which time I can make no arrangements for a fresh Supply of Boots or any other Articles.'[46] The result was that the regiment served throughout the 1812 campaign in their old uniforms, benefiting only from the arrival of the overalls that Steuart had ordered the previous year, and were not fully re-equipped until the following winter. On Christmas Day 1812, Lieutenant John Vandeleur wrote to his mother and mentioned that 'All the new clothing has come out except the caps, which we expect every day', but not until January 1813 could he inform her that 'all our men have got the new pattern clothing, and chacos'. Vandeleur was not entirely enamoured of the change, grousing that 'our neat little uniform is changed to that of the most foreign look', and the complaint that the new light dragoon uniform too closely resembled that of the French *chasseurs à cheval* was a common one. Interestingly, since most depictions show them being grey, Vandeleur described the new overalls as 'dark brown . . . with two stripes of yellow down the sides, the officers to wear two stripes of silver', although when it came to ordering cloth for a replacement pair he did ask for grey.[47] The men at home, meanwhile, received their new clothing at some point in 1812; they had not received it at the spring inspection, but by the autumn all was in conformity with the new regulations.[48]

Having been issued with his uniform and regimental necessaries, the new-made soldier was assigned to one of the regiment's troops. For the bulk of his service, the troop was the financial and administrative unit through which a soldier's military life was managed, but for the recruit under training it did not immediately figure heavily in a day-to-day role. On those occasions that the whole regiment was serving at home, it simply did not make sense to burden a single troop with a whole batch of recruits; nor, due to the need to maintain each troop at a roughly equal strength to permit easy performance of military evolutions, was it possible for one sub-unit of the regiment to be vastly larger than its equivalents. Distributing recruits amongst all of the regiment's troops also facilitated what might be termed the unofficial aspects of their training. The vast amount of kit assigned to each man to equip himself and his horse for service required considerable care and attention if it was to be kept in good order, Steuart specifying that 'Every Recruit when he joins his Troop to be instructed by the Non Commissioned Officers of his Squad in the Care of every article of his Arms, Accoutrements, and Necessaries.'[49] At the same time, so far as formal instruction was concerned, it was clearly necessary to have men under training together so that they could easily be instructed. On those occasions when the bulk of the regiment was overseas, the fact that recruits perforce joined at the regimental depot which was more overtly configured for a training role made things more straightforward. Once six troops were deployed on service in the Peninsula, Steuart directed that two troops of the four remaining at the depot be prioritized for the fittest men and horses, so that they could be sent out to reinforce the regiment if necessary as a fourth active squadron, leaving the last two troops to process new men and horses.[50] Otherwise, and even to a lesser extent at the depot, new men spent their on-duty time away from their troops, undergoing the basic training intended to provide them with the knowledge and drills required to turn them into soldiers. First individually, then in small groups, and then in recruit squads, this training steadily added, layer by layer, the attributes of the soldier. There was no time limit to this process, and Standing Orders emphasized that 'All Recruits must attend Drills till perfected in their Exercise.'[51]

Unlike the infantry, where the large number of men who transferred from the militia to the regular service meant that a large portion of new recruits were already familiar with military life and the basics of drill, cavalry recruits needed training from scratch. It was not even possible to focus recruiting towards men who possessed prior experience with horses, and indeed, of the sample of fifty-two recruits considered above, only one – Charles Oales, an eighteen-year-old blacksmith from Staffordshire who enlisted in January 1815 – gave a trade that demonstrated an obvious equine connection.[52] The most common pre-enlistment trade given by recruits – by 58 per cent of our sample – was simply labourer. Of course, for those with a country background this may well have involved work with horses, but there is no way of confirming this. In any case, there was a world of difference between working a plough or cart horse and riding a cavalry mount, and although the basics of horse care remain unchanged no matter what manner of horse is concerned, even a man used to working with draught animals would have to relearn things the military way. Furthermore, use of labourer in this context, as Edward Coss points out, may well reflect a polite fiction designed to disguise the fact that the new recruit had 'held no significant employment in the recent past'. At best, the term for the most part reflected casual, short-term, unskilled work, which, in the agricultural sector, was likely to be seasonal.[53] With its substantial body of former labourers, followed in second and third place by contingents of erstwhile weavers and shoe-makers, the recruiting base of the 12th Light Dragoons was entirely typical of the British Army as a whole; after these came a smaller number of men from the various factory-based trades, and then one-offs such as Oales the blacksmith, or John McDermot from County Roscommon, who enlisted aged seventeen in October 1814 and gave his former occupation as clerk. Despite appearing a cut above the average recruit, neither of these men stood out in terms of their subsequent careers: both served for nearly two decades, but McDermot never rose beyond private whilst Oales briefly made corporal but was then reduced to the ranks.[54] It was this mixture of material, then, that the regiment was obliged to attempt to turn into cavalrymen.

Summing up the way that training worked in the British Army immediately prior to the period with which we are concerned, historian John Houlding enumerated the various stages of the training process:

> Passing from one element of the drill to the next, the soldier acquired first, at the manual, poise, confidence, and a certain skill with arms, while at the same time coming under the influence of military discipline; next he learned to use his arms in unison with other soldiers and as a response to command; then, well acquainted with his arms, he was taught the basic elements of carriage and regulated movement, individually and then with others in rank and file. Having passed through these first three elements of the training regimen, the private soldier had acquired the three things most essential to the performance of his more advanced tactical role:

knowledge of the use of his weapons, the ability to move in a regulated way, and a docile obedience.[55]

For the cavalryman, of course, this clear progression was rendered altogether more complex and lengthy by the need to perfect mounted as well as dismounted exercise, as well as to learn how to care for his horse. Since these aspects of initial training, and the far more advanced evolutions that became possible once they had been mastered, involved the training of the horse as well as the rider, they are best considered along with other matters equine in the following chapter. What we are concerned with here, then, is the initial training that turned the recruit into a soldier.

With so many recruits being youths with some growing still to do, and a rather greater proportion of the urban and rural poor than the stout yeomanry we might fondly imagine, it is perhaps little surprise that much of the training regime in the first instance was devoted to building up the physical fitness of recruits. This was an Army-wide problem, but the cavalry depot at Radipole Barracks near Weymouth, where the depot of the 12th was stationed between September 1811 and July 1813, was identified by the Army's Medical Board as being a particularly unsavoury location for new soldiers. Realizing that Radipole was merely an extreme example of a wider problem, the Board pointed out that young recruits generally were 'often weakened by this new life' and required 'seasoning'. This was accordingly followed by the recommendation that new soldiers 'are not to be made tender by too much care and confinement, while at the same time the discipline should be mild and conciliatory, and the men at first as little exposed to changes and crowding together'.[56]

Steuart's answer to the question of how to improve the fitness of his regiment, and particularly to build up the strength of its recruits, was reflected in his enthusiasm for instructing the men in the art of cudgelling. The utility of this skill was repeatedly brought up in a series of letters to his subordinates, none of whom seem entirely to have appreciated the value of, or, indeed, fully understood, their colonel's pet theme. Thus, the instruction that men receive such training was repeated time after time – and with particular vehemence to the captains left in command of the regimental depot, whom Steuart may perhaps have felt less likely to oppose his ideas than the regiment's field officers.[57] This culminated in a renewed order in June 1813 to Captain Coles, relative to the planned intake of boy recruits, for whom Steuart felt that the exercise would be particularly beneficial. To this end, Steuart told Coles that he was 'anxious to have a Cudgelling Master in each Troop, it should be a

Corporal, who, as an encouragement, might be exempted from guard mounting or have some other sort of advantage to be thought of'.[58] Coles evidently still failed to get the message, since his reply caused Steuart to bemoan the fact that he could not make himself understood before explaining the virtues of his scheme. Steuart informed Coles that he meant cudgelling:

> [T]o prepare the Body, & facilitate the instruction of all other exercise it gives a Man the use of all his limbs, makes him active and supple, the instruction is best given by way of recreation, in resting times when at Drill for there the body should never be kept long in a constrained position and is much relieved by active exertions. Cudjeling is the fine art of attack and defence when opposed either to the Sword or Lance by tracking to parry and to strike at the [opponent] which if taught with any sharp instrument would injure thus fencing is taught with foils and can not be taught with Swords, the art of carrying an edge with the Sabre is taught by cutting in the air, when an edge is carried the sword will be sharp, when otherwise Sword will not be the same, but I repeat it that the great advantage from Cudjeling is the facility it gives in the instruction of all other exercises. I will instruct a Man in Horsemanship in a far shorter time if he has previously been taught either to Fence or to Cudjel, beside which depend upon it that if you will give a Cavalry Soldier more confidence in action then it is of real utility and even that is a good point. We are fond of imitating foreign Troops in trifles, we should imitate them in essentials, particularly in Horsemanship, they all ride better than we do, and all Cavalry are taught what is called in French L'Espadion which is neither more nor less than Cudjeling.[59]

Mention of French practice may reflect an enthusiasm picked up in Steuart's own military education on the continent, and this sort of mock sword-play with wooden staffs seems logical training for cavalrymen, but cudgelling as a sport was by no means unknown in Britain. Not only did single-stick fighting remain a country pursuit, but in 1800 Captain G. Sinclair of the 42nd Foot had published an illustrated guide to the sport and advertised its utility to officers of both armed services, as well as to those desirous of defending themselves from footpads and the like.[60] Certainly, the whole thing was not simply one of Steuart's fads, and the concept and his justification for it showed a shrewd awareness of what was needed to build up the strength and skills of a recruit. With that being the case, it is rather hard to see exactly what his officers had against the idea, unless Steuart was correct in his assumption that they simply failed to see what he was getting at. In all events, despite their colonel's enthusiasm, cudgelling drill does not seem to have figured as part of the basic training of recruits in the 12th, nor as a recreation for their more seasoned comrades. This deficiency is something that is worth bearing in mind when we look in more detail at the sword exercises that most certainly did form part of every trooper's routine. The idea of rendering the soldier supple, it may be noted, was another enthusiasm, or at least a pet word, of Steuart's, and a term he used with respect to horses as well as men. In achieving this goal, even if not by means of his beloved cudgel exercise, Steuart may reasonably be judged to have been successful: by 1812, the regiment had acquired a nickname for the first time in its history, and that nickname was 'The Supple Twelfth'.[61]

Of course, not every recruit found himself successfully adapting to military life – perhaps in no small part due to the bewildering plethora of drills and exercises – and this, inevitably, led to cases of desertion. Desertion was a significant drain on British military manpower throughout the Napoleonic era, to the extent that the Army lost one man to desertion for every four who fell to sickness or wounds, making it a major cause for concern.[62] Yet it was also a problem that was largely restricted to troops serving in the British Isles: not only was the incidence of desertion on campaign far lower than at home, but the recovery rate – that is to say, the proportion of deserters brought back to their units – was higher.[63] In this respect, the 12th Light Dragoons were entirely typical of the pattern across the Army as a whole. Between June 1805 and December 1815, a total of 115 men deserted from the regiment at home, of whom seventeen were subsequently recovered, but only six men deserted whilst on active service.[64] There are several reasons to explain this. In part, it owes something to the fact that it was an altogether more difficult option to desert in a foreign land without knowledge of the language and – unless one made the ultimate step of going over to the enemy – with no obvious refuge. Desertion at home, on the other hand, offered the chance to merge straight back into the civilian population, elements of which, on occasion, could be induced to aid the deserter either through a personal connection, the potential for profit or as an anti-establishment gesture.[65] The other major factor, however, was that a large proportion of deserters were men who had only recently enlisted, and who had become disillusioned with, or failed to adapt to, a military life; by default, these were men who would not yet be in a state of readiness to be sent overseas. Yet there were plenty of other cases where seasoned soldiers, and even non-commissioned officers, deserted. September 1809 saw the regiment's paymaster serjeant abscond, whilst in October 1813 Steuart was finding it 'rather strange to me that a <u>Trusty Noncommissioned Officer</u> should sell an Officer's Horse, and Desert'.[66]

Of course, as well as those who simply failed to adapt to soldiering, there were those who deliberately deserted so as to re-enlist and claim another bounty, but if possible such men would endeavour to abscond before they had joined a regiment. There are nevertheless several instances of a deserter from the 12th being found out after having enlisted into another regiment – or on one occasion, having joined the Royal Navy – and similarly of men recruited by the 12th being reclaimed by a regiment from which they had earlier deserted. This may, of course, simply reflect a recruit having found himself with nowhere else to go, rather than a deliberate intention to desert and re-enlist for the bounty. Interestingly, whilst deserters who had joined another regiment were returned to that in which they had originally enlisted, Francis Bateman, the deserter who had ended up in the Royal Navy, was retained by the sea service.[67] Others were recovered after long periods in civilian life. William Bywater, who deserted in 1806, must have thought himself well clear of the Army by 1811 but was unfortunate enough to be in Portsmouth when the 12th arrived there to embark for the Peninsula and so was not only reclaimed by the regiment but swept immediately off to war.[68] However, just because a deserter was returned to his regiment did not necessarily mean that he would simply be forgiven and allowed back into the ranks. Britain was short of military manpower but not so short that examples could not be made. In practice, it proved possible to kill two birds with one stone and give a recaptured deserter an exemplary sentence and then commute this in return for service overseas: this typically meant discharge from his original regiment and a transfer to the West Indies. This happened on more than one occasion to men who had deserted from the 12th, but was by no means a typical outcome.

From 1812, the bi-annual inspection reports begin to include abstracts of all regimental courts martial in the six months preceding the inspection. Surviving records show the sentences awarded to eight deserters from the 12th who were brought back to the regiment. In all eight cases a guilty verdict resulted in a flogging, but the number of lashes awarded ranged from 200 to 500. Furthermore, in five of the eight cases, the number of lashes actually inflicted was reduced. One of the men sentenced to 500 lashes received his sentence in full, whereas the other received only 275; other, lower, sentences were also reduced, with the lightest punishment inflicted being 100 lashes, to a man originally sentenced to 300.[69] Certainly, the level of punishment was in part influenced by the amount of time for which a man had been absent: thus, one of the men sentenced to 500 lashes was Michael Tucker, tried by General Depot Court Martial on 25 February 1813 and found guilty of 'absenting himself from Dublin the Head Quarters of his Regiment without leave in June 1804 and not returning until brought back a prisoner on the 20th Feb 1813': a period of nearly nine years.[70] Yet it was Tucker who had nearly half of his sentence cancelled, whereas George McCallum, who was awarded the same sentence and received it without remission, had been absent for less than a month. However, McCallum had deserted from a party on the march, which enabled him to be charged with 'irregular and unsoldierlike conduct' and thus, perhaps, merit the higher sentence. Even then, however, James Lambe who deserted with McCallum and was captured at the same time, was sentenced to only 400 lashes, and had a hundred of them remitted.[71] Without more detailed records of the court's deliberations, the reason for this distinction is not clear: perhaps McCallum was seen as a ringleader, or perhaps Lambe had the better record or someone to speak up in favour of his character. Either is possible, but we have no way of being sure.

Other men who received no remission to their sentence had generally compounded desertion with some other crime. Thus, the charge against Joshua Alsop, who received a full sentence of 200 lashes, notes that he was tried, 'For absenting himself without leave on or about the 6th day of October 1813 & not returning until brought back a prisoner on or about the 1st of November 1813 being disguised at the time of his apprehension in a colour'd Jacket which he had taken with him belonging to an Officer's Servant',[72] whilst Richard Gleeson received 30 lashes for compounding his desertion by also 'making away with his Reg'l Necessaries'.[73] Since Standing Orders laid down that 'No Soldier is permitted to have any other Clothes, than what is Regimental', something that was enforced by a further order that 'old Clothes a Recruit brings to the Regiment are to be sold for his Advantage',[74] the obtaining of civilian clothes, either through direct theft or by making off with items of kit which could then be sold to fund an escape into civilian life, was a clear indication of intention to desert and brought down a heavy punishment as a result. James Henderson even managed to combine both offences, with the records of his Garrison Court Martial, held on 21 March 1812, recording his being found guilty of 'being absent from watch setting and making away with part of his Reg. necessaries 1 pair of Breeches, 1 pair of Reg. Gloves, an[d] suspicion of Deserting having on a round hat & Coloured Cloth[e]s'. Henderson was sentenced to 400 lashes, receiving 200.[75] Punishment was not always draconian, however; Thomas Eadie was found guilty in January 1813 of 'making away with part of his regimental necessaries' and sentenced to 100 lashes only to be pardoned on the grounds that he was a recruit. One of the main complaints of those opposed to flogging was that it left a man marked – literally – as an irredeemable bad character, and it was evidently deemed more effective in this case to let the remitted punishment serve as a warning to a first-time offender who might yet mature into a good soldier.[76]

Throughout the period with which we are concerned, a relatively enlightened approach to discipline seems to have pervaded the 12th Light Dragoons. For Steuart, it was all about leading by example, and he placed the onus of responsibility firmly on the regiment's officers. Steuart was aware that it was Ponsonby's desire to see corporal punishment abolished and, although he had his doubts about the wisdom of this, he reasoned that the commanding officer's wish could best be realized by the continuation of his own creed of discipline. This he made clear in a rather fatherly letter to James Bridger upon that officer taking command of the regimental depot:

> As long as Officers set a bad example it will be followed and punishment will remain unavoidable for the correction of Vice by flogging or otherwise no disgrace ought to be annexed thereto on the contrary it ought to be held out as a purification. Many soldiers are lost to the Service by annexing disgrace to Corporal Punishment, when they have formerly been disgraced by bad conduct and no account taken thereof. If we can not stimulate Officers to good conduct and a strict discharge of their duty from a principle of Honour, how can it be expected from the Common Soldier except by the dread of punishment, having no good example before him.[77]

The same sentiments were also conveyed, in a more abbreviated form, to Blunden upon his succeeding Bridger in the depot command.[78]

Although Steuart never seems to have been satisfied that things were being done quite as he wished – for which he continued to blame his officers – it is an undeniable feature of the successive inspection reports on the 12th that courts martial were few, and punishments, when awarded, light. In 1810, Major General the Hon. Charles Hope noted that 'The Courts Martial have been few and the Punishments Lenient', whilst four years later Major General the Hon. Henry Fane seemed pleased to record that there had been only three courts martial in the second half of 1814, with no corporal punishment at all.[79] Certainly, the remaining cases from the returns of courts martial contain few other serious offences. The heaviest sentence not relating to desertion was that awarded to James Kelly by a Garrison Court Martial of 25 November 1811, at which he was tried 'On suspicion of Entering the Regimental Store of the 13th Lt Dragoons and Stealing out of a chest 3 pair of Regimental Leather Britches'. Found guilty, he was awarded 300 lashes and sentence was carried out in full.[80]

Although other offences also brought the guilty party a flogging, other, non-corporal, punishments were also handed down, with men being awarded a period in solitary confinement or, for more serious offences, incarceration in the 'black hole'. Nor should it be assumed that all trials of private soldiers were a one-sided affair. Military justice as practised at this period was in many ways a far fairer process than the equivalent civil system, with the adjutant responsible for ensuring that all proper preparation be made for regimental courts martial. Within this, the adjutant was specifically tasked with making certain that 'the proper crimes of prisoners are produced' – that is to say, that the charges were correctly framed – 'and the evidence [i.e., witnesses] present, both those on the part of the prosecution, and those for the prisoner'.[81] The fairness of the system can be seen in the acquittal of Joseph Farmer, tried in February 1813, although the nature of the extenuating circumstances are not provided. The charge against him was 'disgraceful and unsoldierlike conduct in overstaying his furlough and getting several large sums of money from Civil Magistrates & others previous to its Expiration'. It might be assumed that in a case relating to financial impropriety that hard evidence would be available to prove the charge, and it is certainly difficult to understand how Farmer could have been mistakenly assumed to have overstayed his leave, but the court nevertheless returned a not guilty verdict.[82]

Of course, only the most serious offences would land the perpetrator in front of a court martial, and it may reasonably be assumed that minor infractions were swiftly dealt with by the NCOs and troop quartermasters. Indeed, there are hints that on occasion too great a reliance was placed on the regiment's non-commissioned leadership. Steuart certainly feared that this was the case, and that ill would come of it, but he was not in daily contact with the regiment and his long-distance diagnoses of its ills cannot always be completely relied upon. More damning is the comment of Major General Anson that he suspected the authority of NCOs to be 'sometimes misapplied', although in the same report he also commented that 'the Non Commissioned Officers are apparently active and intelligent'.[83] Anson, it may also be noted, was reporting on the regiment when it was in winter quarters and a substantial number of the officers had gone on leave, which may explain a greater need for reliance on the NCOs, and it was certainly the case that an inspection of the depot earlier in the year had only praise for its non-commissioned staff. Not only did Major General Jones recommend the 12th's Serjeant Major John Caruthers for further promotion, he also expressed the belief that:

> The other Non Commissioned Officers are well instructed active and intelligent, they are obedient and respectful to their officers, and at the same time support their own authority in a proper manner; they perform their duties at the Drills and in Quarters with promptitude and Energy and by their conduct promote to the best of their abilities the Discipline of the Regiment.[84]

Whilst Steuart certainly expected his officers to take the lead role in running the regiment, he by no means spared the NCOs from a heavy share of duty. In particular, they were to serve as the first link between the private soldiers and commissioned officers, and as such each was to 'keep up that degree of Respect and Command which is due to him from the Men'. As well as the basic duty of instruction already alluded to, Steuart's Standing Orders further required that 'Non Commissioned Officers are to attend Strictly to every Circumstance of a Mans Conduct and Behaviour, and to make it their Business to find out every thing irregular or Suspicious.' Finally, like the officers, they were to lead by example, with Steuart requiring that 'they will be observant in the Case of Arms, Accoutrements and Necessaries; of Cleanliness, and the most perfect Exactness in every Duty of the Regiment'.[85] The same standards, to an even higher degree, were expected of troop quartermasters.[86]

Unlike the commissioned officers, men who obtained non-commissioned rank did so from within the regiment. The unofficial rank of lance corporal permitted a man believed to have promise to be tried out in a position of responsibility – 'In order that the Men may have an Opportunity of qualifying themselves for Promotion' – from which he might subsequently progress to corporal and then on to serjeant. In theory, at least, no man could be given substantive NCO rank without having first served as a lance corporal, but a lance corporal could be reduced back to the ranks at the request of his troop commander should he prove himself unfit for that authority.[87] In order to make the promotion of deserving men easier, a promotion to lance corporal or corporal could be made so as to take a man into a different troop from that in which he had previously served, if there was no vacancy in his own troop. This in turn required a degree of equalization to be factored in, so that a troop would not be drained of all its most promising rank and file.

> When any Dragoon of one Troop is appointed lance Corporal in another, the Commanding Officer of the Troop from which the Lance Corporal is made is to have a Choice of a Man out of the Troop which gets the lance Corporal, the Commanding Officer of that Troop being allowed two Exceptions. In the Appointment of Corporals one Exception is allowed.[88]

By this system, promising men could be advanced as and when vacancies became available, but, even so, promotion was by no means rapid.

Table 3: NCO Ages and Experience, 1809[89]

| | Average Age | Length of Service | | |
		Minimum	Maximum	Average
Quartermasters	38	10	30	19
Serjeants	28	8	35+	12
Corporals	28	5	30	10

This data would suggest that the vast majority of NCOs were experienced, mature men. The close similarity of age and service profiles between serjeants and corporals also confirms a relatively slow rate of promotion, although the presence of three serjeants in their early twenties shows that a truly deserving soldier could still rise accordingly. Six years later, in the aftermath of Waterloo, age and service profiles for serjeants remained almost unchanged, with the average being twenty-nine years of age and twelve years of service; however, this figure includes troop serjeant majors, replacing troop quartermasters, and so the overall average for those in senior non-commissioned leadership roles can be seen to have dropped slightly. Far more apparent, however, is the changed profile for corporals, with an average of twenty-eight years of age but only six years of service. That said, even six years of service covers the entire span of the regiment's Peninsular campaigning with room to spare, so it does not indicate lack of active-service experience in the same way that a similar average in 1809 would have done. What is more, those averages are raised by one man aged over fifty-five and with more than forty years' service, and another man in his late forties – by 1815, the majority of corporals were men in their mid-twenties. Two elderly corporals aside, NCOs were getting younger by the end of the war, and the speed with which it was possible to rise had also increased. Some men had made corporal after only two years, and there were three serjeants on the

1794

Uniform of the 12th Light Dragoons, *c.* 1794.
Detail from watercolour by Richard Simkin.

'The New Costume of the British Light Dragoons.' Engraving by and after Denis Dighton. Issued during the course of 1812, the revised uniform was criticized for making the silhouette of the trooper indistinguishable from that of the French *chasseurs à cheval*.

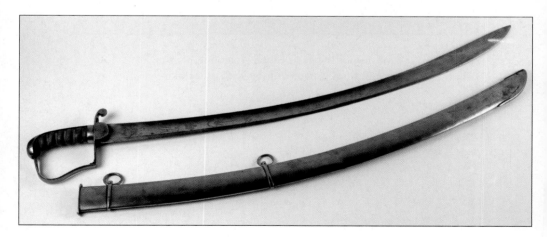

1796-pattern Light Cavalry Sword and scabbard. This officer's version would have been privately purchased and made to a higher quality than those issued to the rank and file. Originally the property of future memoirist Lt William Hay, it was carried by him at Waterloo.

Sir John Ormsby Vandeleur. Oil on canvas by William Salter, *c.* 1835.

Overleaf: Extract from Sir James Steuart's Letterbook, July 1813. Contrast the two memoranda in Steuart's own hand (*top left and middle right*) with the neat copperplate of two different clerks. In these pages matters addressed range from recruitment and procuring horses to a recommendation for the commission made vacant by the death of Cornet Hammon at Vitoria.

Colchester 10th July 1813 —

wrote to Mr. Yarvis to say that I wanted
100 horses that I would go and inspect them
at the birth of Doncaster & Chester but would be most
agreeable your been to Beaton and that I would
make that my good centre for a fortnight or
any time during the months of September &c.
that if he could do no better I depended on
Preston fair —

Colchester 12 July 1813

Sir,

Referring to my letter of the 29th June, address'd to
Commanding Officer and to Capt. Coles letter of the 26 ulto. It appears
that the Recruiting of Boys, can not be taken out of the hands
of Inspecting Field Officers, as I am by no means inclined to take
exclusively on myself

I am Sir
Your obt. humle. Servant
(signed) Jas. Stewart D.
Genl.
Col. 12th L. Dragoons

Officer Commanding
12th L. Dragoons
Depot Weymouth

Colchester 22nd July 1813

Sir.

You will receive instructions from the
Commanding Officer of the Depot of 12th L. Dragoons
proceed to Newcastle on Tyne, there to meet Mr. Thorne
a lot of Horses for my Regiment on the 12th of next month.
You must not buy any above one third of them years old
that is rising five, nor more above six off
You will observe my former instructions, good Bone
and activity.
I hope that the Commanding Officer at Weymouth will
allow to obtain you leave to visit your Friends at Durham
for a short time — Let me hear from you from Newcastle

I am Sir
L. &. &. .
Jas. Stewart D.

Lieut. Phillips
12th L. Dragoons

Coltness 22nd July 1813.

Sir—

By a letter I have just now received from the
[...] the Horse dealer [...] informed that he will
have a lot of Remount Horses for the 12th Lt Dragoons
ready for Inspection at Newcastle upon Tyne on Thursday
the 12th of August next — and as it is not in my power to be
there at that time, you will be pleased to send Lieutenant
Phipps, to inspect the above Horses — He is acquainted with
my general Instructions, to which I have nothing to add, only
that at this season of the year — one third only of the Horses
[...] must be three years old — that is nothing to all the
[...] must be 4 off or upwards not exceeding six years old.

[...] Phipps is anxious to be allowed a short time to see
his friends in the neighbourhood of Durham, and I hope
that you will find it in your power to accommodate him
in that wish.

I am Sir
[...] commanding
12th Lt Dragoons Depot [...]

[...] 27th July 1813 —

Wrote this day to Col [...] and
recommended Mr [...] Reed for a vacancy
in my Regt. in the room of [...]
killed at Vittoria —

Coltness July 31st 1813 —

Sir
This Mornings Post brought me your Letter of the 26th with the
[...] enclosed respecting the inlistment of Boys — I perfectly agree
that the Boys should serve their apprenticeship with the
[...] Tradesmen, by this method very advantage may be expected
[...] System and little will be gained if they are put out — Capt
[...] is correct with respect to the Farrier & Saddler Majors who are
[...] with the Depot but it must be observed that Cavalry
[...] have also Serjant Armourers [...] not at present at
[...] to carry the present System into full & proper effect Govern[ment]
should also allow a Serjant Boot maker and Master Taylor

Re-enactment recreation of troopers of the 12th Light Dragoons from the Napoleonic era. *Above left*: the pre-1812 uniform; *centre*: post-1812 uniform; *above right*: stable dress.

Right and below right: Right and left-hand views respectively of a surviving example of the Tarleton helmet worn by the 12th Light Dragoons from its introduction in the 1780s until replaced by the shako in 1812. Note the Prince of Wales's feathers on the right-hand side, and the regimental name above the peak.

Left: Image pasted into the binding of Steuart's Letterbook, showing the ornate design of watering cap worn by the regiment. Note the two heraldic devices; the Prince of Wales's feathers pinning the tuft into place, and the sphynx badge signifying service in the 1801 Egyptian campaign.

Obverse and reverse of the Military General Service Medal (*above left*) awarded to Serjeant William Summers of the 12th Light Dragoons, with clasps indicating service in Egypt, at Salamanca and at Vitoria. Summers had to wait until 1848 for his early service to be recognized, thirty-two years after receiving the Waterloo Medal (*above right*) for his participation in that battle.

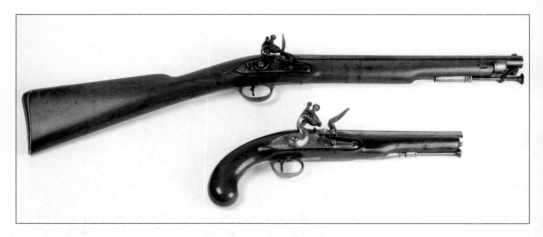

The two main types of firearm issued to Britain's light cavalry during the Napoleonic Wars: the 1796-pattern pistol, and the Paget Carbine. The carbine was introduced around 1808, replacing earlier models carried prior to that date.

strength each of whom had only served for three years. Evidently, the experience of active service gave men a far greater opportunity to show their merit, and be rewarded for it, than did home service.[90]

The NCOs of the 12th Light Dragoons were therefore not men lacking in experience. Yet because they very clearly came from the same sort of background as the body of men over whom their status now required them to exert authority, this to an extent made that authority fragile. When necessary, official punishments were imposed on men who had failed to show adequate respect or obedience to NCOs. Thus Edward Arnos, tried by garrison court martial on 23 July 1813, 'For disobeying the orders of Troop Serjeant Major McCaskle and being repeatedly confined for similar offences' was sentenced to 100 lashes, although this was remitted and he was instead confined in the black hole for seven days. James Sackins, however, did receive a flogging for refusing to obey the orders of Farrier Major Bouton, although in this case the offence was compounded by his having struck one of Bouton's assistants, Farrier William Love. Sackins received 100 of the 300 lashes to which the court sentenced him.[91] It was the same on campaign: less than a month after Waterloo, Philip Aughey was sentenced to 100 lashes, 'For irregular and unsoldierlike conduct & Insolence and disobedience of Orders to Serjeant Major White in the execution of his duty,' although, in the event, a quarter of Aughey's sentence was remitted.[92]

Yet, at the same time as officialdom acted to support non-commissioned authority, the fear remained – in Steuart's eyes, certainly – that NCOs and even troop quartermasters retained the vices of the common soldier and could not entirely be relied upon themselves. It will be recalled, for example, that one of the main reasons that Steuart gave for his support for the abolition of troop quartermasters was the difficulty in finding men of a sufficient moral calibre to fill the role. Indeed, Steuart felt that the fault for any lack of respect for a particular NCO's authority lay with the NCO himself, and that one who failed to secure 'that degree of Respect and Command which is due to him from the Men . . . deserves to be Reduced, as wanting that propriety of Conduct and Behaviour, which will always procure it'.[93] For a troop quartermaster, the security of his warrant guarded against a reversion in status, but for a serjeant or corporal it was quite possible for an error or offence to send him back into the ranks. Sadly, this was not an infrequent occurrence. We have already encountered two NCO deserters, one of them a thief into the bargain, and there were other, if less dramatic falls from grace often with the lubricant of alcohol as a contributing factor.

Nevertheless, particularly on campaign, a valuable NCO could be forgiven a lapse and retained in his rank rather than deprive the regiment of useful junior leadership. Serjeant Flynn, for example, was sentenced to be reduced to the ranks after being found guilty 'being in Liquor and Incapable of doing the duty of Orderly Serjeant of the Regiment on the Morning of the 28 August 1812', but was pardoned by Ponsonby and kept his rank.[94] Similarly, Corporal Peter Lyons was sentenced to 100 lashes and reduction to the ranks for insolence to Lieutenant Frederick Cobbold of the 1st Royal Dragoons, and of disobeying the lieutenant's orders following a roadside encounter on the march into France after Waterloo, but in the event kept his rank and suffered only a week's solitary confinement. Interestingly, Private John Clayme received double Lyons's sentence for the same incident – being awarded 200 lashes but receiving two weeks' solitary – which suggests that Lyons was less to blame, perhaps having been drawn into a confrontation between Clayme and Cobbold.[95] Or possibly the two men were equally at fault and the threatened loss of rank was considered to make up for Lyons's lesser punishment. As with many of these abstract records – as, indeed, with so many aspects of life in the ranks – the details are tantalizingly vague, and a complete understanding remains elusively out of reach.

Chapter IV

Horses and Riders

JUST AS EACH CAVALRY REGIMENT relied upon its own efforts to keep itself recruited up to strength in terms of manpower, so too did each regiment have responsibility for obtaining and training sufficient horses to maintain its mounted strength. As with all areas in which responsibility was decentralized to a regimental level, there were both positives and negatives to this system. On the positive side, a regiment could – within reason – set its own standards of selection, oversee its own training, and in general tailor its buying programme to match its needs. The major negative, however, was that it meant that a regiment that lost its horses had a complex and lengthy task ahead of it to restore itself to full capability. This, for example, was the case for the hussar regiments that were evacuated from Corunna in 1809 and of course for the 12th Light Dragoons after the regiment's return from Egypt. The after-effects of this process were still being felt at the time that the 12th returned from Ireland to England in 1805, with the following year's inspection report noting that part of the regiment was 'obliged to remain in quarters for want of Horses', although the horses that were on the strength were 'very good & in fine condition'. This mismatch between the number of troopers and the number of troop horses was soon redressed by a reduction in the over-large rank and file establishment, but a note in the same report that many of the horses under training – Recruit Horses, as the terminology went – seemed 'much inferior to the old Horses of the Regt.' served as a first sign of problems to come.[1] As the British Army prepared to renew the struggle with France, available horseflesh suitable for military purposes decreased in both quantity and quality. For the next eight years, Steuart would superintend a never-ending struggle to keep his regiment properly mounted.

In order to understand the nature of the problem, it is necessary to understand something of the nature of the horses that were required. The general lightening of the cavalry in the British Army during the second half of the eighteenth century – reflected in the conversion of the last regiments of heavy horse to dragoon guards, as well as the raising or conversion of light dragoon regiments – had led to a resulting lightening of the typical cavalry mount. The old breed of great black horse that had once been the staple of heavy cavalry work in the seventeenth and early eighteenth centuries had, by the start of the nineteenth, been rendered effectively extinct by the introduction of fresh blood-lines. In this way, descendants of this common ancestor had evolved into more specialized types: the hunter, bred as the name would suggest for foxhunting; the coaching type, a fast draught animal whose military use became that of artillery haulage; and the sort of heavy draught animal typified by the Shire horse. With the hunter becoming the staple of all cavalry work, it became necessary to subdivide the type to a degree, and this led to the denomination of light, heavy and medium hunter types. The process that had helped turn the black horse into the hunter was the infusion of thoroughbred blood from the descendants of the eastern horses imported in the 1660s and 1670s as part of Charles II's enthusiastic patronage of the turf, and the continuation of this process – by further infusions of thoroughbred genes – developed the hunter into the charger type that became the preferred mount of such of Britain's cavalry officers as could afford the purchase price.[2]

For the rank and file of Britain's light dragoon regiments, the ideal troop horse – combining stamina, mobility and economy – came from the lighter end of the hunter spectrum, capable of covering seven or eight miles an hour over rough terrain, and sufficiently agile to clear most obstacles. A move towards a distinct light cavalry horse can be identified almost from the first raising of such regiments by the British Army in the 1740s and 1750s, but it took the development of modern foxhunting in the 1780s really to perfect the model for the light dragoon troop horse.[3] Steuart, naturally, had his own specific requirements for the type, which he helpfully outlined in full when informing horse-dealer Hugh Taylor that he would try a batch of fifty horses from him providing they were of sufficient quality:

> I repeat it that I will take no Horse which is not strong and active fit to carry 18 stone on the Road the age from 4 and upwards, one third of that number I will take at four years old next May, young Horses I will take at 14 Hands 2 Inches, but the standard of my Regiment is from 14H 3I to 15 Hands. I prefer dark brown in point of colour – any blacks must have a strong dash of blood.[4]

Black, in this context refers not to the colour as such but to the old type of Great Black Horse, which to be any use for light cavalry work needed a strong infusion of thoroughbred genes – the 'dash of blood' to which Steuart alludes. Indeed, whilst Steuart had a preference for brown horses he was not overly fussy in this regard, going on to tell Taylor that:

> You will observe that altho' I prefer brown Horses I do not restrict you to colour except Grey, but on the whole I prefer dark colour, and I have no objection to Mares. Remember Stout and good Limbs. Stout Backs. Good Feet. Open in the Canter. Good shoulders and well up before. Deep Chested and not light Carcassed, nor too heavy in the hind quarter, but strong in the Gammon and open between the jaws, being particularly necessary for Cavalry.[5]

For once, this was a matter on which the officers of the 12th were fully in concurrence with their colonel, and one of the few things that Steuart found himself in agreement on with the unfortunate Major Wyndham was 'that small compact Horses are the best for Service in general provided such can be procured capable of carrying the weight allowed to them'.[6] The initial ambivalence over mares later swung to a preference for a mixture of mares and geldings, no doubt reflecting experience from the Peninsula, from where Wellington recommended 'that Mares should be sent in preference to Horses, as it has been found that they bear the Work better than the Horses'.[7]

By 1809, when the 12th was fully fit for service, the inspection held in October of that year showed a total of 703 troop horses for 734 rank and file. In size, the animals on the strength showed a great degree of uniformity, almost all being between 14½ and 15 hands: only seventeen animals fell outside this size bracket, reaching up to 15½ hands. Ages were more varied, with two horses still serving at fourteen years of age and fifty-nine three-year-olds, which evidently represented the most recent influx of recruit horses. A little over two-thirds of the troop horses fell into a bracket spanning five to nine years of age.[8] On the whole, this was an entirely adequate complement of horses, but the fact that there were a number of older animals, giving an average age of just under seven years, meant that work would still be needed to keep up the effective mounted strength of the regiment in the future. This need became all the more apparent when the regiment was committed to active service in the Peninsula.

Although Steuart can have harboured few illusions as to the demands that prolonged active service would place on his regiment's horseflesh, the situation must surely have been brought home to him by the order of August 1811 that augmented the established strength of the regiment to 854 effective troop horses.[9] This official confirmation of the need for replacement mounts marked the beginning of a three-year struggle to keep the regiment supplied with horses, which would tax the efforts of both Steuart and his home-based staff. Although a succession of depot commanders would find themselves involved in the process, the key figure alongside the regiment's colonel was its Riding Master, Lieutenant Joseph Philips, who seems to have had the respect of both his seniors and his peers. In addition to Steuart's obvious regard for him, Major General Jones described Philips in successive inspection reports as 'a very diligent and attentive officer', and 'very intelligent and zealous'.[10] Fellow subaltern John Vandeleur – sharing Philips's rank but from a very different background – thought him 'a very quiet good man in every respect', and recommended that his mother pay her respects to him if the Vandeleur family made a mooted visit to Weymouth where the regimental depot was then stationed.[11] Successive inspections of the depot show Philips taking on more and more responsibility there, acting as quartermaster and adjutant and being involved in all aspects of training, reflecting an increasing versatility: indeed, strictly speaking his involvement in the purchase of horses was also beyond the remit of his post as laid down in regulations.[12]

Steuart's use of Philips as his agent for the selection and purchase of regimental horses may in part have stemmed from a certain unhappiness with Captain Bridger's performance in that role: whilst admiring the depot commander's diligence in travelling to Newcastle to purchase mounts he cautioned him that 'in future we must take no three years old'.[13] Certainly, when the time came round to send an officer to Preston Fair in January 1812, where Steuart expected to pick up a large consignment of horses from one of his regular suppliers, Warwickshire-based Thomas Harris, he deputized Philips rather than Bridger to make the trip. This, in part, may have been required by the slightly ticklish nature of the task at hand, since Steuart had received unfavourable reports from the regiment of the quality of the previous batch of horses supplied by Harris, and required Philips both to run an expert eye over the new batch and to return the rejected animals from the old. As if this were not task enough, the letter began with a rare admonition to Philips from his patron, blaming him for accepting the inferior horses in the first place, stressing that 'the Regt. being now on Service requires the best sort of Horse which can be furnished', and warning him that he would be held responsible for any future inferior purchases. After clarifying that Philips should accept 'no Horse from Mr Harris that is not active and fully master of 17 Stone', the letter concluded with a warning, to be passed on to Harris, that Steuart would if necessary cease to employ Harris and take his business elsewhere if he remained unsatisfied, and also a reaffirmation of the high standards that he expected Philips to maintain. In particular, Steuart wanted his regiment's mounts as even in size and quality as possible to which end he warned Philips that 'I by no means approve of the system of taking a bad Horse as a compromise for a remarkable good one.'[14]

Unsurprisingly, Philips's mission to Preston did not bring back horses in the numbers that Steuart had hoped for, although those that were obtained were good and served to restore Steuart's faith in his riding master's ability and judgement. This shortfall, along with the apparent decline in quality of the animals supplied by Harris, was what induced Steuart to seek alternative suppliers, including the Irish dealer Hugh Taylor who received the list of requirements quoted above, to supplement those already providing mounts for the 12th.[15] Yet the inability of Harris to meet the regiment's requirements was indicative of a wider shortage of suitable horseflesh that was affecting the British Army more generally. Since the 1790s, the British Army had been engaged in a series of campaigns that were generally of short duration and which saw the deployment of only limited cavalry forces: now, with a growing force serving under Wellington in the Peninsula, Britain was committed to a campaign that had every indication of being a lengthy endeavour. What was more, the Iberian Peninsula was by no means a favourable climate for horses, so that not only was the initial requirement for horses high but so too was the level of equine wastage. During the Peninsular War as a whole, British forces – artillery and the wagon train as well as cavalry – lost a total of 18,940 horses, all of which needed replacing. Wellington's cavalry force grew steadily as the war went on, with a big increase for the campaigns of 1812 and 1813, so that by the war's end Steuart was one of nineteen cavalry colonels scouring Britain for remounts for their regiments in the Peninsula. Inevitably, this competition meant that the trade in cavalry horses became a seller's market, with animals of a lower quality being offered at the standard price by dealers who recognized that they held the advantage.

Wellington, for his part, entirely appreciated that there was a problem but his response to it was not entirely helpful, expressing the view that the undoubted shortfall of remounts for the regiments under his command was the fault of those at home responsible for their purchase: that is to say, Steuart and his fellow colonels. Noting – this was in April 1813 – that Napoleon had in just three months obtained the best part of 40,000 horses to make good the losses incurred in Russia, Wellington stated himself 'incredulous respecting the difficulties of procuring horses in England'. He was quite prepared to concede 'that the persons usually employed to supply horses, and the ordinary means, and perhaps even the ordinary price, are not sufficient to procure a large supply at the moment,' but felt that with a little alteration things could be made to work. Might regiments not, he mused, purchase horses at the ideal age of five or six years so as to have them ready for instant service? Of course, this would nearly double the purchase price from twenty-five guineas to around forty, but it would serve to fill his immediate need. Otherwise, he felt that regiments not serving in the Peninsula would have to transfer their serviceable horses to those that were already there, and build themselves back up by purchasing young horses. Unsurprisingly, neither option was adopted. Not only was the money not available to buy up older horses, but such animals would in any case still need to be broken to the service. A twenty-five guinea purchase price, when added to the ten pounds per animal that Wellington had earlier calculated it cost to ship a horse out to Portugal, was already quite enough and for colonels to pay more would – unless additional funds were made available – require them to dip into their private purses. As for taking horses from other regiments, this blithely supposed that there was no other worthwhile duty for Britain's cavalry than service in the Peninsula, which was far from the case.[16] No doubt a centralized system of buying horses would have been preferable, but it would have required a great deal of organization, and the whole point of managing matters on a regimental basis was that this work – and expense – was delegated to the colonels.

Steuart, to his credit, continued his efforts even as the demand increased, and strove both to maintain his standards and to hold his own against horse dealers who must have felt their position to control the market grow ever stronger. Following Philips's trip to Preston, an offer was received 'from Mr Guthrie in Yorkshire to provide 100 Horses within the year in Lots of 20', but Steuart weighed up the costs and came to the conclusion that 'unless he would deliver them within a moderate distance of Weymouth it would hardly be worth while to send an Officer to a great distance for 20 Horses'. No further mention is made of Guthrie in subsequent correspondence, although another Yorkshire dealer, John Robson of Catterick Bridge, was offered a similar arrangement but only if he could deliver his batch of twenty horses to Oxford. Robson was also later approached about the possibility of making a delivery at Carlisle. Steuart was also loath to send an officer to Ireland to inspect or collect horses, and although he was obliged by the poor showing at Preston to accept a trial batch of fifty horses from Hugh Taylor, the Irish dealer was obliged to have the animals shipped to Dumfries for inspection. By these measures, which shifted as much of the cost as possible to the dealer, Steuart hoped to make good the equine losses of 1811 and have the regiment back up to its established strength by the summer of 1812.[17] Unfortunately for Steuart's calculations, the campaign of 1812 was the longest and hardest in which his regiment would find itself involved, with consequently severe demands on its horses. Thus, far from representing a peak effort, Steuart's plans to get the 12th back up to strength in the first half of the year were just the start of a process that would continue until the regiment returned to Britain in the summer of 1814.

For the most part, Steuart responded to the challenge by pushing himself – and Philips – harder still, arranging an increasing number of journeys to view and purchase horses. On 18 February 1812 he made a note of his plans for the coming year, calculated on obtaining the bulk of the required horses from Taylor and Harris, topped up by whatever Robson could supply. This note also indicates a first willingness by Steuart to compromise on his previously fixed standards, in that he indicated that he was willing to accept up to half the horses from Robson and Harris at three years old, whilst Taylor was told that if a first batch of a hundred horses proved acceptable he would take a second batch in the autumn and that young animals 'rising 4' would be acceptable.[18] That said, Bridger at the depot was instructed that no horses were to be sent out to the regiment in Portugal that were younger than five or older than eight years.[19] Alas for Steuart's hopes, when he inspected the first consignment of Taylor's horses he found that not only were there only sixty animals presented rather than a hundred, and that, of these, only thirty were worth purchase. What was more, Taylor also supplied horses to the 18th Hussars, and although that regiment took them from him at the standard twenty-five guineas purchase price they also paid a marching allowance for bringing the animals from Portpatrick to Dumfries, which Steuart – conceding that such an extra payment was 'but just and reasonable' – was also obliged to pay. Only by covering their expenses in this way could dealers meet the standard purchase price, and Steuart complained that by paying the standard amount alone it was 'next to impossible to provide the necessary number of Horses'.[20]

Matters continued in a similar vein, with dealers repeatedly unable to deliver the quantity and quality of horses required. Steuart, motivated by the recognition 'that the expenditure of Horses in Portugal is three to one greater than that of Men & we must provide accordingly,' continued to do his utmost to keep the regiment mounted, but was increasingly driven to compromise his standards. Another batch of fifty-nine horses from Taylor was shipped direct from Portpatrick to Weymouth in May 1812, making up the shortfall of the earlier consignment, but Steuart had to warn Bridger that 'they consist of a greater variety than the last lot, many are very good & high priced, some I think indifferent'.[21] This was followed up with an admission that Steuart had been obliged to accept bad horses in order to get good ones at the standard price:

> In the last Lot you will find a good many good Horses which rendered it necessary that I should take some which I really do not approve of but by rejecting them I could not have got the others. By degrees you must find means of getting rid of what is not fit for us, that is by getting them cast [disposed of], I think however that there are very few of that description.[22]

Steuart was also obliged to ask the regimental agents to extend a substantial credit to Taylor 'in order as far as possible to accommodate him and also to enable him to go to some approaching fairs to provide an additional number', as was necessitated by the fact that he still deemed the regiment short by a hundred horses of its requirements for the year.[23]

With ninety-eight more horses delivered by Taylor in June, this seemed to validate Steuart's extension of credit, although his letter reporting this purchase to the depot also includes a rare admission of poor judgement since the colonel allowed that on reflection Bridger and Philips were 'right respecting not taking inferior Horses and afterwards getting them cast'. Steuart did, however, indicate that he would continue to compromise where necessary, if it was the only way of ensuring that sufficient mounts were available, and that whilst he would on this occasion allow Philips to reject one of the horses from the previous consignment and replace it with one from the next, this was not to be considered a precedent. The officers at the depot were henceforth to recognize and accept that 'there must be some inferior Horses in every Lot, and it is better that they should be too heavy than too slight the one may do some work the other can do nothing but fill an Hospital Stable or a Ditch'.[24] At the same time, compromise could extend only so far, and when a belated veterinary inspection – there having been no veterinary surgeon at the depot when the consignment arrived – revealed that three of the horses obtained from Taylor in Carlisle were blind, they, along with the horse rejected by Philips – described as 'heavy a bad mover and altogether an inferior Horse' – were cast and sold at auction, although Steuart assured Taylor that this would entail 'little loss to you, as in other respects their Eyes excepted three of them are serviceable'.[25] Aware that he could not afford to give offence to a man who had almost single-handedly kept the regiment remounted, the unsatisfactory Harris having largely been cut off as a supplier, Steuart warned his depot staff that it would not do to reject further animals without good reason, but that on this occasion he felt that he could mollify Taylor on their behalf. This attitude may have been aided by the fact that this last purchase would in all likelihood complete the year's requirements, with an equal number of recruits and recruit horses left at the depot once the next remount had gone out, and the option of taking a small batch of additional horses in September should circumstances require it.[26]

In the event, Steuart did take another batch of horses from Taylor in the autumn of 1812, although for once he had the advantage of being able to pick his fifty from a larger consignment and affected to tell the dealer that he only took so many as a favour to him.[27] As the equine cost of the 1812 Peninsula campaign became apparent, however, the advantage quickly shifted back to the horse dealers, and 1813 shaped fit to be as difficult a year as the previous one. Weighing up the situation in February 1813, Steuart noted that,

> that part of my Regt. now abroad want about 230 Horses to complete the effectives and there are all together in the Depot but 189, of which 50 at the least can not be fit for service, so that I fear all our exertions will hardly be sufficient to procure an adequate number of remount horses for the service of the next Campaign.[28]

This would require a renewed effort and an increased number of sources to provide the additional horses. Steuart was therefore grateful for a recommendation of a new dealer obtained through a Mr Olphert. In replying to Olphert so as to enable him to acquaint his friend with the requirements and standards of the 12th Light Dragoons, Steuart further indicated the increasing element of compromise in his standards. Whilst maintaining that he would 'positively take no Horse that is not stout and has good action' and – no doubt in light of the trouble caused with Taylor – would not accept 'a fine Horse to make a bad one go down better', he further reduced the weight requirement, already lowered from 18 stone to 17, so as to now accept any animal 'fit to carry 16 stone on the Road'. He was also prepared to compromise on size, stating that 'the standard of Horses must be from 14 Hands 3 Inches to 15 hands. Horses of 3 year old will be taken at 14 2 inches but none above 16 Hands'.[29]

Nor was it just on the standard of horse that Steuart was obliged to compromise. Where once the Yorkshire dealer Guthrie had lost the regiment's business because of his inability to supply horses in sufficient numbers to make it worthwhile for an officer to visit and inspect them, now Steuart and Philips became increasingly active in travelling to seek out prospective purchases. Similarly, whilst it had previously been the case that purchases were concentrated in the summer months so as to best fit the training cycle, horses now had to be purchased when and where they could be found. As Steuart informed Blunden when explaining that Philips would be required to make yet another journey in pursuit of remounts, 'we must take horses at the time the Dealers can assemble them, which can not always be at the periods most convenient for us'.[30] There was at least a more positive development in that the horses being offered for purchase by Harris were now back to an acceptable standard, and this dealer began to assume an increasing share of the burden, reclaiming from Taylor – who rather fades from the picture after dominating the market in 1812 – the lead role in supplying the 12th with its mounts. With the amount of work and expense involved, both with respect to his own activities and the need to coordinate those of the officers at the depot, Steuart was left to observe wryly to Charles Greenwood that 'I find that a Regt. of Lt. Cavalry in Lord Wellington's advanced Posts is no Sinecure'.[31]

Things were becoming harder for the dealers as well, however, since they were now having to scrape up horses to meet a growing demand. Inevitably, there were shortfalls of quality and quantity, and a greater number of mares being offered for sale. Having approved a lot of thirty-one horses in February 1813 – it is not clear whose, although they may have been from the new dealer recommended by Olphert – Steuart explained to Philips that there were twenty-six mares in the batch and only five geldings. Since Philips was shortly to inspect Harris's next batch, then being prepared, Steuart asked him to try if possible to redress this imbalance, noting that 'altho' I have in general no objection to Mares that proportion is too great, you will therefore be pleased to regulate yourself accordingly so as if possible to have the proportions rather in favour of Geldings'.[32] Harris, meanwhile, had restored the quality of his offering but could not keep up the required quantities. Steuart allotted him half of the regiment's predicted requirement for 1813 – 100 horses – and Harris was able to provide forty-two of them to Philips in the spring. The remainder he undertook to have available at Newcastle Fair in October, a meeting that Steuart felt himself unlikely to make and which he therefore deputized Philips to attend in his stead.[33] In the event, Steuart was indeed unable to attend, but, as he told Harris, this was no bad thing as 'I should not like to march between 2 & 3 hundred miles to get 29 Horses', this being all the dealer had been able to procure.[34]

Steuart reviewed the reasons for the failure in a letter to Philips, which also laid out his plans to make up for the shortfall:

Sir, I am glad to have so favourable a report of the sort of Horses you got from Mr Harris at Newcastle altho' disappointed at the number being so small. In general Dealers should not depend alone on particular fairs, but by a proper communication with the Farmers in the Neighbourhood Arrangements should be made with the Farmers for Horses to be brought for the Dealers approbation, I know that is the method many Dealers use.

Spencer now writes me that he expects to get the remainder of the Horses I want at Rugby fair near to Coventry on ye 20th 21st 22nd of this Month and you are to have the refusal of all that he can procure there, you must therefore be at Mr Harris's House at Hunningham on Friday ye 19th and attend to the fair along with him, for which this shall be your authority. I am already acquainted with the Orders of the Commander in Chief respecting the taking of 3 years old Horses but I neglected to repeat it in my former Letter to you, indeed at this time of Year I wish to take as few 3 year old Horses as possible. I have a very good account of our Remount from Lt. Col. Ponsonby and I admit with much satisfaction the credit you have in it.[35]

Typically, even with the Duke of York authorizing a lowering in age standards, Steuart was still keen to compromise only where essential.

By hard work and a judicious flexibility with his standards when the circumstances forced it, Steuart was able to coordinate the continued supply of replacement horses to the depot right through until the peace of April 1814, and the depot in turn to dispatch remount horses of a good quality to the regiment overseas. But, as with the manpower situation, things became increasingly tight as the war neared its end, and it must nevertheless have been with a real sense of relief that Steuart was able to pen the following missive to Thomas Harris in April 1814:

Mr Harris, referring to my last Letter of ye 20th I have now to inform you that I have this Day received Orders from Head quarters of date ye 23rd from the Adjutant General's Office directing that the purchase of Horses for my Regt. shall be discontinued until further Orders you need therefore make no arrangements for a Supply of Horses for ye 12th Lt. Drags. until you receive fresh instructions from me.[36]

A month later, Major General Jones summed up the achievement that Steuart had superintended, reporting the horses he had inspected at the depot 'very good & of sufficient size strength & activity, those fit for service are in

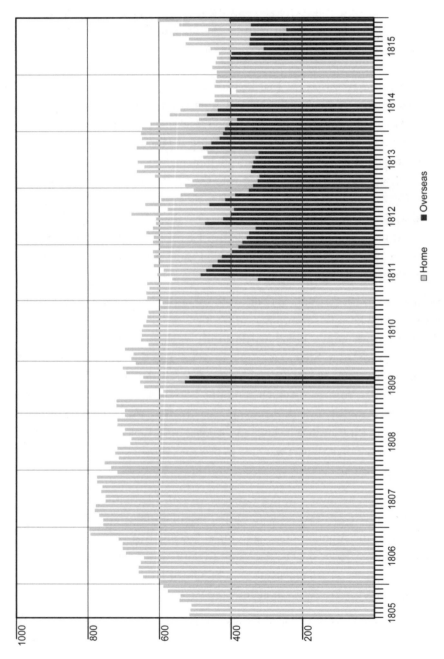

Chart 2: Horse Strength, 1805–1815

good condition & well trained, the remainder are improving'. In continuing his report, Jones confirmed that the depot had, as late as March 1814, 'sent a very large Remount of excellent Horses to the Regiment' and that 'the greatest attention is paid to their training'.[37] This, of course, leads us on to the next part of the story, for it scarcely mattered how many horses were recruited, and what compromises might be allowed over age or size, if the regimental depot could not convert this intake into mounts fit to carry the regiment on active service.

Although horses were purchased at increasingly lower ages as the war went on, there remained an understanding 'that Horses from 5 Years old to 7 are in their prime and answer better than at any age'.[38] However, just as it took time to turn a recruit into a cavalryman, so too did it take time to break an animal to the service and to train the horse – and the rider – so as to render them both fit for service. Taking the horses young ensured that by the time they were trained they were also physically fit for it and in the prime of life. This is seen in the fact that when the regiment was inspected in Portugal, at the end of the 1812 campaign, the full complement of troop horses showed an average age of just under eight years, with no animal younger than five and the majority falling into the six to nine year age bracket.[39] Come the 1815 campaign, when although the regiment as a whole was weaker it had at least been able to make use of the 1814 cut in establishment to keep only the best mounts, the average age had dropped by nearly a year, although the age range as a whole was similar.[40] Thus, with horses ideally being taken from four years of age and upwards, and in practice from as young as three, these figures help demonstrate that the first eighteen months to two years were spent at the depot being prepared for service and this is further borne out by a look at the depot in 1812 which shows 181 horses with an average age of five years, with no animal on the strength older than seven.[41]

This lengthy training time largely mirrors the experience of the regiment's rank and file, and just as new recruits frequently needed their strength building up to prepare them for military service, so too did the horses. One of the main reasons that horses were for the most part taken onto strength in the summer months was to try and have them in the peak of condition when they had been fattened up on fresh pasture rather than having to subsist on the dry fodder that was the only available winter diet. For the same reason, when practical, as many cavalry horses as possible were put out to grass – that is to say, allowed to graze freely on pastureland, which in spring and summer meant green grass high in vitamins A and D, and with their shoes removed to allow free growth.[42] Self-evidently, the same advantages that fresh grazing allowed for a troop horse gone out of condition after a winter on dry forage might also benefit a recruit horse joining the regiment in poor condition. The journey to the depot was generally not conducive to the health of the animals, and the more so if they were transported by sea. Notifying Bridger of the impending arrival at the depot of a batch of Hugh Taylor's Irish horses, shipped first across the North Channel and then put back on board at Whitehaven to be sent round to Weymouth, Steuart warned that 'Most of these you will receive now are much out of condition and have been knocked about on board of Ship, I think you had better give them a dose or two of Phisick on their arrival.'[43]

Once new horses were fit for service, they became the responsibility of the riding master. Whilst in practice Joseph Philips was heavily involved in the selection and purchase of horses for the regiment, his official duties began only once horses were ready to begin the training process. The *Rules and Regulations for the Cavalry* summed up his duties as follows:

> The Riding Master is the responsible person to the Commanding Officer for the breaking of the re-mount horses, and instructing the Young Officers and Recruits in riding, and drilling them on horseback. He is also the person principally to assist the Commanding Officer of the Regiment, and the Officer commanding each Troop, in keeping up the riding of the regiment in general.[44]

In this role, Philips was assisted by a team of rough riders, men skilled in breaking and training horses. Initially provided at a scale of one man per troop, later increased to two when the regimental establishment was expanded, rough riders ranked equivalent to corporals and were paid an additional five guineas per year for their skills. Since they were required to do much of the hands-on work of teaching new soldiers the skills needed to manage their horses, it was required of them that they be men of good conduct as well as skilled horsemen, 'who are very active, and remarkable for a zealous discharge of their duty; and who are likely to carry a proper command in their riding-house business'.[45] The riding master was further enjoined to 'teach them to give the words of command with great spirit and sharpness; at the same time insisting on them keeping their temper, and not swearing or using improper language'.[46]

Notwithstanding the doubling of the allowance for rough riders, this was still a relatively small body of men to superintend the training of the increasing number of horses and men that passed through the depot during the later years of the Napoleonic Wars when the 12th was heavily committed to active operations. The fact that Philips was frequently detached inspecting new horses, and acting in other roles as well as his own even when he was present at the depot, meant that the riding department was stretched even further. Steuart had always made it understood that troop quartermasters, and their successors the troop serjeant majors, were to play a major role in supervising the mounts of their troops, but even this could only do so much to ease the burden. To add insult to injury, it was then ordered that Philips should lose part of the monetary allowance he received for his duties as riding master since he now only had superintendence of the four depot troops – a piece of logic that omitted to take account of the fact that it was through the depot that all new horses passed. Already overworked, Philips evidently did not wish to be underpaid into the bargain and raised his concerns with his colonel, causing Steuart in turn to intervene on his behalf to the Adjutant General:

Sir, I think it is my duty to transmit to you inclosed a letter I have received from Lt. Philips Riding Master to ye 12th Lt Drags & I beg of you to submit it to the consideration of the Commander in Chief with my assurance that I am in the full conviction that if my instructions for the Riding Master of the Depot of that Regt. are attended to as I think & believe that they are no deduction ought in justice to be made in the Riding allowance so long as six Troops of the Regt. remain on Service, 200 Remount Horses and 100 Recruits at least ought yearly to be rendered fit for the Ranks and for Service, and according to my instructions I will venture to say (not in the Ordinary way). The Riding Master has also the instruction of the Officers, who according to my Orders must not be dismissed from the Riding Drills as long as they remain Subaltern Officers, by which means when they arrive at the Rank of Captain they ought to be able very materially to assist in the instructions of the Soldiers.

This I beg leave to observe is more than full employment for one Riding Master whose allowance is hardly sufficient to pay out of it the number of Assistants he should have.

I must say that it is since the six Troops went Abroad I have found additional instructions necessary on the head of the Riding department and from which I expect great benefit will arise to the Service, and I must sincerely hope that his Royal Highness may be prevailed upon to interfere on this occasion, and prevent any deduction being made from the Riding Master's allowance.[47]

A spirited defence of a zealous and effective subordinate, Steuart's plea also helps lay out the full scale of the task that Philips and his assistants faced.

So far as the actual business of accustoming a horse to military service was concerned, terms like 'breaking' and 'rough rider' are somewhat deceptive. Instead, horses were to be treated gently and to be slowly introduced to the features of military life. Captain Robert Hinde in his 1778 *Discipline of the Light Horse* – a work dedicated to a past colonel of the 12th Light Dragoons – recommended that the horse be gradually introduced 'to the saddle and furniture, with the cloak and baggage, to [i]nure them to stand quietly and patiently, and not to be alarmed at their putting on and taking off, to be made much of and cherished, to use them to the appearance of those things'. Thereafter, the new horses were made accustomed to the movements and postures required of them – Hinde recommended for this purpose a cavesson, comprising of a 'headstall, ear band, and throat band of leather, a nose band of iron, jointed and covered with leather, and buckled under the chin in the same manner as the nose band of a curb bridle; it has three rings, one in the middle and one on each side' which would both permit the exercise of the horse on a long rein, now known as lungeing, and the use of the reins to hold the head in the correct posture.[48] Lieutenant Colonel Browne had in 1808 designed a 'Caveson Head-Stall and Collar', adaptable for this and other purposes, which was subsequently furnished to the regiment.[49]

Once a horse was accustomed to moving whilst restrained, the restraints were by degrees to be removed, until the riding master needed only a long whip to control the animal. Further training was required to make the horse change direction and step, after which the animal was fit – assuming its shoulders had been rendered sufficiently supple – to be ridden. This achieved, the movements that had been taught to the loose horse were repeated with a rider mounted, providing the basis for additional training at the end of which it was expected that horse and rider should be able 'to change hands, cross over, form the figure of 8, to rein backwards, to advance in a straight line, to passage or go side ways, to put him upon his haunches, and every other discipline proper for the military service'.[50]

New recruits were treated in much the same way as new horses, with the regiment's eldest and most docile mounts being used for basic training of new riders. A key essential was instruction in the correct posture: the military seat, whose mastery not only ensured uniformity of movements but also allowed the rider to 'yield to the motions of the horse' thus considerably reducing fatigue on a long march. The correct seat was described thus:

A soldier must sit with the small of his back hollow, and body inclining a little, backwards. The inside of the thighs should be turned towards the saddle, the legs hanging easily with the feet parallel to the horse's sides, and the heels a little lower than the toes – the ball only of the foot in the stirrup.[51]

Different techniques for using the sword when mounted – a matter to which we shall return – required a longer or shorter seat, but Steuart, with his usual disdain for changing military fashions, observed that:

[O]n Riding long or Riding short a good Horseman can do either but no man can be a good Military Horseman or Ride short who has not been previously taught to ride long, and the shorter it is the fashion to ride (for all is fashion) the more frequently riding without styrups must be recoursed to.[52]

In Steuart's opinion, one of Joseph Philips's greatest attributes as riding master was that he himself possessed the perfect seat, 'being neither too long nor too short', and Steuart declared that he would be fully satisfied should the rest of the regiment acquire the same posture.

Of course, the novice rider had to be able to control the horse as well as just sit on it, and, what was more, learn to do so using only one hand so as to leave the other free to use his weapons. To accustom the rider to this at an early stage, it was recommended that all work in riding school be performed with a switch held in the right hand, forcing the rider to use only his left to control the horse and also preventing the use of the free hand to correct any failure of balance.[53] As to the movements themselves, Steuart had his own theory of the best means of managing the reins, and in 1806 informed Browne that:

I have ordered Mr Gibson to send you down to the regiment some Running Snaffles which must be kept up out of the Riding Money. I am an old Horseman, having been taught for Eight Years in the best schools in Europe besides having my full share of Military Riding and I know that the running snaffle is by far the best if not the only method of training the Hand of a Cavalry Soldier and making the mouth of a Troop Horse who has previously been well soupled and worked with a plain snaffle.[54]

The point behind this instruction was that the running snaffle enabled the reins more freedom to run freely through eyes in the mouthpiece – hence the name – preventing the application of undue pressure.[55]

The next stage for the rider who had mastered control of his horse was to perfect the sword exercise. Although training with the carbine formed an important part of the soldier's basic training, the value of teaching a cavalryman foot drill had as much to do with instilling a sense of discipline and accustoming the recruit to drill by rote as it did to practical military training. Dismounted work had its place on campaign, but Steuart was in full accord with the ideas of most cavalry officers when he wrote that, 'The Arm which the cavalry soldier has to depend upon is the Sabre he should therefore know how to use it and the blades which are generally neglected should be made as Sharp as possible and constantly kept in that state.'[56] Firearms, though issued as a matter of course on active service, were very much of secondary use and primarily employed in skirmishing rather than on the battlefield.

The weapon with which the troopers of the 12th Light Dragoons were equipped was the 1796 Light Cavalry Sword, introduced as part of a reform of cavalry swords and swordsmanship primarily overseen by the then Major John Gaspard Le Marchant. Le Marchant had seen at first hand during the Flanders campaigns of the early 1790s how inferior British cavalry swords appeared in comparison to those used by their Austrian allies. Although there had been an attempt in 1788 to introduce some standardization of designs, the models of sword then in British use were frequently unwieldy and poorly adapted for the increasingly rapid pace of mounted combat. Le Marchant's answer was twofold: new swords, and a new drill to facilitate their effective use. The weapon that was eventually adopted as the 1796 Light Cavalry Sword, and carried as such by the 12th and their sister regiments through until 1821, was very closely based on a prototype constructed to Le Marchant's specifications. Designed primarily as a cutting weapon, although also able to be used to make a thrust, the 33-inch blade was markedly curved, and was wider at the tip than at the base. Only the top six to eight inches of the blade were sharpened, but it was not uncommon for regiments to have the back of the blade ground down to increase the point and thus increase the utility of the blade for thrusting – albeit at the possible expense of its balance. The sword was furnished with a grip of ribbed wood covered in leather, with a functional iron knucklebow to protect the user's hand. Average weight was a little over two pounds for the standard trooper's sword, although those carried by officers were privately made and often lighter.[57]

Since he entertained a decided preference for the cut over the thrust – as was reflected in the pattern of light cavalry sword that would be forever associated with him – it should come as no surprise that the instructions that Le Marchant produced, issued as the 1796 *Rules and Regulations of the Sword Exercise of the*

Cavalry, emphasized this usage and sought to codify it as part of the basic training of every cavalry trooper. By including a variety of cuts, Le Marchant gave the cavalryman a far more varied combat repertoire than hitherto, since the old preference for the thrust effectively limited the trooper to a single basic gambit. In all, there were six offensive cuts and eight defensive guard postures, all of which were executed with a straight arm so as to give the trooper the longest reach possible and also to keep the vulnerable elbow covered. In addition to these movements, intended for cavalry-to-cavalry combat, the manual also included additional cuts and thrusts intended for use against infantry or fleeing cavalry, in which a bent elbow could be safely risked, and a standard parry intended to deflect infantry bayonets. These drills were taught dismounted on the parade ground or drill square, with troopers facing a target on a wall: to attempt the drills mounted with recruits under training had the potential for disaster, notwithstanding the fact that the cuts were expressly designed to prevent the trooper inadvertently cutting himself or his mount. Under the instruction of more experienced swordsmen, recruits were taught to develop increasingly complex combinations of cuts and parries, carrying out the movements to order. Drills of this nature were a common sight at cavalry barracks across Britain, and John Vandeleur remarked that his father, now retired but once a lieutenant colonel in the 5th Dragoon Guards, would 'be delighted to see the dragoons cutting 5 and 6, etc., in the barrack yard' when he visited the 12th's depot at Weymouth, as 'it will remind him of former times'.[58]

Over and above the standard cuts, Ponsonby's early experience of fighting in the Peninsula, where the French had fielded lancer regiments to good effect, led him to give instructions for additional sword exercises to be taught, intended specifically to counteract this weapon. As his mother explained it, upon his appointment as commanding officer of the 12th he had acquired some lances which he proposed to take with him to the Peninsula in order to make a demonstration of the weapon:

> He has found a serjeant that knows the exercise, and he has drill'd himself in it so well, that he can teach it to his Men; what he wants is, not for them to use it for a continuancy, but to learn it well enough not to be surpris'd at it, and to learn how to attack the Lancers with their swords. He also wants to accustom his horses to the flags, for it was much more the surprise of the Men at this new Arm, and the fright of the horses at the flag, that caus'd the great success of the Lancers at Albuera than any superiority of the weapon.[59]

Ponsonby had evidently also discussed his ideas with his colonel as well as his mother, since Steuart instructed the drills to be practised at the depot as well, noting that the concept was 'highly proper if not carried too far & is confined to the very first class of Horsemen, who should also be taught to defend themselves and attack the Lance Men with the sabre'.[60] Steuart in the same letter also got to the bottom of the logic for such a formulaic means of instruction, recognizing that it helped ensure that success or otherwise in combat was reduced to a matter of good horsemanship. Due to the speed of mounted combat, there was no opportunity for fencing and fancy swordplay: matters had to be decided in the few seconds that opponents were in reach of one and other, and the standardized cuts enabled the cavalryman to fight almost by reflex. What was more, when executed correctly they enabled him to use the impetus of his mount to add force to his blows. With man and horse thus fighting as one, Steuart reasoned – and Le Marchant would surely have agreed – that 'the best Horseman will have the advantage provided their Horses are equally well in hand and are active'.[61]

Over and above training in swordsmanship and the other skills necessary for horse and rider to function effectively in battle, a large part of the trooper's day was taken up by care for his mount. The full routine to be worked through when the regiment was at home was outlined by Steuart in his Standing Orders. So comprehensive are the instructions on what was to be done each day, given under the heading 'Stable Duties', that they are worth quoting at length:

> The first thing is to turn up the Litter under the Manger, Sweep out the Stable, give Water, ¼ of a Pail (when the weather is not too Cold) put some Hay into the Rack and shake it very light, Curry well Body and Legs, after Currying, take a wisp of clean Straw, and wipe him well, after wisping take the Currycomb and Brush, and brush him well – the Currying, Brushing, and Wisping, always to begin at the Neck, and finish at the Croup, against and then with the Lying of the Hair, first the offside, then the near Side. After the Horse is well brushed, take off his Collar, turn him Round, wisp and brush his Head and Neck well, clean his Mane lock by lock with the Brush, put on his Collar, and clean Tail in same Manner. With a Horse Cloth, or Hair Cloth, rub him down Smooth from the Head to Croup with the Grain of the Hair, Shake the Horse

Cloth, put it on, Straw Wisps under the Surcingle, Comb Mane and Tail, litter him down if Ordered, rub his Legs for Eight or Ten Minutes, feed him and Stand by him while feeding. The above Method to be observed and followed at all times when the Horse is dressed.

After exercise, during which the horses were to be watered if possible, more cleaning was required:

At the Stable Time in the Evening, the Stables is again Swept out, the Horses may have a quarter of a Pail of water given them, then Hay, then dressed as ordered, they are anew littered up, legs rubbed then fed. After a Field day or a March, when a Dragoon has arrived at his Stables, he will first unbridle, tie up the Horse by the Collar Rein, take off Clothes, Arms, Cloak and Horse Furniture, and lay them together in the Stable, let out the Sircingle two holes, turn up the Crupper and Breastplate on the Saddle, together with the Stirrups after well wiping them and the Bridle, put up the Litter, take off the Collar and turn the Horse about, rub his Head and ears with a dry wisp, put on the Collar and with a Wisp of Straw in Each hand rub down the Horse thoroughly, Body and Legs, one hand with, and another against the Grain of the Hair, between the legs and under the Belly, pick and wash his feet, and give him some Hay, particularly if the Horses Legs or belly are wet, as no Horse must ever be allowed to stand in the Stables in that Condition, but wiped as dry as can be expected. No Horses legs are ever to be wetted in the Stable by way of Cleaning them.

Take up Arms, Clothes, &c to the Quarters, hang them up and dust them or dry them when necessary, pull off Boots & return to the Stable, and as soon as the Horse is dry and cool, take off the Saddle, and rub his Back with wisps of Straw, Curry him, dress him perfectly clean, give him Hay, litter him down, rub his Legs well and then Carry up the Saddle.[62]

Feeding, too, was discussed in detail, and was to be well supervised, each man watching his own horse under the general supervision of an officer or NCO, and watering was also to be carefully watched, care being 'taken that the horses have not too much Water at a time in cold Weather; two quarts in the morning before feeding, and Gallon before Riding out, is a proper quantity'. In all, it was estimated that care of his mount would take up between five-and-a-half and six hours of each trooper's working day.[63]

On campaign, it was not possible to devote anything like the same amount of care and attention to the horses; something which, along with the greatly increased amount of work expected from them, helps explain the far higher equine mortality rate whilst on campaign. However, a basic level of care was essential if the regiment were to remain effectively mounted, and cutting back on grooming to too great a degree was quickly shown by experience to be a false economy. Steuart, notified of this, agreed that 'the dropping of the Curry comb and Brush' during the winter of 1812–13 'was very ill advised', and going on to remind Ponsonby that 'I well know that on the hardest service and when horses are standing at Picket in cold or wet weather there is nothing more necessary than hard currying and Brushing.'[64] Failure to carry out grooming of this nature meant that the horses' coats rapidly became matted and clogged, blocking pores and leading to sickness. However, the 12th were not alone in trying this false economy: the Household Brigade made a similar attempt to do without around the same time, with equally unfortunate results, and the same had occurred with the heavy dragoon regiments under similar conditions three years previously.[65]

Whilst each man was expected to care for his own horse insofar as the basics were concerned, each cavalry regiment also had its professionals to assist in more specialist matters. Traditionally, the treatment of sick horses had fallen to the farriers, but as of 1796 provision was made for the appointment of a veterinary surgeon, being someone 'who had been educated at, and who had received a certificate from the medical committee of the veterinary collage'.[66] Since what was to become the Royal Veterinary College had only been established five years previously, this was a fairly progressive step and was followed by successive measures to improve the pay and standing of veterinary officers in order to attract men of ability into the service. That the British Army was to benefit greatly from the application of greater scientific rigour is indicated by one of the more strongly worded passages in Steuart's Standing Orders, penned shortly before the institution of regimental veterinary surgeons, which noted that care of horses was to be overseen by troop quartermasters, and that matters were 'not to be left at the Direction of every ignorant Farrier'. Steuart instead required that each troop quartermaster be provided with a copy of Bartlet's *Farriery*, which they were 'to Consult on all Occasions, and follow the Rational Methods of Treatment there laid down. Farriers may be of use in finding out the Nature of the horses Complaints and in the Application of Remedies, but the manner of Cure is there better ascertained, than by their Practice'.[67]

It is telling that the tome whose purchase Steuart encouraged was properly entitled *The Gentleman's Farriery; or a Practical Treatise on the Diseases of Horses*, indicating a time when the farrier was expected to combine the skills of blacksmith and vet.[68] Undoubtedly, many experienced farriers would have obtained, from years of working closely with horses, a great deal of practical knowledge of the symptoms and treatments of the various equine illnesses, but so far as Steuart was concerned the majority of them were 'very ignorant as to the Treatment in Diseases of Horses' and he made it clear that he wished their role in the regiment to be confined as closely as possible to the shoeing of the horses; in cases of illness it was stressed that 'they may advise and give their opinion, but must do nothing without the approbation of the Comm'g Officer of the Troop'.[69]

In this desire, Steuart was reflecting the policy of the Army as a whole, set down in the *Rules and Regulations for the Cavalry*. Both here and in Steuart's Standing Orders it was specified that farriers were to follow the established practice for shoeing laid out by the regiment, which in the case of Steuart's instructions for the farriers of the 12th Light Dragoons required particular care to be taken with trimming the frog – that is to say, the central portion of the hoof, acting in part as a shock absorber – and for the hoof itself to be trimmed down to a greater degree in front than behind. Steuart stressed that this method 'must be strictly attended to . . . and any Farrier who shall presume to deviate from it, may depend on being most Severely Punished', and went on to reiterate that, 'Any farrier who presumes to try on a hot Shoe shall be deemed guilty of Disobedience of Orders in the highest Degree, and will be most Severely punished.' Hot shoeing, whereby the hot shoe fresh from the forge is briefly used to sear the hoof where it is to be set, potentially ensures a better fit if carried out properly, but also risks harm to the horse – Steuart evidently thought the process not worth the risk. Even the farrier who followed regimental instructions to the letter still risked penalties if anything went wrong during the shoeing process: an error that rendered the horse lame would result in his confinement on bread and water until the animal recovered.[70]

Due to the fact that there was only an official allowance of one farrier per troop, 1810 saw the institution of a plan to train an additional four men per troop in shoeing so as to enable them to assist in an emergency, although it proved difficult to keep this up once the regiment was on active service.[71] On the march, and on active service, a farrier was always to be equipped with hammer, pincers and nails.[72] From 1812 onwards, provision was also made for anvils, bellows and charcoal to be carried on mule-back to enable the farriers to make up new horseshoes. Previously, cart-mounted forges had been used but were not fit to keep up with the cavalry and this had led to difficulties in keeping Wellington's cavalry properly shod during its earlier campaigns.[73]

The veterinary surgeon serving with the 12th Light Dragoons for the bulk of their Napoleonic service was James Castley, who exchanged into the regiment in 1809 after two years' service with the 15th Hussars.[74] Although only in his twenties, he seems to have been a competent and successful officer, being described in an 1812 inspection report, whilst serving with the regiment in the Peninsula, as 'intelligent and competent to the Duties of his situation'.[75] During Castley's absence in the Peninsula, the regimental depot shared the services of a Mr Norton, appointed veterinary surgeon to the combined cavalry depots at Dorchester and Radipole.[76] For the most part, the work of the veterinary surgeon was concerned with overseeing the farriers in their shoeing and other duties, and in treating any sick or out-of-condition horses. The range of problems that might be faced, and the recommended treatments for them, take up the bulk of the second volume of Bartlet's *Farriery*, and they amount to quite a catalogue of ailments, with alarming names including 'the Staggers', 'the Strangles', 'the Yellows', and 'the Lax'. Some of these are readily comparable to modern conditions – the last two named being respectively jaundice and looseness of the bowels – but the cures demonstrate little resemblance to modern practice with much recommendation of bleeding and purging, along with a substantial armoury of homespun remedies. For example, if a horse with symptoms of the lax 'voids great quantities of slime and greasy matter', the following drench was prescribed, to be given three times at intervals of two days: 'Take lenitive electuary and cream of tartar, of each four ounces yellow rosin finely powdered, one ounce; and four ounces of sweat [*sic* – sweet] oil: mix with a pint of water-gruel.'[77] Whilst it sounds like witchcraft, there was evidently some sense in what was being recommended, judging by the continued popularity of the work, whilst the directions for dealing with cuts and wounds are straightforward and sensible even if some of the salves and dressings are again a lurch into alchemy.[78] But of all the problems noted by Bartlet and his contemporaries, the one that seems to have caused the most upset was the condition known as glanders.

At the time that Bartlet put together his manual, the work of the Frenchman La Fosse had begun to shed some light on the nature of the condition, prior to which it was noted that 'the cause and seat of the glanders has till lately been imperfectly handled, and so little understood by the writers of this distemper, that it is no wonder it should be ranked among the *incurables*'. Even La Fosse, for whom Bartlet evidently had some considerable admiration, had identified cures for only three of the seven forms the condition was believed to take, the remaining four proving inevitably fatal, although it would seem likely that this was in fact a case of similar conditions being lumped under the same heading, with the common theme being nasal discharge.[79] In fact, true glanders – still a notifiable disease in the modern age thanks to its virulence and potential to spread to humans – is caused by the bacterium *Burkholderia mallei*, with the infection establishing itself in the nasal tract. The condition of farcy, also distinguished at the time by Bartlet and other authorities, and understood to be a linked malady, is caused by the same bacteria causing infection of the skin. In its acute form, glanders causes death in a matter of days through septicaemia, but horses are more likely to contract it in chronic form in which ulcerous nodules develop in the nasal passages and the lungs are progressively weakened by abscesses to the point of eventual death.[80] Since mucus produced as a result of the condition is highly infectious, control is, and was, recognized as being of paramount importance, and animals that were identified as showing symptoms were rapidly shot rather than risk the condition spreading, as can be seen repeatedly in notes to the monthly returns of the 12th and no doubt of all cavalry regiments.

Although Bartlet discusses cures and treatments, these would seem to relate to conditions with similar symptoms rather than true glanders, but this did not stop veterinary surgeons trying. Major General the Hon. Henry Fane, although in the main complementary of Castley's performance of his duties when he inspected the 12th in late 1814, was extremely sceptical when noting that:

> There has been a case of Glanders which the Veterinary Surgeon states himself to have cured; and several cases of Farcy (also cured as he reports). As I have reasons for doubting, at least the cure of this Veterinary Surgeon; perhaps it would be advisable for Mr Coleman [head of the London Veterinary College] to enquire into his practice; and the cases he states himself to have so successfully treated![81]

A mistaken cure could have drastic consequences, since an animal with chronic symptoms remained infectious even if the symptoms themselves had temporarily abated, so Fane was no doubt quite correct to seek a second opinion. In truth, with so imperfect a veterinary knowledge, the only way to deal with the condition was to prevent it taking hold in the first place. Shooting horses suspected of infection was of course key to this, but measures could also be taken to prevent the spread of contagion through isolating horses with symptoms indicative of glanders. This good practice was in marked contrast to the French system, in which sick horses were indiscriminately stabled together, and led to strict instructions being issued for British troops taking over quarters recently vacated by the enemy to take particular care over their cleanliness and in particular that of mangers in stables, where infected horses might well have fed.[82] Even with these precautions, however, glanders alone still killed far more horses than were lost by enemy action, something that the 12th would have to learn the hard way when they came to serve in the field.

Chapter V

Service at Home and Abroad

WHEN THE 12TH LIGHT DRAGOONS RETURNED to England from Ireland in June 1805, Britain's military fortunes were at a low ebb. With Napoleon's invasion barges waiting across the English Channel, and a Franco-Spanish fleet loose in the Atlantic, the naval campaign hung in the balance. The 12th's posting to Romford in Essex did not put them in the first line of defence against invasion, but it formed part of the concentration of troops that would have been called upon to oppose any French advance inland.[1] In the event, of course, the shifting situation in central Europe would cause Napoleon to send his armies against his continental foes rather than his great maritime rival, and the victory of Trafalgar would underscore this change in the focus of the war by ensuring British domination of the seas for the decade to come. Yet Nelson's triumph was soon countered by the lightning campaign that took Napoleon's Grande Armée from Boulogne to Austerlitz by way of Ulm, knocking Austria out of the war and forcing Russia from the fight for the best part of a year. Britain was left with its coasts safe for the time being, and its fleet intact, but with no effective continental allies with which to cooperate. Troops sent to north Germany in late 1805 achieved nothing beyond the acquisition of recruits for the growing King's German Legion and returned in the new year. In the autumn of 1806, Prussia finally joined the war: too late to support Austria and too early to be helped by resurgent Russia, its armies were quickly smashed. Russia fought on alone until defeat at Friedland forced it to submit under the terms of the Treaty of Tilsit in July 1807. All that Britain could manage during this time was to build up its forces in the Mediterranean, striking where it could but unable to prevent the extension of Napoleon's control over Italy and into the Balkans.

For Britain's diplomats and strategists, it was a frustrating time and one that was marked, perhaps inevitably, by political strife and infighting at home. Yet for the British Army as a whole, the lack of a major continental commitment in the years immediately following the collapse of the Peace of Amiens allowed for the reforms that had been ongoing since the turn of the century to be brought to something approaching completion. In the case of the 12th Light Dragoons, there were no major organizational changes, but a series of postings around southeast England during the years 1806–9 allowed the completion of the post-Egypt reconstruction process that had begun when the regiment was stationed in Ireland between 1802 and 1805. After leaving Romford, the regiment moved briefly to Guildford in December 1805, spent three months at Blatchington Barracks in Sussex, and then began a lengthy spell based at Hythe, which lasted until August 1807. After that, the 12th came back to the London area to spend just under a year at the barracks at Hounslow before returning to coastal duties with a posting to Deal in July 1808. During the regiment's time at Hounslow, one of its duties was the provision of escorts for the royal family at Windsor and Hampton Court, something which proved initially diverting but soon paled to boredom. Regimental tradition, however, has it that on one occasion Private Baker found his turn on sentry duty interrupted by an elderly gentleman who enquired as to which regiment he belonged: being informed it was the 12th, the questioner responded, 'Ah yes! George's regiment,' and wandered off. Only later did Baker realize that the gentleman in question was the King, and 'George' the Prince of Wales.[2]

Brushes with royalty aside, the lot of the regiment for the bulk of these early years of the war was training. The 1806 inspection, carried out when they were headquartered at Blatchington, made it clear that the men of the 12th Light Dragoons still had some way to go before the regiment would again be fit for active service. For one thing, and notwithstanding Steuart's efforts to make up for losses during the Egyptian campaign, the inspection report revealed a considerable shortfall in equipment for both horses and troopers. Major General Grey noted that 'the Horse appointments are incomplete in number, but those in possession of the Regiment are very good. The Pouches are all unserviceable, not being large enough to contain the Cartridges suited to the Arms now in use,' that 'The Swords are all in good order, but the Fire Arms are all in so bad a state as to be almost unfit for use, & are very incomplete in number,' and that the regiment had no camp equipment in its possession. The defective ammunition pouches were the second-hand ones received from the 28th Light Dragoons, the poor state of which Steuart was fully aware of, and which he was already seeking to obtain funding to replace. Grey also noted that the most recent batch of new horses were not up to the standard of those that had been longer on the strength. Grey found the troopers physically 'rather a low body of Men' although he qualified this by noting that 'most of them are young and growing'. In terms of their training, he found them entirely proficient in their stable duties, but lacking in experience of the field exercise, which was not aided by the fact that the NCOs were also in need of instruction in this area.[3]

In his study of the training of the British Army of the eighteenth century, John Houlding identified a major flaw in the British military system: the fact that regiments serving within the British Isles were frequently dispersed over a substantial area meant that the opportunities to have enough troops in one place to carry out more advanced training were limited. This led to a situation where the basic military skills – in the case of the 12th, those of drill and horsemanship outlined in the last two chapters – were practised to a high level of individual proficiency but that regiments were left lacking in the advanced training necessary for them to function as effective units. Things had improved by the early nineteenth century, but not by a great deal and Grey cut to the heart of the matter in his report on the 12th when he commented that 'this Corps wants a good deal of instruction in the field, but as the men ride very well I think they would improve fast if they had opportunity of exercising together'.[4]

The problem was that such an opportunity was limited by the regiment at this time being distributed between three separate stations along a sixty-mile stretch of coastline. This was by no means an atypical situation for the 12th: summer 1807, for example, found the regiment even more dispersed, with head-quarters and part of the regiment at Hythe and the rest split between Brabourne Lees, Ashford and Folkestone.[5] Even the posting to Hounslow, which seems to a greater extent to have allowed opportunity for larger bodies to train together, split the regiment's quarters between there and Hampton Court, and the need to provide men for escort duty in London meant that a detachment was also maintained in Kensington.[6] The return to coastal duties in 1808 then saw an even greater dispersion than before, with the regiment scattered across Kent and the largest concentration being the three troops remaining with the headquarters at Deal.[7]

As well as breaking up the regiment into smaller detachments, service at home also imposed a wide range of duties which took up time that could other-wise have been devoted to training. Quite apart from being on hand – at least initially – for anti-invasion duties, the 12th, like all of Britain's cavalry, formed part of the force responsible for maintaining public order at home. Cavalry troopers were, on occasion, employed in a policing role and, more pertinently in the case of the posting of the 12th Light Dragoons along the south-east coast, in support of the revenue and excise services. Both these roles involved some delicate judgement on the part of any officers assigned to them, since they involved military force being placed at the disposal of the civil powers. Rather than risk any ambiguity, Steuart laid down strict instructions on this score:

> When the Officers of the Revenue Calls for a Party of Assistance, a Receipt must be taken from them for the Party delivered, and on Return of the Party the Commanding Officer is desired to have a Return filled up according to the annexed form, Signed by the Revenue Officer, and the Officer or Non Commiss'd Officer who Commanded the Party. The Revenue Officer will also Transcribe his Receipt on the back of the Return. A Role of the Men sent upon such Parties must also be entered upon the back; such Returns to be Transmitted to Head Quarters by the first Opportunity after the Parties have been given, in Order the easier to ascertain what Men are entitled to the Reward given by the Government to Parties who are Successful on the Revenue Service.
>
> Officers and Non Commissioned Officers having the Command of Detachments for the Assistance of Civil Magistrates or Revenue Officers, being ordered not to divide their Parties, signifies that they are not to be Divided without a Civil Officer being Appointed to attend any Detachment made from their Party – but never Otherwise.[8]

On the whole, the application of lethal force in circumstances such as these was extremely rare, and could have serious repercussions for those who ordered it. Steuart's instructions on this matter were rather neatly constructed so as to require any officer sent to aid the civil power to be positive that any order for the troops to open fire must come from the civil authorities:

> [I]t is to be observed by all Officers and Non Commissioned Officers having the Command of any Detachments whatsoever, that they are upon no Occasion to allow their Parties to Cast away their Ammunition by following so Unmilitary and improper a Practice of throwing away their Fire without an Intention of doing Execution. Therefore when any party under the Direction of a Civil Magistrate or Revenue Officer are ordered to fire, that Fire must be made as Effectual as possible. Therefore all Officers having the Command of such Detachments, as well as the Person who parades them, and delivers them over to Such Civil Officers, are heavily desired to inform them of these Orders, so as they may regulate

their Conduct Accordingly, and not order Parties to fire except when they wish Execution Should be done.[9]

There is no record of men of the 12th being obliged to open fire in support either of the revenue or the civil powers. Certainly, however, the regiment was actively employed in this manner, and in 1813 a payment of £11 9s 4d was made over to Quartermaster Richard Sidley, acting as depot paymaster, 'for aiding the Officers of the Revenue'.[10]

Even without the excitement of a clash with smugglers to enliven things, the coast duty in support of the excise was a further diversion away from time that could be spent on training, and the dispersal that it forced on the regiment further limited opportunities for the whole unit to train together as a body. Even when the regiment could be more readily brought together, however, the range of training that was actually provided was fairly basic, which in turn reflected a fairly simple doctrinal concept of what cavalry was for. Although light cavalry had been originally raised for outpost service, and had performed effectively in this role during the American War of 1775–83, this focus had largely been forgotten – or deliberately set aside – by the turn of the century in much the same way as that conflict's lessons in light infantry tactics. Campaigns since 1793 had led to a growing rediscovery of the fact that light cavalry would be required in practice to spend much of its time on outpost duty, skirmishing with the enemy and carrying out reconnaissance rather than engaging in head-on combat, but most theorists of cavalry tactics continued to fixate on the charge.

This fixation, in turn, was reflected in the drills and manuals produced for the cavalry, both the official publications sanctioned by Horse Guards and – with a particularly relevant exception to which we will return – the musings of various theorists, both professional and amateur. Thus, the official *Instructions and Regulations for the Formations and Movements of the Cavalry* devoted nearly 300 pages to the increasingly complex evolutions essential to manoeuvre a regiment and the squadrons within it, and for the whole to function as part of a larger force, but had only fifteen pages dealing with the successive sub-headings of 'Skirmishing', 'Advanced guards', 'Advanced posts, and 'Patroles'.[11] Of course, the value of the formal movements must not be underrated; they provided an essential foundation on which to build the wider range of skills needed for action both on and off the battlefield, and without them a regiment could have functioned solely as a cloud of mounted skirmishers, no more effective on the field of battle than Russia's Cossacks. At the same time, however, it cannot be denied that these formal drills and evolutions loomed large – perhaps too large – in the thinking of officers of light as well as heavy cavalry.

This preoccupation existed across the Army, so the officers of the 12th Light Dragoons were no more or less at fault than their brethren in other regiments. Furthermore, the formal drills necessary to perfect these squadron and regimental manoeuvres were an obvious extension of the more basic modes of training that were required to fit the soldier for service in his troop, and the troop for duty as part of a larger whole. Steuart was, in this, as guilty as the rest – not once in his correspondence or Standing Orders is there any discussion of skirmishing or outpost work – but if he conformed to the majority view of seeing the role of light cavalry primarily as a battlefield force, he did at least retain sight of the fact that all the training and manoeuvring had the intended goal of making the regiment fit for combat, and was not simply an end in itself. His views on the futility of the sort of training that could only ever serve to make an impressive show for an inspecting general were expressed in a typically direct manner:

As to the rapidity of movements now so much in fashion I have no objection very far from it but that must be in proportion to the expertness of Individuals in Horsemanship and aught never to supersede the correctness of formation particularly when the object is to form the line to attack which must always be perpendicular to the object of attack as cavalry cannot Charge in any other direction, but having recommended it to you and to the officers of the Regt. the peculiar Study of His Majesty's Regulations I need say no more on this subject except to recommend to you the reading with attention Books of Science on the Subject of Military Tacticks and particularly Sir David Dundas's original great Work on the Principles of Military Movement Illustrated and Exemplified by a Short account of Prince Ferdinand's Campaigns during the Seven Years War, I will only make one more remark on the Rapidity at present so much in fashion in Cavalry formations.

The attack of Cavalry at the Charge is generally the result of all Deployments into line, the Moment the line be formed it should be ready to Charge without any time being necessary for corrections in order to ensure correctness in the march to the front and being able to proceed to the Charge with all the velocity that the Horses are capable of without confusion. If the Deployment into line is made with such rapidity as to blow the Horses, the Charge must suffer from it. If to prepare for attack is not the object of any particular Deployment Rapidity in that formation becomes less necessary. There are many other reasons I could give against this over grown practice but I think the above is sufficient to strike you of the impropriety of following a practice which is established on no Principle and is really so by fashion. I have lately seen Crack Regiments Deploy into line at the rate of Twenty Miles an Hour who did not afterwards Charge above two hundred yards at any moderate rate: they could not indeed do otherwise what with the horses being blown the line of formation being taken up at random and the Charge not directed on any perpendicular Point.[12]

If the home training of the 12th Light Dragoons was too heavily focussed on the charge and the manoeuvres leading up to it, Steuart's injection of realism into proceedings at least helped to ensure that his regiment would perform these manoeuvres in a manner that could be readily translated into effective battlefield performance.

Based simply on the lack of attention seemingly paid to the matter by the regiment's officers, it would be too great a leap of faith to assume that no training whatsoever in outpost work or skirmishing was carried out by the 12th Light Dragoons prior to their departure for the Peninsula in 1811. However, anything beyond the most perfunctory exercises of this nature would have rendered the regiment practically unique amongst its contemporaries. William Tomkinson, who served through most of the Peninsular War as a lieutenant and later a captain in the 16th Light Dragoons, a regiment that served frequently alongside the 12th, offered the oft-quoted opinion that:

> To attempt giving men or officers any idea in England of outpost duty was considered absurd, and when they came abroad, they had all this to learn. The fact was, there was no one to teach them. Sir Stapleton Cotton tried, at Woodbridge in Suffolk, with the 14th and 16th Light Dragoons, and got the enemy's vedettes and his own looking the same way. There is much to be learnt in service which cannot be done at home, though I do not mean to say nothing can be taught in England.[13]

Tomkinson would also have assured himself of Steuart's approval, for his critique of cavalry training also included a well-argued case against the injurious practice of emphasizing movements at the gallop, which he considered completely unrepresentative of combat conditions but which was still in vogue even when Tomkinson wrote up and annotated his wartime diaries in 1819.

Other than Cotton's well-intentioned but ultimately farcical efforts to instil some realism into the training of his command, the only other significant attempt to develop and pass on a doctrine of outpost work for Britain's light cavalry came in an 1801 publication entitled *Duty of Officers Commanding Detachments in the Field* by John Ormsby Vandeleur, then a lieutenant colonel in command of the 8th Light Dragoons. Vandeleur had served extensively with his regiment during the campaigns of the 1790s; particularly notable in the context of his experience in outpost work was service from 1796 at the taking of the Cape of Good Hope and subsequent operations in southern Africa. Vandeleur argued that most, if not all, existing military texts either dealt only with minutiae of tactics and drill, or else were written for generals and dealt with the art of war on a grand scale. A large portion of his own text is in fact not dissimilar to those that he critiques, with extensive padding taken from the works of continental historians and theorists, but the first sixty pages drew on his own African service – and a recognition of what had taken place in America a quarter of a century earlier – to lay out an excellent primer on how to manage a light cavalry regiment on outpost duty.

Vandeleur made the distinction between the outposts that covered the front of an army, and the outlying picquets that covered the main outposts: both duties being those that typically fell to the lot of light cavalry, although the outposts as a whole might well also include light infantry and these might even be posted to the outlying picquets if the country was rough. Noting that a small picquet might well be commanded by a junior officer of limited experience, Vandeleur offered a range of practical suggestions such as moving the post slightly under the cover of darkness so as to fool any opponent who might be planning a night attack, and stressed the wisdom of keeping a reserve – however small – in any fight so as to have the power to threaten an enemy's flank. As well as the largely defensive duties of the picquet, Vandeleur also covered the duties to be expected of light cavalry on patrol, stressing in particular the importance of delivering detailed and accurate reports both on the terrain and on any enemy forces encountered. Finally, it might also be necessary to force a reconnaissance against enemy picquets, or to clear them away in preparation for an advance, and here Vandeleur tied his hints on the *petit guerre* back to the more formalized training for action by squadrons and larger bodies, suggesting a range of manoeuvres that might readily be adopted for this purpose.[14] So far as the story of the 12th Light Dragoons is concerned Vandeleur and his book are important for two reasons: firstly because the publication of his ideas demonstrates that there were officers even before the Peninsular War who had begun to rediscover a light cavalry doctrine that extended beyond the battlefield charge, and secondly because the regiment was twice brigaded under his command during its Peninsular and Waterloo service, where it would have to put that doctrine into practice.

If opportunities for advanced training of any sort when the whole regiment was at home were limited, the situation became even more adverse once the majority of the effective manpower was deployed on active service. Not only did the troops constituting the regimental depot contain by definition the officers and men most in need of training, but the lack of numbers meant that opportunities to train at anything beyond the troop level were practically non-existent. In order to compensate for this, once it became clear that the Peninsular War represented a long-term commitment and that the regiments serving there would not be coming home for some years, measures were put in force to bring together the home-based depots of the various cavalry regiments in order to facilitate their training and better superintend their organization. From autumn 1811, the depot of the 12th Light Dragoons was shifted to Radipole Barracks at Weymouth along with those of the other light cavalry regiments serving in the Peninsula, and from there, in August 1813, the whole contingent was shifted to Dorchester. The consolidated depot as a whole was placed under the command of Major General Oliver Jones, an experienced light cavalry officer who had commanded the 18th Hussars during the Corunna campaign before his promotion to major general in January 1812. William Hay found him 'a great martinet', but also quick to recognize and reward merit in those under his command: Steuart, perhaps reflecting agreement on both counts, also thought highly of him and was pleased that the 12th's depot 'should be brigaded under so good an Officer'.[15] Consolidation of the light cavalry depots enabled the services of specialist officers to be shared between regiments so that, for example, the 13th Light Dragoons supplied a veterinary surgeon, whilst Joseph Philips had even more duties added to his workload by functioning as Jones's adjutant.[16]

In terms of advanced training, Jones's reports indicate that all troops within a given depot who were fit to take the field were formed into composite squadrons in order to practice regimental-scale manoeuvres and thus provide at least a modicum of advanced training before men were sent out as reinforcements to their regiments.[17] Indeed, in one sense the men who completed their instruction at the Consolidated Depot may have received a more rounded course of training than those who did so with the regiment before it embarked for service. In 1812, although bemoaning the limitations that he was working under due to shortages of equipment, Jones reported that:

great attention is paid to the riding of the Officers and Men, they are likewise taught the Sword Exercise and perform it well, every day the Men
fit for Service of the Consolidated Depot are assembled, and the Officers
attend, where they are instructed in the cavalry Movements on foot,
likewise skirmishing, forming advance rear Guards and side Patroles.[18]

These were exactly the sort of duties that Vandeleur had covered in his book,
and which were now in demand in the Peninsula. Of course, Jones had himself
commanded a light cavalry regiment at war and was able to pass on the practical
experience that he had thereby gained. Furthermore, as time went on, increasing
numbers of the officers serving under him were men who had themselves
returned from a spell on active service with their regiments. These advantages
were simply not available in the years prior to 1811.

By the time the 12th Light Dragoons returned to duties along the Kent coast
after their time at Hampton Court and Windsor, the fortunes of the ongoing
war had again begun to shift. Attempting to eliminate the last potential threats
to his power on the continent, Napoleon had turned his gaze in the aftermath
of Tilsit to Denmark and Portugal. In the former case, a British expedition had
seized the Danish fleet in a pre-emptive strike before the French could act, but
this operational success had the unfortunate – if understandable – side-effect of
driving the Danes into the French camp. In Portugal, on the other hand, the
French struck first and, with Spanish help, had occupied Lisbon by the end of
November 1807. The Portuguese royal family fled with their fleet to Brazil, and
the occupying French set about disbanding the country's army. Thereafter,
however, Napoleon's plans to consolidate his hold on the Peninsula by placing
his brother Joseph on the Spanish throne quickly went awry in the face of
growing popular insurrection. British troops were soon on their way to the
Peninsula to take advantage of this new foothold on the continent, and by the
end of August 1808 Portugal was liberated thanks to Lieutenant General Sir
Arthur Wellesley's victories at Roliça and Vimeiro. Wellesley's little army was
only the first wave of a substantial British military commitment, command of
which eventually passed to Lieutenant General Sir John Moore after the original
British commanders were recalled to face an enquiry into the generous terms
allowed to the defeated French. In Britain, plans were afoot to reinforce Moore,
who now led his troops into Spain where additional cavalry would be particularly

needed. Orders were given for the formation and dispatch of five cavalry brigades, of which only one arrived in time to participate in Moore's campaign. The component regiments of four of these brigades were named, whilst the fifth was to be composed of unspecified regiments of light cavalry: whether the 12th would have been amongst them is unknown, but perfectly plausible. In the event, however, these plans were cut short by Moore's retreat to Corunna in the face of overwhelming French forces, culminating in the battle of 16 January in which Moore was killed, and the subsequent evacuation of his troops.[19]

Although the return to Britain of Moore's survivors meant that the year started on a bad note, as 1809 progressed the balance seemed to shift yet further in Britain's favour. Austria, rebuilding its armies after the defeats of 1805, saw the new war in the Peninsula as the perfect distraction on which to capitalize in order to strike back against the French in Germany, whilst Britain's continued toehold in Portugal offered it the chance to rebuild an army there and continue the fight alongside its Iberian allies. However, the situation in central Europe also gave Britain opportunities closer to home, and ultimately a two-pronged strategy was decided upon. There would be reinforcements for the Peninsula, with Wellesley restored to command, but the main thrust would be elsewhere. In the years since Trafalgar, Napoleon had sought to rebuild his fleet, and one of the major sites of his construction programme was Antwerp. A British expedition to the Low Countries, it was thought, would have the twin effects of functioning as a diversion in favour of Austria and as a means of eliminating the threat that Antwerp and its shipyards posed to British control of the seas. This expedition, land-based command of which would be invested in Lieutenant General the Earl of Chatham, would form Britain's main military commitment for 1809.

In total, Wellesley's and Chatham's armies would together amount to some 63,000 men, of whom 51,000 needed to be furnished from troops then in the British Isles.[20] Moore's erstwhile command naturally formed a large portion of the available troops, and almost all his infantry battalions were re-employed for the new campaigns. However, Moore's five cavalry regiments had returned from Spain minus their horses, rendering them unfit for service and forcing Horse Guards to look elsewhere for regiments with which to reinforce Wellesley and to provide Chatham with a mounted contingent. In this search, orchestrated by General Sir David Dundas, recently appointed Commander-in-Chief to replace the Duke of York who had been temporarily forced from office after the Mary Anne Clarke scandal, one of the cavalry regiments identified as fit for service was the 12th Light Dragoons.[21]

By the time that the 12th received their orders to join Chatham's command, six cavalry regiments had already departed for the Peninsula. However, four of these had already been under orders to join Moore, and so now joined Wellesley instead, requiring only two more regiments to make up a strong cavalry division. Although hindsight tells us that the Peninsula was the main theatre, at the time it was Flanders that was intended to be the principal focus of Britain's war effort, so it is difficult to see any slight in the selection of the 12th for this service rather than to join Wellesley. The eventual structure of Chatham's command created seven divisions, First through Fifth, Light, and Reserve, although this organization was soon modified once the troops had landed. After various changes to the cavalry component of the force, and a reduction in the number of mounted troops to be sent, Chatham was assigned the 3rd Dragoons, 9th and 12th Light Dragoons, and 2nd KGL Hussars. The 2nd Dragoon Guards were also slated to take part in the operation, but never actually sailed. With the exception of the 9th Light Dragoons, which was attached to the Fifth Division, the cavalry regiments were to form a brigade under Major General Baron Karl von Linsingen, which was in turn posted to the Light Division under the command of Lieutenant General the Earl of Rosslyn. Rosslyn was, of course, a former commanding officer of the 12th, familiar with cavalry duties, whilst Linsingen was a veteran officer from the old Hanoverian cavalry service who had joined the KGL upon its formation and most recently served in the Copenhagen expedition.[22]

The initial orders sent to the 12th, dated 21 June 1809, called for eight troops to be prepared for active service; three days later, this was amended to six. This change is an interesting one, since the regiments that had gone out to the Peninsula earlier in the year had all done so with an active establishment of eight troops and only two troops left in depot. Later in the war, Wellington would cut his cavalry regiments from eight to six active troops, retaining the rank and file of the other two but sending the officer and NCO cadres back to the regimental depots, reflecting the fact that it was impossible for the regiments to keep eight troops up to strength on active service. However, it is unclear whether the decision to send only six troops per regiment with Chatham represents Horse Guards coming to a similar conclusion, or if it simply reflects the fact that a campaign around the forts and islands of the Scheldt estuary did not require large bodies of cavalry. Indeed, it may even simply be indicative of the confusion that seems to have accompanied much of the planning for the expedition. Whatever the reasoning behind them, on receipt of these orders Lieutenant Colonel Browne assumed command of the six troops bound to join

Chatham, seconded by Major Spicer, whilst Major Blunden took charge of the four to stay at home. Of the home troops, two remained at Deal and the other two at Sandwich. In addition to those officers who accompanied their troops on active service, Captain Charles Morland joined the expedition as ADC to the Earl of Rosslyn, whilst Captain Thomas Dickens was appointed as an assistant quartermaster general on Chatham's staff. Morland had been Rosslyn's aide for some time already, and his connection with the 12th was shortly afterwards severed for good following his 25 July appointment to a majority in the 17th Light Dragoons. Lieutenant John Vernon benefited by moving up to fill the vacant captaincy, only to be himself appointed shortly afterwards to be assistant quartermaster general on the home-based staff of the Eastern District.[23]

In the haste to get away, no one thought to alert the regiment's colonel to what was happening – Browne having apparently assumed that Blunden would see to it, and the latter having neglected to do so – leaving Steuart mortified that 'I have now no further information on the Subject than what I receive from the Newspapers' and demanding an up-to-date account of what force had been embarked.[24] The answer, when it reached him, would have informed Steuart that the six troops embarked as part of Chatham's army – the so-called 'Grand Expedition' – totalled 524 rank and file; 9 trumpeters; 28 serjeants including the armourer and saddler serjeants; the regimental serjeant major; and 5 troop quartermasters. As well as the two field officers, each of the troops had a captain in command and two lieutenants to second him; the sole cornet then on the strength remained at home. Regimental staff officers taking part in the expedition comprised the adjutant, the paymaster, the surgeon and his assistant, but no veterinary surgeon to look after the 528 troop horses.[25]

The business of shipping that quantity of men and horses, even for a short passage across the North Sea, was by no means an easy one. For almost the entirety of the Napoleonic Wars, with the twin exceptions of the closing campaigns in the Peninsula and the Hundred Days, Britain was never able to field a cavalry force in proportion to the amount of infantry it was able to put into the field, and the primary reason for this was the lack of shipping capacity. For a start, cavalry regiments required specialized transports for the horses, whereas infantrymen could be – and on occasion were – loaded aboard just about anything that would float. Secondly, to move a whole regiment and its horses required a substantial amount of shipping, since even the largest cavalry transports could carry only in the region of forty or so horses.[26] Taken together, this meant that cavalry transports had to be shuttled about when needed, potentially delaying the departure of regiments going overseas as had been the case with the reinforcements being prepared for Moore in 1808.[27] Nor, for the men and their mounts, were matters aboard the transports any easier to organize. Simply getting the horses on board could be difficult enough, requiring hoists and slings and generally serving to upset the animals and bring out the worst in them, and they then needed to be kept in a fit state during the passage. A long spell cooped up aboard transports was damaging to the health of men and horses alike, but whereas the worst the men were likely to suffer from bad weather were the horrors of seasickness, a pitching and rolling ship meant distressed horses and – more likely than not – broken legs and the resulting destruction of the animal.[28]

At the time, then, the officers and men of the 12th Light Dragoons were no doubt left frustrated by the turn of events once the great armada arrived in the Scheldt estuary. Whilst the Left Wing of the army, under Lieutenant General Sir Eyre Coote, landed on the island of Walcheren on 30 July, quickly establishing itself ashore and beginning to move against Middelburg and Flushing, the remaining troops were kept aboard their transports waiting for the opportunity to get ashore.[29] For the cavalry of Linsingen's Brigade, however, that opportunity never arose. Although Middelburg quickly fell, Flushing held out until 14 August, by which time a large Franco-Dutch army had been assembled to cover Antwerp. With Austria out of the war following Napoleon's victories at Eckmuhl and Wagram, there was nothing to stop further French troops being brought to face the British, and any hope that Chatham's operations would serve a useful diversionary purpose was now gone. Elements of the army's Right Wing landed on South Beveland, but there was no need for cavalry and so the 12th and their companion regiments remained aboard their transports until, when it was clear that nothing more could be achieved, the main force was withdrawn leaving only a garrison to hold Walcheren itself. By this stage, many of the troops who had gone ashore were crippled by fevers, which would ultimately claim some 4,000 lives – around 10 per cent of the total force – as against only 106 men lost by enemy action. A further 12,000 men were on the sick lists, many of whom would never fully recover.[30] The Grand Expedition had proved to be a damp squib, and by September the whole of the 12th Light Dragoons were reunited with regimental headquarters once more at Deal Barracks.[31]

In retrospect, whilst the Walcheren Expedition was a fiasco for the British Army as a whole, the 12th Light Dragoons escaped from it without any ill effects. There was only a single fatality amongst the men embarked, and also one horse lost. Only a handful of men were reported sick during the regiment's time aboard transports, and although two men were discharged as unfit upon the regiment's return home, and a further eleven transferred to the 11th Royal Veteran Battalion, there is no indication that this was directly connected to the late campaign, or even if the men discharged had participated in it. In fact, service at home was as dangerous – relatively speaking, more so since there were fewer men at home – as service with the expedition, since the four home-based troops also lost one man and one horse whilst the rest of the regiment was away. The circumstances relative to the loss of the horse are not recorded, but the fate of Cornet Thomas Bateson made him perhaps the most bizarre casualty of the whole war, the *Gentleman's Magazine* recording that his death on 28 September 'was occasioned by a mortification of the bowels, occasioned by eating an immoderate quantity of nuts on the proceeding Saturday, on which day he came of age'.[32]

All in all, the regiment got off very lightly from what could have been a debilitating service. Just how bad things could have been is exemplified by the unfortunate case of the 9th Light Dragoons, who, as the sole cavalry regiment attached to the Left Wing, not only took part in all the operations on Walcheren but also furnished part of the garrison force left there through the autumn. Not only did the 9th lose heavily to the fevers at the time, but the sickness became so ingrained in the regiment that even as late as the winter of 1812–13, when it had been some time in the Peninsula, the after-effects of Walcheren remained a problem. Its efficiency and health fatally undermined, the 9th served for only twenty months under Wellington before being recalled to Britain after which it saw no further action in the struggle against Napoleon.[33] For the 12th, on the other hand, when the regiment was inspected in the spring of 1810 Major General Hope found them 'in every respect in high order a fine Body of Men well appointed and clothed[,] ride well and are active and well instructed[,] they are very well mounted and their Horses perfectly equal to any duty', going on to note further that 'both Officers and Men are Stout and Active in the Field they have been well instructed and are attentive to every party of their Duty'.[34]

By the end of that year, things were better still and Major General Robert Bolton found nothing to fault. The officers and NCOs were fully equal to their duties; the men were clean and healthy, 'well drilled, appear attentive, & are reported to be sober & well conducted, & no Man is kept on the strength of the Regiment who is not Clothed & who does not do his duty as a soldier'. The horses, meanwhile, were 'in good Condition, well broken & of a good Description as to Shape & Strength'. Bolton further found that,

The Field Exercise & Movements of this Regiment in the Field are performed with precision & according to the established Regulations & with a tolerable degree of celerity, & the several Troops & Squadrons act tolerably well together. The Officers are well mounted & with the Non Commissioned Officers & Men ride well & appear to understand the Management of their Horses. They are also expert in the Sword exercise.

Bolton seems to have a had a fondness for the word 'tolerable', which peppers the whole of his report, but in the context of the regiment's speed of manoeuvring his use of the term, rather than simply bestowing unqualified praise, would suggest that Browne was following Steuart's line of thinking and training the regiment to carry out its evolutions at a pace suited to the battlefield rather than one calculated to impress inspecting generals. Not surprisingly, after detailing so many positives, Bolton concluded his report by stating it his opinion that 'The Regiment may be considered fit for immediate Service.'[35]

Whilst the good state of the 12th Light Dragoons as identified by Major General Bolton in the autumn of 1810 was perfectly creditable to the regiment and its officers, it is also hardly to be wondered at. After all, the regiment had been deemed perfectly fit for service as far back as the spring of 1809, and had actually been sent on service that summer, only to return to Britain without ever disembarking from its transports. With the war still raging in the Peninsula, events seem rather to beg the question of why the 12th was not sent out post-haste to Portugal once it returned from the Scheldt, rather than being deployed, as it was in reality, for a further year and a half of duty along the south coast of England. After all, infantry units that had served with Chatham began disembarking in Lisbon as early as April 1810.[36] The answer lies in the course of events in Spain and Portugal after Sir Arthur Wellesley assumed command of Britain's forces there in April 1809. Initial operations were in the north of the country, culminating in a British victory at the Second Battle of Oporto that removed the threat posed by Marshal Soult's II Corps and pushed it back over the mountains into northern Spain. Thereafter, Wellesley moved into Spain to cooperate with the Spanish in a combined advance on Madrid. The allies were victorious over the forces of Joseph Bonaparte at Talavera on 27–28 July – the battle that saw Wellesley ennobled as Lord Wellington and that taught Ponsonby to be more respectful of French infantry – but were then forced to retreat when a reinforced and re-equipped Soult moved against their communications. By the end of the year, the British were back on the Portuguese border and the Spanish, after a stunning French offensive into Andalucía, left holed up in Cadiz. Wellington, fully aware that the allied failures in central Europe during the course of 1809 would enable the French to reinforce their armies in the Peninsula in time for the next campaigning season, restricted his goals to holding Lisbon as a base for further operations.

Whilst more cavalry could well have been useful during the Talavera campaign, their effectiveness would have been severely compromised by the chronic supply problems that plagued these operations. Such concerns were also in Wellington's mind as he prepared for the campaign of 1810, which would be fought in the far more enclosed terrain of Portugal and, ultimately, from behind the defensive works that were being constructed to cover Lisbon. Accordingly, having sent the cut-up 23rd Light Dragoons home after their disaster at Talavera but having also been joined by the 1st Royal Dragoons and 13th Light Dragoons to give him a total of seven British cavalry regiments, plus the 2nd KGL Hussars with the British garrison at Cadiz, Wellington requested that, for the time being, no additional cavalry be sent out to him. All that he desired, he informed the Secretary of State for War and the Colonies, Lord Liverpool, was that the regiments that he currently had under his command be brought up to strength in horses so as to render them fully effective.[37]

Not needed in the Peninsula for the time being, the 12th settled back into their old routine duties along the south coast through the course of the winter of 1809–10, before moving in the April of the latter year to take up new quarters in Essex. Headquarters was at Romford Barracks where four troops were also stationed; a fifth was quartered in the town, and the remainder spread between Waltham, Hornchurch, Woodford, Epping and Ilford.[38] Meanwhile, in the Peninsula, the French Armée de Portugal under Marshal André Massena had begun its offensive against Lisbon by capturing the border fortresses of Ciudad Rodrigo and Almeida prior to advancing into Portugal. Wellington gave the French a bloody nose at Bussaco on 27 September but continued his retreat and by 10 October had withdrawn inside the formidable Lines of Torres Vedras. Thanks to a thoroughly implemented scorched-earth policy, Massena's troops found themselves unable either to capture Lisbon or to maintain themselves outside the lines, and eventually fell back to Santarém on the Tagus. Finally conceding that his campaign had failed, Massena began a further retreat on 5 March, intending to extricate his troops from Portugal and withdraw to the Spanish border. Wellington, his forces having been steadily reinforced throughout the course of 1810 to give him an army of 48,000 British troops and 24,000 Portuguese, immediately followed up the French retreat, harrying Massena's rearguard. However, a French offensive in the south, where Soult was now in command of the French Armée du Midi, threatened the strategic fortress of Badajoz, forcing Wellington to detach forces to try and prevent its fall. Too late to prevent the surrender of the fortress on 11 March, this southern contingent of 21,000 men under Sir William Beresford, the British officer seconded to retrain the Portuguese Army and who now held the rank of marshal in that nation's forces, began a new campaign aimed at retaking Badajoz. Having sent three of his British cavalry regiments south with Beresford, along with the majority of the Portuguese cavalry, Wellington now found himself increasingly short of mounted troops just as his army was beginning to recommence the sort of active operations in which a strong cavalry force was needed.

Wellington could hardly be faulted for his stance on not desiring any further cavalry reinforcements during the winter, since so long as the army was behind the Lines of Torres Vedras there was neither employment nor forage for them. What was more, there were only a limited number of light cavalry regiments back in Britain that were then fit for service, and since it was light cavalry for which Wellington had expressed a preference this led to an unconventional – and, for the 12th Light Dragoons, devastating – means of quickly bringing the Peninsular regiments up to their maximum effectiveness. Lord Liverpool, 'desirous of informing you as soon as possible of the arrangements we have made for keeping your cavalry effective', explained the scheme to Wellington in a letter of 7 May 1811:

> The 11th light dragoons are embarked for Lisbon, and only waiting for a fair wind : they are one of the most complete, best appointed, and best disciplined regiments in the service. The severe shock which the cavalry received in Sir J. Moore's retreat in the year 1808 has placed us in this predicament, that the 12th light dragoons is now the only regiment of that description in this country which has seasoned horses. If the other regiments are suffered to remain in their present state till next year, they will be fit for any service; but it would be a serious detriment to them, and no adequate advantage to you, to move them at present. It has therefore been determined to dismount the 12th light dragoons, and to send the greater part of their horses to complete the light dragoon regiments at present in Portugal.[39]

Thus, all the work that had been done by Steuart and the regiment's officers over the past decade in order to bring the 12th to a state of readiness would, at a stroke, be undone and the regiment would end up no better off than it had been upon its return from Egypt. The horses would, at least, be put to good use – although, since a portion would need to go to the three regiments of heavy cavalry then under Wellington's command, not always to the use for which they were best fitted. However, the only proposed service for the men was for four troops to be sent to do dismounted duty as part of the garrison on Sicily.[40]

Wellington throughout his Peninsular command can be faulted for a too-narrow focus on his own immediate requirements, and on an expectation that Horse Guards and the War Office would sacrifice their own long-term Army-wide priorities in order to meet his needs. The plan to dismount the 12th, coming only months after Wellington's request to be sent horses for his existing regiments rather than new complete units, represents one of the few occasions that those at home gave in to his entreaties. Possibly it is no coincidence in this respect that this was still the era of Sir David Dundas as Commander-in-Chief; once the Duke of York returned to the post in May 1811, Wellington would find that Horse Guards was far less inclined to acquiesce meekly to his wishes.[41] Quite what Steuart thought of all this is unclear – he must surely have been furious, but since there is a gap in his correspondence for the period in question we have no way of knowing. Surely, however, it was as a result of this unprecedented upset that Steuart paid a personal visit to the regiment at Romford, and his presence meant that he was personally aware of the stream of orders and counter-orders that now descended upon the 12th as its future was finally settled.[42]

The first set of orders, dispatched on 10 May and received by the regiment a day later, called for the dispatch of four troops; those of Captains Dickens, Stawell, Morgan, and Erskine were selected for the service and sent down to Portsmouth in May 1811 under the command of Major Wyndham. On the face of it, giving the command to a newly arrived junior field officer – Wyndham having only been appointed to the regiment less than a month before he was sent on service – seems illogical. However, with Browne on the point of leaving the regiment, his promotion to major general being formally gazetted on 4 June, the only other available field officer was Blunden, who, as the senior major, naturally took command of the larger portion of the regiment: that is to say, the six troops remaining at home. At this stage, the intention still seems to have been for the four service troops to be shipped first to Lisbon, where their horses would be handed over for distribution amongst Wellington's cavalry regiments, and then re-embarked for Sicily.[43]

However, at some point prior to the troops sailing, common sense at Horse Guards prevailed and it was decided that not only the horses but also the men were to disembark in Lisbon and join Wellington's command, Wellington being informed of this in a letter from the Military Secretary at Horse Guards, dated 28 May.[44] Then, in order to bring the active portion of the regiment up to strength, 29 May saw orders given for the dispatch of two additional squadrons, adding another four troops to give a total of eight under orders for the Peninsula. Three days later, the orders were changed again and now only two additional troops were to be sent rather than two additional squadrons; it is not clear whether this represents the correction of an error in the initial order, or yet another change of heart. In all events, the troops of Captains Saunders and Sandys were dispatched to join the four already under Wyndham, Major Blunden going out with them to take command of the regiment. This left the troops of Captains Bridger, Vernon, Wallace and Barton to form the depot, which was shifted to Norwich with Wallace in command pending the arrival of Bridger who had been recalled to the regiment from Ireland where he had been serving as an aide-de-camp to Major General Sir James Affleck. The threat of dismounting had thus been avoided, and the regiment was now at last presented with the chance to demonstrate its prowess in the field for the first time in a decade.[45]

Chapter VI

To War in the Peninsula

WHEN THE 12TH LIGHT DRAGOONS arrived there on 25 June 1811, Lisbon had been at the centre of world events for four years, and had played host – not always willingly – to soldiers of half the armies in Europe.[1] At the start of 1811, with Massena's French army still stalled outside the Lines of Torres Vedras, war had come perilously close: now, as summer drew on, the threat was receding again but Portugal's capital was left full of the refugees uprooted by Wellington's scorched-earth policy. Any initial gratitude for the deliverance that had been bestowed by the British had largely dissipated, and the foreign soldiers seemed now to be seen primarily as an annoyance and a source of income.[2] Lisbon, however, was only the port of disembarkation for British reinforcements arriving in the Peninsula; the true base of Wellington's ever-growing command was the great base-depot outside the city at Belém. Each regiment maintained a detachment there to function as an advanced depot, and in this the 12th Light Dragoons were no exception. Once things had settled down, this contingent was left to the supervision of Quartermaster Abel Hammon, who took charge from March 1812 onwards. For the regiment's first few months in the Peninsula, however, sufficient of the regiment's officers were posted at Belém due to the state of their health – this also being the location of the Peninsular army's main base-hospital – that one convalescent or another was always available to oversee such horses and men as were detached there. Indeed, for these first few months, it was mostly convalescents who made up the regiment's rear-area details; only when reinforcements began to be sent out, along with replacement uniforms, weapons and accoutrements for the men still serving, was a more formalized structure necessary, coinciding with Hammon's appointment to oversee its running.[3]

Arriving in Portugal, the 12th fielded a respectable strength of 23 officers, 32 serjeants, 6 trumpeters, 480 rank and file, and 484 troop horses.[4] Even upon

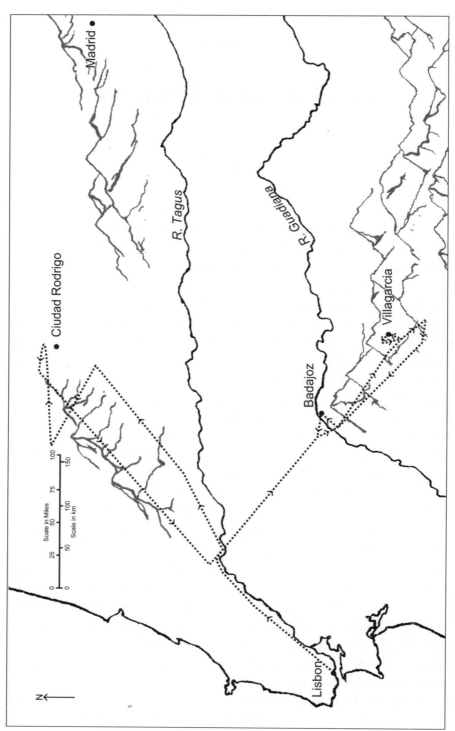

Map 1: Peninsular Operations, June 1811–April 1812

landing, however, seven troopers were already on the sick list, and this total quickly grew during the first few weeks on service. This process of acclimatiz-ation was something that affected all new regiments joining the army in the Peninsula, and was an understandable reaction to sudden exposure to a climate and diet very different to that which almost all of them would have been accus-tomed to. Only the handful of Egyptian veterans still in the ranks would have experienced anything of the like before, but for most of the 12th the midsummer heat of Portugal would have come as quite the shock. After a ten-day wait at Belém, the regiment began the move up-country to join the main field army on the Spanish frontier. The pace was not forced, and travelling was timed to avoid the heat of the day: even so, a month after landing by which time the 12th had reached Castello Branco – 140 miles from Lisbon and only two-thirds of the way to their destination – forty-three troopers and four officers had been left behind as sick, with a further six men listed as sick but able to remain with the regiment. Three of the officers, Captains Erskine and Saunders and Lieutenant Chatterton, had either never made it beyond Belém or else had been quickly obliged to return there, whilst Paymaster William Otway had been left behind at Abrantes. In addition to those of their comrades placed on the sick list by whatever germs were lurking within them, the waters of Portugal also claimed two victims by rather more direct means with two men returned as drowned in the Tagus.[5]

The regiment's horses had fared equally badly, for whilst only one animal had been lost during the voyage out, the march up to Castello Branco cost the lives of no fewer than seventeen. Of these, seven had been shot due to glanders and farcy, very likely contracted from being stabled in quarters vacated by the French during their retreat earlier in the year, notwithstanding the orders for particular care under such circumstances. A further eighteen horses were sick but still with the regiment.[6] After exposure to disease, the main debilitating factor was the manner of forage available in the Peninsula, which was very different to what the horses were accustomed to. In light of this, it had long before been recognized that horses would need to be weaned onto the Iberian forage. A General Order of 5 May 1809 required that those animals that would accept the local forage be fed exclusively on it; for the rest, 'The Commanding Officers of dragoons and artillery will give directions that all their horses may be accustomed to the corn and forage of the country, by being fed at first in the proportions of half English and half Portuguese corn; then two-thirds Portu-guese and one-third English; and, lastly, wholly of Portuguese.' As well as being unfamiliar, Iberian forage was also deemed less nutritious, as reflected by the fact that fourteen pounds of it were needed in order to replace ten of English hay. Along with the hay or straw, twelve pounds of barley or Indian corn made up the ration of dry forage by the time the 12th arrived in the Peninsula. When green forage was available, it was issued at a rate of twenty-eight pounds per horse. Three days' worth of corn was to be carried as a matter of course, to bestow at least a modicum of self-sufficiency upon the cavalry, but despite this there were frequent shortages during the course of the war, to the inevitable distress of the horses.[7]

As well as the various officers, men, and horses lost to illness or accident along the way, by the time the 12th Light Dragoons reached Castello Branco they had also lost their commanding officer. Having brought out the two extra troops added to the initial four ordered on service under Major Wyndham, Major Blunden had returned to England. Indeed, it would seem that he never even left Lisbon, but handed the command over to his junior before the regiment began its march inland. On the face of it, with Ponsonby appointed as the new commanding officer, it made sense for one of the three field officers to return home to take charge of the depot, but Blunden's unseemly haste to depart left the regiment under the command of the inexperienced Wyndham at a critical moment. For although Ponsonby's appointment to command the 12th was made on 11 June, before the regiment even arrived at Lisbon, the new commanding officer was sick: although the monthly return of 25 September listed him as being on the regiment's strength it also noted that he was at Belém due to his illness. Indeed, so bad was his health that Ponsonby was eventually obliged to return to England and it would not be until early 1812 that he would finally assume command of the 12th. Other officers who had initially gone sick were eventually able to recover and resume their duties, but others fell ill in their turn, including Surgeon Robinson himself, which cannot have done much for the medical care available to the others since Assistant Surgeon Thomas Cock was also detached from the regiment. In the end, Assistant Surgeon John Perkins of the 26th Foot had to be attached to the 12th in order to give the regiment a medical officer, a transfer that was later made permanent when Cock resigned his appointment the following year and Perkins was appointed in his place.[8]

Wyndham, too, fell ill and was absent as a result for part of November 1811, command falling to Frederick Dickens as senior captain. Wyndham was back in command the following month and remained with the 12th long enough to hand over to Ponsonby in person, but he then obtained two months' leave with effect from 16 February 1812 and, in the event, did not return thanks to his subsequent promotion out of the regiment.[9] Before his departure, however,

Wyndham wrote home to his colonel on 28 August, by which time the 12th had joined the main army, reporting on the parlous state of the regimental accoutrements. So shocked was Steuart to receive this missive that he in turn wrote directly to Wellington, expressing his

> . . . great surprise that the appointments sent with the last Squadron which marched from Romford were so extremely bad as to oblige him to request I should send out without delay a Supply of at least one hundred Sets of appointments complete as there are a vast number of Horse Appointments so bad that in the course of a very short time they will be totally unfit for Service. Major Windham further states in a Subsequent Letter to me dated ye 26th of August the necessity of an immediate supply of boots for that those the Regt. have at present will not last a fortnight before the Enemy when the men can never take them off.

This, to Steuart, was a self-evidently ridiculous series of complaints, which, had he taken them at face value, would have represented a damning criticism of the means by which the regimental supply of accoutrements were furnished. Mustering his arguments and, one suspects, fighting to keep his temper in check, Steuart continued his letter to provide Wellington with a rebuttal of Wyndham's case:

> I have desired my Agents Messers Greenwood & Cox to remonstrate against this demand at Head Quarters on different grounds and particularly on these contained in a statement given in by Major General Brown a Copy of which I beg leave to inclose to you. I must in addition observe that the last squadron which marched from Romford last May appeared to me to be perfectly well appointed for any Service, and that no complaints were made either on their arrival at Portsmouth or at Lisbon. That squadron as well as the other two had a pick of the appointments of the Regt.
>
> Major Windham complains that the Horses had suffered considerably by Sore Backs on the March from Lisbon to Abrantes three weeks after their landing in Portugal and <u>that</u> from the badness of the saddles . . . I have served 50 years in the Cavalry both at Home and Abroad and know that Sore Backs must proceed from neglect and want of discipline provided that the Saddles have originally been well made and that the Trees are Correct. The Saddles of my Regt. are furnished by Messers Gibson & Peat in London and none better can be made.

> I feel most anxious for the honour of ye 12th Lt Drag's as well as for
> the propriety of his Majesty's Service and particularly for that part of it
> now under Your Lordship's Orders on which so much depends, but I must
> claim your justice that I may not be made responsible for defects which do
> not originate with myself or proceed from the neglect of others.[10]

Wellington would respond by ordering a board of officers to inspect the items
that Wyndham had reported as being unfit. This would take some time to
implement, and, as we shall see, would ensure that the matter would drag on
and on, to the eventual discomfiture of just about all parties concerned.[11]

Wyndham's report of inadequate appointments marked the beginning of an
ongoing battle between Steuart on the one hand and the regiment's officers on
the other over the state of the regiment's kit. For his part, Steuart clung
inflexibly to his peacetime manner of dealing with things: equipment would be
purchased only in sufficient quantity to equip the effective strength of the
regiment; furthermore, it would be expected to last until the next yearly issue
and anything that was lost, damaged or destroyed prior to that would fall to the
charge of whoever was responsible for its loss. Going through Wyndham's letter
point by point, Steuart noted that,

> If the Regt wear out their Boots every two months it will not be in my
> power as Colonel to supply them. If the tear and wear of Boots and
> Appointments on the Service in Portugal is beyond all former example
> the allowance to the Colonel from Government should be in proportion.
> The same remark will apply to the list of Appointments applied for by . . .
> Major Windham.[12]

From a point of view of Steuart's personal finances, this was an entirely
reasonable stance, but from the point of view of regimental efficiency it most
certainly was not. Yet when Steuart in the past had spent his own money to
improve the efficiency of his regiment by replacing worn-out items, he had
received no financial recompense for doing so and had been left badly out of
pocket. Indeed, by early 1812 Steuart would be obliged to ask for the aid of the
agents in clearing bills of £4,873 owing to Gibson & Peat, manufacturer of the
regiment's saddles, leatherwork and associated items. Apparently directing his
comments to Charles Greenwood in person, although the letter was addressed
to the firm as a whole, Steuart complained that:

> You gave me to hope at one time that a Regt. of Lt. Cavalry was worth
> about £2200 a year I fear I shall fall very short of any such thing, and if

matters go on as they seem to do at present my private fortune must materially suffer so for God sake my good friend take the matter into your consideration and give me some comfort if you can.[13]

With such a financial crisis brewing, it is small wonder that Steuart was unprepared to sanction any additional expenditure to remedy the defects reported by Wyndham. The whole affair clearly highlights the principal inadequacy of the outsourcing of regimental purchases to regimental colonels rather than ensuring that such matters were dealt with centrally: that no allowance was made for sudden contingencies that might cripple the finances of an individual colonel but which could be far more readily absorbed at a central level.

At the same time, however, Steuart was no fool and was with some justification suspicious of the rapidity with which so many items had been rendered in need of replacement. The fact that the regiment was initially to be sent out dismounted does lead to the unworthy thought that the first four troops were issued with old kit in order to pass it on to whichever regiment was to receive their drafted horses, but there is no indication that this is what took place and certainly Steuart continued to insist vehemently that all six troops had gone out to Portugal with the best equipment that could be provided. Pending the investigation that Wellington had ordered, this would have to be accepted. But if the 12th had indeed been as well equipped as Steuart insisted, some explanation was certainly required with respect to what had gone amiss with the regiment. Steuart raised the whole affair with Ponsonby, in terms that made it abundantly clear that he considered that Wyndham had, at best, demonstrated that he was too lacking in experience for the command that had been left to him.

Steuart began by expressing at the same time his sorrow 'to find that your ill state of health has oblig'd you to return to England' and his 'hope for your speedy recovery and your return to take Command of my Regt. in Portugal'. He then went on to explain that he had referred the whole matter of the regimental appointments to the agents, and referred Ponsonby to Charles Greenwood in order that the agent might bring him up to date. Having reviewed matters as they stood, Steuart now told Ponsonby how he wished things to proceed in the future:

> On hearing from Major Windham of your intended return to England, I wrote to Mr Greenwood immediately to communicate with you on the Subject of the Supply necessary to be sent out to the Regt, and whatever arrangements you make with him for the future regular Supply shall have

my sanction, without however taking any thing from the responsibility of the Commanding Officer that strict discipline shall at all times be observed and that there shall be no waste. I am perfectly sensible that the tare and wear must be very great, it is therefore the more necessary that great attention should be paid to that particular branch of the Œconomy of the Regt. and I expect that you will make proper arrangements for that purpose & I highly approve that the Supply of Appointments should be sent three times a year – February, June, and Oct – but those Supplys must be in consequence of a most careful general inspection, at which the Commanding Officer himself must be present and whereof a Return must be sent to the Agent for my information, the articles lost or destroy'd between one Supply and the other must be accounted for in a satisfactory manner in a separate Return so as to give me a Claim on Government for proper remuneration. As to the Boots I perfectly agree with you that when on Out Posts they seldom can be taken off, but Troops are not always on Out Posts, and I fear the Opportunity's they have of taking off are frequently overlooked and expediency gives way to fashion. At the date of Major Windham's Letters it does not appear to me that ye 12th had been within sight of an Out Post or had moved a Hundred Miles in Portugal.[14]

For the time being, this is where matters were left. So far as Steuart was concerned, though, the sooner he saw Ponsonby fit and able to get matters in Portugal in hand, the better.

Notwithstanding the impression gained by a review of the illnesses and deaths of man and beast which litter the monthly returns of late 1811 and early 1812, nor the dire tone of Wyndham's letters home, the situation of the 12th during their early Peninsular service was much akin to that of other recently arrived cavalry regiments, and representative of the acclimatization process for new troops joining Wellington's command. Only the ongoing problems of equipment represented something out of the ordinary, and would remain unresolved for some time to come.[15] Certainly, newly appointed Lieutenant William Hay was favourably impressed with his new regiment when he first saw it shortly after the 12th joined the field army on the Spanish frontier. Hay came from the Scots landed gentry, being born in 1792 on the family estate near Dunbar. The eldest son, he stood to inherit in due course but his father – himself a former soldier – sought to prepare young William for a military career. Study at the Royal Military College was followed by a commission in the 52nd Light Infantry with which Hay served in the Peninsula from September 1810 onwards. By the summer of 1811, Hay was expecting to succeed to a vacant lieutenancy in his own regiment, so that when Major Charles Rowan congratulated him on his promotion he first assumed that this had been duly gazetted. Instead, Rowan informed him that the promotion was into the 12th Light Dragoons – Hay's father having made the requisite arrangements – something that Hay initially refused to credit. Upon an offended Rowan convincing him of its truth, Hay deemed the appointment 'an utterly unexpected piece of good luck': a worthwhile compliment to the 12th, since the 52nd was one of the finest infantry regiments in the service, in which Hay considered his time as having been spent 'as a child in a happy and well-conducted family'.[16]

For Hay to take up his appointment, however, was a rather more complicated process than simply riding across and reporting for duty with the 12th. The 52nd was engaged in a running outpost battle with their French counterparts, and Hay's commanding officer, Major Edward Gibbs, felt that he could not in fairness expose the newly made lieutenant to the danger of combat when he no longer belonged to the regiment. Gibbs therefore applied to Major General Robert Craufurd, commanding the Light Division, for permission for Hay to join the 12th at once rather than wait for a formal appointment. Craufurd, typically, refused, leaving Gibbs mortified and Hay obliged to wait for orders to join his new regiment. However, Hay was known as an excellent horseman – at least by his own account – and Gibbs saw an opportunity in this, pointing out that the 12th were quartered only thirty miles away and that Hay might at least take the opportunity to visit his new regiment so long as he could be back with the 52nd by the following morning. Gibbs also pointed out that Hay on his ride would pass the headquarters of Lieutenant General Sir Stapleton Cotton, commanding the cavalry, the hint being that Cotton would likely be able to get Hay's orders to join the 12th expedited. This, indeed, was swiftly achieved and Hay rode on to meet the regiment, where he was 'most kindly received' by Wyndham and his new fellow-officers. As for the regiment itself, Hay found 'the men in new uniforms, and the horses and appointments in the best condition', the whole making a favourable comparison with the ragged state of the 52nd and rather undermining Wyndham's complaints to Steuart. Cotton having issued the required orders, Hay made his way down to Lisbon to get himself fitted out for cavalry service, but there fell ill and was ultimately obliged to return home to recover his health. After his brief introduction, it would now be several months before Hay, the only member of the 12th subsequently to publish his memoirs, would be able to re-join the regiment.[17]

By the time of Hay's first – brief – encounter with his new regiment, it had been assigned to the First Cavalry Division and brigaded along with the 1st Royal Dragoons under the command of Major General John Slade. At this time, the Peninsular cavalry force was in something of a state of organizational flux as it began to grow for the first time since 1809. The original single cavalry division had now spawned a second to encompass the mounted troops operating in the southern theatre of operations, and new brigades were being created, and regiments shuffled between them, in order to make best use of the available troops. The posting of the 12th to Slade's Brigade allowed the transfer elsewhere of the 13th and 14th Light Dragoons, allowing the creation of a new brigade which brought the First Cavalry Division to six British regiments in three brigades, plus a brigade of Portuguese. Cotton retained personal command of the division whilst delegating day-to-day responsibility for the new Second Cavalry Division – two more British brigades and one Portuguese – to Major General Sir William Erskine.[18] The fact that Slade's Brigade contained a regiment apiece of heavy and light cavalry was something of an oddity, indicative both of the shortage of heavy regiments in the Peninsula and the doctrinal blurring of roles between Britain's heavy and light cavalry, but if this was a potential hamper to the brigade's effectiveness it palled in comparison to that brought on by the inadequacies of the brigadier.

Wellington's cavalry generals have come in for a rather bad press over the years, which – when applied to the body of men as a whole – is rather undeserved. Cotton, who led the cavalry for most of the Peninsular War, was a thoroughly competent commander whose reputation has suffered not for his actions in that role but for his unjustified pretensions to higher responsibility.[19] Beneath him, brigade commanders such as John Le Marchant, Henry Fane, John Ormsby Vandeleur and Richard Hussey Vivian all distinguished themselves. Yet this is largely passed over by historians who concentrate on those who did less well: William Erskine, Robert Long, and most of all John Slade. Yet on the face of his record, 'Black Jack' Slade should have been the ideal commander of a cavalry brigade. Born in 1762, he had entered the Army as a cornet in what was then the 10th Light Dragoons, and rose steadily through that regiment's ranks before taking command of the 1st Royal Dragoons in 1798. Appointed a brigadier general on the home staff in 1804, he went out to the Peninsula to command one of Moore's two cavalry brigades and it was here that his inadequacies began to become apparent. Prior to the Battle of Sahagún on 20 December 1808, Slade spent so long delivering an inspirational speech to his old regiment – now the 10th Hussars – that he and they missed the fighting. Five days later, in a skirmish at Mayorga, he spent so long adjusting his stirrups that Lieutenant General Lord Paget, commanding Moore's cavalry, was obliged to intervene and personally order the 10th to charge. Nor did Slade play any appreciable part in Paget's last victory, at Benavente on 29 December. Although his conduct had demonstrated dubious command abilities and questionable personal courage, by October 1809 seniority had carried Slade to major general and he was back in the Peninsula as a brigadier of cavalry. There he continued in undistinguished vein, contributing along with Erskine to the poor performance of the cavalry in the pursuit of Massena's retreat from Portugal. Remarkably, despite further subsequent failings, including the disaster at Maguilla in June 1812 that provoked Wellington's 'galloping at everything' quote, it would not be until April 1813 that Wellington was able to secure Slade's recall to Britain.[20]

Thankfully, the 12th's spell under Slade's command would be short-lived, with the regiment spending only six months as part of his brigade, and during this time their commander's peculiar genius for catastrophe would remain in check. This period as a whole was nevertheless an active one, and if the 12th was not exposed to any heavy fighting the regiment did begin to grow accustomed to the long marches and sometimes irregular supplies that characterized the resumed mobile warfare of this period. This process, notwithstanding Lieutenant Hay's largely positive impression of the state of the regiment when he saw it, would see things get worse before they began to get better.

By the time the 12th Light Dragoons had reached the front, the two major battles of the year had already been fought. During 3–6 May at Fuentes de Oñoro, Wellington successfully countered a renewed offensive by Massena's Armée de Portugal aimed at relieving the fortress of Almeida. Although the battle saw several tactical blunders on the allied side, the French were nevertheless defeated and abandoned Almeida shortly afterwards. Massena had had his last chance and was replaced by Marshal Marmont who fell back on Salamanca to rebuild his command. Meanwhile, in the southern theatre, Beresford had begun siege operations outside Badajoz but was soon forced to turn and face a relief force under Soult. Joined by a sizeable Spanish contingent, Beresford gave battle at Albuera on 16 May, leading to the bloodiest action of the Peninsular War. Neither side held any clear advantage, but Soult's nerve gave way before his adversary's and the French withdrew after a two day face-off. Thus, by the end of May, Wellington had secured the Portuguese frontier but could not operate in Spain until he had taken the two fortresses barring his way: Ciudad Rodrigo guarding the northern road, and Badajoz the southern. For the best part of a year, Wellington would repeatedly shuffle troops between the northern and southern theatres, hoping to achieve a concentration of force long enough to besiege one of the fortresses successfully before the various French field armies could concentrate against him.[21]

Ciudad Rodrigo was garrisoned and covered by the French Armée du Nord under Général de Division Dorsenne, and Badajoz by Soult's Armée du Midi. Neither of these forces could put enough men into the field to oppose Welling-ton alone, but both could be reinforced by Marmont's Armée de Portugal. Already, by the time the 12th Light Dragoons had joined Slade's Brigade, Wellington had been obliged to give up a renewed attempt to capture Badajoz when Soult and Marmont combined their forces and forced him to raise the siege. Now, the focus shifted back to the northern sector where Wellington began a blockade of Ciudad Rodrigo. Marmont, following the allies back north, planned to combine with Dorsenne and raise the blockade, allowing the fortress to be provisioned, and also, if all went to plan, cut off and destroy the blockading force. In this, the French were only partially successful; the blockade was lifted for a time, but the Third Division at El Bodón made a fine fighting withdrawal in conjunction with the light cavalry of Alten's Brigade, allowing the army to regroup around Fuente Guinaldo. Slade's Brigade was held in reserve during these initial operations, but was now brought up to join this troop concentration, which was complete by the evening of 25 September. However, with the French coming on in force, Wellington elected to make a further withdrawal which was accomplished without interference. On the 27th, Marmont made a probing attack at Aldea de Ponte, which was covered by the infantry of the Fourth Division and by two cavalry brigades under Slade and Colonel Sir Granby Calcraft. The four cavalry regiments skirmished on and off with their French counterparts under Général de Division Pierre Watier, who was initially successful in driving in the British outposts but unable to press home the advantage. The 12th, still under Wyndham's command at this juncture, was not heavily engaged but managed to lose four men taken prisoner, presumably when the outlying piquets were overrun in the initial French attack. As Oman summed it up, in the cavalry action 'neither party had any appreciable losses, nor gained any marked advantage'. Still, the 12th Light Dragoons had at least now been blooded, but for the most part the fighting that day was infantry work and this was performed with distinction by the Fusilier Brigade of the Fourth Division, who forced a French withdrawal. The following day, Marmont brought his whole force up, but by then the allied position was too strong to risk an attack, and the French withdrew.[22]

With the conclusion of these operations, which coincided with the onset of heavy rains that presaged worse weather to come, both armies began to settle into winter quarters. Those of Slade's Brigade were in the villages around Celorico in the Mondego Valley.[23] For the cavalry, this respite came none too soon, for many of the regiments were in a bad way, and those that were newly arrived particularly so: Lieutenant Tomkinson of the 16th Light Dragoons met the 12th on the march as they withdrew to winter quarters, and reported that 'never were horses in such a state'.[24] The worst case was reckoned by Wellington to be the 4th Dragoon Guards, whom he described as looking 'more like men come out of the hospitals than troops arrived from England', but he noted that the other recent arrivals were 'in nearly the same state'.[25] So bad were matters that the spectre of dismounting again returned to haunt the 12th, with Wellington discussing with Cotton the possibility of taking horses from them, as well as from the newly arrived 9th Light Dragoons, in order to mount the 2nd KGL Hussars who had recently joined the field army from Cadiz. Noting that it was established practice that all cavalry regiments had one-tenth of their strength dismounted as a matter of course – allowing for men absent in hospital or detached at Lisbon or Belém – Wellington required that Cotton should continue to use this as a basic rule of thumb, but that 'if you find a regiment very sickly, you may dismount more if you think proper, and transfer the horses to other regiments whose men are more healthy'.[26]

With respect to the 12th, Wellington's proposal would not have meant dismounting the whole regiment, merely reassigning any surplus horses, but since the 12th had nearly a quarter of its troopers in hospital at the time, and, after detachments, could put only 274 men into the field, it is clear to see why Wellington saw it as a likely donor of mounts for more deserving regiments. Quite possibly the saving grace was the fact that the regiment's horses were in an equally bad way, and many of them not worth transferring elsewhere. Even with the arrival of an early remount – twenty horses, conducted by a serjeant and ten rank and file – only 291 could be found fit for duty, and Cotton was able to convince Wellington that the 12th could not give up any more mounts. Indeed, he advocated that, if possible, a portion of those that remained with the regiment be put out to grass so as to recover their fitness.[27] This was implemented but, even so, substantial numbers of animals continued to die or to become so weak as to be cast as ineffective; in November, twenty-eight were lost to 'general debility' as well as one to glanders. Not until December did things begin to show any appreciable signs of improving.[28]

By 25 January 1812, two things had happened that would signal the beginning of a change in fortunes for the 12th Light Dragoons: Frederick Ponsonby had assumed command of the regiment, and Ciudad Rodrigo had fallen to the allies. The two events were, of course, unconnected, with the capture of the fortress coming after a swift winter campaign in which the cavalry were relegated to a screening role while the infantry struggled in the trenches and, on the night of 19–20 January, successfully stormed the two breaches that had been blown in the walls. Wellington had taken advantage of the fact that the Armée de Portugal had been temporarily depleted by the detachment of reinforcements for French operations against Valencia, and was thus in no position to interfere with his siege operations. By seizing this opportunity, albeit at the cost of 1,100 casualties, Wellington had swung the operational initiative in his favour and was now able to consider a move against Badajoz with a far greater force than in the previous year, trusting to the fact that with both Ciudad Rodrigo and Almeida in allied hands the northern route between Spain and Portugal could be covered by a skeleton force. These developments ushered in a new phase in the Peninsular War, in which the allied forces would adopt an increasingly aggressive strategy that was ultimately aimed at driving the French out of Spain.[29]

As a consequence of the move towards offensive warfare, and in order to incorporate additional reinforcements, particularly of heavy cavalry, that had arrived during the winter, Wellington instituted a substantial reorganization of his mounted troops. One of the consequences of this was that Slade's Brigade ceased to be a mixed formation and received two additional regiments of heavy cavalry. This in turn allowed the transfer of the 12th to Anson's Brigade where it joined the veteran 14th and 16th Light Dragoons, two regiments which, along with the 1st KGL Hussars, had borne the brunt of light cavalry work under Wellington since 1809. This policy of mixing veteran regiments with newer troops was a key feature of the 1812 reorganization, and would be repeated with the next batch of reinforcements the following winter. Allowing newer troops to benefit from the lessons learnt by those who had been longer in the theatre, it served to improve the efficiency of the cavalry as a whole.[30]

The formation to which the 12th found themselves posted was designated Anson's Brigade after its regular or incumbent commander, Major General George Anson, the same officer under whose command Ponsonby had served at Talavera with the 23rd Light Dragoons. Anson was not a colourful character in the mould of some of his contemporaries, but he was an experienced cavalry officer with long Peninsular service and could certainly be deemed a safe and reliable brigadier, albeit one who preferred a cautious and conservative approach to one of dash and initiative. His application to leave the Peninsula in 1813 at the same time as Wellington managed to get rid of several of the more obvious duds amongst his cavalry brigadiers has led some historians to lump him in unfairly with those officers, but this assumption is entirely unjustified.[31] Prior to his Peninsula service, which saw him fight throughout the campaigns of 1809–11 as a regimental and then a brigade commander, Anson had served consistently as a light cavalry officer, rising through the ranks of the 16th and 20th Light Dragoons after his initial appointment as a cornet in the former regiment in 1786.[32]

However, at the time of the January 1812 reorganization, Anson was on leave and, indeed, would remain so for the first half of the year. This meant that, in his absence, the brigade command would fall to the senior commanding officer of its component regiments, who happened to be Frederick Ponsonby. Thus, within a month of gaining a new commanding officer, the 12th had lost him again. Clearly, he did not disappear from their sight, and as acting brigadier he was still part of the regiment's chain of command and in a position to oversee its activities, but, equally, he was not in a position to exercise day-to-day control. Notwithstanding that his temporary appointment to act in Anson's stead gave him a larger command than he had ever held before, Ponsonby's mother reported that he was in 'high Spirits', after receiving two letters from him written during the early spring of 1812.[33]

With Wyndham gone, regimental command of the 12th again fell to Captain Dickens, who continued to exercise it throughout the time that Ponsonby had the brigade, notwithstanding the fact that Major Blunden returned to the Peninsula in the spring of 1812. Quite what Blunden was trying to achieve at this point is unclear: he had made it plain to Steuart upon returning home the previous year that he wished for a regimental command, yet now, having the opportunity to take up such a role with the 12th while Ponsonby was filling in for Anson, he seemingly baulked at it. Arriving at Lisbon in April, he made it no closer to the front than Belém, where he served with the advance depot for a mere two months before obtaining leave to return to England. Quite possibly, Blunden had already shifted his ambitions from the military to the political arena following the failure of his petition for promotion, and was keen to secure his position in the aftermath of the 11 May assassination of Prime Minister Spencer Percival and the run-up to General Election that autumn in which he would be a successful candidate. Whatever the major's motivation, his apparent unwillingness to take the field meant that the 12th had no active field officer other than Ponsonby until September when Major the Earl of Walde-grave joined the regiment.[34]

In the immediate aftermath of the capture of Ciudad Rodrigo, the harsh winter conditions made it imperative to get the cavalry back into winter quarters where the regiments would be able to obtain better food and shelter for their horses. The three regiments of Anson's Brigade were all assembled by 1 February with headquarters at Seixo, where Ponsonby assumed the command in place of Lieutenant Colonel Felton Hervey of the 14th Light Dragoons who had held it since Anson's departure. On 16 February the 12th were shifted down to Tomar, which was reached after five days on the road. Tomkinson, whose regiment marched by the same route as the 12th, thought it to be 'the third best town I have seen in Portugal', something that he attributed – no doubt unfairly – to the fact that the inhabitants had been more pro-French than their compatriots and had thus been spared the desolation that Massena's army had inflicted elsewhere.[35] Although he may well have been at fault when it came to the patriotism of the people of Tomar, Tomkinson is generally a reliable and informative eyewitness, and since his experiences as an officer of the 16th Light Dragoons mimicked those of the 12th so closely for the months to come, his account helps fill the gap that would otherwise exist in the eyewitness record at this point in our story.

Notwithstanding the swift return to winter quarters, the effective strength of the 12th in both men and horses continued to remain low. A comparison of manpower effectiveness with the brigade's two veteran regiments is particularly telling, with the 12th in February 1812 having 24 per cent of its rank and file strength on the sick list, as opposed to 15 per cent in the 14th and only 11 per cent in the 16th. Clearly, the process of acclimatization for the 12th was still ongoing.[36] February did see the beginnings of an improvement for the regiment's horses, with those mounts that had been sent to grass returning to regimental duty. However, with sickness still prevalent amongst the men this was not immediately reflected in a proportionate increase in the mounted strength since there were insufficient fit men for all the troop horses – 292 men to 306 horses as of 25 February. With only twenty animals sick and twenty-nine detached at this time, this was a creditable sickness ratio so far as the troop horses were concerned, the more so due to the great difficulties experienced in obtaining sufficient forage, even after the return to more productive lands after the deployment to the Spanish frontier during January. Tomkinson explained the nature of the ongoing problem, and the amount of work it entailed for the troopers of the brigade:

> The procuring of forage through this winter for the horses was attended with the greatest difficulty, both to men and horses. The detachments left their quarters soon after daylight, and were absent from six to eight hours generally, and frequently until dark. The peasants hid their straw with the greatest care, being the only chance they had of keeping what few oxen remained to them, for the purpose of agriculture, alive until the spring. They hid their straw behind stores of wood laid by for fuel, which two or three dragoons would remove with several hours' work, and possibly not find above three or four days' supply for three or four horses. The carrying it away was always attended with the complaints and lamentations of the women, who followed us out of the place saying then their oxen must now die.[37]

Tomkinson relates how the dragoons entered a battle of wits with the peasantry in order to obtain sufficient forage for their mounts, an area in which the experienced men of the 14th and 16th Light Dragoons would no doubt have been able to teach their comrades of the 12th a trick or two.

The brigade's rest around Tomar lasted for only six days before orders were received to move south as part of the shift that would culminate in the opening of siege operations against Badajoz. However, the march was made in easy stages, passing through Abrantes to the village of Sousel in the Alentejo region where there was another halt.[38] All three regiments benefitted from the onset of spring, which saw a rapid improvement in the quantity and quality of forage that was available. Tomkinson noted that they 'began to use the green forage, which we got in great abundance. The barley was just fit to cut, and improved the horses a good deal.'[39] Continued inroads of this nature into any available green forage would ultimately bring down a rebuke from Wellington, concerned that the short-term gain would mean nothing being left for later in the year, but the immediate results were certainly beneficial for the army's horses, if not for the local farmers.[40]

As with the operations leading up to the capture of Ciudad Rodrigo, there was next to no role for mounted troops in the coming siege of Badajoz, except perhaps for the handful of troopers detached from each regiment and employed as orderly dragoons carrying messages for and between the army's general officers: monthly returns indicate that the 12th generally had around a half-dozen troopers detached on this duty throughout the regiment's time in the Peninsula. For the most part, the role of Wellington's cavalry was one of providing a screen of outposts behind which the siege forces could operate, and as such they formed the outer layer of a protective cordon that also included substantial bodies of infantry. Because the threat in the north had been minimized by the capture of Ciudad Rodrigo, Wellington was able to bring nearly his whole army to the operations around Badajoz, and this allowed him to assign two powerful forces – each an army corps in all but name – to guard against the approach of a potential relief army. Lieutenant General Sir Thomas Graham with the First, Sixth, and Seventh Divisions and two brigades of cavalry operated south of the Guadiana, whilst Lieutenant General Sir Rowland Hill had the Second and Portuguese Divisions under his command, along with the Second Cavalry Division, and operated to the north of that river. There were only two French divisions in the area, along with supporting cavalry, detached from the Armée du Midi and under the combined command of Général de Division Jean-Baptiste Drouet, Comte d'Erlon. This was far too small a force to resist the allied advance, and Graham and Hill were easily able to clear the area around Badajoz of French troops, allowing Wellington to move out from his advanced base at Elvas on 14 March, and to begin siege works in earnest two days later.[41]

When the siege operations began, Anson's Brigade, along with the newly arrived heavy dragoons of the KGL, were still on their way south and were brought no closer to the front than the town of Vila Viçosa, some miles within Portugal. There both brigades remained until 30 March when they were brought up to Elvas, and then on the following day to Olivenza. Finally, on 3 April, the three light dragoon regiments were sent up to join Graham's corps, a movement that served to reunite the bulk of the First Cavalry Division and to provide Graham with some much-needed light horsemen for outpost work to relieve the heavy dragoons and dragoon guards under Slade and Le Marchant that had previously been his only mounted troops. Brigade headquarters were established at Los Santos, where the 12th were also stationed, with the other two regiments of the brigade at Villafranca de los Barros. Tomkinson, reviewing the measures in force to provide a screen of outposts, felt that with the French now showing signs of activity greater precautions would be necessary lest there be a surprise attack. Noting that 'we are only just come to the country; the enemy have been here for the last two years, and know every lane hereabouts', he suspected that the preference for mobile detached parties rather than a chain of posts could well result in the capture of an outlying party.[42] Sure enough, the arrival of the light cavalry allowed additional measures to be set in motion, and Lieutenant Henry Andrews of the 12th became one of the select body of Observing Officers assigned to keep a close watch on French movements out ahead of the main outposts. Such an assignment indicated official recognition of the growing competence in outpost and reconnaissance work of the officers and men of the regiment.[43]

In his perception that the French were on the move, Tomkinson was quite correct. Soult had pulled together a field force of 13,000 men from the Armée du Midi, and had begun to move towards Badajoz. Combining with the troops already in the area under d'Erlon, this gave him 25,000 men which, although a respectable force, was still insufficient to raise the siege without help from the Armée de Portugal. Marmont, for his part, had at first prepared three divisions to aid Soult, but orders from Napoleon had caused him instead to mount a foray into northern Portugal in the false hope of obliging Wellington to redeploy troops to meet it.[44] Nevertheless, with the French on the move and aware that he was under pressure of time, Wellington pushed forwards his siege operations and launched an assault on the night of 6–7 April. Despite heavy casualties in the breaches, secondary assaults by escalade were successful and Badajoz was in allied hands by morning. In an ideal world, Wellington could now have turned on Soult's relief force and attacked it in overwhelming force; as it was, however, the time taken to restore order in Badajoz and the need to respond to the threat to Ciudad Rodrigo caused by Marmont's movements in the north meant that any further large-scale offensive operations in the southern theatre were not possible.[45]

Having obtained intelligence that Badajoz had fallen and that the Spanish had reopened active operations in Andalucía, Soult at once set things in motion to return to Seville with the troops that he had brought north with him. Soult left d'Erlon with his old command at Llerena, eighty miles south-east of Badajoz, with orders to fall back on Seville if he was pressed. Graham's command, including Cotton's three cavalry brigades, had maintained Soult's troops under observation throughout their time in the north, and Graham remained keen to strike a blow if at all possible. Wellington, for his part, wished only to convince the French that he meant to move on Seville, thus blinding the enemy to his real intentions, but when Graham sought permission for a more offensive stance the commander of the forces replied that he had 'no objection to the cavalry pressing a little on Soult's rear guard without over-working the horses'. With this permission, Graham on 10 April ordered Le Marchant's Brigade of heavy cavalry, and Bull's Troop of the Royal Horse Artillery, to join Cotton, who was already with Ponsonby on the outposts. Cotton's third brigade, Slade's, was ordered up to Villafranca in support, whilst Graham's infantry remained in the rear: none of these troops would play a part in the coming fight, which would see the 12th Light Dragoons committed to a major action for the first time since their arrival in the Peninsula.[46]

Facing the outposts of Ponsonby's three regiments was the 1er Division de Cavalerie of the Armée du Midi under the command of Général de Brigade André-Thomas Perreimond. Perreimond's command comprised a brigade of light cavalry, only a single regiment of which was present at Llerena, and a brigade of dragoons under Général de Brigade François-Antoine Lallemand. The veteran Perreimond was on the point of retirement, whereas Lallemand was a younger officer only recently promoted from a regimental command, and this marked contrast of personality types would have some impact on the coming clash.[47] Although the bulk of d'Erlon's forces, and all his infantry and guns, were deployed around Llerena, an outpost was maintained around Villagarcia by Lallemand's two dragoon regiments. Thanks to the open nature of the inter-vening terrain, the French troops in Villagarcia were visible – with the aid of a good glass – from the observation post maintained by the British atop the tower of the church at Bienvenida. Ascending to view the scene for himself, Cotton quickly recognized the vulnerability of Lallemand's position and issued orders to concentrate all three cavalry brigades at Bienvenida in order to bring an overwhelming force to bear on the French.[48]

Cotton's initial scheme seems to have been for an uncomplicated frontal attack, with Ponsonby and Le Marchant making the main offensive movement and Slade coming up as a reserve. Le Marchant was ordered to make a night march so as to arrive at Bienvenida by dawn on the 11th, which was no small matter since his brigade was eighteen miles away at Zafra and Los Santos, whilst Ponsonby, whose command was at Villafranca and thus had even further to come, was to move up during the afternoon of the 10th. Almost immediately, however, things began to go awry as the 16th Light Dragoons were awaiting a ration issue when Cotton's dispatch arrived and could not move out as ordered; this meant that Ponsonby could bring only the 12th and 14th with him, with

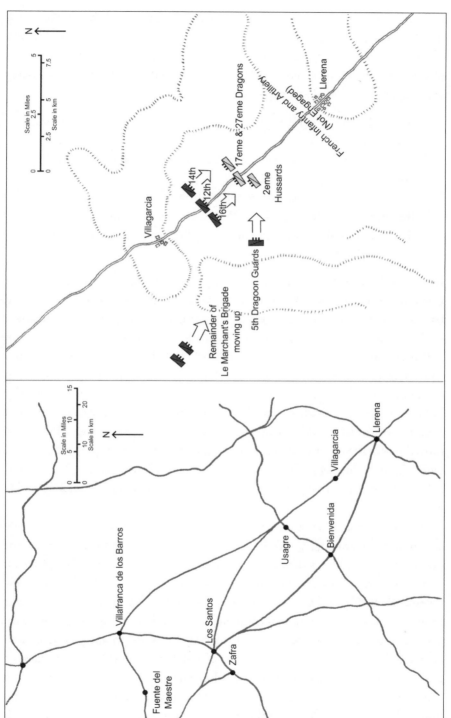

Map 2a: Area of Operations, April 1812

Map 2b: Battle of Villagarcia, 11 April 1812

the 16th following later. Then it was learnt that the French had pulled back from Villagarcia, which forced the abandonment of the original plan. Since it seemed as if the French were withdrawing, Cotton needed to attack as soon as possible and therefore issued the following order to Ponsonby, the second paragraph apparently added as a postscript:

> Should the enemy not occupy Usagre in force, you will move from your present quarters and occupy it this evening. Should he occupy it, you will bivouack in rear of the town, and advance at daylight the following morning.
>
> I wish we had been allowed to follow them this day. I fear it is too late. The enemy have left Villa Garcia. Push Cocks on in the morning to Villa Garcia, and let him send on patrols to feel the enemy, whose rear, I think, he will find in Berlanga.[49]

Major the Hon. Edward Charles Cocks, a noted intelligence specialist, was at this time responsible for the outposts of Anson's Brigade, his command being two detached squadrons furnished on a rotating basis by the three regiments.[50]

Once the French cavalry had been located, presumably somewhere between Villagarcia and Llerena, an attack could then be launched. This would require some hard marching through the night if all was to be in place by the morning of the 11th, and the need to hurry, lest the French fall back and the opportunity be lost, meant that Slade's Brigade and Major Bull's horse artillery, though ordered forwards, would not be able to participate. Accordingly, Ponsonby moved under the cover of darkness to Usagre with the two regiments at hand, whilst Cotton, having overseen the movement of Le Marchant's Brigade and collected the late-arriving 16th as they reached Bienvenida, moved up in his wake.

In making use of what was available, Cotton's initial plan was conceptually sound, but unfortunately, once Ponsonby was on his way, a further refinement occurred to him. This led to a last-minute modification to the plan of attack that threatened to throw the whole operation out of kilter. In Cotton's new scheme, Ponsonby was now to delay his movement in order to give Le Marchant time to work around the French left flank; this would hopefully enable the heavy cavalry to get between the French dragoons and their infantry support and enable the whole enemy force to be cut off and destroyed. Lieutenant Luard of the 4th Dragoons was dispatched with Ponsonby's revised orders but, by the time Luard reached Usagre, Ponsonby and his command were no longer there. Thus, when Cotton rode out on the morning of the 11th at the head of the 16th

Light Dragoons, it was found that 'the 12th and 14th had moved from Usagre a short time before us, and driven the enemy's vedettes off the rising ground in front of Villa Garcia just before we made our appearance'.[51] With Le Marchant still some way in the rear, and with his brigade's horses worn from their overnight march, this meant that Cotton was now irrevocably committed to an action that had opened under conditions very different to those that he had anticipated.

Ponsonby, of course, had every belief that he was acting entirely in accordance with Cotton's wishes, in compliance with which he had sent Cocks forward a squadron apiece from the 12th and 14th. Ponsonby then brought up the remaining four squadrons in reserve, those of the 12th being under Captain Dickens and those of the 14th under Lieutenant Colonel Hervey. As of the most recent monthly returns, those of 25 March, the 12th had an effective rank and file strength of 262 and the 14th of 409. Using the same figures, the 16th, when they came up, would add a further 351 men to give the brigade a theoretical strength of 1,022 troopers, but it is likely in reality that strengths for all three regiments had fallen since the date of the last return and most narratives allow only 600 men for the 12th and 14th combined.[52] Cocks had no difficulty in driving in the French outposts, which were pursued back through Villagarcia, but as his force of around 200 men crested the high ground beyond the village they found themselves faced by Lallemand's two dragoon regiments. The exact strength of the French force is difficult to establish. Tomkinson thought that they fielded around 2,000 cavalry in total, and Cotton reported 2,500, but this is almost certainly an over-estimate of the forces actually engaged.[53] Lallemand initially had only the 17eme and 27eme Dragons with him, both regiments three squadrons strong. On 1 July 1812, by which time both regiments had also been engaged at Maguilla, their combined strength amounted to 644 men. Allowing for losses in that action as well as those suffered at Villagarcia, this suggests that Lallemand probably had around 800–850 heavy dragoons under his immediate command on 11 April, to which Perreimond would later add something in the region of 350 reinforcements in the three squadrons of the 2eme Hussards.[54] Undeniably, however, the force that Major Cocks encountered on the far side of Villagarcia outnumbered him by a comfortable margin, and the two advanced squadrons quickly fell back on Ponsonby's main body. Since the 12th are recorded as operating as a three-squadron regiment later in the battle, it may be inferred that both detached squadrons fell in with their respective units at this point. With the 12th on the right and the 14th on the left, Ponsonby then renewed his advance and moved forwards to engage Lallemand.

Although Cotton would later complain that Ponsonby had thrown the operational plan adrift by attacking too early, the latter was actually performing very well in his first action as a brigade commander. It was, after all, through no fault of his own that he had not received Cotton's revised orders, and his actions were entirely in accordance with the only orders that he had received, which required him to push aggressively past Villagarcia. At the same time, it was clearly not a sensible option for British light dragoons to attack a superior force of French heavy cavalry and Ponsonby therefore contented himself with a defensive stance, falling slowly back with his skirmishers out to delay the French. Those accounts that credit the French with 2,000 or more horsemen in the field would indeed be correct in asserting that Ponsonby's position was perilous at this juncture, but even if the 2eme Hussards had already joined the fight at this point – which is by no means clear – the odds were still only two to one in the French favour and Ponsonby was aware that there were four more British regiments on hand to support him. As Cotton's dispatch makes plain, by the time the divisional commander arrived only Ponsonby's outposts were seriously engaged and the situation was by no means critical.[55] Indeed, the main bodies of each side were still some distance apart, with Tomkinson describing how 'when we came on the top of the hill, there were the 12th and 14th on our left, close in front of Villa Garcia. The enemy formed a quarter of a mile from them.'[56]

Even if he complained about the situation later, Cotton wasted no time in recriminations when he arrived on the field and instead sought to adapt his plan to the situation that he now faced. Le Marchant's Brigade was still not up, but Cotton had ordered his Assistant Adjutant General, Lieutenant Colonel John Elley, to lead the heavy cavalry into position to outflank the French left as planned. To facilitate this, it was necessary to distract the French by maintaining the fight to their front, and Ponsonby was therefore instructed to keep three squadrons engaged while Le Marchant got into position. Exactly how long this continued skirmishing lasted is unclear, and indeed accounts of the battle as a whole are remarkably quiet so far as the issue of time and timings are concerned. Tomkinson seems to imply that the 16th went straight into action as soon as they arrived on the field, and that this was in turn near-simultaneous with Le Marchant's intervention, which suggests that Cotton may well have ridden ahead of the 16th rather than bringing them onto the field in person and that skirmishing continued at least until the 16th came up. In all events, once the additional British troops reached the scene the action rapidly became general. Le Marchant's lead regiment, the 5th Dragoon Guards, was spotted by the

French before the remaining heavies were able to get into position, although Thoumine's questionable account has Perreimond refusing to be convinced of the threat despite Lallemand's warnings, allowing the British to gain a more advantageous position. Upon realizing that he had been discovered, Le Marchant ordered the 5th to charge at once notwithstanding their horses being blown after their long approach march, and at about the same time the 16th came into action on the right of the 12th and the three light dragoon regiments went forwards in a general attack.

Exactly what happened next is unclear, since both heavy and light cavalry claimed the honours of breaking the two French dragoon regiments, but the heavier casualties suffered by the 5th Dragoon Guards relative to the regiments of Anson's Brigade would tend to suggest that the heavies charged first and were initially checked, and that it was the combination of attacks from two directions that brought about the discomfiture of the French. Indeed, Fortescue's account of the fight, drawing on an unpublished account by a trooper of the 5th, suggests that the dragoon guards made two charges, the first being brought to a stop by mounted fire from the French. This in turn would serve to reconcile the conflicting versions put forward by the champions of the two brigades by suggesting that Ponsonby's attack coincided with the second, successful, charge by Le Marchant and the 5th.[57] In all events, the result of this sweeping attack was to break the French dragoons and tumble the whole lot into a headlong flight across the open plain towards Llerena.

The fight had not yet completely gone from the French however, and Lallemand was able to take advantage of a ditch mid-way between Villagarcia and Llerena in order to make a stand. Cotton seems to have been determined to keep his command well in hand and prevent the sort of over-enthusiastic pursuit that had marred earlier mounted actions, in which desire he was successful. Thus, although Lallemand was given an opportunity to regroup, Cotton in turn was able to tackle the new French position with his troops in good order. Two squadrons of the 16th were dispatched to turn the flank of the position whilst all three squadrons of the 12th attacked head-on. Cotton himself took part in this charge, and was badly bruised when his charger was brought down attempting to cross the ditch. With Le Marchant again committing the 5th Dragoon Guards – his other regiments left far in the rear – to bring a total of eight squadrons into action with four more in close support, the French were overwhelmed and broken for a second time and pursued almost to Llerena itself. Only the presence of d'Erlon's infantry and artillery served finally to check the pursuit and allow the remaining French cavalry to make good their escape.

Although the French force was not cut off and destroyed as Cotton had hoped, there is no denying that the action at Villagarcia was a crushing victory for the British cavalry. French casualties were calculated at 189 killed, wounded and taken prisoner, with Cotton estimating that the captures alone amounted to 150 men – including four officers – as well as 130 horses.[58] Tomkinson reported how 'the prisoners were dreadfully cut, and some will not recover', and also remarked that 'a French dragoon had his head nearer cut off than I ever saw before; it was by a sabre cut at the back of the neck'.[59] All this would suggest that the bulk of the action, apart from the initial charges and the second assault organized to drive the French from behind the ditch where Lallemand had attempted to rally, involved the pursuit of a fleeing enemy. This is reflected too in the extremely low British casualties relative to those of their opponents: Cotton lost fourteen killed, forty-two wounded and two missing, with the majority of these casualties being from the 5th Dragoon Guards. In the 12th, the only fatalities were Troop Serjeant Major Robertson and three private dragoons.[60] In contrast to the good management of the action by Cotton and his brigade commanders, the French seem to have made a poor showing, with Perreimond committing his reserve – the 2eme Hussards – too early and thus having no supports on hand when his lines broke. Thoumine suggests that there was dissent in the French command, and it is certainly the case that Lallemand, cast in the subordinate role this day, was a far more competent officer than his chief, as he would demonstrate a month later at Maguilla when his brigade comprehensively defeated that of John Slade.[61]

In the aftermath of the cavalry fighting, evidently convinced that Cotton's division was the advance guard of an allied offensive towards Seville, d'Erlon ordered a withdrawal from Llerena with his whole force, thus bringing to an end the field operations linked with the siege of Badajoz. Within days, the 12th Light Dragoons would be on the road north along with the rest of their brigade. Both the regiment and its commanding officer had been successfully blooded in a field action, but the campaigning season of 1812 was barely begun, and still greater things lay ahead.

Chapter VII

To Burgos and Back Again

THE FIGHT AT VILLAGARCIA represented a last swipe at the Armée du Midi before Wellington shifted his attention to Marmont's Armée de Portugal. At first the allied commander was concerned only to secure northern Portugal, and was still mooting a return south to tackle Soult, but by the end of May he had set upon seeking a decisive confrontation with Marmont.[1] With Napoleon having begun to pull troops out of Spain to participate in his new war against Russia, the opportunities for the various French armies to cooperate against Wellington's growing Anglo-Portuguese force were not what they had been. The Armée de Portugal remained strong, but the Armée du Nord had given up substantial numbers of troops and was now largely restricted to holding its ground against the growing menace of Spanish guerrillas. The small Armée du Centre, based around Madrid under the personal command of King Joseph Bonaparte – now also a very nominal commander-in-chief for the others as well – was similarly constrained, whilst Soult's Armée du Midi was largely tied up with holding down Andalucía. Wellington therefore had the opportunity to tackle Marmont on something like equal terms. Furthermore his growing number of mounted troops, if well handled, gave him a potential edge on the open terrain of Old Castile. As a result, the campaign of 1812 would make greater demands on Wellington's cavalry than ever before.[2]

In the aftermath of the fighting at Villagarcia, both sides withdrew and Anson's Brigade returned to cantonments in Villafranca and Zafra. Any chance to rest was short-lived, for on 14 April orders were received for the brigade, and that of Le Marchant, to move north to re-join the main army. For the 12th, the route north took them through Badajoz, Elvas, Estremoz, Niza, and thence to Castello Branco. By then it was clear that the French had withdrawn from northern Portugal, and since further operations were not immediately pending the cavalry were shifted back into cantonments in the Alentejo. Here the 12th remained until 19 May, when, along with the rest of Graham's command – now consisting of the First and Sixth Divisions and the cavalry of Ponsonby and Le Marchant – it was shifted to Mérida to act as a covering force for Sir Rowland Hill's strike against the French-held crossing of the Tagus at Almaraz. Hill successfully completed his mission without any need of Graham's support, in doing so severing the main line of communication between the armies of Soult and Marmont, and this allowed the 12th to return again to billets at Canno. There they remained until 1 June when, along with the rest of Anson's Brigade, they began a march of ten days to join the main body of Wellington's army around Ciudad Rodrigo in preparation for the offensive against Marmont.[3]

Although it was of course necessary for Graham's troops to retrace their steps in order to provide a covering force for Hill's operations, the fact that much of May and early June was thus spent on the road rather than in cantonments served to hinder what was otherwise a steady increase in the effective strength of the 12th Light Dragoons. Whilst the regiment had now indisputably proved its merits on the battlefield, the health of its men and horses remained uncertain, and continued care was needed to ensure that matters did not again deteriorate. To set against this, the regiment also received its first major reinforcement since deployment to the Peninsula, with Captain Barton bringing out a remount of 150 horses along with a manpower infusion totalling 4 other officers, 1 troop quartermaster, 2 serjeants, a trumpeter and 89 rank and file. On the negative side of the ledger, 1 serjeant and 11 rank and file were sent home and, once Barton's remount had marched up from Lisbon to join the regiment in the field, 39 horses were transferred to the 4th Dragoons on the orders of Lieutenant General Cotton. Nevertheless, the 12th were the gainers overall, and once these various changes had taken place the regiment was able to begin Wellington's offensive into Spain with an effective strength of 309 rank and file and 319 troop horses. Major General Anson was on his way back from leave to resume command of his brigade which, when he arrived, would allow Ponsonby to return to his regimental duties, but for the opening moves of the new campaign Captain Dickens remained in command of the regiment and Ponsonby of the brigade. Although Ponsonby had certainly done well during his stint as a brigade commander, the 12th were undoubtedly in need of him since with only four captains present for duty, and no other field officers, there was a definite shortage of senior leadership. Captain Samson Stawell had been serving since April as aide de camp to Lieutenant General Christopher Tilson-Chowne, commanding the Second Division, and Captain Arthur Saunders had retired. So long as Dickens continued in command, this meant that the three remaining captains were each required to lead a squadron and thus that troop duties were left entirely to the subaltern officers of whom nine were present as of 25 June.[4]

For his campaign against Marmont, Wellington led an allied army of 48,000 men – including 3,500 cavalry – and 54 guns. A small Spanish force under Don Carlos d'España formed part of the main army and, as the campaign progressed, the Spanish Sixth Army, operating out of Galicia, would add a further 16,000 troops. The main army under Wellington's command began its march into Spain on 13 June, with its objective the city of Salamanca, which, as the main operational base of the 50,000-strong Armée de Portugal, represented a direct attack intended to bring on a general action with Marmont.[5] In order to co-ordinate the advance, the force was divided into three columns, the right under Graham, the centre under Beresford, and the left under Lieutenant General Thomas Picton. Each column had a regiment of light cavalry assigned to form its advance guard, leaving the 12th and 16th Light Dragoons further to the rear as part of the centre column. Not until 16 June were the first French outposts seen, by which time the allies were well on their way to Salamanca, and it soon became clear that Marmont did not intend to make a fight for the city. Unable to call in all his outlying troops in time, and particularly weak in cavalry, the French commander withdrew to the north leaving only a small garrison in Salamanca to hold three makeshift forts. On 17 June, Wellington marched a token force into the abandoned city, to the cheers of its inhabitants, and then sat down to besiege the forts. His hope, it would seem, was that Marmont would march to their relief, but when his adversary did just that the result was a face-off rather than a battle. Wellington had taken up a strong position on the heights of San Cristóbal north-east of Salamanca, and Marmont, who had still only been able to muster 43,000 troops by 21 June, baulked at attacking. But Wellington, for his part, refused to risk things by coming down from the heights, and so at length the French withdrew unmolested. For the remainder of the month, Wellington concentrated on trying to take the forts and Marmont on a series of feints intended to distract him and buy time for reinforcements to come up. After the repulse of a first mismanaged assault on the night of 23 June, the forts fell on the 27th and Marmont, still unreinforced, withdrew northwards once again.[6]

The role of the 12th in these operations was limited and, for the most part, unexciting. When the French initially evacuated Salamanca Ponsonby's command was shifted across to form the advance guard of Picton's column, and spent 17 June skirmishing with the French rear-guard as it withdrew past San

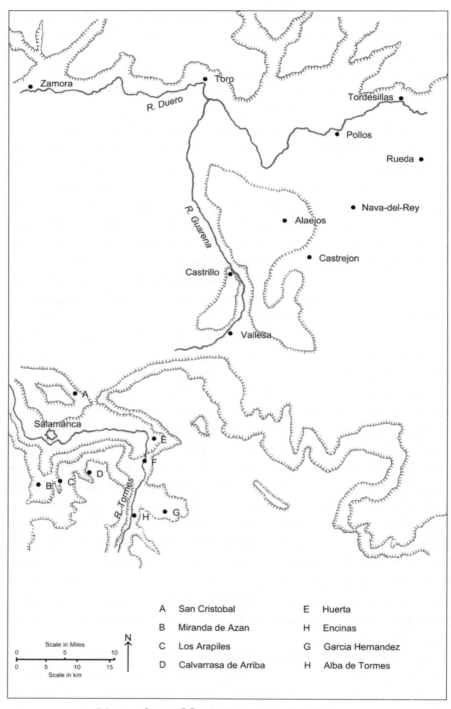

Map 3: **Area of Operations around Salamanca**

A	San Cristobal	E	Huerta
B	Miranda de Azan	H	Encinas
C	Los Arapiles	G	Garcia Hernandez
D	Calvarrasa de Arriba	H	Alba de Tormes

Scale in Miles
0   5   10

0   5   10   15
Scale in km

N

Cristóbal. For the 12th at least, this does not seem to have been the occasion of any serious fighting, and no casualties were reported. Thereafter the brigade remained around San Cristóbal and formed a screening force for the allied left flank during Wellington's stand on the heights; again, they were not heavily engaged and suffered no casualties. Once the French withdrew for a second time, the brigade moved forwards to occupy the ground in front of the heights and provide a screen of outposts for the main force.[7] There they remained until 29 June, when the army as a whole began to move north in pursuit of the French. Anson's Brigade formed the vanguard on the Toro road, and eventually caught up with the enemy around Alaejos late on the 30th. There was some hope of the French being brought to action there, but they decamped under the cover of darkness and so the pursuit continued. Contact was regained on 1 July around Nava-del-Rey, at which place Major General Anson finally caught up with the brigade and resumed command of it.

The same pattern of movements was repeated the following day, with the French never lingering long enough to be brought to action. Both British brigades of light cavalry, Alten's as well as Anson's, were engaged in what Ponsonby described as 'a good sharp skirmish' near Rueda, but Alten's Brigade bore the brunt of the affair so far as the allies were concerned, with Anson's remaining in support. Since Wellington refused to allow the cavalry to become heavily engaged until the infantry were up, the action eventually petered out after an artillery bombardment of the French, who subsequently again withdrew.[8] Having kept successfully one step ahead of Wellington, Marmont now withdrew behind the line of the River Duero, and there settled down to await reinforcements. The last of his own eight infantry divisions was still on the march from the Asturias, and he also entertained an expectation of assistance from the Armée du Nord, although in the event this would not be forthcoming until it was too late to make a difference. Until he had increased his forces Marmont had no intention of risking his army south of the Duero, whilst the strength of the French position north of the river made Wellington unwilling to risk an attack. As Ponsonby put it, 'we have been looking at each other, without our being able to get at them, or their wishing to come to us'.[9] In the meantime, the allies made the most of the rich and relatively untouched countryside south of the Duero in finding forage for their horses, although the need to cover a lengthy front with several potential river crossings meant that the light cavalry were kept hard at work on outpost duty.

Wellington also took the opportunity of making some organizational changes in his army, in part necessitated by the fact that both Graham and

Picton had had to return to England due to the state of their health, which led to the abolition of the temporary distribution of the army into columns. Within the cavalry, the 14th Light Dragoons were removed from Anson's Brigade into Alten's, with the 11th Light Dragoons being posted in exchange. According to Tomkinson, now a captain on Cotton's staff, this was apparently the result of the poor performance of the 11th in a minor action on 30 July in which several men were taken prisoner, leading Cotton to declare that the 11th should be transferred. The inference here is that since Alten's was numerically the weaker brigade, having only two regiments, it required that both those regiments be reliable whereas Anson's Brigade could more easily cope if one regiment out of three was a little shaky. In reality, Tomkinson suggests that there was no real failing in the 11th and that Cotton's decision to make the transfer was unfair. All this does imply a recognition of the 12th as now being considered as being amongst the more reliable of the army's light cavalry regiments, if their presence in the brigade was deemed by Cotton a suitable counter to the deficiencies he perceived in the 11th.[10]

The two armies continued their face-off across the Duero for a fortnight, with the generals searching for the opportunity to catch the other side at a disadvantage whilst the men cheerfully fraternized across the water. At length, having brought together all his own troops but still lacking any reinforcements from outside his command, Marmont prepared to renew the offensive. In order to try and steal a march on his adversary, Marmont enacted a clever feint, first ostentatiously shifting two divisions south of the river at Toro on the far western extremity of his lines, and then withdrawing them under cover of darkness and throwing his whole force over the river further east on the night of 16–17 July. Wellington, who had been moving troops to meet the anticipated French advance from Toro, was badly wrong-footed, and forced to try and rescue matters before his whole force was compromised. In this, he was aided by the fact that the valley of the River Guarena ran roughly north–south to enter the Duero a little to the east of Toro. If he could defend the line of the Guarena, Wellington had a good position from which to fend off a French attack, but unfortunately the speed of Marmont's offensive had left the allied right wing – the infantry of the Fourth and Light Divisions, and the majority of Cotton's cavalry – on the east bank of the Guarena. Badly exposed and some distance from support, these troops were extremely vulnerable to attack by the Armée de Portugal which, by nightfall on the 17th, was concentrated between Rueda and Nava-del-Rey. The following day would therefore be a critical one for the outcome of the campaign.[11]

Through seniority, command of the isolated allied force east of the Guarena fell to Cotton, who at dawn on 18 July sent out Tomkinson – now back on regimental duty with the 16th Light Dragoons – with a patrol to establish the nature of the French troops facing him. Tomkinson quickly established that the French were on the move in force and, along with a supporting squadron from the 11th Light Dragoons, fell back on the main body of Anson's Brigade at Castrejón. The artillery accompanying the French advance swiftly unlimbered and went into action, causing some loss amongst all three of Anson's regiments and driving them from the village. Tomkinson though it 'the sharpest cannon-ade, for the time, we were, or I, was ever exposed to', and commented that its intensity rendered it 'almost impossible to get the men away in complete order'.[12] Even the Registry of Services for the 12th, normally a dry record of marches and postings, remarked that 'a very heavy Cannonade took place in which the Brigade suffered'.[13] By this point, around seven in the morning, Wellington had arrived on the scene and ordered Cotton to cover the retreat of the infantry, leading to fighting that was characterized by Ponsonby as 'two hours' sharp cannonading and skirmishing'. Thus covered, the allied infantry were able to cross the Guarena successfully and link up with the Fifth Division which had been brought up to help secure the position, allowing the cavalry in turn to begin to withdraw. This was timely, as the French were pushing their infantry up in some force and the retreating allies had a race on their hands to get safely across the Guarena. The French attempted to follow up their advantage by trying to cross the river near Castrillo, but their advance guard was counterattacked and roughly handled by Alten's Brigade and the infantry of the Fourth Division, allowing Wellington to end the day secure behind the Guarena.[14]

Other than a passing – and, when compared with official returns, inaccurate – note of the regiment's losses, Ponsonby's account, written after the Battle of Salamanca and therefore understandably concentrating on the main event rather than the preliminary skirmishing, has little else to say about the fighting on the 18th. Indeed, he even gets his chronology out of order and has events taking place a day late. Actual rank and file losses in the 12th amounted to five killed, twelve wounded, and one missing, plus Lieutenant Gitterick wounded for a total of nineteen casualties rather than the sixteen given by Ponsonby.[15] Given that when he wrote this letter he had been several days in the saddle and had fought in a major battle, it is hard to criticize Ponsonby for giving a poor account of the fighting at Castrejón, or for getting his figures wrong. However, it does mean that we are left to look elsewhere for detail of the 12th's involvement in the day's events and, in particular, on an incident early on in the fighting that, had things gone a little differently, could have had truly disastrous results.

During the French cannonade on the morning of the 18th, a squadron apiece from the 11th and the 12th were employed on the far left of the allied position, covering two guns of Major Ross's 'A' Troop, Royal Horse Artillery. Due to the ferocity of the French bombardment, the allied force as a whole was still in some disarray and this confusion seemingly extended well up the chain of command. Tomkinson picks up the story:

> The squadrons were supporting one another, and on the advance of some of the enemy's cavalry (inferior to the two squadrons), the one in front went about. Some of Marshal Beresford's staff seeing this, conceived the guns were in danger, rode up to the retiring squadron, calling 'Threes about!' This of course put the other squadron about in the place of front-ing the one already retiring. One person gave one word, one another, and the enemy's cavalry came up to the guns. There was no harm done, and our dragoons (the 11th) immediately advanced and drove them back.[16]

If the squadron that was turned about, and subsequently rallied, was that of the 11th, it of course follows that the one which was already retiring was that of the 12th.

The whole business seems a classic case of order; counter-order; disorder, but the consequences were potentially far worse than just the loss of Ross's guns, for as the confused mass of cavalry and horse-gunners tumbled backwards they swept up with them not only Beresford's staff – including the anonymous officer whose order had thrown things adrift – but also Wellington himself. The conse-quences of Wellington's wounding or capture at this critical juncture do not bear thinking about, but thankfully the supporting squadron, that of the 11th, was able to recover its order and drive back the French. This in turn allowed the squadron from the 12th, which had also been thrown into some confusion, to regroup also and join in the rout of the attackers. Although the situation was thereby restored, and no error was perpetrated by the 12th who were already falling back when the mistaken order was given, both regiments nevertheless came in for some criticism, and it is perhaps not to be wondered that Ponsonby chose to draw a veil over the whole affair in his letter home, and concentrate on the altogether more creditable events of the days that followed.[17]

With his army safely back across the Guarena, Wellington had successfully thwarted Marmont's attempt to defeat him in detail, but the campaign of movement was back on in earnest and the coming days saw both generals stretch their skills to the limit. As Marmont extended his left, moving southwards along the east bank of the Guarena, so was Wellington obliged to extend his right to match him. The two armies began a parallel march to the south, being drawn closer and closer together as the river valley narrowed and eventually dwindled away to nothing. With the two sides in such close proximity, one false move by either commander could have spelled disaster, but both armies kept closed up and neither general saw the opportunity for an attack. Finally, late on 20 July, Wellington began to open up the distance between the two forces and by the following day had again taken up his favourite defensive position on the heights above San Cristóbal. Marmont, however, again refused to be drawn and instead continued moving to the south, crossing the River Tormes and assuming a position south-east of Salamanca. Wellington moved south to match him, leaving only the Third Division and some Portuguese cavalry north of the river to cover Salamanca itself, and the two armies spent the night in close proximity and sharing the demoralizing effects of a heavy thunderstorm that drenched both and caused havoc in the British horse lines. Spooked by the thunder and lightning, several horses of Le Marchant's Brigade broke loose and could not be recovered, but the disorder does not seem to have spread to the light cavalry and certainly the 12th returned no loss from amongst its mounts.[18]

History of course records that the thunderstorm on the night of 21–22 July 1812 – like that which soaked the troops on the Mont St-Jean ridge just under three years later – was the harbinger of a great victory for Wellington's army, but it is unlikely on the morning of the 22nd that the troops on either side had any idea that this was likely to be the case. Indeed, it initially seemed that the French had the advantage. Marmont, however, became overconfident and allowed his army to become strung out as he again sought to turn Wellington's right flank. This moment's mistake was all that was needed, although the chance disabling of the French commander by a lucky shell early in the day extended the window of opportunity in which the allies could strike, and Wellington set in motion a classic oblique attack that rolled up the exposed French left wing in short order. To all intents and purposes, this strike by the Third and Fifth Divisions and Le Marchant's Brigade, covered by the bulk of the allied light cavalry, was the decisive moment in the battle. Le Marchant was killed, but his charge completed the destruction of three of Marmont's eight divisions and left the remainder – now under the command of Général de Division Bertrand Clausel – at an impossible disadvantage. Clausel nevertheless put in a strong counterattack against the allied centre, which took some hard fighting to check, and when the French eventually withdrew it was under the cover of an effective rear-guard that enabled the surviving troops to get away in reasonable order. Nevertheless, with the French having lost 12,000 men, twelve guns, and two Imperial Eagle standards, as against allied losses of a little over 5,000, Salamanca was a crushing allied victory that sealed Wellington's reputation as a general and wrecked the Armée de Portugal as a fighting force.[19]

It will be noted that this account of the Battle of Salamanca, whilst a necessarily brief summary, makes no mention of the role of the 12th Light Dragoons. This, however, is for the very good reason that the regiment played no part in the main action, being instead engaged in a battle-within-a-battle away on the eastern flank. Initially, the section of the field in which the 12th was engaged represented the southern extremity of Wellington's line on the morning of the battle, facing east and looking towards the French on the heights of Calvarassa de Arriba. As the day went on, both armies extended their lines to the west, until what had been the left of Wellington's position became its right, extending north at right angles from a line that had shifted from a north–south to an east–west axis. The fighting that decided matters was all along the long side of this new L-shaped alignment, but throughout the day the allied Light Division faced off against Général de Division Maximilien Foy's French troops on the heights. Both armies, as they wheeled to the south-west, had left detachments of cavalry to cover the open flank to the north of Calvarassa de Arriba. Marmont, at a significant disadvantage in mounted troops, left only a single regiment, the 15eme Dragons, but Wellington could afford to detach a larger number of horsemen: not only was Bock's Brigade positioned well to the north, but an ad hoc detachment of light cavalry was posted to cover the immediate left of the Light Division. This detachment was commanded by Lieutenant Colonel Ponsonby and composed of all three squadrons of the 12th Light Dragoons as well as one belonging to the 14th. That these units ended up where they did seems to have been as much chance as deliberate selection – something reinforced by the fact that the 12th and 14th were now in different brigades – as the 12th had initially been deployed further to the north and been brought down to link up with the sole squadron of the 14th at some time in the mid-morning.[20]

Whilst this semi-independent command placed Ponsonby and the 12th in a position of some responsibility, it also renders it difficult for the historian to reconstruct exactly what the regiment did. The only thing that can be said with any degree of certainty, beyond the details of the casualties suffered, is that the regiment – or part of it – charged against elements of the French rear-guard in the closing stages of the battle. The main sources for exactly what happened are contained in the Leveson-Gower correspondence in the shape of Ponsonby's own letter home describing the battle and a subsequent account by his mother based on a third-hand account ultimately emanating from Captain Lord Clinton, the bearer of Wellington's victory despatch. Ponsonby's own letter relates how,

> it was getting very dark when Lord W. advanced the light divisions and first against their Right. I covered them with a squadron of the 12th and one of the 5th: we charged twice, and in the last went thro' two battalions of Infantry. I was unfortunate enough to lose Dickens in this charge; he was leading a Squadron, and received a ball in his left breast. Just as we came up to the enemy's columns the officer who commanded the other Squadron was also shot in the breast, but not killed.[21]

Lady Bessborough's version of events then further complicates things by giving a different composition of Ponsonby's command and invoking the presence of Wellington himself to direct operations:

> Lady Bathurst was told by Lord Clinton that Ld. W. order'd F. [Frederick Ponsonby] to command the three Squadrons he mentions – 12th, and 5th, and 1st – and to accompany him and take his orders directly from himself. Ld. Clinton added: Never were orders more clearly given or more correctly executed, and that two charges particularly Lord Wellington quite exclaim'd at, and said, 'That is gallantly done – nothing can be better.' Is not this a delightful thing to hear – to know that F. had the advantage of being directed by the greatest general that ever liv'd, and the glory of being approv'd by him?[22]

These accounts, then, leave us with a number of questions to be answered as to just which units took part in the charges, who they charged against, and who directed the manoeuvres.

For the 12th itself, the record is pretty clear as the unfortunate death of Captain Dickens, who Ponsonby mourned as 'a most excellent officer', confirms that it was his squadron of the regiment that was engaged, but the identity of the squadron or squadrons that charged alongside it is less obvious, as Ponsonby makes it clear that only Dickens's of the 12th was engaged. Both letters mention the '5th', but the only cavalry regiment on the field with that number was the 5th Dragoon Guards of Le Marchant's Brigade, all three squadrons of which were some distance away. It seems more obvious, as Rory Muir suggests in his history of the battle, that the other squadron was that detached from the 14th and that the number has been somehow mangled in the telling. This is not an entirely satisfactory answer as no officer of the 14th was returned as being wounded, but it is quite possible that the injury that Ponsonby mentions was less severe than he had assumed and was not formally recorded. Certainly, all those cavalry regiments that did return officer casualties can be safely accounted for elsewhere on the field at this point. Mention of the '1st' in Lady Bessborough's account may just possibly refer to a squadron of the 1st KGL Dragoons from Bock's Brigade, but is more likely a red herring stemming from some misunderstanding during the successive re-tellings by which the story reached her. The family had just been hit by scandal when Ponsonby's sister, Lady Caroline Lamb, ran off with the poet Lord Byron, and under the circumstances Lady Bessborough can be forgiven for being sufficiently distracted to confuse the minor details of a military engagement. In all probability, then, Ponsonby led a series of charges by Dickens's squadron of the 12th and the attached squadron of the 14th Light Dragoons. Whether they were specifically ordered on by Wellington as Lady Bessborough believed is unclear, although Wellington certainly did order the general advance by the Light Division and supporting troops, and remained in the area afterwards where he was struck by a spent ball as is mentioned by several eyewitnesses.[23]

The other question that remains is what they charged against. Ponsonby states that the second charge, in which Dickens was killed, 'went thro' two battalions of Infantry', but this is not corroborated by the French divisional commander, Foy, in his account of the combat. For two squadrons of light cavalry to have charged two formed battalions of infantry would, in any case, have been something of a tall order, and would certainly have been attended by a greater loss than the 12th actually suffered. Other than Dickens, casualties in the battle amounted to Troop Serjeant Major Key and one other man killed, and two men wounded, which is hardly suggestive of a desperate fight against a large body of formed troops.[24] Still, Ponsonby was not simply making things up, so this begs the question of what actually happened. The answer, or at least the best one that can be produced to reconcile the conflicting evidence, lies again with Foy's account of things from the French perspective. He reports that in covering the French retreat he was assailed by a large force of infantry, '1,500 cavalry', and six guns. This is clearly the Light Division and Ponsonby's horsemen, but since the latter amounted to, at best, 450 all ranks, Foy's description also emphasizes the fact that darkness magnified the number of troops for all concerned and may therefore have added some inadvertent exaggeration to Ponsonby's account too. However, the most important fact that Foy mentions is that whilst his division was repeatedly charged they kept their order but that other troops in the area were by this stage broken.[25] Whilst it remains unrealistic to expect the two British squadrons to have gone through two battalions of formed French infantry, two battalions-worth of fugitives is quite another thing, and this seems the most likely explanation of what happened during the evening of 22 July.

On the face of it, this all sounds rather less dramatic than the stirring image of a full-blown cavalry charge suggested by an initial reading of Ponsonby's account. Yet what it seems the 12th did that evening was exactly what light cavalry were supposed to do, as indeed had been the case with the regiment's participation in the whole battle. Having spent most of the day screening the infantry of the Light Division, the regiment – and its attached squadron of the 14th – had then successfully harassed and pursued a defeated enemy and in so doing taken part in the only effective pursuit of the Armée de Portugal. Commanded after Dickens fell by the newly promoted Captain Henry Andrews, and apparently still accompanied by Ponsonby, the advance squadron of the 12th joined the infantry of the Light and First Divisions in their pursuit to Huerta and remained with them there until the following day.[26]

As a result of the detachment of the 12th Light Dragoons to Wellington's left wing, and subsequent dispersal during the course of the abortive post-battle pursuit, the regiment was absent when the rest of Anson's Brigade supported Bock's Germans in their epic charge at Garcia Hernandez the day after the victory at Salamanca. Here the KGL Dragoons broke the squares of Foy's rearguard infantry, completing the rout of the Armée de Portugal and putting the seal on Wellington's triumph. Only later in the day were the various squadrons of the 12th reunited with each other and with the rest of the brigade. Although victorious, the allied army as a whole had suffered a not-inconsiderable loss in their defeat of Marmont, and Wellington was particularly short of senior commanders. Graham and Picton had been invalided home before the battle and Lieutenant Generals Cole, Leith and Cotton were all wounded during it, thus depriving the army of three more divisional commanders. Major General Baron von Bock of the KGL – brave, but extremely short-sighted – replaced Cotton as acting head of the First Cavalry Division. Hampered by these command losses and the inevitable dislocation that follows a major battle, Wellington did not launch a vigorous pursuit but instead sought only to follow the line of the French retreat towards Valladolid on the Duero. The city was

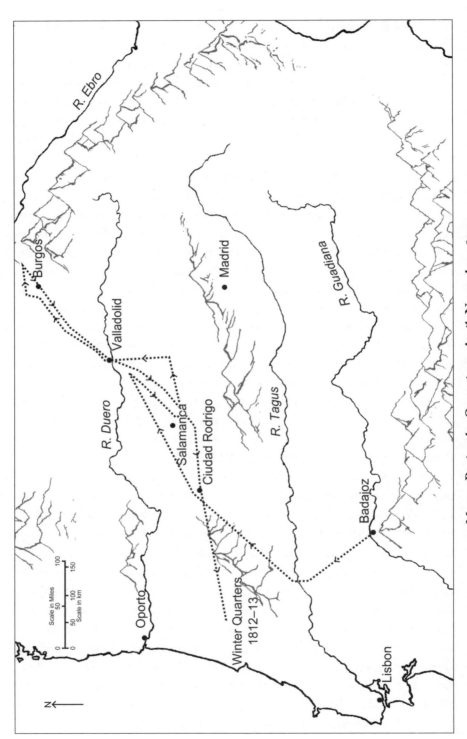

Map 4: Peninsular Operations, April–November 1812

R. Ebro

Burgos

Valladolid

Madrid

R. Duero

Salamanca

Ciudad Rodrigo

R. Guadiana

R. Tagus

Oporto

Badajoz

Winter Quarters
1812–13

Lisbon

Scale in Miles
Scale in km

N

occupied without a fight, yielding up a portion of the sick and stragglers from Clausel's retreating army, and Anson's Brigade was then left to cover Wellington's northern flank along the line of the Duero. Leaving the Sixth Division and elements of the Spanish Sixth Army to support the cavalry outposts, Wellington took the rest of his forces back southwards to occupy Madrid.[27]

Although there was no fighting in Valladolid itself, the southern approaches to the city were contested by the French. As Ponsonby described it in a letter home, 'I had the advance, and was close up with them, harassing their rear with about forty of my best riders; but on coming to the bridge, they blew it up. Fortunately, we clear'd it in time, and lost only three horses.'[28] After this hair-raising start, the regiment was rewarded with the duty of escorting Wellington in his entry into Valladolid, and Ponsonby in a second, more detailed, letter related that,

> Ld. W.'s reception was very fine; I escorted him with two Squadrons of the 12th, the only troops that enter'd the town. We were met at every turn by bands of music, people of all descriptions, high and low, especially Ladies, bearing streamers and trophies, crowns of Laurel and wreaths of flowers, with which the way was strewed, every house decorated as you have seen them formerly in France for the fête Dieu. Women of all ranks bringing refreshments, even to the privates, walking by the side of our horses; and if Ld. W. would have let them, they would have knelt and pray'd to him; whilst on every side were heard acclamations of *Viva el Gran Capitan, Viva los Heroes Ingleses los Salvadores*.[29]

Interestingly, Oman notes that Valladolid was supposed to be one of the most pro-French towns in all of occupied Spain, so either there was some speedy back-tracking going on here, or else the loyal inhabitants were making sure to compensate for their *Afrancesado* brethren![30]

Anson's Brigade would stay on the Duero for some time to come, remaining north of the river until 12 August when the French reoccupation of Valladolid forced a relocation to the south bank. There they remained until early September.[31] Although the early French counteroffensive came as a shock, Clausel showed no desire to push south of the Duero, and so for the most part the cavalry were allowed a period of rest. Evidently there was some skirmishing, one man being recorded as killed in action on 18 August, but for the most part things remained quiet.[32] This, indeed, was not before time, since Ponsonby reported that there was growing sickness in the army and that his own regiment was 'much reduced in numbers, though what there are, are in pretty good order'. Effective strength as of 25 August was 271 rank and file and 289 troop horses, but officers remained in short supply and Ponsonby was still the only field officer, although he told his mother that 'I expect Lord Waldegrave up every day.'[33]

The rest could last only for so long, however. Wellington, having concentrated all his Anglo-Portuguese forces, including Hill's command brought up from Extremadura, at Madrid, now returned his attentions to the north. Wellington's intention was to move on Burgos in order to counter the renewed aggression of the Armée de Portugal, the power of recovery of which he had perhaps underestimated, and he took with him from Madrid the First, Fifth, and Seventh Divisions along with the two brigades of heavy cavalry, leaving Hill in command of the remainder. Moving north and crossing the Duero on 6 September, he picked the Sixth Division and Anson's Brigade up as he did so, and thereafter Anson's three light dragoon regiments would function as the vanguard of the advance. The respite on the Duero was over, and the toughest phase of the campaign yet was about to commence.[34]

As the main body of the 12th joined Wellington's advance on Burgos, another detachment was already on the way to link up with them. It will be remembered that 1812 saw the beginning of substantial efforts by Steuart and the officers of the regimental depot to increase the number of horses being readied for service, and this now allowed for the despatch of another strong remount, not quite on a par with that sent out during the spring but by no means insubstantial either. In addition to 94 troop horses, the detachment also included 3 officers, the regimental serjeant major, 2 serjeants, 1 trumpeter and 33 rank and file, and arrived in Lisbon on 18 September after a remarkably swift passage. By chance, two of the officers with this detachment were the pair whose memoirs and letters respectively serve to open up a far greater understanding of life in the 12th on active service than has been hitherto possible through the sparse and frequently laconic letters of Lieutenant Colonel Ponsonby. Our future memoirist, William Hay, we have already briefly encountered upon his transfer to the regiment back in 1811: notwithstanding medical advice to the contrary, he had decided that he was fit enough to return to the field and after some effort managed to convince Major General Jones at Radipole to include him in the draft.[35]

Our letter-writer, on the other hand, requires some introduction although his letters have already been cited on a handful of occasions in this work. He was Lieutenant John Vandeleur, second cousin and near namesake to Major General John Ormsby Vandeleur, the author of *Duty of Officers Commanding Detachments in the Field*, who was now also in the Peninsula commanding an infantry brigade in the Light Division. Originally commissioned into the 71st Highland Light Infantry, Vandeleur junior had served with his regiment during the Portuguese campaigns of 1810–11. The culmination of these operations was the hard-fought action at Fuentes de Oñoro, in which the 71st were heavily engaged and where Vandeleur was seriously wounded. During his convalescence he was awarded a lieutenancy, without purchase, in the 12th and joined the regimental depot in April 1812.[36] In many ways, the two young men were similar: both came from good families; both had started their careers as light infantrymen; both had useful connections in the Army that would lead them into staff postings in the future. However, Hay's memoir was composed some years after the fact, while Vandeleur's letters home to his mother were only published after his death and are thus a plain and unvarnished account of what he had done and seen.

The detachment with which the reinforcement for the 12th had been convoyed to Lisbon was a substantial one, amounting to 'remounts for nearly every dragoon regiment employed',[37] and Hay's and Vandeleur's account of its progress through Portugal and into Spain gives a good feel for day-to-day life on active service. All three officers of the 12th had served in the Peninsula before – the third, Lieutenant William Dowbiggen, having like Hay transferred from the 52nd Light Infantry – and so knew what to expect on campaign. Nevertheless, the impoverished and devastated state of much of Portugal after the French invasion of 1810–11, meant that all that experience was put to good use. By contriving always to be billeted on the priest of whatever town or village the detachment was halted in, the three officers were generally able to obtain good rations, but there were occasions when such comforts were not available. Then the young gentlemen were obliged to prove whether they had the qualities required not only to lead by example on the battlefield but in quarters as well. As Vandeleur explained to his mother, the detachment

> ... marched on the 29th [September] to Vilha Velha, the worst march
> without exception that I ever had in Portugal, it was about twenty miles,
> and when we got there we found but three or four houses which were in
> a wretched state and only held eight or ten horses. It was a very rainy cold

night and every one wished to be one of the ten, therefore, to prevent any discontent, I slept out myself with my horses and they all did the same. We had no sort of cover nor a single tree to make a fire with.[38]

That was perhaps the worst of things, although food and quarters remained patchy throughout the march, but it is refreshing to see proof of the willingness of British officers to share the discomforts as well as the perils of their men.

Conditions improved as the remount detachments entered Spain, where the towns and villages, although until recently under French occupation, had at least been spared the worst of the fighting. However, extra food to supplement the rations became harder to come by, just a little milk and honey, and the rains continued to soak the troops. The Spaniards made a good first impression, however, with Vandeleur catching something of the spirit that had saddled the French occupiers with such a sapping guerrilla war:

> The Spaniards are undoubtedly a noble-looking people – fine, straight, tall, well-made fellows. Their houses are remarkably clean, they give us beds every night, and shew a good deal of blunt civility. The Spaniard will not submit to be ill-treated. They are extremely tenacious of everything, and jealous to the greatest degree.[39]

At length Salamanca was reached, and shortly afterwards there took place a parting of ways with Vandeleur conducting the remounts for Anson's Brigade to their regiments whilst Hay was detached to a cavalry depot 'at a town called, I think, Revelo (or Riedo)' – it seems in fact to have been Arevalo – to oversee those horses unfit to go onwards.[40] Vandeleur did not, however, have much further to go, since his detachment met up with the rest of the brigade at La Seca, on the Duero near Valladolid, at the beginning of November.[41]

Since we last saw the 12th heading north across that river two months previously, we need now to return to the regiment to establish what it had been doing in the meantime, and why it was that it, and the army, were back where we left them.

At first, the advance to the north had gone well. The Armée de Portugal, dispersed thanks to a futile effort to relieve Astorga and other places under siege by the Spanish, fell back once more and at first the only French who were encountered were stragglers. A more serious attempt to delay the allied advance was made at the crossing of the River Pisuagre on 7 September, where, in a re-run of events two months previously, the bridge was blown up just as Ponsonby was about to lead a squadron over it. On the 12th, Anson missed – in

Tomkinson's opinion at least – an ideal opportunity to cut off part of the French rear-guard and instead only followed it up, giving the French a chance to counterattack the British advance guard. The forces amounted to a squadron apiece from the 11th and 16th but they were directed, due to a shortage of field officers, by Lieutenant Colonel Ponsonby. The French made their move at dusk, and Tomkinson related how, because of the enclosed nature of the country to either side, the attack was restricted to the road along which the British were advancing,

> which made our small numbers equal to theirs. They came down the road
> at a trot, trumpeting to charge. We stood still, and they halted within
> thirty yards, firing volleys at us. When we moved forward they retired,
> and we kept our ground till dark. Colonel Ponsonby spoke highly of our
> squadron, and we can with equal justice bear testimony to his conduct.[42]

Four days later, the brigade's outposts – this time a squadron apiece from the 12th and 16th, under the newly joined Major Lord Waldegrave – drove in the picquets of the 22eme Chasseurs à Cheval, and on the 18th the French evacuated Burgos leaving only a garrison in the castle that overlooked the town. Although the omens were otherwise – Tomkinson judging from the conduct of the 22eme that the French were still demoralized after their defeat at Salamanca – this would prove the high-water mark of Wellington's 1812 campaign.

As a matter left to the infantry, artillery and engineers, the sorry tale of the siege of Burgos has no place in this narrative. Suffice it to say that Wellington attempted too much with inadequate resources, in appalling weather, and with the looming threat of intervention by the regrouped French armies. For the Armée de Portugal – now under Général de Division Joseph Souham – stood to be reinforced by the Armée du Nord, whilst Soult had evacuated Andalucía and taken his Armée du Midi to link up with King Joseph and the Armée du Centre near Valencia. For thirty-three days, Wellington's infantry struggled in the trenches and in a series of desperate assaults that cost the life – amongst 2,100 others – of Major Cocks who had so ably led Ponsonby's advance guard at Villagarcia. Only on 20 October did Wellington come to accept that there would be no further advance this year, and that the siege must be abandoned and his force reunited with that around Madrid under Hill, if anything was to be saved from the year's operations.[43]

Whilst the siege operations were still going on, Anson's Brigade was shifted, as of 22 September, to a position thirteen miles north-east of Burgos with headquarters at Fresno de Rodilla. There they were ideally placed to guard against any advance down the Great Road, which ran from the French border to Madrid by way of Vitoria and Burgos. The 12th were initially deployed in an advance position near Monasterio de Rodilla, described in the regimental Registry of Services as 'a very dangerous post' that was frequently under attack. Accordingly, at the beginning of October, the 12th were relived of this duty and ordered to move back to brigade headquarters whilst elements of the other two regiments took a turn of the outpost duty. However, on 2 October, before this change could be made, the regiment's outposts at Castel Piones came under attack and, as Tomkinson described, the 'advanced piquet was so surprised under Lieutenant [Richard] Fulton, of the 12th, that he had scarcely time to mount his men'.[44] Unable to form up in time to make any resistance, the picquet was tumbled back towards the rest of the duty squadron and the whole body obliged to beat a hasty retreat from which they were rescued by the one squadron of the 11th Light Dragoons that had been retained on the outposts. Ultimately, it was a case of all being well that ended well, but Fulton had made a serious error in allowing his men to dismount in so dangerous a post, and it was more by luck than judgement that things did not get any worse.

Summing up the day's action, Tomkinson highlighted the narrowness of the margin between success and failure, and the potential consequences if the French thrust had not been more successfully resisted:

> The enemy's intention was to surprise the advanced squadron, in which they failed, and retired again to their former posts. Had not it so happened that the 11th were turned out to relieve them I have little doubt they would have taken the greater number of the 12th, and gained Monestario before the troops there could have turned out. The two squadrons took from the enemy one captain and twelve men, and lost one corporal and one man from the 11th, with eleven privates from the 12th.[45]

Fulton had been on duty with the regiment in the Peninsula since January, so there was really no excuse for his not having taken better precautions against an attack of this nature. What would seem to be the case was that so long a period of continuous service was beginning to wear down officers and men alike: just as the infantry before Burgos performed far less effectively in the trenches than in the earlier sieges, so too did the cavalry on the outposts begin to lose their edge as well.

In light of the growing French pressure along the Great Road, infantry support was brought up to reinforce the cavalry, and the outposts pulled back to the line of a small river near where the action of 2 October had reached its climax. The French continued to attack this position, mounting a serious reconnaissance in force on the morning of 13 October with 1,500 infantry and 600 cavalry. In resisting this attack the 12th suffered the loss of Lieutenant Colonel Ponsonby, who was wounded and obliged to leave the regiment in order to receive treatment. With the help of the infantry of the Brunswick-Oels Regiment, the French were driven off, but Wellington was deprived of another experienced commander in a campaign that had already cost him too many veteran officers.[46]

Colonel the Hon. William Ponsonby, Frederick's cousin, who had led the 5th Dragoon Guards at Salamanca and taken over Le Marchant's Brigade after the general's death, wrote home to Lord Bessborough to explain what had happened:

> As you will no doubt hear from various quarters that your son Frederick has been wounded, I have thought that it would be satisfactory to you, and might prevent much uneasiness on your part as well as Lady Bessborough's, to be assured from me that no serious consequence is at all to be apprehended from his wound.
>
> On Wednesday morning last, in a skirmish at the advanced posts he received a musket shot in the thigh, which was however immediately extracted. The bone is certainly not injured, nor has there been any inflammation or fever, so that there is every reason to hope that he will be very shortly on his legs again.[47]

Ponsonby himself wrote home that he was 'quite well in health only kept very hungry, which you know does not suit me', and expressing the hope that his parents would 'not be in a great fuss about this scratch of mine'.[48]

With Ponsonby wounded, Lord Waldegrave assumed command of the regiment, and it was under his leadership that the 12th, along with the rest of the brigade and Bock's KGL dragoons, formed Wellington's rear-guard as the siege of Burgos was abandoned and the allies fell back to the line of the Duero. Having become greatly worn down by their extensive outpost service – the regiment returning only 156 effective rank and file as of 25 October, and 135 troop horses – the 12th was temporarily reorganized in two squadrons rather than three for the remainder of the campaign.[49] Being weakened, however, the regiment played only a supporting role in the last major cavalry action of this phase of the campaign, which took place at Venta del Pozo on 23 October.

Although the notes to the 25 October monthly return indicate that the regiment suffered casualties on the date in question, the only mention of the fight in the regimental Registry of Services is a brief note that 'A sharp affair of cavalry took place near Quintana de Puente in which the British Cavalry suffered.'[50] The apparent distinction between the 12th and the cavalry as a whole would seem to confirm a limited involvement only, but with Ponsonby wounded and both Hay and Vandeleur still not having joined, there are no eyewitness accounts of exactly what the regiment was doing. We cannot even, on this occasion, fall back on Tomkinson, since he was at this time on his way to the rear in the grip of a high fever. Cotton, who had just returned to the command of the cavalry although still by no means recovered from his Salamanca wound, commanded a rear-guard comprising Bock's and Anson's Brigades, two battalions of KGL light infantry, and a mixture of regular and irregular Spanish cavalry. Although able to conduct a respectable fighting retreat despite being outnumbered, Cotton mistimed what could have been a decisive counterattack by Bock's German heavies, and the allies were eventually forced back with substantial losses.[51] What seems likely, based on the fact that the 12th was certainly in action on the day but is not mentioned in accounts of the main fight, is that it participated in the initial fighting retreat but not in the abortive counterattack and subsequent confused melee. This is further corroborated by the fact that at least some of the casualties in the 12th were men taken prisoner, since such prisoners as were taken from Anson's Brigade during the action were lost during the early stages of the fight. Also, total casualties amounted to only twenty men out of 116 in Anson's Brigade as a whole.[52] Considering their numerical weakness, a reserve role for the 12th would make sense; certainly Hay confirms that, a little later in the campaign, the regiment was temporarily stood down due to its attenuated state.[53]

The French cavalry that attacked Cotton at Venta del Pozo represented the combined mounted forces of the Armée du Nord and the Armée de Portugal, confirming the wisdom of Wellington's decision to fall back to the Duero. At first it was hoped that the French might be contained north of the river and that winter quarters could be maintained within Spain, but with the Armée du Midi and Armée du Centre also closing in Wellington was left substantially outnumbered and with the flanks and rear under pressure. Still, with combined British, Portuguese and Spanish forces totalling some 75,000 men, the French with just over 90,000 could not afford to be overconfident and their moves in the final stages of the campaign would remain circumspect.[54] Although Anson's Brigade was left, yet again, to cover the retreat when Wellington fell back towards Salamanca on 5 November, Vandeleur remarked that the French 'let us off that day very quietly to Nava del Rey, where we bivouacked; and the next day we saw nothing of them until the evening, when they shewed their pickets. They followed us very close, but did no mischief till we got near Salamanca.'[55]

Wellington initially hoped to make a fight of it north of the Tormes, where perhaps the French might at last be tempted to attack his favoured position at San Cristóbal. Instead, however, Wellington found on 14 November that he had been outflanked to the south and that the French had gained a crossing over the Tormes. This necessitated that he shift his own forces south of the river, and by the evening of 14 November the allies were established in a new position covering the old Salamanca battlefield and the heights to its west.[56] The extrication of the allied forces from their successive defensive lines was not completed without confusion, and Lieutenant Hay related a series of adventures before he was able to re-join the 12th south of Salamanca. Hay, it will be remembered, had been left to oversee the regiment's unfit horses at the depot in Arevalo, which was under the command of Captain John Johnstone of the 3rd Dragoons. By Hay's account, Johnstone was not up to the task: when orders came to evacuate the post and remove the several hundred horses there to a place of safety, he at first lingered until his own personal preparations were complete and then, when it became clear that the French were close, absconded and left Hay to take charge of the detachment. With only one man to every five horses, the little convoy made but poor progress, until Hay eventually realized that they were now in a sort of no-man's-land between the two armies. This necessitated the destruction of several badly unfit horses and an overnight march to get the remainder of the detachment back behind friendly lines. There, Hay sent a report to the regiment – he says to the colonel, but in reality it was still Lord Waldegrave in command – with the information that he had several recovered horses belonging to the 12th in his charge and requesting permission to re-join, which, to his joy, was granted.[57]

The regiment that Hay joined, however, was by this stage of the campaign in a pitiful state. Not only were its numbers greatly reduced, but the horses and men were in a sorry condition:

> The men's clothes were actually in rags, some one colour, some another; some in worn-out helmets, some in none; others in forage caps or with handkerchiefs tied round their heads; the horses in a woeful state, many quite unfit to carry the weight of the rider and his baggage.

All in all, it made a sad contrast with the 12th as Hay had last seen them the previous year. Nevertheless, he concluded that 'the edge was indeed off all but the spirit of the dragoons and the blade of his sabre; these continued the same ever, under all privations, willing and ready to work'.[58] Although the army was tired and outnumbered, Vandeleur, too, commented that they had every expectation of a fight, and a successful one at that, once the French launched an attack on Wellington's latest position. However, the French seemed unwilling to oblige: on the 14th 'the rascals would only skirmish with the cavalry', and on the following morning, after the allies had stood to their arms all night, 'to our disappointment at day's dawn we perceived large columns of cavalry moving away along our front in the direction of Ciudad Rodrigo, which caused the whole of our army to retreat on that road'.[59]

Thus began the last, and hardest, stage of the retreat from Burgos. Soult, who had assumed the direction of the combined French armies, baulked at attacking the allies in their defensive position south of Salamanca – although he made preparations to receive an attack if Wellington had been foolish enough to try one – and instead attempted to repeat Marmont's July strategy of turning the allied right and threatening the lines of communication back to Portugal. Unlike Marmont, Soult had a numerical advantage and a strong force of cavalry at hand, enabling him to keep his forces well closed up and thus safe from the defeat in detail that Marmont had suffered on this same ground. Realizing that he was outmanoeuvred, Wellington settled on a further retreat and by midday on 15 November the allies were trudging west through the rain on the road to Ciudad Rodrigo. Under ordinary circumstances, a fighting retreat was a hard thing to manage, with the constant need for vigilance on the part of the rear-guard. Here, however, additional factors made the five days that it took to get the army back over the Portuguese frontier a particular ordeal. Firstly, the weather was atrocious, with an incessant cold rain soaking and chilling the soldiers and turning the roads to mud. Secondly, mismanagement by the army's Quartermaster General – an officer foisted on Wellington against his wishes – meant that food supplies for the troops were practically non-existent, with regiments sent by one road and their rations by another. Thirdly, the bulk of the troops had been engaged in active operations for months, during which time several major actions had been fought; this meant that not only were the men individually tired out, but that the attrition of the campaign had left gaps in the army's command structure from senior generals down to the regimental level. Lastly, as a result of the first three factors, morale understandably suffered and, in some units at least, discipline began to crumble as officers and men put food and shelter before their military duty.[60]

All in all, it was a sad and sorry state of affairs, but the 12th seems to have come out of it, by and large, better than most. No doubt it helped that, with the remount brought up by Vandeleur and Hay now having joined, the regiment again had enough mounts – and fresh ones at that – for all its effective troopers. Being, inevitably, in the rear-guard, Anson's Brigade was engaged in an on-and-off running skirmish with the French cavalry for much of the retreat, and whilst this in one sense added to the ordeal it also served as a reminder to all concerned of what they were about and of the likely fate of anyone who fell out of the ranks. Vandeleur offered a succinct summary of the experience:

> We were all wet to the skin, and had to skirmish with those fellows all day long, and the same thing for five successive days – out the whole of every night in the most severe, cold, rainy weather, and often without a morsel of wood to cook our ration of meal, which we were as often without as with; and entirely without bread, or corn for our horses.[61]

Hay, indeed, thought that in total the 12th had been a full week without any rations being issued to the men or the horses, circumstances which he felt entirely to have justified the unofficial foraging: most infamously a large-scale shooting of pigs on 17 November from which he himself benefitted by the purchase of a leg of pork. Hay did, however, take some comfort in the fact that the persistent rain had the rather beneficial side-effect of acting 'like the fashionable "water-cure"' in driving from him the recurrent fever which, notwithstanding his assurances to Major General Jones back at Radipole, had continued to torment him since his return to the Peninsula. In having something positive to say for the November weather, Hay must surely be unique amongst survivors of the retreat![62]

In the final days of their withdrawal, the 12th caught up with their commanding officer, who had been making his way back to Portugal by easier stages since his wounding the previous month, and who now resumed command of what was left of the regiment. On 19 November, Soult called off the pursuit, and two days later the allies, secure behind the Portuguese border in the rear of Ciudad Rodrigo, began to disperse into winter quarters. The Anglo-Portuguese forces collectively returned the loss of 4,752 men during the retreat, plus an unrecorded number of Spanish.[63] In the 12th Light Dragoons, five men and five horses were returned as having died during the period 25 October–24 November, and in addition a further twenty-four horses were listed as cast, having been captured by the enemy. On the positive side, one horse, reported lost in the fighting around Venta del Pozo, turned out to have been in the possession of the 2nd KGL Dragoons and was now reclaimed, and one man who had been taken prisoner during the fighting around Burgos made his escape and re-joined. Nevertheless, the 12th still had only 258 effective rank and file out of 442, and 251 effective troop horses out of 387 at the end of the retreat. Worn out by a year's hard service, the regiment was undeniably in need of a substantial break from active campaigning in order to get itself back in order.[64]

Chapter VIII

The Hard Road to Vitoria

THE ENDING OF THE 1812 CAMPAIGN after the retreat from Burgos marked an absolute nadir in the Peninsular fortunes of the 12th Light Dragoons. Not only was the effective strength of the regiment shrunken in both horses and men, but an inspection by Major General Anson on 12 December 1812 identified other serious problems. Many of these were an inevitable consequence of the extremely taxing campaigning of the past year, Anson noting in particular that the horses, though of a good size and active, needed 'great care and good feeding to keep them in condition'. Since this had not been possible during the retreat, and remained difficult even in winter quarters, it had in turn led to a fall in standards of horsemanship in the regiment, with Anson concluding that,

> I cannot say much in favor of the Movements and Exercise of this Regiment the Men have a great deal of dash amongst them but ride ill. It is difficult in this country to find even ground & move a Squadron; were it practicable the condition of the horses at this season of the year would not admit of it, consequently the field exercise cannot be attended to with that regularity which is required.[1]

The situation with respect to forage was not aided by the apparent incompetence of the commissary officer attached to the regiment, who was removed from his post by a General Order of 4 December 1812 on account of 'great neglect of duty'. The officer in question was Acting Deputy Assistant Commissary General Matthew Willock, who was actually a lieutenant in the 103rd Foot serving on attachment, and who had been with the 12th since June. Exactly what Willock's failing was is unclear, but the 3rd Dragoons, 9th and 13th Light Dragoons, and 'A' Troop of the Royal Horse Artillery all saw their commissaries removed as well by the same order and for the same cause, which suggests that the neglect of these five officers related to the complete failure to provide forage and rations during the withdrawal from Salamanca to Ciudad Rodrigo. Since Willock's regiment was not in the Peninsula he was ordered to settle his accounts and return to Britain, although this was evidently a complex process as he did not in fact go home until March 1814. Willock's departure allowed for the return of Deputy Assistant Commissary General William Myler, who had already served briefly with the 12th during the spring of 1812. Myler was described by Hay as 'a very excellent commissary and a great favourite with everyone', who 'moved about as a commissary had a right to do, with many more comforts than would have been consistent with the equipage of a fighting officer, and amongst others a wife'. Commissary and Mrs Myler would play frequent host to the officers of the 12th during the winter and in the campaign that followed.[2]

Despite approaching the inspection with what feels from the tone of his report to have been slightly jaundiced eyes, Anson still had good things to say as well. Of Ponsonby, he reported that 'this officer has been repeatedly and most deservedly noticed by the Commander of the Forces for his Ability, Judgement, and gallant conduct in the Field'; however there was a sting in the tail since although Anson felt that Ponsonby had 'paid every attention to the Discipline of the Regiment' since assuming command, the 12th were nevertheless 'not well versed in the Manoeuvers, having been originally badly instructed'. As with some of Anson's other complaints, it is hard to understand exactly what he was getting at, a situation not helped by the fact that this was the only formal inspection of the 12th that was carried out while they were in the Peninsula, giving us little else to make comparison with. Anson did have rather more justice when he noted that, since Lord Waldegrave had now left the regiment upon his promotion, 'an active Major would be a great acquisition to the Regiment', but with the newly minted Major Bridger on his way to join from the depot this was something that was already in the process of being rectified. The other officers were generally deemed satisfactory, as were the NCOs, although the trumpeters were 'but indifferent'.[3]

As for the rank and file, Anson thought them, 'a good body of Men, of a proper standard and healthy in their appearance. They are well set up on Foot, and attentive when on duty, rather loose in their conduct at other times, and require a tight hand over them.' Since the only recent regimental court martial, relating to a case of theft of items from a military store, had resulted in a flogging for the offender, it is again difficult to see quite where Anson was coming from with this.[4] Certainly there are no other suggestions that discipline was lax, although, as we have seen, Ponsonby was strongly opposed to corporal punishment. A possible clue, however, comes from Hay's memoirs. Here he writes of the regiment's 'great good fortune' to have Ponsonby as a commanding officer, since he was 'not only a most gallant soldier, but most kind and considerate alike to men and officers'. Therefore, at the time of Anson's inspection, and indeed throughout the regiment's spell in winter quarters, Ponsonby's main concern was to allow his command the maximum possible opportunity to rest and recuperate:

> His great anxiety at this time was to get his regiment into order, after the long hard work it had gone through, and to do so by giving as little trouble as possible. Troop-watering parade daily was all the military duty we were called on to perform, all were for a time to rest and amuse themselves.[5]

Hay goes on to say that 'the men fully appreciated their colonel's kindness and gave no trouble', but it is easy to see why this approach, which required and was rewarded by a high level of trust between all ranks, may have appeared somewhat lax to an outsider.

For the most part, Anson's report paints a picture of a regiment that needed a chance to rebuild itself after hard service. There might well be some areas on which the brigade commander and the regimental officers were at odds as to the best approach to things, but there was certainly nothing that suggested any serious problems to come. Nothing, that is, except the one matter upon which Anson, Ponsonby and the troop officers of the 12th were entirely in agreement, and which was addressed in Anson's report under the heading of 'Clothing Accoutrements and Appointments'. The general covered the first item quickly, confirming that the new pattern uniforms had been received 'in due time and in good condition'. Then, however, he turned his attention to the remainder of the heading:

> The appointments of this regiment have not been attended to sufficiently in former days; some of the saddles were so bad as to materially injure the Horses backs. The supplies of saddles have not been sent to the Regiment according to the Return of the Annual Inspection 1811. They have lately received one hundred saddles which they should have had before they came to this country. Lieutenant Colonel Ponsonby has written home frequently for the information of his Colonel reporting the real state of things. As far as the effectives they are now complete, but more attention should be paid to the annual inspection return transmitted home and

signed by the Commanding Officer and the Two Senior Captains, that the deficiencies therein specified might be immediately supplied.[6]

This was a serious matter, and resurrected an issue that Steuart seems to have long considered closed. What was more, it did so in a manner that placed the blame squarely on the regimental colonel and, in doing so, on the decentralized administrative system that had left him with the responsibility in the first place.

It took time for Anson's report to make its way up the chain of command, first to Wellington and then back to Horse Guards, and it was not until the following July that the London-based Adjutant General, Lieutenant General Sir Harry Calvert, raised the matter with Steuart and copied to him the offending passage quoted above. Steuart had already managed to get himself at crossed-purposes with Horse Guards earlier in the year after attempting to enlist official help in compelling officers of the 12th who were home on leave to report themselves to him as their colonel. This had been interpreted as an attempt to interfere with the instructions of the Adjutant General and Steuart had been compelled to write a conciliatory letter to justify himself.[7] This earlier clash notwithstanding, Steuart nevertheless took a firm line in his response to Calvert, seeking to demolish point-by-point the assertions made in Anson's report. Any problems stemming from inadequate care of appointments, he justly argued, 'must rest to be accounted for by the different Commanding Officers and I have on this subject to refer to my repeated orders which are to be found in the Regimental Books'. Blame thus shifted, Steuart then outlined his methodology for keeping the regiment equipped:

> On my receiving Annual Inspection Returns I immediately order the supply for the Effective Men and Horses in conformity thereto, and I give credit to the Commanding Officer of the Regiment for what may become necessary for the non effectives between one Inspection Return and another so that they may be supplied by the Tradesmen as the Commanding Officer may require, this was observed as usual in the year 1811, every article was ordered by myself in conformity to the Annual Inspection Return. And the Saddlery was ordered from Gibson & Peat by my letter dated seventh of February, credit was at the same time given to the Commanding Officer with all the Regimental Tradesmen for what might become wanting for the Non Effectives this will appear by my letter also of the 7th of February addressed to the Commanding Officer which may be seen in my letter Books now with the Regiment and with the Depot.[8]

As for the supposedly poor quality of the saddles with which the 12th had embarked for the Peninsula, Steuart was quick to take the offensive, remarking that Calvert need only consult Major General Bolton's 1811 Confidential Report to confirm that the squadrons sent on service 'were then completed to their full establishment with every article of appointment, having had the pick of the whole Regiment'. If the saddles had subsequently become unusable, Steuart stressed that he had 'great doubts of the attention which was paid to the care of the appointments from the time of their Embarkation until the Regt. joined the Army in the field, or indeed until Lieutenant Col. Ponsonby took the Command', and concluded his defence by highlighting the lack of communication from the Peninsula and the delays imposed by the issue of the new pattern of uniforms:

> The supply of a Hundred Saddles accompanied with a Hundred sets of different articles of appointments were sent out at the desire of Lt. Col. Ponsonby and I considered them as the Annual Supply for 1812, no Annual Inspection Return for that year having ever reached me. You will also be pleased to recollect that an order was issued the date of which I do not at present remember, that all supplys for Regts. of Cavalry should be postponed until the new patterns should finally be fixed upon which occasioned a considerable delay.

Finally, Steuart emphasized that he had had no notification from Ponsonby that matters were amiss, and had dealt promptly with those letters that he had received from the 12th's commanding officer. He was, however, 'glad to find that the effectives are now complete and more attention can not be paid by me', and assured Calvert that matters were now in hand for the 1813 issue notwithstanding a three-month delay in receiving Ponsonby's report of what was required.

Insofar as it went, Steuart's rebuttal was largely valid. By his standards, he had done everything that was required of him as regimental colonel, but the problem was that those standards had been set by years of service during peacetime or during the decidedly limited warfare in which Britain had engaged prior to 1808. Even his reply to Calvert concluded with what was no doubt meant to be a comforting assurance that 'every thing has been ordered accordingly for the Effectives and I hope by this time are on their way; credit has also been given as usual to the Commanding Officer for articles which may become necessary for the Non Effectives'.[9] The old soldier does not seem to have grasped that the intensive warfare of the Napoleonic era meant that greater provision needed to be made for losses on campaign. That said, such a policy of anticipating requirements would have required a far greater financial outlay on Steuart's part, and, as his own experience continued to indicate, there was no certainty that he would ever get his money back. Yet if the system of delegating the provision of equipment to regimental colonels was inefficient, the fact that the change to the new patterns of clothing and saddlery had been so delayed – such, indeed, that the 1812 issue was only received by the troops in the field after the conclusion of that year's campaigning – suggested that central management by Horse Guards was no better. More than any point of personal culpability, the issues raised in Anson's report really serve to underline the fact that Britain simply lacked a system of military organization sufficient to cope with the demands of what had, by 1812, effectively become a world war.

The only thing that undermines Steuart's case was the fact that the board of officers appointed by Wellington to look into the state of the accoutrements of the 12th had found that things back in 1811 had been every bit as bad as Wyndham had asserted. Steuart had been informed of this in a letter from Wellington dated 29 January 1812, and although he complained of the time that it had taken for a decision to be made, and confessed that 'I should and do draw a very different conclusion,' he nevertheless declared that if the board's findings were good enough for Wellington – 'the only Officer we have seen in this Country since the Duke of Marlborough' – then they were good enough for him and that replacements would be ordered.[10] This correspondence resulted in the dispatch of the hundred saddles mentioned in Anson's report, although this does raise the point that if Steuart had accepted Wyndham's complaints at face value they could have been ordered, and delivered to the regiment in the field, far sooner. Nevertheless, it should be stressed that it was the findings of the board of officers set up by Wellington, and not Anson's later inspection report, that set matters aright for the 12th, and ensured that the regiment was fully equipped to take the field when operations resumed in 1813.

Anson's report had reopened old wounds, and Steuart – whilst unprepared to argue with Wellington on the subject – evidently felt that the latter's board of inquiry had been wrong and that the fault for all the problems lay with Major Wyndham and not with him. Only two days after his reply to Calvert, which had itself hinted at mismanagement prior to Ponsonby's taking command of the 12th, Steuart made his criticism explicit in a less formal letter to Charles Greenwood, in which he observed that at the same time as Wyndham made his 1811 complaints, no similar problems were encountered by the four troops left in Britain, notwithstanding that the six on active service had supposedly had the pick of the accoutrements:

> The two Squadrons which remained at Home under the Command of Capt. Bridger Marched first to Norwich from Romford, and from that to Weymouth, a distance of 300 Miles without sore backs or any complaints what so ever that I heard of. The others by the time they got to Elvas in Portugal and long before they had been near the Enemy complain'd of sore backs &c &c &c and particularly reported not in a very regular or Military Manner that the Appointments were in a miserable state, from which I judged there had been a great want of Discipline and regularity in the conduct of that part of the Regt.[11]

Steuart does not seem to have grasped, even now, that the main concern – and, indeed, his personal priority as regimental colonel – should never have been to establish whose fault it was that the appointments had become unfit for further use, but to see that they were replaced as soon as possible. By hammering home the point that Wyndham was culpable, long after it had ceased to matter whose fault the original deficiency had been, Steuart demonstrated that he had, for once, allowed his own interests to take primacy over those of his regiment.

In blaming Wyndham, Steuart could at least take comfort that with Ponsonby now in charge there would be no repeat performance. But it is evident from his letter to Greenwood, in which Steuart seems rather to have unburdened himself to the agent, that relations between the colonel and commanding officer had been dealt something of a blow by the implication of duplicity on Ponsonby's part that came from Steuart's reading of Anson's report. Steuart stressed that whilst he did not know what letters Greenwood might 'have received from Lieut. Col. Ponsonby for my information & reporting the real state of things as it is called in the confidential Report . . . nothing unpleasant has ever been communicated to me in that or any other way until I received the Copy of the confidential Report', and that he was therefore unable to 'conceive that Lt. Col. Ponsonby would have given foundation to so mistaken a statement' as that which Anson had included in his report. Steuart also begged the agent,

> that you will give to the Adjutant Genl. such further information as you may think necessary in order to remove any unfavourable impression which the confidential Report may have made on the mind of the Duke of York. Such Reports when made confidentially should be correct for if his Royal Highness had not been so good viz fairly to order the Report to

be communicated to me I should not have had an opportunity of giving my Statement and an unfavourable impression might have remained unknown to me.[12]

If necessary, Steuart concluded, he would face an inquiry if that was what it took to vindicate himself, for 'the State the Appointments may be in that must depend on circumstances – but as to the Supply I feel myself correct'. Thankfully for all concerned, things never reached such a pass, and the matter was finally closed. Thereafter, however, it is clear that whilst Steuart retained a full appreciation of Ponsonby's professional qualities, the warmth that had been apparent in their earlier correspondence henceforth disappears, and, indeed, the majority of subsequent communication, at least from Steuart to Ponsonby, took place via the agents rather than directly.

The fact that the breakdown in relations between Steuart and Ponsonby was delayed until the summer of 1813 meant that the two men were able to cooperate effectively throughout the crucial first six months of that year, during which time Wellington used the battered veterans of the 1812 campaign as the nucleus around which a larger, even more formidable force could be built so as to achieve the goal of throwing the French out of the Peninsula for good. Part of this process was simply to give the allied forces a good rest, as Ponsonby was already doing with the 12th, but Wellington also felt the need to address several problems that had made themselves apparent in the previous year's campaigning. A strongly worded letter, intended for divisional and brigade commanders but soon circulated amongst the whole army, called for an all-round tightening up of discipline. Steuart, needless to say, thought it 'well deserved' and preened himself on the thought that such a system was already in place in the 12th, but the circular had the immediate effect of giving considerable offence to regimental officers across the army.[13] Following on from this, stringent efforts were made to root out officers of all stations who were unfit to fulfil the roles in which they were serving. John Slade was one of several general officers who were sent home, but the cull continued down to the lowest level, as seen in the removal of commissaries from the 12th and other cavalry regiments.[14] Wellington had been trying for some time to obtain greater control over officer appointments, and was gratified to have got his way on this matter, but he was less pleased to find that Horse Guards had recalled to Britain a number of worn-down regiments of infantry and cavalry. Most of the infantry he eventually managed to retain, but on the cavalry he had to give way and the 4th Dragoon Guards, 9th and 11th Light Dragoons, and 2nd KGL Hussars were ordered to turn over their horses to other regiments prior to returning home. In their place, two complete new brigades, one of hussars and the other comprising the 1st and 2nd Life Guards and the Royal Horse Guards, were sent out from home. Now consolidated into a single large division, this collection of eighteen British and KGL regiments in eight brigades would be the most formidable mounted force that Wellington would ever control.[15]

This period in extended winter quarters also saw the arrival of more new equipment, Steuart having acted promptly on receipt of Ponsonby's requests for those items needed to make up the shortfall existing after the Burgos campaign. Even so, this latest issue was still subject to delays, with Steuart as late as August informing the agents that, as of the previous month,

> the Chacoes & Cloaks for the Regt. had not been received, I can not account for this delay as I understood they were ready when I left Town in April. It appears also that you have some arrangements to make with Col. Ponsonby respecting the short Boots formerly sent out to the Regt. they did not answer the purpose and now stand to be charged to the Regt. and to be reconciled to me. I hope that the Boots I ordered from Mr Powis have been sent out long ago, Col. Ponsonby makes no mention of them, I beg that on receiving this you will write him a full explanation of those matters that no blame may attach to me. I beg of you also to inform me at what time the Chacoes Cloaks and Boots were sent to the Packers.[16]

As well as being keen to avoid any blame for these delays, Steuart was also clearly sensitive to any lack of quality in accoutrements being supplied to the 12th, informing Gibson & Peat, the regiment's saddlers, 'that Capt. Coles now in Command of the Depot of the 12th Lt. Drags. at Weymouth states, the Horse Collars, Curbs & parts of the Bridles last sent to the Depot not to be of a good quality', and that Steuart expected 'that any of the above Articles which may be returned not having been used will be replaced by others of an acceptable quality'.[17]

Amongst Wellington's changes and innovations for the coming year's campaign was one that would have an additional effect on the 12th, over and above its general utility for the army as a whole. This was the formation of a new unit called the Staff Corps of Cavalry. With a strength of around 200 all ranks, this mounted unit of headquarters guards and orderlies had an intended role somewhat akin to that of the French Gendarmerie and was very much part of Wellington's plan to improve the discipline of the force under his command. The duties of officers in this new corps having strong administrative overtones reminiscent of an adjutant's work, there were few commissioned volunteers for the new unit but John Gitterick of the 12th was one of them, trading in his years of experience as adjutant for a captaincy in the new unit.[18] In the long term, as we have already seen, the vacancy was filled by the commissioning of Regimental Serjeant Major Griffith, but Griffith was at the depot when Gitterick's promotion and transfer were announced, so that it would be some time before his appointment could be confirmed, and longer still before he could join the regiment on campaign. By chance, however – or, to be more strictly accurate, as the result of some well-motivated but ill-informed meddling on the part of Sir James Steuart – the 12th had in the Peninsula a newly gazetted cornet possessed of exactly the sort of experience required to act in Griffith's absence. This was Abel Hammon, for years the regimental quartermaster, but to follow the bizarre story of his promotion we need to step back almost two years, to the point when the 12th had just arrived in Portugal under the command of Major Wyndham.

Hammon was, by all accounts and reports, an extremely competent and energetic officer, who had done a sterling job running the regiment's advanced depot at Belém for much of the time that the 12th had been serving under Wellington. Wyndham, it would seem, was forced during his time in command to rely heavily on his quartermaster's experience, and to show his gratitude sought to obtain him a further promotion. Steuart was at first unwilling to recommend Hammon for a cornetcy, informing Ponsonby, who had now succeeded Wyndham in command, that:

> Qr Master Hammon I know to be a very deserving Man but I have not heard of any addition to his Merit during Two Months Service in Portugal, and his Merit has lately been rewarded by his appointment as Regimental Quartermaster, a Situation both honourable and lucrative and for which he is better qualified than for that of a Cornet.[19]

There matters might well have rested, had Steuart not been then seized by a laudable but misguided notion that Hammon – for whom the regiment as a whole seems to have had a high regard – might receive a cornetcy without having to give up his quartermaster's role. This assumption led Steuart in March 1812 to include Hammon's name in a series of recommendations to Horse Guards, noting that:

Cornet Goldsmid having been promoted without Purchase to a Lieutenancy I now further beg leave in the strongest manner to recommend
& to solicit from the Duke of York that the appointment to the Cornetcy
without Purchase may be in favour of Regimental Qr Master Hammon
as an Officer of superior merit in his line and a very old Active and good
Soldier.[20]

Steuart sought to make it clear that he did not intend it to establish a
precedent, informing Captain Bridger at the depot, who had apparently made
a recommendation on behalf of one of the 12th's remaining troop quartermasters, that,

> I doubt I shall not immediately succeed in my application for a Cornetcy
> for Mr Hammon, until then I can make no other application, and I
> confess it must be from very particular merit indeed that I can be induced
> to recommend Serjeants for Officer's Commissions, and had Mr
> Hammon not held a Commission already as Quarter Master I should
> never have consented to Recommend him.[21]

Steuart was correct in his belief that it would take time to get Hammon's
promotion approved: the application that he receive the cornetcy made vacant
by Goldsmid's promotion was turned down, as was a second for a vacancy
created by the promotions following Captain Dickens's death at Salamanca, but
Steuart resolved to keep trying, noting that whilst 'there is I think a very proper
objection, to the carrying Quartermasters forward to the rank of officers' an
exception might be made for Hammon since 'as regimental Qr Mr he already
has the King's commission'.[22] Having developed this argument, Steuart used it
in a renewed application to Horse Guards on Hammon's part, first in general
terms for any future vacancy, and then specifically for that created when Cornet
Stanhope obtained his lieutenancy in March 1813.[23]

On this occasion, Steuart was at last successful, and he obviously took some
pleasure in writing to Hammon in his new rank, informing him that,

> my last recommendation in your favour by my Letter of ye 14th Inst. has
> been attended to by his Royal Highness the Commander in Chief and
> that your appointment to a Cornetcy in my Regt. being without purchase
> was last night officially notified to me. I hope that this mark of his
> Majesty's favor will stimulate your further zeal and that you will use your
> additional Rank with discretion.[24]

It is evident from the tone of this letter that Steuart had not yet realized that Hammon's cornetcy would not be 'additional' to his existing appointment, and that he could not simultaneously be a cornet and a regimental quartermaster. On finally being acquainted with his misapprehension, Steuart passed the resulting quandary on to Ponsonby:

> I now write to you on the Subject of Qr Master, now Cornet Hammon, new Gazetted. It was in consequence of my application and as a reward for his good conduct as Regimental Quarter Master, not being aware at the time that he can not hold a double Commission, the same as the Adjutant, but that being the case I fear it will not be an advantageous change for him. Should he be of the same opinion I can get the Commission cancel'd so that he may retain, or rather return, to his former situation of Regimental Quarter Master. Pray let me know your Sentiments and his on this point without delay for if the Commission is to be cancelled no time must be lost in making the application. Should Hammon prefer keeping the Cornetcy I shall recommend of Qr Master Sidley to succeed him as Regimental Quarter Master if you have no objection of which I beg you will inform me without delay.[25]

Troop Quartermaster Richard Sidley was apparently the man whose merits Bridger had earlier been promoting. Certainly, Bridger made an application for a cornetcy in Sidley's favour at around the same time as Hammon's commission was gazetted, which prompted Steuart to stress that the best Sidley could hope for was the regimental quartermaster's post should Hammon prefer to retain his cornetcy.[26] For this post, pending Hammon's decision, Sidley was duly recommended, with Steuart citing his thirty-seven years of 'unblemished reputation having been frequently employ'd in active & confidential Situations' and current good service as paymaster to the regimental depot.[27] Nevertheless, it was indicative of the social gulf between commissioned officers and the old troop quartermasters that Steuart still had to ask the clerks at Greenwood, Cox & Co. to find out from their records Sidley's Christian name.[28] Since Hammon elected to keep his cornetcy, Sidley in turn rose to be quartermaster, although he remained at the depot and did not join the regiment in the Peninsula. Hammon, meanwhile, assumed the acting responsibility of adjutant pending Griffith's arrival. The seemingly obvious solution, that Hammon be recommended for the adjutancy rather than Griffith, does not seem to have crossed anyone's mind.

By the time that Hammon took over as acting adjutant, the active portion of the regiment also had a second field officer with it, the newly promoted Major

Bridger having come out to the Peninsula in February.[29] There seems to have been something of a mixed reception for Bridger when he joined, with Hay describing him as 'a good old man in his way, but not an active soldier',[30] which seems a rather odd characterization with Bridger only being thirty-four. True, this was rather older than most of the officers, and older even than Ponsonby whose thirtieth birthday was still some months away, but Bridger seems to have fitted well into the society of the regiment's younger officers. Indeed, he was one of the participants, along with Lieutenants Vandeleur and Calderwood, in a deception practised on the Archbishop of Braga in which the three officers, having wandered into the archiepiscopal palace during the festivities surrounding the illumination of the city, succeeded in convincing the aged but patriotic prelate that they were all Catholic Irishmen and on being then offered a sample of the palace cellars, doing their best to drain them.[31]

With the addition of Bridger and several other officers either newly joined or returned from leave, by the time that active campaigning recommenced in May 1813 the 12th could muster a commissioned strength of two field officers, six captains, ten lieutenants and a solitary cornet, plus the paymaster, one assistant surgeon and the veterinary surgeon. All in all this represented a considerable improvement on the rather overstretched officer corps that had brought the regiment back from Burgos six months previously. Rank and file strength on the same date amounted to 337 effectives, with 314 troop horses. For the most part, this resurgence had been the product not of infusions of manpower from home, but the recovery to effectiveness of those who were already in the Peninsula. Whereas the number of men reported sick in December 1812 amounted to 27 per cent of the strength, this figure had dropped to only 7 per cent six months later. The fact that there were more fit men than horses as of May 1813 indicated that things were not as promising in this regard, but this is most likely accounted for by the fact that the regiment had the previous month received a draft of thirty-eight horses from the 11th Light Dragoons upon that regiment being sent back to Britain. Certainly, the proportion of effective horses had been improving prior to this addition, and would continue to improve through the coming summer. Additions to the manpower strength had also come from within the Peninsula, in this case in the return of twenty-two men who had been struck off the regimental returns after being reported as being taken prisoner during the Burgos campaign. Although there are plenty of accounts of men escaping from captivity throughout the Peninsular War, the numbers involved here suggest that at least the majority in this case were actually stragglers or men who had been cut off from the main body during the skirmishes on the retreat and who had now made their way back to the army.[32]

Throughout their six-month period in winter quarters the 12th had been in peaceful billets in central Portugal, first to the rear of Ciudad Rodrigo and then, once it was clear that the French had also retired into quarters, in the more sheltered country of the Mondego valley. There they would likely have remained until campaigning resumed, but a shortage of feed for the horses occasioned a shift further north, first to San Pedro de Sul on the Vouga, and then to Aguida, between Coimbra and Oporto, with billets being shifted every month or so to make the most of what forage was available.[33] As spring came on, however, more and more of Wellington's forces were shifted to the north of Portugal, as preparations for the next campaign began in earnest. With the French having abandoned Andalucía in order to concentrate against Wellington in 1812, the whole centre of gravity of the war had been shifted northwards, but Wellington now intended to move things even further in that direction by throwing his army through the mountains of the Tras-os-Montes and thence onwards towards the Ebro and the Pyrenees.

Although the French armies in Spain were much depleted as a result of heavy drafts taken from them to rebuild the Grande Armée after the Russian debacle, taken together they nevertheless amounted to a respectable force of 140,000 men. Soult having been called back to Germany, the French were under the direct command of Joseph Bonaparte, with Marshal Jean-Baptiste Jourdan as his chief of staff, and although the four distinct armies that had cooperated in the 1812 campaign retained their names and identities they were now closer in size to corps formations. In the case of the Armée du Midi and Armée de Portugal, which remained the two largest formations at Joseph's disposal, the names were now complete misnomers, for the French had abandoned any pretence of occupying or even threatening Portugal and south-western Spain. Joseph had his headquarters at Valladolid, so that even Madrid was now more an outpost than a capital city within Napoleon's empire. For his part, Wellington had under his direct command not only his Anglo-Portuguese field army, now 81,000 strong, but also a further 39,000 Spanish troops to give a total force of 120,000.[34] In order to catch the French off-balance, Wellington divided his main force in two, pushing a weak right wing under Hill ostentatiously into Spain in order to distract attention away from the concentration of forces in northern Portugal that was to form his main blow. Commanded by Sir Thomas Graham, these troops were to outflank the French position and prevent them from uniting their forces without risk of being cut off from France. With plans already afoot to shift the army's axis of supply from Lisbon to the Biscay ports, Wellington's strategy was intended to avoid the difficulties that had bogged down his 1812 campaign, and to drive the French from Spain for good.

Typically, after so long in settled quarters, the orders to move out came in a hurry on 26 April, and the last days of that month saw the 12th making their way to Oporto. There, the regiment received a month's pay: not always something that could be relied upon, and therefore extremely timely since it allowed the purchase of any unofficial extras that might serve to make life on campaign that bit more bearable. On 30 April the regiment again set off, leaving the city to the acclamation of the populace. Vandeleur recorded how,

> We were all in our best for the occasion; the inhabitants were truly grate-
> ful, giving bread, wine, etc. to the soldiers and officers. The young girls
> threw roses and laurels under our horses' feet, every one, old and young,
> shaking our hands and kissing them, some pitying us, others exulting at
> our departure to expel their enemies.[35]

Unfortunately, pride came before a fall, since the regiment was hardly clear of the city, and still in their finery, 'when one of the most dreadful showers I ever encountered blew right in our faces and wet our new coats and hats, to take the glaze off'.

The regiment's destination was Barcellos, two days' march to the north, but thankfully overnight accommodation was available in a sizeable Benedictine monastery, where the monks provided bread and tea, and later gave a dinner for the regiment's officers. However, possibly due to the amount of port wine furnished by the monks that evening, the following day's match saw the regiment miss its route and eventually travel double the ordinary distance before finally reaching its destination. There it would remain until the troop concen-tration was complete and Wellington able to open his campaign in earnest.

That moment came on 20 May, and caught the French completely off-guard. Hill moved on Salamanca that day, occupying the city six days later and serving to distract the attention of the French – already preoccupied by guerrilla activity along the Biscay coast – from Graham's command which moved out a day after Hill set off. Wellington himself rode initially with this southern column, furthering the impression that this was his main move, so that when Graham's six divisions crossed the border into Spain on the same day that Hill occupied Salamanca, only scattered French forces were in the area to resist them. Pressing forwards, Graham's divisions were able to concentrate at Toro by 3 June, which, along with Spanish troops, gave Wellington a block of 80,000 men safely north of the Duero and perfectly poised to threaten the French line of communications.[36]

To describe the movement of Graham's troops so simply is, however, to detract considerably from the great achievement that it undoubtedly was. Spearheading the advance of the allied right wing were three cavalry brigades – Anson's, now composed of just the 12th and 16th Light Dragoons, was one – later joined by a fourth. The greatest problem for them, however, was not the enemy but rather the terrain, for there was then a complete absence of lateral roads providing a link between Portugal and Spain. As a result, even getting as far as the frontier required a series of hard marches across terrain where the roads were either poor or non-existent. Hay, perhaps not wishing to recall the ordeal, passes over this phase, but Vandeleur's letters capture things vividly. The initial march, to Braga, where the regiment enjoyed the illuminations and some of its officers imposed themselves upon the Archbishop, were easy enough, but once that city was left behind on 14 May, things rapidly became more trying:

> On the 15th we had a terrible march, though only 4 leagues; we were on horseback nine hours. The roads were very bad and uncommonly hilly. One of the guns, a six-pounder, upset down a precipice and hurt two of the horses so badly that they were obliged to be immediately shot. One of the riders had his thigh broke and otherwise so dreadfully hurt, that he is given over. Several of our horses fell, but none hurt. We have repassed the river Cavado, and entered the province of Tras-os-Montes, which literally signifies Cross over Mountains, and well it might be called so, for in all my life I never beheld such mountains or such roads. We arrived at Rivaens, worse, if possible, than the former village, thatched houses built of mud, nothing to buy but milk and Indian corn bread. This place is 4 leagues from the former. We continued our march on the 16th to Alturas, five leagues, a bad road, and bad village. On the 17th we marched 3 leagues to Boticas, which was rather better than the former places; here we were able to get some white bread and eggs for breakfast. The people, seeing us in the new dress, took us for French Dragoons, and the greatest part of them fled to the neighbouring mountains, of which there was no *scarcity*. We were ordered to halt in this village. On the 18th,

unfortunately, some of the inhabitants left their wine-houses open, which was soon found out by the 12th, who lost no time in conveying it away in camp kettles, canteens, earthen pots, etc., they all got rather intoxicated in the course of the evening.[37]

Only on 19 May, when Chaves was reached, were decent billets again available, but the regiment was then back on the road and did not get a proper rest until they reached Benavente on the 23rd, where they had a two-day halt and the officers 'destroyed an immense quantity of pigeons for food – in fact, for nearly a week afterwards there was nothing but roast, boiled, stewed, broiled, etc., and in every way'.[38]

All this, it should be remembered, mostly took place before the campaign was properly under way, and when the advance into Spain began in earnest the result was more hard marching in bad weather and on poor roads. From leaving Benavente, the French cavalry were in evidence, but with only a single regiment of dragoons at the front there were simply not the forces at hand to enable the allied advance to be contested, and the main enemy continued to be the foul weather. The worst came with the crossing of the River Esla on 31 May, when several KGL and Portuguese horsemen were swept away by the high waters. Anson's Brigade was preparing to cross when, to some relief, one of Graham's aides arrived with orders to cross at a safer location. Says Vandeleur,

> We were then ordered down to the other ford, which was two leagues down the river. We had already marched 5 leagues. The sun was tremendously hot, everyone fatigued and hot and sleepy. However, we continued our march, crossed the river, marched back the two leagues on the other side and arrived at a little village at 8 o'clock that evening, which concluded a march of 9 leagues (about 36 English miles) that was performed in the space of 20½ hours, over a terrible hilly country.[39]

Still there was no rest, although all in the 12th had been hoping for one, and with the French outposts now evident in growing numbers there was now a greater need of cavalry for all kinds of duty. As a result, elements of the 12th were 'constantly on some duty or other, observation duty, patrols, carrying confidential letters', leaving both horses and men 'sadly knocked about'.

Not until 18 June would the hard slog be rewarded by a chance to take the frustrations out on the enemy, when elements of Graham's column clashed with part of the Armée de Portugal. By this stage in the campaign, Wellington's speedy advance and the dispersed nature of the French forces had enabled the

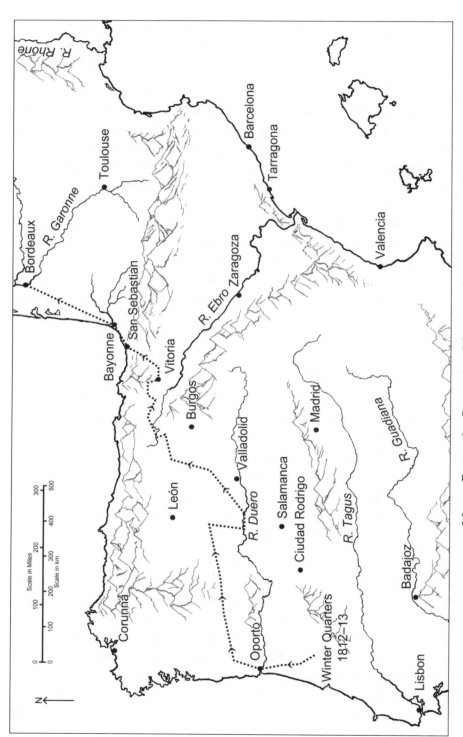

Map 5: Peninsular Operations, May 1813–April 1814

allies to press on continuously and turn the northern flank of successive positions that the French might otherwise have been able to hold. Thus the castle at Burgos was blown up, and the town abandoned, on 13 June, and by the 17th Wellington had his army comfortably into the rear of the French positions along the Ebro and was moving to cut the Great Road at Vitoria. As the various allied columns fell in with one and other, Graham's contingent assumed the lead, his orders for the 18th being to take the road through Osma to Orduña. Under his command were the First and Fifth Divisions, two Portuguese infantry brigades, and Anson's light dragoons. As the leading allied troops passed through Osma, however, they encountered what proved to be three divisions belonging to the Armée de Portugal under Général de Division Honoré Reille, sent to try and link up with French forces operating along the Biscay coast. Such an operation, inadvertently throwing as it did Reille's 16,000 men straight at Wellington's advancing masses, showed how fully Joseph and Jourdan had been taken aback by the speed of the allied advance.[40]

The 12th were at the head of Graham's advance, with Vandeleur taking his turn on outpost duty ahead of the regiment. With three men he rode into Osma itself,

> where, just as I arrived, I saw about 12 dragns. coming towards us. I had but three men, we halted and they halted, I took them for Spaniards, but they fired a shot and retired. Col. Ponsonby came up with the remainder of the picquet, and ordered me to skirmish, which I did with them for 2 hours, supported by Capt. [William] Webb, who had his horse wounded. They retired about half-a-mile into a thick wood, where they had a number of sharpshooters concealed. I followed no further than the edge of the wood.[41]

To support the cavalry – according to Vandeleur, it was at Ponsonby's request – Graham sent the KGL light infantry forward to bolster his mounted vanguard while he deployed the remainder of his forces, supporting them with the guns of Captain Norman Ramsay's 'I' Troop of the Royal Horse Artillery. Part of the 12th was required to go forward with the guns in order to cover them against any French attack, much to the frustration of Lieutenant Hay:

> The squadron to which I belonged was all the day employed in one of the most irksome and trying duties a dragoon can be exposed to – covering guns. There you have to sit on your horses, inactive, exposed to the fire of the artillery, and losing horses and men.[42]

Thereafter it became an infantry battle, although battle is perhaps too strong a word for it. Reille made a show of defiance but his heart does not seem to have been in it, and in any case the French position was soon rendered untenable by the unexpected arrival by a side-road of the allied Fourth Division. Outflanked and outnumbered, Reille swiftly disengaged and fell back towards the main body of the French forces.

Shocked into a true understanding of things by Reille's encounter at Osma, and by a second action fought the same day at San Milan, Joseph now ordered a concentration of all available forces around Vitoria where he hoped to make a stand at least sufficient to allow the successful extrication back to France of the extensive convoy of baggage – official and unofficial – that represented the fruits of five years' occupation of Spain. By 19 July, Joseph had the bulk of his available troops – the Armée du Midi and Armée du Centre, plus elements of the Armée de Portugal – assembled. The Armée du Nord and the remainder of the Armée du Portugal were operating against the Spanish along the Biscay coast, and although Joseph hoped that they would reinforce him before battle was joined this hope proved illusory. Thus, he was able to bring a total of only 63,000 men to the coming fight, against which Wellington, who had dropped off the Sixth Division and the bulk of his Spanish troops to cover his flank and rear, could still field 73,000 Anglo-Portuguese and a further 8,000 Spaniards.[43] The position that Joseph hoped to defend was a rectangular area of relatively flat land in the Zadorra valley, roughly seven miles by four on an east–west axis. The Great Road from France entered this plain, along with the Zadorra, by a pass at the north-east corner, and both left by a second pass at the south-west. However, whilst the road, once it had passed through the town of Vitoria, ran directly across the valley bottom, the river hugged the northern edge of the plain for the bulk of the time, and then swung south in a series of lazy loops. Joseph deployed his forces in three successive north–south lines, blocking the anticipated allied advance along the axis of the Great Road. Wellington, meanwhile, had the bulk of his troops concentrated in the hills to the west by the evening of 20 July, ready to attack on the morrow.[44]

Wellington, of course, had no intention of throwing his forces head-on up the valley and into the teeth of Joseph's prepared defences. Instead, he prepared to replicate, on a tactical scale, the methods that had served him so well in the opening of the campaign. Hill, commanding the allied right with a division apiece of British, Portuguese and Spanish, would attack the Puebla Heights at the south-western extremity of the valley, and in doing so hopefully attract the attention of the enemy, whilst the rest of the army, in three columns, would hook around to the north and come down on the French flanks. Two of these columns would make a fairly direct attack, under Wellington's own eye, but the last, on the far left, would make a more circuitous march so as to emerge from the mountains almost at the north-eastern extremity of the valley where it could threaten the French rear. This column was formed by Sir Thomas Graham's command, its infantry component still organized as in the clash at Osma three days earlier but with its mounted element reinforced with the KGL troopers of Bock's Brigade as well as Anson's two regiments, operating in conjunction with a strong force of Spanish semi-regular infantry under the guerrilla chief Francisco Longa. Some controversy exists over whether Graham was to function, like Hill, primarily as a distraction that would permit Wellington to make his main attack with the best advantage, or whether his troops were intended to cut the Great Road and block the French line of retreat. The latter, certainly, would have been an advantageous move had Graham's troops managed it, but there is no evidence to suggest that it formed a formal part of his orders, which, for his infantry at least, would prove quite enough of a challenge as things were.[45]

Graham's troops were on the road at eight o'clock on the morning of 21 July, having a lengthy march to make. Longa's Spaniards were out in front, and as Graham's troops began to descend into the valley of the Zadorra after two hours on the march, they found that the French had deployed

> ... from 4,000 to 5,000 infantry, and about six squadrons of cavalry, occupying strong hills to the left of the road, and with reserves in the villages of Gamarra Mayor, and Abechuco, covering the passes over the Zadorra river.[46]

It would therefore be for the infantry to clear the way for the passage of the river before the cavalry could move across and exploit, and Anson's command thus had little to do during the early stages of the battle. The 16th this time drew the unenviable task of covering the artillery, but the 12th were ordered to detach a squadron to serve as an advance guard to Major General John Oswald's Fifth Division, which, reinforced by a brigade of Portuguese, was to form the mainstay of Graham's assault. The late start and light employment of his regiment was, it may be said in passing, no bad thing for Lieutenant Colonel Ponsonby, who was that morning afflicted with a bout of fever. Accompanying Lieutenant Hay on a reconnaissance in advance of the whole column, Ponsonby became so ill that he was obliged to rest for several hours, charging Hay to continue the patrol but to report to him the moment the 12th were called upon since, ill or not, he had no intention of letting his regiment go into battle without him.[47]

Thankfully for Ponsonby, it was some time before the 12th would be called upon. Graham was keen not to attack too early and thus took his cue from the main action that was developing off to the south-west, which, thanks to the clear day and the open bowl-like nature of the valley, was all readily visible to Graham and his troops. At length, Major General Denis Pack's Portuguese infantry, still with a squadron of the 12th attached, were ordered to clear the hills on the north bank of the Zadorra, which was done to good effect. However, as the French infantry retired, some of their cavalry moved up to cover the withdrawal, leaving the single squadron of the 12th at risk until Tomkinson's squadron of the 16th was shifted across to reinforce them. In the event, however, the French cavalry showed no aggressive intent and quickly followed their infantry across the river as soon as the latter were safely across.[48] This withdrawal freed Graham to move up the Fifth Division to try and force a crossing, but to do so meant capturing the bridge at Gamarra Mayor, which in turn meant capturing the heavily defended village. An operation that had initially seemed to be going like clockwork now soon bogged down into a vicious close-quarters action. As a result of this fixation on a single crossing, no attempt was made to force one elsewhere, so that it was not until five in the evening, after heavy losses for the Fifth Division, that Gamarra Mayor and its bridge were secured.[49]

Whilst Graham's column had been fighting their way across the upper Zadorra, the main battle was taking place off to the south-west. Here, though not without loss, Wellington had been able to break the French positions and roll back the successive defensive lines until the whole French force, elements of the three different armies all mixed up together, was tumbling back towards the town of Vitoria. Joseph now ordered a retreat by a variety of minor roads, whilst assigning Reille – who had been commanding the troops facing Graham – to form a rear-guard with his detachment of the Armée de Portugal. It was at this point that Graham's troops were at last in a position to intervene in the main battle and fall upon the fleeing enemy but, having opposed them all day, Reille's troops had no intention of letting them do so without a fight, and continued to block the allied efforts to debouch from the bridgehead that had been won at Gamarra Mayor.

The French rear-guard was composed of one regiment of infantry – the 36eme Ligne, two battalions strong – and two of cavalry, the 15eme Dragons and the 3eme Hussards. They were initially opposed by Longa's Spaniards – who had got across the river further upstream – and by the advance squadrons of Anson's Brigade, one apiece from each regiment, that had gone forward earlier in the day to screen the infantry.[50] It is not clear who commanded the 12th's squadron, but Tomkinson of the 16th seems to have been the senior cavalry officer present. He relates how, after being briefly engaged with the Spanish infantry, the French began to withdraw, at which point the two British squadrons moved after them:

> My squadron was in advance, and on arriving on the plain formed immediately and advanced to the charge. All was confusion, all calling 'go on' before the men had time to get in their places. We got half across before I was able to place them in any form, and had we been allowed one minute more in forming, our advance might have been quicker, and made with much more regularity.
>
> The enemy had about six squadrons in line, with one a little in advance, consisting of their *élite* companies. This I charged, broke, and drove on their line, which, advancing, I was obliged to retire, having had a good deal of sabring with those I charged and with their support. A squadron of the 12th was in my rear, and in the place of coming up on my flank, followed me, so that they only added to the confusion of retiring by mixing with my men.[51]

The rest of the brigade now came up, but the lead squadron of the 16th likewise pitched straight into the melee, and by the time that order had been restored, and the brigade properly deployed, the French had fallen back.

Once Anson had got his command into order, and with the French showing no signs of withdrawing, the stage was now set for a full-scale charge by the whole brigade, an attack on a scale such as the 12th had not been engaged in since Villagarcia over a year previously. Anson drew up his brigade with the 16th Light Dragoons on the right and the 12th on the left, and with each squadron echeloned back from the one to its right: Hay, from whom we have the best account of this episode, was commanding the left-most troop of the 12th and was thus on the flank of the whole brigade:

> In this order we advanced, first at a trot then at a canter, and soon came in sight of the French cavalry. On seeing our advance, advantage was taken of some broken ground at the extreme end of the plain over which we were advancing towards them, to halt and form for our reception.
>
> As we drew closer this appeared madness, as their numbers did not exceed half ours. Our trumpet sounded 'The Charge', when, on coming

up to what seemed a regiment of dragoons awaiting their doom, their flanks were thrown back and there stood, formed in squares, about three thousand infantry. These opened such a close and well directed fire on our leading squadrons, that not only were we brought to a standstill, but the ranks were broken and the leading squadrons went about, and order was not restored till a troop of horse artillery arrived on our flank and, within about a hundred yards, opened such a fire of grape shot on the French infantry that at the first round I saw the men fall like a pack of cards.[52]

Hay's account, written years after the fact, is suspect on one count, in that he states that the brigade was three regiments strong rather than two, forgetting that the 11th, which regiment he asserts to have taken part in the battle, had in fact been recalled to England some months previously. This, in theory, should have entitled the 12th, as the senior regiment, to hold the place of honour on the right of the brigade, but it is apparent from other evidence that on this occasion the 16th took that post. The gunners who came up belonged to Ramsay's horse artillery troop, and their fire now negated the advantage that the French had held through their well-placed infantry, enabling Anson's Brigade to re-form and charge again.

Anson's initial charge had been broken not so much by enemy fire as confusion stemming from the realization that formed infantry lay to the front of the brigade. Such losses as had been sustained had fallen primarily on the 16th, the leading regiment, which incurred nearly double the casualties of the 12th this day. The 12th did, however, suffer the loss of its newly promoted acting adjutant, Abel Hammon, killed outright by a musket shot. The death of this popular and well-respected officer seems to have enraged the men of the regiment, and when they charged again they were out for vengeance. Vandeleur explained how,

> The death of the adjutant so exasperated the men, that they spared nothing, but cut and slashed about them like madmen. The Col. with all his coolness and intrepidity could not check the impetuosity of the charge, but charge upon charge was continued as long as we had light, and had not it failed us so soon, we should have massacred every soul of them.[53]

Interestingly, Stewart's history of the regiment accuses Vandeleur of employing 'the exaggeration of youth' in this account, taking his cue from the poor performance of the cavalry more generally, and it is true that Hay in his version of events makes no mention of a second charge. However, Vandeleur's account would seem to be confirmed by the commissary officer attached to the 16th Light Dragoons, Alexander Dallas, who was a witness to the brigade's charge and used it as a set-piece in his 1818 memoir-cum-novel, *Felix Alvarez*. Here, after relating the initial repulse and then the collapse of the French infantry, Dallas described how 'the cavalry pursued them close, sacrificing numbers, and taking many prisoners'.[54] Whether or not all six of the brigade's squadrons charged again after the initial attack is, of course, another matter, and indeed good practice would require that some of them be held back as a reserve. Since Hay remarks that the brigade as a whole 'bivouacked for the night nearly on the ground on which we were brought up by the French squares', this does rather confirm the impression that by no means the whole formation charged for a second time, and thereby reconciles the conflicting accounts.[55]

Other than Hammon, the only other fatality in the 12th was Private George Moore, a former weaver from Leitrim. However, Private Thomas Moore died of wounds on 5 July, raising the total deaths to three. A further eight men were wounded.[56] Hammon's death was particularly tragic, not only in coming so soon after his promotion but also because of the state in which it left his family. Upon receiving the news, Steuart promptly sent a memorial to Horse Guards, directed to the Duke of York in person and summarizing Hammon's career as well as detailing his fate. Steuart went on to explain that,

> By his death a Wife with five Children have become destitute the pension of a Cornet's Widow excepted.
>
> May I therefore earnestly entreat your Royal Highness that the price of an Ensigncy, at least, may be appropriated for the benefit of the Children of the late Cornet Hammon, allowing the life rent only to go to the Widow for the support and education of the Children, the capital being secured to them.[57]

Notwithstanding Steuart's well-argued case, the application, and others, were unsuccessful, leaving Steuart to inform the regimental depot – they being in contact with Hammon's family – 'that the only thing we have to expect is from the Charitable fund the application being supported by his Royal Highness the Commander in Chief', and asking that the number of Hammon's children be ascertained for this purpose.[58] By this stage, the fate of the family had taken an even worse turn, Mrs Hammon having also died, but even so Steuart was only able to secure a one-off payment of £40 for the children, with the possibility of this being renewed annually. Richard Sidley was appointed guardian of his late friend's family, and tasked 'to correspond with Mr Birnie at

Mr Greenwood's Office on the subject and the sum applied for the benefit of the Children'.[59] Sidley himself died in 1824, still serving as regimental quarter-master, but his will makes no mention of the wards he had inherited from his predecessor, who vanish from the record.[60]

In that they maintained a pursuit into the darkness, the 12th performed more diligently than the bulk of their sister regiments, for such of Wellington's cavalry that got into action at all quickly became diverted by the huge haul of plunder to be had from the abandoned French baggage train. Thanks to this distraction, and the lateness of the hour, the French were able to disengage successfully and make their escape, but in doing so they abandoned not only all their baggage but all bar two of their artillery pieces as well. In addition to these material losses, Joseph's forces lost in excess of 8,000 killed and wounded, as opposed to only 5,158 allied casualties.[61] Undeniably Vitoria was a crushing victory for Wellington's forces, but the manner in which the battle closed meant that there was much work still to be done in the coming days.

Chapter IX

Over the Pyrenees

RATHER IRONICALLY, HAVING OBTAINED THE SERVICES of such a large and effective force of cavalry, Wellington now found that the speed of his advance to Vitoria had carried his army into territory where the utility of mounted troops was decidedly limited. For several months the war would bog down in the Pyrenees, and Wellington would eventually send many of his mounted regiments to the rear over the coming winter. The 12th, however, were destined – in part through the continued need for light cavalry on outpost work, and in part through the pushiness of their commanding officer – to play a more active role in the coming operations than most regiments, and the closing months of the Peninsular War saw them employed in an often taxing variety of roles.

In the immediate aftermath of Vitoria, the priority was to complete the victory by mounting an effective pursuit of the defeated French. However, this was thwarted from the outset by a combination of factors: partly the failing light on the evening of 21 June and the fact that the French had fled along several small roads, but primarily the lure of the captured enemy baggage which drew the attentions of officers and men alike. The 12th, having been more closely engaged with the French rear-guard than most regiments, missed out on the plunder and Hay was therefore able to take the moral high ground in his memoirs and condemn those who did seize the opportunity to fill their pockets. However, a party under Serjeant Blood of the 16th came upon a small military chest – perhaps belonging to one of the regiments with which Anson's Brigade had been engaged – whilst on patrol during the night and on the general's orders the contents of this were distributed amongst the brigade as unofficial prize-money. With the amount graded by rank, Hay recorded that his share as a subaltern came to thirty-three dollars.[1] With all the distractions, it was not until 10 o'clock on the morning of 22 June that Wellington set his army in motion to pursue the enemy, initiating a week of confused marches and fighting as both the survivors of Vitoria and those French units that had missed the battle – notably the Armée du Nord, now under Clausel – sought to extricate themselves from the grasp of the victorious allies. For Anson's Brigade, these operations saw them continue to work as part of the allied left wing under Sir Thomas Graham.

The initial pursuit proceeded well enough, although the main body of the French had had too good a head start and only stragglers were encountered on the roads. However, the next day, 23 June, saw a descent into confusion as some generals moved their commands forwards without orders – assuming, not unreasonably, that the pursuit was to be pressed – so that Wellington was obliged to recall them and reorganize matters. Anson was one of the guilty officers, being redirected by a furious Wellington and sent further to the west.[2] The weather had again taken a turn for the worse, and the pursuit was now taking the allies into the Pyrenees proper, which together made for some very hard marches. Tomkinson recorded of 23 June that, when eventually set on the right road, the brigade 'marched four leagues in incessant rain, which made the mountains so slippery that many horses came down, and it almost prevented the infantry moving at all'.[3] Things did not improve the following day, and Vandeleur told his mother how the 12th 'endeavoured to pass a mountain, that took us from 2 o'clock p.m. until past 11 at night to get to its summit, where we were obliged to halt from the excessive darkness of the night and the badness of the descent, which was bad enough next morning to get down'.[4] More and more French troops were encountered, and Graham's infantry were frequently in action, but with the terrain not only being as precipitous as described by Vandeleur but also heavily wooded, there was little scope to use the cavalry for anything but reconnaissance work. Only when the French made a stand at Tolosa on the 25th were Anson's regiments called upon to take part in a more general action, but even then their role was restricted to screening the movements of the artillery.

On 1 July, the French completed their withdrawal from Spain, falling back across the Bidassoa River. Captain Henry Andrews's troop had moved up with the infantry, who had a hard fight with the French rear-guard, but again there was little scope for cavalry work. This did not, however, prevent two of the 12th's officers claiming a rather cheeky 'first' for the regiment, Vandeleur relating how, after the French had finally withdrawn,

> Capt. Andrews and I remained and rode to Fuenterabia, where we crossed
> the river in a row boat at a short distance from their picquets and actually
> landed in France; but mark, we immediately stepped into the boat again

General Sir James Steaurt.
Watercolour by Richard
Dighton, *c.* 1836.

Lieutenant Colonel (later
Major General) Frederick
Cavendish Ponsonby.
Watercolour and pencil by
Thomas Heaphy, *c.* 1813.

Sword practice. Watercolour by G. H. Brennan after Denis Dighton. Although this image depicts a trooper of the 13th Light Dragoons, men of all regiments trained in dismounted sword drill so as to familiarize themselves with the standard cuts and parries.

Dismounted trooper of the 12th Light Dragoons, c. 1801. Watercolour by Jacques Brouillet. Although British cavalry rarely fought on foot, dismounted drill played a large part in conditioning new recruits to orders and routine.

Monument to Cornet Thomas Bateson, 12th Light Dragoons, at St George's Church, Deal. The victim of a surfeit of nuts, Bateson was the regiment's first commissioned fatality of the Napoleonic Wars.

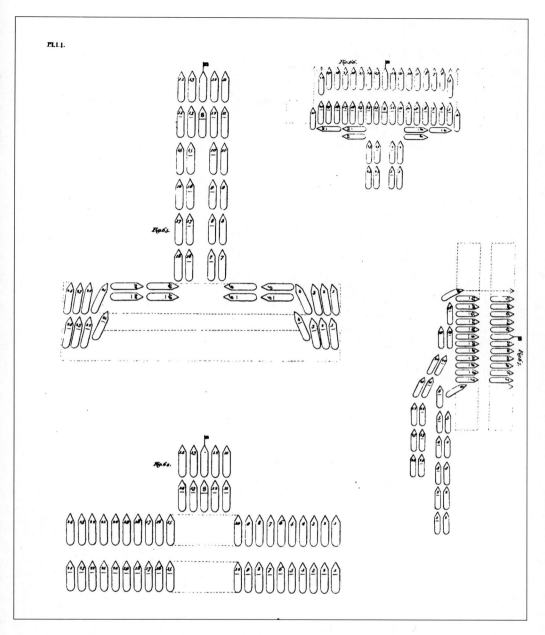

Advanced training, once the trooper had mastered control of his own horse, required knowledge of the evolutions needed to operate as part of a troop or squadron. These figures from the 1803 *Light Horse Drill* show deployment to and from a column of fours.

Left: Stapleton Cotton, 1st Viscount Combermere. Watercolour by Thomas Heaphy, 1817.

Below: Battle of Salamanca, 22 July 1812. Engraving by G. Lewis after John Augustus Atkinson. Most of the cavalry work fell to Le Marchant's heavy brigade, seen right, but note also the light cavalry officer to the far left of the image, wearing the pelisse often adopted on campaign. His shako, however, is incorrect for the date, for although in use at home by this time, light dragoon regiments in the Peninsula did not receive their new issue until after the campaign was over.

British Field Battery and Light Dragoons. Anonymous ink sketch. Covering artillery was a common – and detested – duty for regiments such as the 12th, depriving them of mobility whilst exposing them to enemy counter-battery fire.

View of Bayonne from the left bank of the Adour, 12 March 1814. Engraving by Matthew Dubourg, after Lt George Willis. The 12th spent much of the final stages of the Peninsular War engaged in operations around Bayonne.

Left: Henry William Paget, 1st Marquess of Anglesey. Pencil and watercolour by Henry Edridge, 1808. As the Earl of Uxbridge, Paget commanded Wellington's cavalry during the Hundred Days until wounded at Waterloo. His partiality for the hussars, whose uniform he habitually wore as here, caused some concern amongst officers of the light dragoon regiments.

Below: Battle of Waterloo. Aquatint by William Thomas Fry, after Denis Dighton. Showing the final British advance, with Vivian's hussars in the foreground supported by Vandeleur's light dragoons, this scene captures much of the confusion of the fighting on such a confined battlefield.

Above: 'Field of Waterloo, as it appeared the morning after the memorable battle of 18th June 1815.' Aquatint by Mathew Dubourg, after John Heaviside Clarke. Many of the wounded from the 12th, including Lt Col Ponsonby and Captain Sandys, spent the whole of the intervening night on the field; whilst Ponsonby eventually recovered, Sandys did not.

Right: Memorial plaque to the officers and soldiers of the 12th Light Dragoons killed at Waterloo, St Joseph's Church, Waterloo.

This Monument was erected by the 12th L.t Dragoons to the Memory of the Officers and Soldiers belonging to the Regiment who were killed at the Battle of WATERLOO 18th June 1815.

CAPTAIN EDWARD SANDYS
LIEUTENANT LINDSEY BERTIE
CORNET JOHN E. LOCKART

SERJEANT MAJORS

ROBERT NELSON　　　　　　　　THOMAS SCANLON

SERJEANTS

| WILLIAM BAIRD | THOMAS FINLEY | JAMES KIRBY |
| WILSON COX | | WILLIAM TOOLE |

CORPORALS

| WILLIAM HORSTON | WILLIAM MARSH | SAMUEL NICHOLS |

PRIVATES

ISAAC BISHOP	JOHN GLASS	JAMES McLASHER
WILLIAM BURLEY	EDWARD GROWCOCK	EDWARD McDONALD
JOHN BAXTER	JEREMIAH HICKEY	JOHN NUGENT
CHARLES COCHRAN	GEORGE HURST	FRANCIS PERCY
CHARLES CLARE	THOMAS HALFORD	MICHAEL RAINSFORD
THOMAS CLARKE	ROBERT KELLY	HUGH SMITH
HUGH DONNEGAN	JOHN KING	WILLIAM STEWART
WILLIAM DAXTER	FRANCIS LANG	JAMES SIVELL
GUY DEVITT	DANIEL MURPHY	RICHARD SLADE
EDWARD EADIE	PHILIP MURPHY	JOSEPH WILLIAMSON
JOHN EARLY	ROBERT MATTHEWSON	JAMES WIGGINS
FRANCIS FOSTER	JOHN MACFARLANE	JAMES WILMOT
JAMES FISHER		JOHN WELSH

Samson Stawell. Oil on canvas by William Salter, *c.* 1835. Stawell served with the 12th in the Peninsula and at Waterloo and later went on to command the regiment after its conversion to lancers, in which uniform he is shown here.

12th Lancer, *c.* 1820. Lithograph after William Heath. As well as giving them a more ornate uniform, conversion to lancers began to take the 12th away from their roots as outpost troops, reinforcing the preference for the mounted charge over other cavalry duties.

and went back; but we can say that we were the first two men of the allied army that landed in France.[5]

The French withdrawal allowed Wellington to consolidate his position south of the frontier, and, in particular, to reduce the fortresses of San Sebastián and Pamplona. Since Graham's troops were already in the area of San Sebastián, they were assigned the task of capturing the place, and siege operations were commenced on 7 July. This slowing of the operational tempo came at a good time for the 12th, who had been on the march for the best part of two months with very little respite. Now they settled down into quarters around the village of Zubieta, where they remained until 9 July when a shortage of forage compelled the whole brigade to remove to quarters around Tolosa and Villafranca de Ordicia. Prior to their departure, the 12th had been compelled – for want of anything else – to make do with cutting the ripe wheat to feed their horses, which was not only fodder of a poor quality but which was of course also completely destructive so far as the local farmers were concerned.[6]

Before moving down to their new quarters, the 12th and 16th had witnessed the arrival of a new brigade commander, one of a number of changes that took place in the organization of the British cavalry in the aftermath of Vitoria. Several of these had already been in the pipeline before the campaign began, but had been held up pending the return from England of Sir Stapleton Cotton, who had gone home over the winter in order to recuperate fully from his Salamanca wound, and whose return had been delayed by adverse weather. With his cavalry chief expected daily, Wellington had delayed making organizational changes until Cotton could be consulted in person, but Cotton only reached the front on 25 June, with his absence at Vitoria having perhaps contributed something to the less-than-stellar performance of the cavalry as a whole in that battle.[7] One of the changes in urgent need of approval, since it had been pending since the spring, was the posting of Major General John Ormsby Vandeleur to replace George Anson. Anson had requested a home posting as early as February 1813, in order to attend to family affairs, and this was now authorized – along with the appointment of Vandeleur to replace him – as of 2 July.[8]

The new brigadier's arrival four days later, 'riding in with a servant and a pair of saddle-bags, without bag or baggage, all of which has since come up', was naturally most welcome for the 12th's Lieutenant John Vandeleur, who excitedly told his mother that the general,

> immediately wrote to Sir T. [*sic*] Cotton to get me appointed A.D. Camp.
> He has not yet received an answer, but there is no doubt I will get the

> appointment, as Genl. Anson had an extra A.D. Camp also. I am now
> living with him, and I trust it will make you and my father very happy to
> hear of my success.[9]

Unfortunately, this was not to be, since Wellington unaccountably refused to grant the appointment, notwithstanding the fact that, as Vandeleur complained,

> only a few days before he granted the same request to M. Genl. Ponsonby,
> a junior officer who commanded a brigade that never was or is intended
> to be on outpost duty, and another thing, the very officer who the Genl.
> succeeded (Anson) was allowed an extra, altho' he never gave them
> anything to do, but always employed and used the regimental officers
> upon every service of difficulty, and pampered his two A-D-Camps in
> the most shameful manner. However, the Genl. has no particular interest,
> therefore he is refused everything he asks, and has no redress.[10]

Wellington's decision notwithstanding, Vandeleur junior nevertheless did act for the remainder of the war as an unofficial extra ADC to his cousin, his detachment from regimental duty having been approved by Lieutenant Colonel Ponsonby as soon as the general sent in his initial request. Since Vandeleur's regular ADC, Lieutenant William Armstrong of the 19th Light Dragoons, was frequently ill during the period, this was probably no bad thing for the effective functioning of the brigade, and his new job gave Vandeleur a greater grasp of events outside his regiment, which in turn is reflected in the content of his remaining Peninsula letters.

While all this was going on, the French had not been idle. As had been the case after Salamanca, Wellington had underestimated the power of recovery of the troops he had defeated, and would shortly receive an unpleasant reminder. With Joseph and Jourdan in disgrace, Marshal Soult was sent back from Germany to take command of the survivors of the Vitoria debacle, which were now reorganized into a single Armée d'Espagne, 79,000 strong. Opening operations on 25 July, Soult drove through the Pyrenean passes with the goal of relieving the garrison of Pamplona. His troops got to within sight of the fortress before being brought to a stop and then thrown into retreat in the First and Second Battles of Sorauren on 28 and 30 July.[11] For the 12th, Soult's counteroffensive did not involve any fighting, but it did disrupt the line of communications between Graham's corps and the rest of the army, this not being reopened until part of the regiment was able to link up with the infantry of the Light Division on 29 July.[12] Soult's campaign also caused considerable disruption of the siege works at San Sebastián, which did not recommence in earnest until late August. The town finally fell after a bloody storm on the last day of the month, but not until 5 September did the castle, into which the surviving garrison had withdrawn, finally capitulate.[13] During the second siege, both regiments of Vandeleur's Brigade were initially posted out along the coast road to watch for a renewed French advance: Graham believed that they would be of great use if the enemy made a direct attack but it quickly became apparent that so large a mounted force could neither be maintained nor profitably employed in the rough terrain, and the bulk of the brigade was withdrawn, leaving only a single squadron of the 12th on outpost duty at Rentería, seven miles east of the fortress on the River Oiartzun.[14]

On the face of things, the relatively leisurely conduct of Wellington's operations during the summer months of 1813, particularly when taken in contrast with his initial rapid offensive, seems hard to understand. However, the Peninsular War was part of a wider conflict, and further operations had to be conducted with an eye on the progress of events in Germany where Napoleon was in the field against the Russians and Prussians. For much of the summer, an armistice was in force in Germany, and it was not until this ended in mid-August, and Austria came in on the side of the allies, that Wellington knew that he could safely move into France without fear that Napoleon might send reinforcements to Soult. Once acquainted with events in Germany, however, Wellington was quick to strike, launching his forces across the Bidassoa and into France on 7 October. Graham's corps, being still deployed along the coast following the fall of San Sebastián, would form the left wing of the attack, taking advantage of a low tide to cross the Bidassoa estuary. Again, this operation was largely an infantry affair, but the 12th moved up to help screen the attacking troops of the First and Fifth Divisions, and remained with them once they were established on French soil so as to furnish them with a chain of outposts.[15]

Having crossed the Bidassoa, the 12th were now occupying some of the most advanced positions held by Wellington's forces, but this was an honour that was not necessarily appreciated, with Lieutenant Vandeleur describing a rather rough and ready existence:

> The forage is all consumed. We are the only dragoon regt. up here. We have been doing duty for some time. All the rest of the cavalry are up to their bellies in fine hay and straw, doing nothing, as far back as Pampeluna, but Col. Ponsonby is such a man that he is never quiet unless we are in the middle of everything.[16]

The only saving grace was that the days remained warm, but the nights were growing increasingly cold and since even the brigade commander's staff had only a hovel and a tent for their accommodation this did not bode well with winter coming on. Ponsonby, however, was clearly in his element, although his mother feared for his safety after having learned that her son was 'most eager to get into action, because he says he is asham'd of his Medals and has not earn'd them,' a sentiment that may well explain his zeal for offering up the 12th for any adventurous service.[17]

Still, notwithstanding the fact that their commanding officer's zeal meant that life was rather harder for them than for most of their comrades in other regiments, the horses and men of the 12th were in excellent condition now that they had recovered from the hard marches that carried them to Vitoria. Whilst the siege of San Sebastián was still going on, Ponsonby had proudly told his mother that his command was 'in such big order, discipline, health and spirits, so well hors'd and accoutred, that I quite long to shew it to the Bayonne People before another winter's Bivouacking has thrown it back again'.[18] Not only was the regiment in good order, but it had also been reinforced: thanks to the capture of the Biscay ports, a draft had been shipped directly to Bilbao under the command of Captain William Coles, where it was met on landing by a party from the regiment. Spared the long march up from Lisbon that had faced Hay and Vandeleur the previous year, the new horses and men were soon at the front, so that total rank and file strength was increased to 482 as of 25 September, 441 of these being present and fit for duty. Total strength in troop horses was likewise increased to 453 fit for duty out of a total of 476, although whereas the number of effective troopers would remain high for the rest of the war, the difficulty in keeping the horses fed and healthy over the winter would soon see the mounted strength fall again. In addition to Coles, three subalterns came out with the remount, whilst John Griffith, having been gazetted Cornet and Adjutant, joined the regiment in October.[19]

After the crossing of the Bidassoa, matters again stabilized as Wellington waited until Pamplona had fallen and for positive news from Germany that the campaign against Napoleon was going in the allies' favour. Soult was now holding the line of the Nivelle, another strong position, and Wellington sought to deceive his enemy with a feint attack in the west so as to draw the French focus away from the eastern sector where the main blow was to fall. The left wing, now under the command of Lieutenant General Sir John Hope after Graham had been obliged to return home on sick leave, was to make an attack on French positions south of the Nivelle, which flowed into the sea at St-Jean-de-Luz.[20]

The attack opened on the morning of 10 November, with the terrain again placing the burden of assault upon the infantry, and leaving the 12th to the hated role of covering the allied artillery. On this occasion, however, the work was less dangerous than dull, so that Ponsonby rode forward to observe the infantry action and left Bridger in temporary command. Although the 12th were not themselves visible to the French gunners, being tucked neatly behind a reverse slope in the rear of Ramsay's horse artillery, they remained vulnerable to random 'overs' from the French counter-battery fire that came bowling over the crest. Some of the regiment's 'young and thoughtless' junior officers, noting that Bridger had taken the precaution of placing himself behind a stout willow, sought to have a little fun at the major's expense, as Hay related:

> At the top of the hill, just in range of the French forts and the willow, was a dry ditch, into which we got into, one of the party keeping a look out with a spyglass, and the rest got onto the top facing the ditch; when the one with the glass saw the fuse put to the gun, he gave the word 'Down', we jumped into the ditch safe enough, but the shot struck the top of the hill in line with the tree under which [Bridger] sat and then went right through the branches. This foolish amusement we continued till his resting place became quite unsafe, and [Bridger] finding out the cause, an order was of course given for us to desist.

It can hardly be conceived that Sir James Steuart would have approved of such antics amongst his officers, but in any case the participants in the prank soon received a reminder of the seriousness of affairs. Evidently wishing to show that he retained his sense of humour notwithstanding the potentially deadly joke played on him, Bridger invited Hay and his companions to dine with him:

> A large piece of salt beef was provided, round which about eight officers were seated on the ground, when one of the shots we had been provoking from the battery, came right into the midst of us, knocking the beef and plates about our ears, rebounded and took the arm off an orderly, who was in the act of putting a nosebag on his horse, and killed the animal. We were sitting close together, and it was quite a miracle some of the party were not killed.[21]

Throughout the day, this was as close as Vandeleur's Brigade came to the fighting, but when operations were resumed on the 11th the call at last came for the cavalry to move to the front. Hope's infantry had carried the French positions, and it was hoped that a swift pursuit would allow the cavalry to seize the bridge at St-Jean-de-Luz before the French could either secure or destroy it. Lieutenant George Gleig of the 85th Light Infantry, which had just captured the village of Urrugne and the entrenched positions beyond it, was alerted by a cry from the rear of 'Make way for the cavalry!' as his battalion began to move onwards. Thus alerted, the 85th 'accordingly inclined to the right of the road, when the 12th and 16th light dragoons rode past at a quick trot, sending out half a troop before them to feel their way'.[22] Even this necessary precaution of an advanced guard did little to slow the cavalry pursuit, but their efforts were still to no avail, for the French had fired the bridge and were thus able to make good their retreat. A crossing was eventually made by a ford further upstream, and Vandeleur's Brigade pushed forwards in the pursuit but was unable to prevent the French from completing their withdrawal into the entrenched camps around Bayonne. The Battle of the Nivelle was another clear-cut victory for the allies, and seemed to establish a good position in which to place the army into winter quarters. Even so, outposts were still needed, and the 12th remained at the front, maintaining positions in advance of Hope's infantry until they were relieved by the 16th on 24 November and pulled back to Urrugne to recuperate.[23]

The pull-back came not a moment too soon, for winter – the first storms of which had already served to delay the launching of the Nivelle attacks – now set in with a vengeance. Hay remembered that although the allied advance had carried Wellington's forces clear of the mountains, 'we had not improved our condition either in regards quarters or forage for our horses': as long as they remained on the outposts, and to an extent once they were withdrawn, the officers and men 'were nearly starved to death with cold; and our nags were only kept alive by eating chopped whins'.[24] The French, despite their defeats, also remained full of fight, and the regimental Registry of Services records that 'several skirmishes took place' whilst the 12th were on outpost duty.[25] However, for the most part, common sense prevailed and the opposing picquets and vedettes cooperated to prevent unnecessary casualties and to allow both sides to concentrate on keeping themselves warm and fed. Arrangements for obtaining forage from villages between the lines were even formalized to the extent that the French 'generally went first, and after helping themselves, rang the church bell, as a sign we might come on'.[26]

So far as the troops were concerned, it would no doubt have been quite acceptable had this temporary truce gone on until spring, but Wellington was not entirely happy with the position occupied by his forces, whose further advance northwards was now barred by the fortress of Bayonne on the Adour River. Directly covered by Soult's field army, still 60,000 strong even after its earlier defeats, Bayonne would be a difficult obstacle for the 1814 campaign. Even if a major attack would have to wait until the new year, something might still be done in the last days of the old to place the allies in an improved position. As things now stood, the allies were facing the French along a relatively narrow front between the River Nive and the sea. The Nive flowed north-west to enter the Adour at Bayonne, so that the closer the allies advanced to the north, the narrower their front became between the river and the sea. Wellington accordingly decided to establish a bridgehead east of the Nive so as to be able to advance on Bayonne from both sides of that river, but this was a potentially risky undertaking since Soult was in a position to shift his forces rapidly from one bank of the Nive to the other via the bridges of Bayonne, whereas Wellington was obliged to use the fords at Cambo, some distance to the south.[27] The resulting operations would present the allies with a major challenge, offer Soult a useful opportunity, and see the 12th Light Dragoons take part in their last field action of the Peninsular War.

Wellington began to shift Hill's corps to the east bank of the Nive at day-break on 9 December, covered by a feigned advance by Hope with the First, Fifth, and Light Divisions on the opposite bank. Having pushed forwards during the day, almost up to the entrenched batteries covering Bayonne, Hope then withdrew the main body of his command under the cover of darkness and left only a line of picquets to hold the ground that he had occupied. Unfortunately, the bulk of Hope's infantry was pulled too far back, almost as far as St-Jean-de-Luz, and this would prove a costly error the next day for Soult, always a canny manoeuvrer even if his tactics once on the field sometimes let him down, elected not to do the obvious and attack Hill's corps in its new position but instead to strike the weakened forces remaining west of the Nive. Attacking at daybreak, the French quickly overran the allied picquet line that had been established the night before, and pressed on hard against the Fifth Division. Outnumbered, the infantry were driven back with some loss – many of the picquets being taken prisoner – and only when the First Division could be brought back into the fight was the situation stabilized.

Forming part of the outpost line, the 12th were in the thick of the action from the outset, having pushed patrols out towards Bayonne during the night, and detected the initial French advance before first light. Against such numbers there was little that could be done by the two regiments of

Vandeleur's Brigade, and the cavalry were therefore kept back as a final reserve in the event that the infantry could not hold. Throughout the day, the French were successfully contained, but by late afternoon a determined push seemed likely to swing matters in Soult's favour. Lieutenant Vandeleur was at the side of the brigade commander, and provides a vivid account of the confused fighting:

> The French brought up guns and used every effort, but could not move until nearly 4 o'clock, when they succeeded in driving in the infantry skirmishers pell-mell on top of the cavalry and artillery. Everybody then rode forward and exerted themselves to get the infantry on. At this unfortunate moment, while I was endeavouring to rally the infantry, my horse was shot through the lungs. The enemy were coming on fast, and I had to run as hard as my legs would carry me to avoid being taken. I ran to the 16th Drgs. and got a troop horse and returned to the fight. I met Armstrong on foot, whose horse had been shot dead; he was going for a troop-horse also. I joined the Genl., who by this time had succeeded in getting the infantry and the picquets of the 16th Dragoons to charge, which turned the scale, and everything was going well; but the fire was very hot and lively. Unfortunately, the Genl.'s orderly, who was close to us, was knocked down by a ball thro' his neck; he is still alive, but I am afraid he will not survive it. The Genl. was extremely fortunate . . . his horse got a graze, but it did no harm . . . The fighting continued extremely hard until night put an end to it.[28]

As well as darkness, it was the timely return of the last of the troops who had been withdrawn too far south that checked the French advance, but when night fell Soult's forces were holding the ground from which they had driven the allied picquets that morning, and both sides had suffered heavy casualties. The only positive for the allies was that Hill was now firmly established on the opposite bank of the Nive.

On the afternoon of the 11th, the French made another attack, again catching the Fifth Division at a disadvantage. Although the cavalry as a body were not engaged, Major General Vandeleur happened to be in the rear of Colonel de Rego Barreto's Portuguese infantry brigade when part of its line began to falter, and quickly sought to intervene:

> [The French] came down with the bayonet, shouting and drumming. The Portuguese gave way, and there was general disorder for some minutes.

The Genl., with great presence of mind, took his small picquet to the rear of the fugitives and charged them and beat them most unmercifully until we made them stop, and again advance. Supported by the British they regained their ground and, as before, night put a stop to the proceedings.[29]

Now forced back twice, the French took a much less aggressive stance after their second repulse, and on the 12th there was only skirmishing between the infantry outposts. Hope had now been reinforced, and the position west of the Nive was now quite evidently too tough a nut for the French to crack. However, Soult was not ready to give up yet, and took advantage of the interior lines afforded to him by the bridges at Bayonne to shift his forces across the Nive under the cover of darkness in preparation for an attack on Hill's corps the following morning.

Hill had had several days to establish a strong position, and a pontoon bridge had been thrown across the Nive to allow easy communication between the two wings. Alerted by the sounds of French artillery rumbling through the streets of Bayonne, Hill had his men in position to meet the French attack when it came on 13 December, but during the night the Nive rose by a considerable margin, and the pontoon bridge was rendered impassable. Nevertheless, and despite some early setbacks, Hill obtained a creditable victory against the odds and inflicted double the casualties that he received. Unable to cross until the pontoon bridge was replaced, the 12th could only listen to the cannonade off to the east, but as night fell new orders were received that directed them to reinforce the troops on the opposite bank. The regiment, along with the 16th, was ordered to Cambo, in the rear of Hill's position, in consequence of reports of a French force threatening his rear. As Lieutenant Vandeleur recorded, 'the distance was about 16 miles, but the state of the road was so excessively bad, that we could not arrive until 12 next morning, altho' we marched all night, which unfortunately was both dark and stormy'.[30]

The French force they were being sent to oppose was a flying column operating on Soult's far-left flank under Général de Brigade Marie-Auguste Paris, who had made a diversionary movement against the allied rear. The shifting of Vandeleur's Brigade to Cambo was part of a concentration of cavalry ordered in response to Paris's move, and also brought up the brigades of Major General Victor von Alten and Major General Lord Edward Somerset. Both these formations were composed entirely of hussar regiments and, other than the veteran 1st KGL Hussars under Alten, they were all fresh out from home and had as yet seen little service. Indeed, Somerset's three regiments – the 7th,

10th, and 15th Hussars – had come up from the rear having been pulled out of their winter quarters. The opportunity for comparison was too good to be missed, Vandeleur recording that the hussars

> . . . came up yesterday morning in beautiful condition, and well they might, for since they came into the country, they have been fed with English Hay and never done a day's duty. Since the 12th have been in this country they have always had the out-post duty of that part of the army which they were attached to, and never were quartered in the rear of the army to regain their condition except last winter, when every man in the army was in quiet quarters at a great distance from the enemy.[31]

Vandeleur had every right to be proud of his regiment, but they would now at last – with Soult pinned back in Bayonne and Paris's force having been dealt with by troops already at hand – be themselves allowed to settle into winter quarters.

On 18 December, having been relieved by Somerset's hussars, the brigade returned to the west bank of the Nive. The 12th was then posted to the outpost line for a few days longer, until on Christmas Eve they were relieved by the 16th and went into winter quarters at Urrugne.[32] It was no doubt a fairly spartan Christmas, but it was at least a break from active operations and ensured that the regiment was in something like a fit state, albeit with insufficient horses to mount its full effective rank and file strength, when operations resumed. The number of horses dying – primarily as a result of bad weather and insufficient fodder – did drop whilst the regiment was in winter quarters, but this did not cease completely with four dead horses in January and another eleven the following month. Three deaths amongst the rank and file were also recorded during the period, but two of these related to men who had only now been confirmed as casualties of the earlier fighting.[33] However, in addition to the one trooper who did expire of natural causes during the winter, the regiment also lost its popular commissary, William Myler, who died on 5 January 1814.[34]

In the aftermath of the Battle of the Nive, Soult had withdrawn the bulk of his field army some distance to the north-east, leaving only a reinforced garrison in Bayonne and its surrounding entrenched camps. Preparing to recommence active operations as soon as the weather permitted, Wellington produced a daring plan to throw a force across the Adour not upstream, where Soult might interfere with operations, but rather downstream of Bayonne. This entailed crossing a wide tidal estuary, for which purpose arrangements were set in motion for the famous 'bridge of boats' constructed under the supervision of Lieutenant

Colonel Henry Sturgeon of the Royal Staff Corps, with the cooperation of sailors from the squadron under Rear Admiral Charles Penrose then operating off the Biscay coast. The troops detailed to carry out the actual crossing, and to establish a bridgehead on the north bank of the river, were the infantry of the First Division – two brigades of Foot Guards and one of KGL infantry, under Major General Kenneth Howard – and Vandeleur's two light dragoon regiments. The rest of Hope's corps would support the crossing whilst the remainder of the army conducted a feint further upriver and the Spanish field forces, until now little employed north of the Pyrenees for fear of the retribution they would exact on the French civilian population, would be brought up to mask Bayonne itself.

The operation began during the night of 21–22 February, with Hope advancing his troops over the same ground that they had taken and then lost during the Battle of the Nive. Unfortunately, the British flotilla conveying the boats intended for the bridge – adapted from French fishing vessels – was unable to enter the river as planned. It seemed that this would prevent the crossing being made, but Hope's troops had brought several smaller boats overland on carriages. These boats were used to establish a ferry across the Adour by means of which eight companies, drawn from the Foot Guards and the riflemen of the 5/60th, were carried across the river during the course of the 22nd. That night, they came under a heavy French attack, but this was beaten off, and the following day it was possible to continue the operations and expand the bridgehead. Amongst the troops sent across were a squadron of the 12th, who 'were obliged to swim our horses across, carrying the men and saddles in the boats'. The bridgehead thus established was a dangerous post, although covered by the fire of heavy guns and Congreve Rockets emplaced on the south bank, but, as Vandeleur put it, 'we made so good a resistance that the enemy thought that we had a very strong force across the river, and therefore retired, and let us alone for that night. We worked hard all night and got about 1,000 men across the river. They never molested us after.'[35]

Thankfully, a change of wind on 24 February allowed the larger boats intended to construct the bridge to be brought safely into the estuary, and after two days' work the structure was completed and Hope could bring across sufficient troops to complete the investment of Bayonne. Thereafter, his corps would remain detached from Wellington's main field army, which headed eastwards after Soult, beating him again at Orthez on 27 February and pursuing him to Toulouse. Hope did not press a vigorous siege operation, preferring to let the blockade take its toll, and so although his two cavalry regiments were required for outpost work this was fairly light duty since the main French field army was now some distance away. Hay, certainly, was pleased that the shift to the north bank of the Adour meant that 'we had now established ourselves in rather a better country, where the houses, though in many instances deserted by the inhabitants, were more comfortable and the natives more civilised than the Basque peasants'.[36] The 12th were given the task of covering the road into Bayonne from Bordeaux, clearing a detachment of the Garde National from the town of Dax on 1 March.[37] Later that month, Hope would report to Wellington that 'Vandeleur has pushed his patrols already a very considerable way in the direction of Bordeaux, and cannot hear of a French soldier being in his front'.[38] Yet again, though, any rest for the regiment was to be but short-lived, for although their share in the serious fighting was now over the 12th had one last major duty to carry out before their Peninsular War service came to an end.

The city of Bordeaux had long had an ambivalent relationship with the successive regimes in Paris, having lent its support and the name of its river estuary to the moderate Girondin faction during the French Revolution and seeing its representatives suffer accordingly when the Jacobins triumphed. An initial acceptance of Napoleon's rule had quickly turned sour once it became apparent that his resumption of the war with Britain would cripple the maritime trade upon which the city depended, and so by 1814, after a decade of blockade and with the conscription laws growing ever tighter, there were few in the city who had much love left for their Emperor. This dissatisfaction ultimately led the Mayor of Bordeaux, Jean-Baptiste Lynch, to make overtures aimed at delivering the city into Wellington's hands in the name of Louis XVIII. Since the British had not yet adopted a policy on what to do when Napoleon fell – although a Bourbon restoration was certainly beginning to look like the lesser of a multitude of evils – Wellington felt unable to accept Lynch's terms, but when the Mayor agreed to hand the city over anyway, orders went out for the detachment of an allied force to take possession of Bordeaux. This corps would be under the command of Sir William Beresford, and would comprise the infantry of the Fourth and Seventh Divisions as well as Vivian's Brigade of cavalry.[39] As he marched north, Beresford also picked up two squadrons of the 12th Light Dragoons, leaving the third, along with the whole of the 16th Light Dragoons, to look after Hope's outposts around Bayonne.

The orders for the two squadrons to march north came unexpectedly and in the midst of a heavy snow-storm, so that the journey itself, through 'wild and uncultivated country' of the Pays des Landes, was a hard one. However, it also took the riders out of the area that had been stripped of forage by the two armies, so that for once there was sufficient fodder available – notwithstanding the hard winter – to give the horses a good feed. Bordeaux itself, once Beresford's troops entered it on 12 March, was also welcoming, and provided good quarters. The cavalry were still obliged to provide troops for outpost duties, detaching a squadron at a time for this purpose, but such French troops as were in the area were conscripts or units of the Garde National, and posed little threat to the allies. Accordingly, once Bordeaux was secure, Beresford departed on 15 March along with the bulk of the troops that he had brought north, leaving only Lieutenant General Lord Dalhousie's Seventh Division to garrison the city, with the 12th attached to provide a sufficient cavalry force.[40] On 17 March the missing squadron was also ordered up from Bayonne, reuniting the regiment; until they arrived, one squadron of Vivian's Brigade was retained at Bordeaux.[41]

Having occupied Bordeaux, Dalhousie's initial preoccupation was to secure the navigation of the Gironde to allow the city to be used as a supply port for the allied forces. This entailed the elimination of the French naval force in the river and the reduction of the fortress of Blaye. Difficulties in clearing the Gironde did not, however, prevent the arrival in Bordeaux of the Duc d'Angoulême, nephew of the Bourbon claimant Louis XVIII, who sought to raise the surrounding area for his uncle. Dalhousie had already been using the 12th to furnish outpost patrols between the Garonne and Dordogne, the two rivers that meet immediately north of Bordeaux to form the estuary of the Gironde.[42] However, Angoulême persuaded him that a greater military presence between the two rivers might swing the whole area behind the Bourbons. Accordingly, on 28 March, Dalhousie led a force, including a squadron of the 12th, on just such an expedition, but elected not to press beyond the Dordogne and returned to Bordeaux after a sweep through the lands where Angoulême had assured him that the populace would rise, but where, in fact, no such thing occurred.[43] Hay, in his memoirs, claims that he was instrumental in saving the life of the Duc during these operations by detecting an ambush, as a result of which Hay subsequently 'received marked attention from him, he frequently sending me an invitation to his dinner-parties'. Hay, however, is always the hero of his own adventures, and whilst it may well be that he did indeed unmask a concealed French battery as he relates, whether or not this had indeed been emplaced as part of a plot to ambush the Duc is another matter entirely.[44] The other two squadrons took part in a subsidiary move up the Garonne to La Réole in company with the infantry brigade of Major General William Inglis.[45]

Dalhousie now elected to make a more serious attack on the fortress at Blaye, which until this point had only been kept under observation. On 5 April he therefore moved out of Bordeaux a second time with a force similar to that which had accompanied his earlier foray. Major Bridger's squadron of the 12th, composed of the troops of Captains Andrews and Sandys, again took part in the expedition which also included six battalions of infantry – two British, three Portuguese and one of Brunswickers. Hay had by this time, like Vandeleur, traded his family connections for a staff position, having made use of an acquaintance with Dalhousie that dated back to childhood to obtain an appointment as one of the general's orderly officers. In this capacity, he was well placed to describe the advance of Dalhousie's little column, which, after an overnight halt 'at a neat, clean village on the main road', moved out again on the morning of 6 April, turning onto a lesser road to approach Blaye from the northeast. Patrols, composed of troopers from the 12th backed up with riflemen of the Brunswick-Oels Jägers, went ahead of the main body and before long it was reported that a French force had been encountered, blocking the advance. Further reconnaissance quickly established that this was indeed the case, but with the French having occupied the pine forest on either side of the road with their skirmishers it was not immediately clear what size or manner of troops were faced. Only after the Jägers had driven the French from the woods was the main force revealed, described by Hay as being composed of 'several battalions of French infantry drawn up in line, supported by a squadron of cavalry'.[46]

Since we have just seen evidence of Hay's tendency to exaggerate matters when it suits the purposes of his narrative, it is worth noting that on this occasion his account of the forces present at Étauliers under the command of Général de Division François l'Huillier is confirmed by the historian Sir Charles Oman, who notes that the French had three battalions of conscripts belonging to the 27eme, 105eme, and 120eme Ligne, and not one but three squadrons of cavalry, these being provisional formations created from depot troops.[47] Although verging on 2,000 strong, l'Huillier's motley contingent was little match for Dalhousie's veterans. Major General John Gardiner's brigade – 1/6th Foot, 3rd Provisional Battalion, and the Brunswick-Oels Light Infantry – formed line and launched a direct attack, with Bridger and his squadron in support. The majority of the French force broke at the first contact, many of the unwilling conscripts taking the opportunity to desert, but at least one battalion managed to form something approaching a square as the 12th spurred forwards, leading to what Hay described as 'one of the most animating sights I ever beheld'.

Serving in his staff capacity, Hay was not with Bridger's squadron himself, although he had a small escort from the 12th with him, with which he had already taken a number of prisoners during the early stages of the fighting. Dalhousie had ordered up his artillery and, as Hay told it,

> When the guns were brought to bear on the French square, the 12th advanced at the charge in a most gallant style, and with the small number of men (one hundred and fifty) not only broke the first square of six hundred men who laid down their arms, but prepared to attack another body. But the general, to save so much bloodshed, had the guns brought close up . . . so prudence was thought the better part of valour, and the French engaged agreed to lay down their arms.[48]

This all sounds very dramatic, but alas it would seem that Hay's account once again over-states things. Only 320 men were taken prisoner in the action as a whole, so the capture of 600-plus related by Hay is a clear exaggeration, but more to the point the casualty figures do not suggest an action of this ferocity, with Dalhousie suffering the loss of only twenty killed and wounded. What we have here is a situation much like that at Salamanca, with a charge against a force that was already broken. Whilst this does not sound quite so glorious as Hay's version of events, it must again be remembered that this is exactly what light cavalry were supposed to do. Furthermore, Dalhousie's use of Bridger's horsemen to pin the French in square until his guns could be brought up sufficiently close to make surrender the only viable option represents an effective use of combined arms in action, demonstrating the growing sophistication of cavalry tactics based on the experience of war.

In all events, the fight at Étauliers was a neat little victory, and a fitting end to the active involvement of the 12th Light Dragoons in the Peninsular War. The defeated l'Huillier fled the five miles south to Blaye with about 500 survivors from his shattered command, and Dalhousie quickly followed. The fortress proved a difficult place to take, however, and its commander, Contre Amiral Louis-Léon Jacob, who had just overseen the scuttling of the surviving French warships in the Gironde, was disinclined to accept the entreaties made to him to raise the Bourbon colours. On the other hand, news of the victory at Étauliers had at last brought the countryside out in support of Louis XVIII, and with hostilities so clearly drawing to a close Dalhousie saw no need to waste lives in further active operations. Finally, confirmation was received of the abdication of Napoleon and the consequent conclusion of peace, at which even Jacob at Blaye hauled down the tricolour.[49] Ponsonby, having missed the excitement of Dalhousie's miniature campaign, volunteered to take the news onward to Wellington; too late to prevent the needless Battle of Toulouse on 10 April, he joined the subsequent festivities in the captured city.[50] There would be yet more unnecessary bloodshed when the French garrison at Bayonne launched a sortie against the besiegers, but with these final shots the Peninsular War was now at an end and the 12th Light Dragoons could, in common with the rest of Wellington's victorious troops, think about going home.

During April and May 1814, Bordeaux became the focal point for the Anglo-Portuguese army as it began to break up into its constituent parts. The city also became the centre of a social hubbub – 'full of our own officers, both naval and military, theatres every night, and pleasure parties every day'[51] – as men celebrated their victory and prepared to take their leave of old friends. Not least of those friends were the army's Portuguese allies, who soon began the long march homeward, but the British contingent too was to be split, for whilst the war in Europe was won Britain remained at war with the United States, and it was felt that nothing would serve better to put down the upstart Americans than a few brigades of Wellington's veterans. The North American conflict, however, was one fought largely by infantry, and although the 14th Light Dragoons had the unenviable assignment of accompanying the troops bound across the Atlantic, the rest of Wellington's cavalry were under orders for home. There was no means of shipping such a number of horses and men, however, even had the reinforcement for the Americas not taken priority for the transports: instead the cavalry was to march overland across France, making their final return to home shores by means of a cross-Channel passage from Calais or Boulogne. In all, with the cavalry, horse artillery and the draught animals of the Royal Wagon Train, this amounted to 11,300 horses and was quite the logistical exercise.[52]

Vandeleur's Brigade, to which had been added the 13th Light Dragoons, led the column destined to embark at Boulogne, which they eventually reached on 5 July only to find themselves redirected to Calais after all. Arriving there the following day, they were then transported to Dover in a relay of small ships over the course of the coming week.[53] Not all the regiment went home that way, however. A few officers had been able to obtain leave and depart early, whilst Lieutenant Hay was now a permanent member of Lord Dalhousie's staff and sailed home with the general and the rest of his entourage.[54] Others were either on the sick list, or else left without a mount by the equine losses of the winter or the casting of horses deemed unfit to make the march across France. Under Captain William Patton, this group amounted collectively to four other officers,

Surgeon Robinson, seven serjeants, and eighty-nine rank and file, all of whom sailed home from Bordeaux. Eleven men newly returned from being held as prisoners of war by the French also likely formed part of this contingent.[55] There was one group, however, who neither marched with the regiment nor sailed down the Gironde, and that was the Spanish and Portuguese women who had followed the army through its campaigns. Although many soldiers in all regiments had taken up with local women, only those who had been formally married were entitled to accompany their menfolk back to Britain, and Bordeaux was the scene of many a heart-breaking parting.[56]

If the partings at Bordeaux meant that the Peninsular War ended on a sour note for the 12th, they could at least take some pride in what they had achieved in their three years' service under Wellington. A few months before the peace, Lieutenant Vandeleur had written to his mother with the proud claim that, 'We can boast of what no regt. in the army can, except the ones that came out the other day, that we never lost a single man by surprise, not a picquet or patrole has ever been taken, nor a man deserted or even tried by a Genl. Court Martial.'[57] So far as Vandeleur's own service with the regiment was concerned, this was actually true, for although a total of six men had deserted early on there had not been a single case since January 1812. Similarly, although there had been surprises early on, the 12th had quickly become adept in outpost work with only the action at Castel Piones during the siege of Burgos as a blot on an otherwise entirely creditable record. None of this had been achieved without casualties, of course, and a total of 180 officers and men had lost their lives, the great majority of them as a result of illness rather than enemy action. The losses in horses were even more staggering: 614 dead and a further 66 cast as unserviceable, which, when added to the 399 troop horses still on the strength at the war's end, meant that a total of 1,079 animals had been needed to mount a regiment whose strength in horses at any one time averaged a third of that number.[58]

The men of the 12th who had come back with the horses via Calais were first posted to Hounslow, where they were reviewed by the Duke of York, before proceeding to join the depot at Dorchester Barracks where the whole regiment was reunited and where they would remain until the following spring.[59] This was certainly pleasing to Steuart, who had earlier requested that Horse Guards bring them together at this location.[60] Even before the regiment was fully reassembled, though, orders had already been issued for the reduction of the regimental establishments, which cut the number of troops back from ten to eight, with the surplus men being discharged, surplus horses cast, and the most junior officers in each rank placed upon half-pay. Ordered on 12 August, this had largely been completed by the 25 August monthly return, which recorded the discharge of seven serjeants, two trumpeters, and 142 men. Remaining man-power was redistributed to create eight troops, all having a total rank and file strength of 62 or 63 men, although in terms of men present and fit for duty the discrepancies were rather larger, effective strengths ranging from 39 to 56 troopers.[61] Captains Patton and White had left the regiment to go on half-pay, as had Lieutenants Bertie, Lane, Hawkesley and Stanhope, but the two cornetcies that were lost in the reduction had never been filled in the first place.[62] As well as the six officers sent on enforced leave as a result of the reduction, a number of others sought the opportunity for one sort of absence or other during the course of 1814. Not all simply went home, however: Lieutenant Vandeleur spent some time in Flanders, where his cousin the major general had been given command of an infantry division in the small British army retained in the Low Countries until the peace settlement was finalized. Lieutenant Dowbiggen also spent some time in Flanders, whilst October saw Lieutenant Fulton detached from the regiment for service with the 19th Light Dragoons in Canada, thus making him the only member of the 12th to participate in the War of 1812.[63]

It may be inferred that the regiment took the opportunity provided by the reduction to get rid of its unfit men and bad characters. Certainly this was Steuart's intention when he informed the commanding officer that 'I have been applied to some time ago for the discharge of Corporal Wilmer of Capt. Barton's Troop, I fancy that he would be no material loss to the Regt. if so I should not be sorry to get his discharge at the expected Reduction.'[64] As a result, the 12th received a favourable report when they were inspected in December 1814, Major General Fane finding little to fault beyond the state of the horses – although the problem was not those animals that had returned from service in the Peninsula, but rather the last batch of remounts purchased before the peace – and the proficiency of the men at their riding. As a result of these points, Fane reported that he had expressed 'to Major Bridger his approbation of the general appearance of the 12th', going on to note that,

> The exertion that has been made for their re-equipment since they returned from foreign service is highly praiseworthy and creditable as also is the state of their interior œconomy. He thinks, however, that a little more attention to the grooming of the troop horses, would be advantageous to their condition. He recommends that assiduous attention should be paid to the riding of the regiment during the winter; as much improvement is practicable in that department.[65]

It was telling, however, that it was to Bridger that Fane's praise had been directed, and earlier in his report the general had remarked that 'The Commanding Officer of this Regiment being one of the Aides de Camp to His Royal Highness the Prince Regent has been but a very few days with his Corps since its return from Foreign Service. It has been commanded by Lieut. Colonel Blunden and Maj. Bridger chiefly by the latter.'

As well as his attendance on the Prince Regent, Ponsonby, like Blunden, was also frequently absent to attend Parliament, where he had served since 1806 as member for Kilkenny.[66] Unlike Blunden, he had put his military duties ahead of Parliamentary and other concerns so long as there was a war to be fought, but now that peace had returned it was time to take up his role as part of one of the nation's Whig political dynasties. However dashing and effective his wartime leadership, Ponsonby seems to have been satisfied to leave the peacetime drudgery of regimental soldiering to the reliable Bridger, intervening primarily during this period to indulge the request of the regiment's officers that the 12th might form a band. In this, he promptly incurred the ire of his colonel, who was already concerned that discipline was suffering now that peace had returned, and who saw such pandering to fashion as entirely counterproductive. In one of his first recorded letters to Ponsonby since the upset over the regimental appointments, Steuart gave a particularly pungent answer to the commanding officer's proposal:

> I am sorry you should think of giving way to the ill considered wishes of the officers of my Regiment, respecting a Band, I should prefer their taste for discipline to that for music, if a bad band may be so called. The first thing I did on getting the Regiment was to dismiss the Band they then had, and to destroy the instruments, the expense will be great but do as you like. I only object to the Trumpeters being made a part of the Band, so far as to take them from their respective Troops, and they must go along with them when the Regiment is dispersed in Cantonments.[67]

Soon, however, such matters would cease to be Steuart's concern, for his departure from the regiment to assume the colonelcy of the 2nd Dragoons was now imminent, being gazetted on 12 January 1815, and he formally took his leave of the 12th in a letter dated six days later.[68] His replacement as colonel was Lieutenant General Sir William Payne, who had briefly commanded the Peninsular cavalry during the 1809 campaign before returning home in early 1810. Prior to his command in the Peninsula Payne had also taken part in the Flanders campaign as a junior officer, but otherwise his service had been at home or in Ireland, his regimental duty having been with the 1st Royal Dragoons and then the 3rd Dragoon Guards. Although Payne was a heavy cavalryman by training, the heavy dragoon and dragoon guards regiments were amongst the most prestigious regimental colonelcies, and Payne had therefore been slowly working his way towards a more senior post by occupying a series of light dragoon colonelcies, beginning with his appointment to the 23rd in 1807. In 1814 he rose to the colonelcy of the 19th Light Dragoons, and then to the 12th on Steuart's removal to the 2nd Dragoons: he would eventually obtain the colonelcy of his former regiment, the 3rd Dragoon Guards, in 1825.[69] As might be inferred by his butterfly-like flitting from one regiment to another, Payne was far more typical of regimental colonels than had been his predecessor, viewing the appointment very much as a sinecure and source of prestige rather than as a duty. If he made any mark upon the 12th after replacing Steuart, there is certainly little record of it, and the regiment was therefore left to face the extreme challenges of the coming year without the watchful eye of its former chief to ensure all was as it should be.

Chapter X

Waterloo

FOR THOSE OFFICERS of the 12th Light Dragoons who remained with the regiment through the winter of 1814–15 – and there were not that many of them, the number dropping as low as thirteen in January 1815 – the main threat to their existence seemed to be boredom. William Hay, who had returned to regimental duty upon the termination of his appointment to Lord Dalhousie's staff, recorded that Dorchester 'was the most horrid, dull, stupid inland town I had ever known', and found peacetime barrack soldiering not at all to his taste.[1] Before 1815 was very old, however, the unsatisfactory nature of the peace settlement would provoke a series of events that would take the 12th away from quiet Dorchester and set them on the march again.

The first call, however, came in order to meet not a foreign foe but a domestic one, for the return of peace had served to precipitate something of an economic crisis, which, thanks to some badly received new legislation, saw the outbreak of substantial domestic unrest. The legislation in question was the Corn Law, intended to favour British farmers by fixing the price of grain and thereby keeping out cheap foreign imports. This was all very well for farmers and landowners, but disastrous for the urban poor who relied heavily on bread as a staple of their diet. In combination with the discharge of substantial numbers of men from the armed forces now that hostilities were at an end, the result was substantial urban unrest. Hay remarked that,

> bread was dear, and the restless disposition of the people became roused by the sudden change that had taken place, from a long and protracted war; symptoms of disturbance, in and about London, were the consequences. Troops were ordered to the neighbourhood and others to hold themselves in readiness to march for the metropolis; in the latter case was the 12th Light Dragoons, I for one was delighted at the prospect of breaking ground from Dorchester, be our destination where it would.[2]

Their destination, in fact, was not London – where a substantial number of troops had flooded the streets and largely put an end to any rumblings of dissent – but Berkshire. Towards the end of February – even the Registry of Services for once fails to give an exact date – the 12th were ordered to make a forced march from Dorchester to Reading. As had been the case in London, the arrival of troops in large numbers quelled any riotous tendencies, but the regiment remained in the area in order to keep the peace, having on 25 March four troops at Reading and two apiece at Maidenhead and Henley.[3] They were still there when news from the continent arrived of a threat altogether more serious than that posed by the agitators of London or Berkshire. Hay described how the regiment's officers were awaiting orders at the inn that had been adopted as their mess, and that when a coach-guard informed them that he brought news for them the assumption was that he had the route-orders to take the regiment back to barracks. In reply, the guard told them that he brought 'the route in earnest, old Bonny [*sic*] has broken out again and got to Paris', which electrifying intelligence was swiftly followed by the arrival of instructions from Horse Guards for four troops, each to be made up of seventy-five mounted and five dismounted troopers, be held in instant readiness to embark at Ramsgate for service on the continent.[4]

Such was the confusion inherent in the response to the news from France, that within a day the orders had been amended. Now six troops would go instead of four, forming three squadrons, but the mounted strength of these troops would be cut to only sixty rank and file.[5] Later still, the embarkation plans would be changed as well, so that the 12th marched first to Canterbury – where the depot was to remain – and then to Dover where they embarked at once for Ostend. Hay remarked in his memoirs that 'the news gave me the greatest satisfaction, as I had no liking for the life of a soldier in idleness,' and it was no doubt widely welcomed amongst the regiment's officers – in particular those who had been put on half-pay by the peacetime reductions, and who returned to duty when the old establishment of ten troops was restored on 5 April.[6]

Lieutenant Colonel Ponsonby assumed command of the regiment with Major Bridger as his second-in-command, along with fifteen troop officers and a commissioned staff comprising Paymaster Otway, Cornet and Adjutant Griffith, Surgeon Robinson, Assistant Surgeon Smith and Veterinary Surgeon Castley. Lieutenants Bertie and Lane joined from home the following month after being recalled from half-pay, and Captain Alexander Craufurd of the 2nd Ceylon Regiment joined the 12th as a volunteer so as to see action in the coming campaign.[7] The non-commissioned element bound for active service amounted to 27 serjeants, 3 trumpeters and 393 rank and file, with 398 troop horses – both figures giving totals rather in excess of the numbers that had actually been requested, and with no dismounted men. The downside of this extensive commitment was that once the sick and men on recruiting duty were accounted for, there were only sixty-six effective rank and file left at the depot, and a mere fifteen effective horses. Although emergency measures were set in motion to increase the strength, these, as we saw in Chapter III, did not take effect until hostilities had ended.[8]

Having landed at Ostend on 3 April, the regiment marched at once for Bruges, and then on the 6th to Ghent and finally two days later to Renaix.[9] There, on 20 April, they were reviewed by Wellington, himself newly arrived in the Low Countries, after which inspection Ponsonby issued the following regimental order:

> The Duke of Wellington has desired Colonel Ponsonby to express to the Regiment his approbation of their appearance this day, His Grace is happy at having again under his Orders a Regiment which was distinguished for its gallantry and discipline, he has no doubt if occasion offer they will continue to deserve his good approbation as on the former and he hopes every Man will feel a pride in endeavouring to support the credit of the Regiment in the latter.[10]

Wellington was no doubt pleased to have all the veteran troops that he could muster for his new campaign, but with a large portion of his old Peninsular infantry still on their way back from North America there was no chance of immediately re-creating the army that had dispersed from Bordeaux a year previously. Still, many of the cavalry regiments that had served in Spain and Portugal were available for the new campaign, giving the Duke a powerful body of mounted troops. However, there was a decided preponderance of light cavalry over heavy, and of the seven regiments of heavies that did deploy to Flanders only the 1st Royal Dragoons had seen any appreciable Peninsular service.

In all, Wellington would muster for this campaign twenty-one regiments of British and KGL cavalry, organized into seven brigades. These, along with a single brigade of Hanoverian cavalry, were formed into one large division which was, however, referred to as the Cavalry Corps. Independent of this was the Netherlands Cavalry Division with seven regiments in three brigades, and the Brunswick cavalry which was equivalent to another weak brigade. Wellington had hoped again to have Stapleton Cotton, now ennobled as Lord Combermere, to command his mounted troops. Instead, though, the post went to Lieutenant General the Earl of Uxbridge, who, as Lord Paget, had commanded Sir John Moore's cavalry in the Corunna campaign. A veteran cavalry officer, Uxbridge had been barred from returning to the Peninsula by the fact that he had outranked Wellington; however, since the latter had been made a Field Marshal after Vitoria, this restriction no longer applied and left Uxbridge free to serve in 1815.[11] As the officer who had commanded the original Hussar Brigade, and being colonel of the 7th Hussars whose uniform he habitually wore, the new chief of cavalry was naturally perceived to have a preference for the showier cousins of the light dragoons, and it was expected by officers of the 12th that Uxbridge would ensure that the hussars got all the glory of the coming campaign.[12]

If Uxbridge was an unknown quantity, the 12th at least had a familiar face as their brigadier. Although he had held an infantry command during the peace, the resumption of hostilities saw Major General Vandeleur return to cavalry service, and, in a nice touch, he was reunited with his old Peninsular brigade. What was more, the third regiment in the new Fourth Cavalry Brigade – a return having been made to distinguishing brigades numerically rather than by the name of their commander – was the 11th Light Dragoons, which although it had not served under Vandeleur before had been the brigade-mate of the 12th and 16th under Anson for the 1812 campaign.[13] Yet again, Lieutenant Vandeleur sought an appointment on the general's staff, and yet again his efforts got him nowhere. On this occasion the problem was the well-meaning intervention of Vandeleur's father, who wrote to the Duke of Wellington on the lieutenant's behalf but in doing so managed only to complicate matters, since he pre-empted any formal approach and the Major General in any case preferred not 'to be under an obligation to the Duke, and . . . will not condescend to ask a favour'. John Vandeleur would serve in the coming campaign as a troop officer.[14]

The Cavalry Corps was stationed in the villages around Ninove, fifteen miles west of Brussels, and was frequently brought together for reviews and field days. As well as providing a great spectacle, this enabled Uxbridge to assess, and where necessary work to improve, the efficiency of the regiments and brigades under his command, from which he ultimately expected 'every thing that can be attained by Discipline, Bravery, and a high sense of honor'.[15] As a rule, field days were held twice a week as April turned into May and the build-up of forces continued. However, whilst the field days concentrated on perfecting the manoeuvres that the cavalry would need in a clash on the battlefield, both Major

General Vandeleur and Lieutenant Colonel Ponsonby were acutely aware that the light cavalry would be required to perform outpost and reconnaissance work once the advance into France began, and a series of orders were issued to outline the responsibilities of all ranks in these situations. Covering the duties of orderlies and vedettes as well as larger formations, these orders included a standard form for the recording of any intelligence, warned against drunkenness and plundering, and in the case of Ponsonby's regimental orders concluded with a requirement that emphasized an obvious appreciation for the trustworthiness and the intelligence of the rank and file:

> It is hoped that the Non Commissioned Officers and Men will endeavour to get sufficiently acquainted with the French Language to ask questions and to understand the Answers – to describe places carefully, and in every respect to be alert and intelligent, as many of them were in the last Campaigns.[16]

As if further evidence were required, this was a statement that placed the troopers of the 12th at a far remove from the stereotypical 'scum of the earth' – truly, in Ponsonby's conception, the men of whom this was expected were clearly 'fine fellows'.

Notwithstanding the extensive social scene that had grown up around Brussels, with so much going on to prepare the army for the coming campaign many regimental officers found that they lacked the time and energy to do much beyond some localized sight-seeing, and this became more pronounced as the weather grew hotter until by early June the heat made for 'severe work'.[17] The bringing together of so many regiments did, however, make it easy to look up old comrades from the Peninsular days, or family acquaintances serving in other regiments, and young Vandeleur wrote home to his mother with an account of officers with whom he had dined whilst she, in turn, seems to have kept him informed of new arrivals whose company he might wish to cultivate. All in all, it was a peaceful, if busy, time, and even in mid-May, Vandeleur could tell his mother that, 'It is the report of the day that we are to have no fighting. The French are very quiet; I cannot conceive how it will end.'[18]

For the rank and file, the delights of Brussels remained beyond reach, but the local drink was cheap and there were inevitable courts martial for drunkenness. May 5th seems to have been marked by a particularly riotous session, as a result of which Privates Powers, Lyman and Harmsby all received the rare award of a flogging. Only Edward Powers, however, who had compounded his drunkenness by being 'Insolent to Serjeant Bull in the execution of his duty', received a heavy sentence. A month later, Powers – described as 'one of the worst characters in the whole army, but cool, determined, and brave to a fault' – would distinguish himself at Waterloo, taking prisoner three French cuirassiers and underlining as he did so the inherent contradictions in conduct that seem to have characterized many of Wellington's rank and file.[19] Harmsby, meanwhile, had his whole sentence of 100 lashes remitted, but on this occasion Ponsonby's well-intentioned desire to avoid corporal punishment may have been interpreted as weakness, since within a week Harmsby was again on trial, this time 'For irregular conduct in being drunk and rioting in his quarters on the night of the 11th inst and making his escape from Serjt. Payne when ordered by him to the Guard Room on the morning of the 12th inst.' This obtained him an award of 300 lashes, but again the sentence was ultimately remitted although not, perhaps, until Harmsby had been left to sweat a good while.[20]

The campaign that would culminate at Waterloo is perhaps the most written about of the whole Napoleonic Wars. Certainly, from the point of view of the 12th Light Dragoons, the historian has a far greater range of eyewitness accounts to draw upon than the fine but limited selection covering the regiment's time in the Peninsula. It is nevertheless important to place the actions of the 12th in the context of the wider campaign, and to fill in the background of events in order to make sense of the regiment's involvement in them. As part of the allied plan for a combined advance into France in the summer of 1815, two major forces had been assembled in the United Netherlands. One was the Anglo-Dutch-German army commanded by Wellington, 112,000 strong; the other was composed of 120,000 Prussians under Generalfeldmarschall Gebhard von Blücher. Ultimately these two armies would cooperate with an Austro-German army operating on the upper Rhine, with a Russian contingent moving up as a reserve. However, Napoleon had no intention of waiting to be over-whelmed and launched a pre-emptive attack in the hope of defeating the two enemy forces representing the most immediate threat. Concentrating the bulk of his available field forces in the 123,000-strong Armée du Nord, Napoleon opened his offensive at dawn on 15 June.[21]

Wellington's forces were deployed to the west of Blücher's, with the Brussels–Charleroi Road serving as a rough demarcation line. Napoleon, after crossing the border around Charleroi, pushed his forces up this road and in so doing gained the central position between the two allies. Wellington had anticipated potential attacks from the south as happened, or from the south-west through Mons, and had deployed his forces to meet either. However, a breakdown in his intelligence systems, and the speed of the French advance, left him famously 'humbugged' and by the time it was established that the Charleroi attack was Napoleon's main offensive, valuable time had been lost. Because Wellington was slow to assemble his forces Napoleon's opening gambit was successful, allowing him to concentrate against Blücher at Ligny on 16 June. Wellington hoped to come to his ally's aid but Marshal Ney, commanding the French left wing, had pushed up troops to threaten the vital crossroads of Quatre Bras where Wellington's line of march crossed the Brussels Road. The Prussians, with three of their four corps concentrated at Ligny, made a hard fight of it but were eventually overwhelmed and forced to retreat, whilst Wellington fought Ney to a standstill at Quatre Bras but, with his troops committed piecemeal as they arrived on the field, did so only at the cost of substantial casualties.

Ponsonby had been invited to the Duchess of Richmond's famous ball on the evening of the 15th, but having been alerted to news of skirmishing on the frontier had decided to remain with his regiment. This was wise, for at three in the morning on 16 June the 12th received orders to move out.[22] Stationed well to the north-west, the British cavalry had a hard march towards the sound of the guns as Wellington sought to concentrate his forces. Dawn saw the bulk of Uxbridge's command gathered at Enghien, a position from where the option still remained for them to move either south-east to reinforce the Prussians or south to meet an advance through Mons. There the horses were given a good feed, and the cavalry remained for the remainder of the morning as the infantry slogged through on their way to the front. In the afternoon, the regiments were again set in motion, moving through Braine-le-Comte towards Nivelles. Eventually, the shortage of mounted troops at Quatre Bras, where Wellington had fewer than 2,000 Netherlands and Brunswick cavalry on the field, required that the cavalry move forward more rapidly, but with the infantry still clogging the roads this required a more circuitous advance. Still a mile or so short of Nivelles, Vandeleur's three regiments were 'directed to separate and to be led through unfrequented paths by the commanding officer of each regiment, to meet at a given rendezvous, fixed on by the quartermaster-general'.[23]

Notwithstanding these exertions, however, the brigade did not reach the field of Quatre Bras until the fighting there had drawn to a close. Napoleon having called Ney's reserves away to Ligny, the French had been unable to carry the allied position and Wellington was now able to concentrate his forces around the crossroads. As the first British horsemen to arrive, the Fourth Cavalry Brigade was progressively shifted further to the left of the line to make room for more regiments as they came up, and thus much of the night was spent on the move. This did, however, give them a good chance to take a look at the field of battle, with Ponsonby taking the opportunity to satisfy his curiosity as to whether or not the steel breastplates worn by the French cuirassiers were bullet-proof. The British had never faced Napoleon's heavy cavalry before, these elite regiments never having been deployed against Wellington's troops in Spain, and their armour was an object of some speculation. Evidence from the field, however, served readily to demonstrate that, although impressive, the cuirasses would not stop a musket ball. As well as a series of moves that lasted at least until midnight when the final troops came in, the night was rendered more uncomfortable by the shortage of food – the troops having out-marched their supplies – and of water. Even after the brigade as a whole had settled down for what remained of the night, elements were required for picquet duty, and the outpost line was maintained through until dawn.[24]

Whereas the action at Quatre Bras had been trailing off towards dusk, the fighting at Ligny had continued into the darkness, as the defeated Prussians attempted to disengage. Matters were not helped by the fact that Blücher, having led a cavalry charge in person, had been unhorsed and was missing for some time, so that it was his chief of staff, Gneisenau, who organized the retreat. Distrustful of Wellington, whom he felt had betrayed the Prussians by failing to come to their aid on the 16th, Gneisenau was in no hurry to keep his ally informed of matters, so that the Prussians were well on their way to Wavre before Wellington gained an accurate appreciation of what had befallen them. Naturally, it was impossible for Wellington to remain at Quatre Bras with his left flank wide open, and once intelligence of the Prussian retreat was received, orders were swiftly given to pull the British and their allies back to the ridge of Mont St-Jean. This was as an excellent defensive position, but it meant a with-drawal of nine miles. To cover the infantry and guns, Uxbridge was ordered to remain at Quatre Bras until the rest of the army was safely away, and then form a rear-guard for the retreat. Thankfully, the French had suffered considerable losses in the fighting on the 16th, as well as some dislocation of command structures, so that it was late in the morning before Napoleon had his troops in motion: Marshal Grouchy was to go after the Prussians, whilst the Emperor turned on Wellington in person.

Once the infantry and foot artillery were safely away, Wellington left Uxbridge to handle the rear-guard, something the latter subsequently described as 'the prettiest Field Day of Cavalry and Horse Artillery that I ever witnessed'.[25] As the infantry filed off, the cavalry were pulled in until Uxbridge had them arrayed in three lines, his favourite hussars to the fore, the two brigades of heavies in the second line, and the remaining brigades in support. Around two in the afternoon, in the shadow of an impending downpour, the massed French cavalry at last moved forwards to be met by the fire of the Royal Horse Artillery. As the rain finally came down, so the cavalry too began to retreat, but although the initial withdrawal of the reserve units was orderly, they soon found themselves pressed to go faster by those in their rear, who were in turn being pressed by the French. This was easier said than done, for the route assigned to Vandeleur's three regiments, and the hussars of Major General Vivian's Sixth Cavalry Brigade who followed them, ran well to the east of the Brussels Road, taking instead 'a narrow cross-country road, full of holes and of broad, deep ruts full of water from the recent rains'. The fresh downpour now turned the road surface into 'stiff, slippery clay' that impeded progress even further, so that many men were forced, with their mounts, off the roadway and into the ditches.[26] All in all, it was perhaps as well that the French had concentrated their advance up the Brussels Road, where a stiff fight developed around the village of Genappe, although the 12th did briefly come under fire from a Dutch artillery battery whose gunners took them for French *chasseurs à cheval*. Vivian's hussars, to the rear, were lightly engaged with the French, and some dissatisfaction was later expressed that the light dragoons had not turned to support their comrades. This, however, seems to have stemmed from a false expectation of what was wanted from the cavalry that day, and a misunderstanding in the hussar regiments as to what orders had been given to their supposed supports. In fact, Vandeleur's orders called for him to move his brigade swiftly across the River Dyle so as to clear the path for the hussars, and this – albeit with some delay by virtue of the appalling conditions underfoot – is what transpired.[27]

Once the allies were across the Dyle, the French pursuit petered out, as did the rain, and the cavalry were able to complete their withdrawal without further molestation and link up with the rest of Wellington's troops at the Mont St-Jean position. There the brigades of Vandeleur and Vivian remained on the left wing, deploying on the high ground immediately north of Papelotte. Much of the area was covered in standing corn, which, although trampled down in places where many troops had passed through, was for the most part at its full height. As Hay related, 'from the rain that had fallen and the height of the corn, it was like riding through a pond'. Accordingly, since the brigade was deployed along the line of an east–west road that intersected the Brussels Road just north of

La Haye Sainte, insofar as possible the three regiments were spread out along the road to keep them out of the fields. This, though, was only a relative improvement:

> As to lying down to rest, it was out of the question, as the road was knee deep in mud and water; consequently, the night was spent uncomfortably. We heard, the whole night long the moving of the French troops into position. Fires we had none, from lack of fuel, so the camps looked more dull than usual.

Hay, who furnished the above description, did eventually manage to get some sleep wrapped in his cloak, but on awakening found that he had 'sunk some six or eight inches deep in the water and clay'.[28]

There is neither the space nor the necessity to give any more than the briefest accounts of the dispositions at Waterloo, nor of the course of the battle as a whole, but a basic overview is required so as to understand the role that the 12th Light Dragoons would play. The bulk of Wellington's forces were deployed west of the Brussels Road, with that portion of the line to its east being held by the Fifth Division under Lieutenant General Sir Thomas Picton and the 2nd Netherlands Division under Lieutenant General Perponcher-Sedlnitzky, one of whose two brigades was thrown forward to cover Papelotte. Two brigades of the Sixth Division were deployed in support, and behind them, straddling the Brussels Road, were the two British heavy cavalry brigades and the Netherlands Cavalry Division. The brigades of Vandeleur and Vivian served to support the far left flank of this position, with Vandeleur the senior officer present. Off on the other side of the Brussels Road, the Third and First Divisions held the ridgeline as far as the Château of Hougoumont, supported by the Second Division and part of the Fourth; the rest of the cavalry, along with more Brunswick, Netherlandish and Nassau infantry, were in reserve on the reverse slope. Napoleon, for his part, had I Corps and IV Cavalry Corps in line east of the Brussels Road and II Corps and III Cavalry Corps to the west, with his remaining forces – VI Corps and the Imperial Guard – in reserve behind his centre. His plan called for a feint against Hougoumont and then a major attack east of the Brussels Road where the terrain was less favourable to the defenders. Wellington, who had elected to fight after receiving assurances that the regrouped Prussians were matching to his aid, planned for a defensive battle although – as he famously reminded Uxbridge – 'Bonaparte has not given me any idea of his projects: and as my plans will depend on his, how can you expect me to tell you what mine are?'[29]

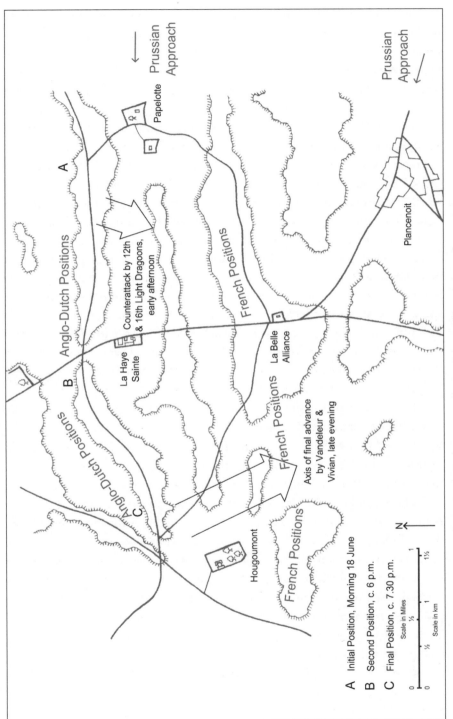

Map 6: The 12th Light Dragoons at Waterloo, 18 June 1815

Prussian Approach

Prussian Approach

Papelotte

Anglo-Dutch Positions

Counterattack by 12th
& 16th Light Dragoons,
early afternoon

French Positions

La Haye
Sainte

B

A

Anglo-Dutch positions

C

La Belle
Alliance

French Positions

French Positions

Axis of final advance
by Vandeleur &
Vivian, late evening

Plancenoit

Hougoumont

French Positions

N

A Initial Position, Morning 18 June

B Second Position, c. 6 p.m.

C Final Position, c. 7.30 p.m.

Scale in Miles

½   1   1½

Scale in km

0

½   1

0

Nevertheless, Wellington refused to dance to Napoleon's tune when the battle opened late in the morning of 18 June. The heavy rains had inconvenienced the French just as much as they had the allies, and it took time for their forces to get into position: in particular, the thick mud delayed the deployment of the French artillery. Eventually, a little before noon, elements of the French II Corps began the diversionary offensive against Hougoumont, but Wellington did not commit his reserves and the action in fact served to draw in additional French troops. Around 1.30 the French I Corps – commanded by Peninsular veteran d'Erlon, whose troops the 12th had faced at Villagarcia – moved forwards. D'Erlon's corps was composed of four infantry divisions, of which the central pair made the main assault whilst those on the flanks moved against the farm complexes of La Haye Sainte and Papelotte. Already in action, seeking to soften up the target, were the forty guns of d'Erlon's corps artillery, spaced out along the infantry lines. With cavalry also moving up in support it was a formidable, if unsophisticated, attack, and was aimed at what was probably the most vulnerable point in the allied lines. Not only did the defenders lack the cover that was available elsewhere on the battlefield, but three brigades facing the attack were depleted by casualties taken at Quatre Bras two days previously. Some battalions wavered, others were pushed back, but the line held long enough for Wellington to order Uxbridge to launch the two heavy cavalry brigades into a counterattack.

This was a key moment in the battle, for the initial charge successfully checked the advance and then sent the French reeling back. West of the Brussels Road, the Household troops of the First Cavalry Brigade swept aside two regiments of cuirassiers to crash into the French flanking infantry, whilst, to the east, Major General Sir William Ponsonby – cousin of the 12th's Frederick – led the Second Cavalry Brigade head on against d'Erlon's main body. With a regiment apiece from England, Ireland and Scotland – the last-named being the 2nd Dragoons or Scots Greys, of which Sir James Steuart was now colonel – Sir William's command was popularly known as the Union Brigade, but it did not remain united for long as the three regiments cut their own paths through the French infantry. Two eagles were taken, along with over 2,000 prisoners, and a good half of d'Erlon's infantry were knocked out of the fight. Then, however, rather than rallying, the victorious troopers continued their charge. Joined by elements of the Household regiments, they turned their attention to remaining French infantry and their artillery supports. The 2nd Dragoons over-ran some of the French artillery, cutting down the gunners, but were unable to spike or remove the cannon they had captured. As squadrons and regiments sought their own objectives, with some officers leading their men on whilst others sought to rally and re-form, the great charge finally stalled, leaving the best part of the two brigades badly dispersed and with their horses blown. Uxbridge, who had charged with the First Cavalry Brigade – perhaps unwisely given that his doing so left him now unable to exercise much in the way of overall control – sought to restore order, but to little avail. To the watchers on the heights – including Major General Vandeleur – it became worryingly apparent that, having charged so far into the valley between the French and allied lines, with substantial bodies of French infantry still unbroken and the French cavalry moving up for a counter-charge, the British heavies were now fatally exposed. Subsequent events would see the 12th Light Dragoons hurled into the maelstrom as Vandeleur sought to avert the looming disaster.

Inevitably, conflicting accounts make an exact chronology of Vandeleur's intervention in the fighting hard to reconstruct. There is also some debate over exactly what orders he and Vivian had received, and the extent to which they may or may not have exceeded them. Certainly, Wellington did not approve of any movement that took place without orders, as events in the aftermath of Vitoria had made clear, but on this occasion Uxbridge had given the two brigade commanders discretion 'to engage the enemy whenever they could do so with advantage without waiting for orders'. This rather calls into question the account of the Prussian Generalmajor Karl von Müffling, who claims that neither commander would take his brigade into action without orders for fear of prosecution, although Vandeleur's account does confirm that the only other order which was received was to close up with the infantry. Writing two decades after the fact, he could not recall if this order came from Uxbridge or Wellington, but in either case its intent was purely defensive, making it implicit that when Vandeleur did order a charge, it was on his own initiative.[30]

Inevitably, once the action commenced in earnest, the different impressions of those involved were necessarily focussed on their own activities, and at times are often wildly contradictory. Siborne's collected *Waterloo Letters* mean that we can add the recollections of Captain Barton of the 12th, Major General Vandeleur and several officers of the 11th and 16th to the usual suspects whose recollections have illuminated the battles of the Peninsula. On some points, it is clear to see where an eyewitness writing well after the fact has made an error – Hay, for example, asserts that Vandeleur's charge took place *before* that of the heavies, which makes a nonsense of its whole *raison d'être* – but even by discounting such anomalies there is an inevitable element of synthesis in the following narrative, which attempts as far as possible to reconcile all accounts.[31]

Undoubtedly, the decision to commit the Fourth Cavalry Brigade to the action was the correct one. Not only was the British heavy cavalry hard pressed, but since the heavies, in falling back, had masked the left-front of the British infantry, Vandeleur's light dragoons were the only troops immediately available to intervene. Furthermore, they were ideally positioned to clear a route by which the surviving heavy cavalry might withdraw. Nevertheless, the general was determined not to make the same mistake that had led to the discomfiture of the heavies and thus committed only the 12th and 16th Light Dragoons to the charge, holding back the 11th as supports. Still, on such a crowded battlefield, it was necessary to judge matters to perfection, as the timing and direction of the charge created a multi-dimensional puzzle to be solved. Vandeleur considered 'that it was impossible to form a line perpendicular to the Enemy's flank in order to charge him in flank perpendicularly without exposing the left of the Brigade to a flank attack by a part of the Enemy's Column. The two regiments were therefore ordered, "Squadrons Right half wheel, charge".'[32] The 'Column' to which the general referred was most likely the 85eme Ligne, which had been assigned to cover the right flank of the French gun-line: the regiment was part of the French 4eme Division, the remainder of which had been involved in the attack on Papelotte and had therefore avoided the attention of the British heavy cavalry. As the left-hand of Vandeleur's two attacking regiments, the 12th were directly threatened by the presence of this body of infantry, and this would have a considerable impact on their involvement in the charge. Apparently unsuspected by the British, the French infantry were supported by the 3eme Chasseurs à Cheval, a squadron of which was already engaged with the British heavies.

Vandeleur had earlier given his brigade the order to dismount so as to avoid the 'overs' from the French artillery that were reaching their position, but the men now swiftly returned to the saddle. Because of the nature of the terrain, it was simply not possible to make a direct charge from the brigade's start-line, and it was first necessary to cross an intervening 'ravine' – in fact one of the sunken lanes that cut across the field – before the two regiments could form up. Having already been ordered to close on the infantry, Vandeleur brought his brigade almost up to the positions held by the Fifth Division, requiring Major General Pack, commanding the Ninth Brigade, to risk his life in stopping his rattled infantry opening fire on the allied horsemen.[33] By the time these moves were complete, the left-most squadron of the 12th was only eighty yards from the unbroken French infantry of the 4eme Division, which had formed square in response to the threat posed by the allied cavalry; furthermore, having led the way across the lane, the 12th were some distance ahead of the 16th, which in turn contributed to the eventual separation of the regiments once the charge began.

Having been dismounted beyond the crest of the allied position, the regimental officers did not benefit from the overview of events that had been available to their brigade commander, and some at least were not aware of the presence of French cavalry in the dead ground of the valley floor. On the far left of the brigade, Hay naturally assumed that their objective was the French infantry immediately off to his left, notwithstanding that these were already in square. On hearing the command to move forwards, he immediately turned his troop in that direction,

> and in a moment would have dashed at the square next me, when I heard called out to me '*Not* that, *not* that, Hay!' I then, for the first time discovered just in our front were moving over the flat ground several squadrons of French cavalry.[34]

Although they did not charge this body of infantry, the left squadron of the 12th nevertheless rode so close past the flank of the formation that they came under fire as they did so, whilst forcing the French skirmishers to beat a hasty retreat. Meanwhile, the centre and right squadrons also found infantry in their path, but these were broken troops of the 46eme Ligne, one of the regiments driven back by the initial charge of the heavy cavalry, who were now charged for a second time as the 12th crashed through their disordered ranks.[35] The left-hand squadron of the 16th may also have engaged the French infantry at this point; certainly something separated it from the other two squadrons of that regiment, creating space for a large body of survivors from the 2nd Dragoons to retire through the gap. Several eyewitnesses with the 12th came out of the action believing that only one squadron of the 16th had charged with them, but in fact their sister-regiment was fully engaged and charged the French cavalry head-on whilst the centre and right squadrons of the 12th caught them in the flank.

In conjunction with two regiments of Netherlands light cavalry which also counter-charged the French horsemen, Vandeleur's intervention helped secure the retreat of the survivors of the Union Brigade. However, it also exposed the charging regiments to counterattack, and the 12th, being on the exposed left flank, were left particularly vulnerable. Two squadrons of the 3eme Chasseurs à Cheval had thus far remained unengaged, and now caught the British in the flank. With a roughly two-to-one numerical advantage, and the benefit of striking a flank, the French got the better of the clash – interestingly, too, Hay claims that the French had the advantage of being on heavier horses, which is rather at odds with those secondary sources suggesting that the French cavalry were badly mounted in this campaign. It is possible that elements of the 3eme and 4eme Lanciers were also engaged at this point, but it seems more likely that these two regiments – which did considerable execution against the retiring heavies – were committed further to the west. It is most likely that those men of the 12th who were engaged with lancers came from the right and centre squadrons: so far as the left squadron is concerned, Hay is definite that its assailants were chasseurs, and Ponsonby also specifies chasseurs in one of his accounts.[36]

Whoever the French cavalry were, this engagement – apparently broken off by mutual consent, for it took place in a no-man's land under crossfire from both sides – separated the left squadron from the rest of the 12th, and Ponsonby ordered it to fall back and rally on the infantry whilst he re-formed the remainder of the regiment. Vandeleur had ordered that neither the 12th nor the 16th push far into the valley, but the exhilaration of the charge, and a succession of targets, meant that things had got rather out of hand. Ponsonby realized this, and sought to restore order, but he had no sooner ridden after the centre squadron when he was attacked by a French cavalryman and wounded in both arms by sabre cuts, following which 'my horse sprung forward and carried me to the rising ground on the right of the French position, where I was knocked off my Horse by a blow to the head'.[37] Bereft of direction, the rest of the 12th continued their charge and crossed the low ground to the opposite crest where stood the abandoned guns that had earlier been captured by the 2nd Dragoons. Having pushed this far, these three squadrons – the left squadron of the 16th having also apparently remained with them – found themselves at the mercy of the French lancers, and were roughly handled before they could extricate themselves. In this, they were aided by the fact that the 11th Light Dragoons, and Vivian's three hussar regiments, were available to support them, and also by the oft-ignored intervention of the Netherlands Cavalry Division.

Although Vandeleur's charge fully achieved its objective of relieving the pressure on the heavy cavalry and facilitating their withdrawal, it did so only with heavy losses. These, in no small part, were caused by the fact that a large portion of the brigade – at the least, two squadrons of the 12th and one of the 16th – charged further than had been anticipated. Tomkinson wrote that there was

. . . difficulty in preventing the men of the 16th from attacking in small bodies, after the charge, those parties of the enemy which had pursued the 2nd [Union] brigade. Had they done this, we should have got into the same scrape; at least, we could not have covered the retreat of the others, but must have retired to form ourselves.[38]

Like the 12th, the 16th lost their commanding officer in the charge, so to an extent a lack of leadership added to the confusion, but the 16th had the brigade commander with them to give direction, and, being closer to their supports, came off in better order than the 12th. Ponsonby, at the point of his being wounded, was on his way to restore order to the centre and right squadrons of his regiment, having already given orders for the battered left squadron to withdraw and re-form, but he freely admitted that the other two squadrons had charged too far.

Writing two decades after the battle, Ponsonby gave historian William Siborne a reasoned account of why events had panned out as they did:

A good many men fell on the crest of the French position. I know we ought not to have been there, and that we fell into the same error which we went down to correct, but I believe that this is an error almost inevitable after a successful charge, and it must always depend upon the steadiness of good support to prevent serious consequences. In a great battle the support is at hand, and I am therefore firmly of opinion that although we sustained a greater loss than we should have done if our Squadrons had remained compact, the Enemy suffered a greater loss, was thrown into more confusion, and required more time to re-establish order, than if greater regularity had been preserved.[39]

This, then, was no brainless galloping with nothing held in reserve, but a calculated risk by a first-line commander who knew himself to be well supported. It should also be remembered that the 12th charged into a fluid and fast-moving battle, fought over rolling ground that concealed large bodies of the enemy. Inevitably, the regiment became broken up, and with substantial casualties amongst its officers it is hardly to be wondered that not all elements remained under control. If it is possible to make any charge of indiscipline, it needs to be directed at the junior officers who were keen to charge anything in front of them – even, in Hay's case, a steady square of French infantry. Then again, though, those junior officers were unaware of their actual objective in the first place, as an unfortunate but inevitable consequence of the speed with which Vandeleur had been compelled to throw his brigade into action. Ponsonby, though ending up well to the fore, had been carried there whilst trying to restore order, and his reputation certainly did not suffer for his conduct. Tomkinson – a great critic of any senior officer he considered to have erred – retained unaltered his opinion that Ponsonby was 'one of the best officers in the service', whose services in command of cavalry would be most desirable in any future war.[40]

For the time being, though, Lieutenant Colonel Ponsonby was lost and feared dead, and it was Captain Stawell who rallied what was left of the 12th as the brigade re-formed. Major Bridger was alive but unhorsed, and it was a little while before he was able to procure himself a replacement mount and re-join the regiment, of which he then assumed command.[41] There were not many of them, so much so that it was only possible to form two weak squadrons from the residue of the three strong ones that had gone into action – the one mustered 24 files and the other 23, for a total of 94 troopers still in the saddle. This represented a huge reduction from the 310 rank and file present when the battle opened, but in reality many of those missing were just that – missing – and would re-join once they had found their way back to the regiment, or procured a new mount to replace one lost or lamed in the charge.[42] Nevertheless, the 12th had suffered severely, with casualties for the day as a whole amounting to 2 officers, 6 serjeants and 39 troopers killed and 3 officers, 3 serjeants and 55 troopers wounded. The majority of these losses were sustained during the charge and its aftermath. Lieutenant Lindsey Bertie and Cornet John Lockhart were dead, and Ponsonby and Captain Edwin Sandys were both feared so, only to be later brought in horribly wounded: Lieutenant Dowbiggen was less severely injured.[43] Ninety troop horses were lost, and at least two dogs also charged with the regiment and failed to return. One was Lieutenant Hay's setter, Dash, who had been left with the baggage but had escaped from the care of Hay's servant and followed his master into battle only to be killed by a musket shot. Dash was a recent present from Hay's father, but Hay remembered the death at the same time of 'another dog that had attended the troop to which I was attached, [which] had followed the 12th from the regiment's landing in Lisbon, in 1811, and was present in all the actions and during the several campaigns in the Peninsula'.[44]

There was, at least, plenty of time for Bridger to get the regiment back together, since once the last of the allied cavalry had extricated itself from the valley both sides concentrated on re-forming their lines and restoring some sort of order. Although it had taken the commitment of almost half of Wellington's cavalry to achieve it, d'Erlon's attack had been comprehensively defeated, and the scope for French offensive action east of the Brussels Road neutralized. Already aware that the Prussians were on the march, Napoleon shifted his right wing to a defensive stance, moving reserve infantry formations eastwards and extending his lines southwards from Papelotte to cover his flank. Meanwhile, the French offensive shifted west of the Brussels Road, where a series of cavalry charges pinned much of Wellington's centre in square but, without infantry support, failed to make any gains. All the while, though, the French artillery remained in action, and there was a steady closing to the right as allied units shortened their fronts to fill the gaps caused by casualties. By early evening, although the brigades of Vandeleur and Vivian remained on the far left of Wellington's line, their position had shifted so that they were now on the ground where Picton's infantry had stood at the beginning of the day. There they remained as the Prussian reinforcements were drawn into a grinding street-fight in the village of Plancenoit and the French infantry, having regrouped, at last drove the defenders from La Haye Sainte. With the Imperial Guard forming up for a final French attack, this marked the crisis point of the battle.

By this stage in the fighting, between six and seven in the evening and with the Prussians already on the field, orders had already been given for all Wellington's remaining cavalry to concentrate in the centre and help hold the line along the ridge west of the Brussels Road. Of Vandeleur's three regiments, only the 11th Light Dragoons was still fresh, and so the brigade was posted to support Vivian's three hussar regiments, which had seen no action this day. The two brigades were initially sited immediately west of the Brussels Road, but were subsequently moved again to the right of Wellington's line, above Hougoumont. Their role, which the other cavalry brigades had been performing throughout the afternoon, was to support any portion of the infantry line that seemed to be wavering, but in the event, although the attack of the Imperial Guard came in places very close to success, the infantry held their ground and the guardsmen were stopped in their tracks. With the Prussians having taken Plancenoit and on the point of breaking through at Papelotte, it was clearly all over for the French, and all that remained was for a pursuit to turn the defeat into a rout.

With a wave of his hat, Wellington ordered his whole line to advance, and such of the cavalry who were still fit and mounted spurred forwards into the midst of the broken French. As the Imperial Guard fell back, the whole of the troops behind them also crumbled, so that, as Hay related, 'we actually rode over the flying masses, who had nearly all thrown down their arms, the difficulty being to get our horses over the heaps of dying and dead'.[45] Captain Barton was even more vivid in his description of the ground immediately in front of that section of the line held by Major General Maitland's brigade of Foot Guards, which had been charged over by the French cavalry during the afternoon, and where the main attack of the Imperial Guard had been repulsed, writing that 'bodies were lying so close to each other that our horses could scarcely advance without trampling on them, and a great many were wounded in the fetlocks from the bayonets and other weapons that were scattered about on the field'.[46] Barton was unsure, what with the smoke and gathering dusk, which side the brigade passed of the Hougoumont farm complex; however, he believed that they had remained east of it, which fits with having advanced from a position in the rear of the British Foot Guards.

Initially the lead role in the pursuit was taken by the three fresh hussar regiments of Vivian's Sixth Cavalry Brigade. However, being deployed to the left of Vandeleur's light dragoons, who were on the far right of the advancing line, the hussars were more heavily engaged and eventually Vandeleur took the lead. The Earl of Uxbridge had been badly wounded during the crisis of the battle, leaving Vandeleur in command of all the allied cavalry whilst Lieutenant Colonel James Sleigh of the 11th assumed command of his brigade. Although Vandeleur remained with his own brigade and did little at this late stage in the day to exert any wider control, he was evidently disinclined to have his new authority questioned, and there seems to have been some dispute between Vandeleur and Vivian at this point. Isolated infantry and cavalry – the latter including the Grenadiers à Cheval of the Imperial Guard – attempted to delay the allied pursuit by presenting a bold front, and much of the French artillery remained in action for as long as possible, with the 11th Light Dragoons over-running one of the last batteries to be silenced. For the 12th, confined to a supporting role by their lack of numbers even after their brigade took over the lead, the pursuit mostly entailed picking up prisoners from the broken French regiments, many of whom, like the staff officer who yielded his sword to Lieutenant Hay, were seemingly all too pleased to enter the safety of captivity. At length, when darkness prevented any further pursuit, the advance was halted, only for a final alarm when the 1st KGL Hussars, having become separated from Vivian's other two regiments, loomed up suddenly from the rear and were momentarily taken for a French unit.[47]

After nightfall, the Prussians continued the pursuit while Wellington's battered forces rested and began to secure the battlefield. This allowed the rounding-up of men and horses who had become separated during the fighting, as well as the recovery of those men who had been left wounded on the battlefield. Lieutenant Hay received the former task – albeit with ill grace, since it meant a journey well to the rear to search out skulkers as far back as Brussels – whilst Lieutenant Vandeleur took it upon himself to search for the regiment's missing commanding officer. Ponsonby was assumed to be dead, but Vandeleur 'asked leave to go look for his body among the dead; every body said I would never find it, but I was determined to find him, and I did, but he was nearly dead. I took a canteen of water with me, which revived him a little.'[48]

Ponsonby's ordeal is one of the epics of Waterloo, and he himself gave several accounts of what befell him. It will be recalled that, whilst in the act of rallying the regiment after its charge, he was first cut about the arms and then knocked unconscious. When he recovered his senses – which cannot have been long after, as he recalled still seeing soldiers of the 12th in the valley across which the regiment had charged – he unfortunately attracted the attentions of a French lancer who stabbed him in the back, penetrating his lungs and rendering it difficult for him to breathe. Thereafter, the French infantry reoccupied the position, and the luckless Ponsonby was successively plundered, given brandy by an officer who also propped him up on a knapsack but could not arrange his evacuation, and used for cover by 'a young Tirailleur who fired over me [and] talked the whole time always observing that he had killed a man with every shot he fired'. The French, at length, were driven off, but Ponsonby's ordeal was still not over as he now found himself ridden over by a squadron of Prussian cavalry, and then plundered a second time by his supposed allies. Eventually a British soldier found him, and kept him company through the night but could provide no water to assuage his raging thirst. Only when it became light was he discovered by a trooper of the 11th, who in turn alerted Lieutenant Vandeleur to his presence.[49]

Ponsonby's was a horrific ordeal, from which he was incredibly lucky to recover, but it is only fair to say that his was only one amongst thousands of similar stories, many of which lacked the happy ending of rescue and recovery. Captain Sandys, it will be recalled, had, like Ponsonby, been left for dead on the field. Commanding the centre squadron of the 12th, Sandys had charged into the heart of the French positions only to be cut down by multiple wounds to the body. Eventually picked up, he was taken to Brussels where Hay, in the course of rousting out stragglers and checking on the regiment's wounded, found him on 21 June. Sandys 'complained bitterly of not receiving attention from any medical man', and asked Hay to find him a doctor. This Hay was eventually able to do, but his search revealed to him the horrors of the army's general hospitals where the overworked surgical staff were swamped by the sheer volume of casualties. Eventually, however, a doctor was located:

> Accompanied by him I returned to poor Sand[y]s, who said, on my going into his room: 'Oh! I am so sorry I gave you the trouble, I feel much better, all the pain has left me, I suffer only from coldness in my feet.' I retired to let the doctor look at his wound, who, after a few minutes, followed me, saying: 'I regret to say your friend cannot live many hours, mortification has set in, and his sufferings will soon be at an end.' His words were only too true, at 8 p.m. he breathed his last.[50]

Of course, although Waterloo was a crushing and decisive victory, the battle did not, in itself, bring about an instant end to the war. Marshal Grouchy, who had been engaged with the Prussian left wing at Wavre, still had his forces in good order and was able to extricate them successfully once he received news of his Emperor's defeat, whilst Soult, whose talents had been rather wasted as Napoleon's chief of staff, helped rally the survivors of Waterloo. With Napoleon having hurried back to Paris in an attempt to regain his political credibility and raise fresh forces, an advance into France was still necessary to bring matters to a close. That said, it was also imperative that the allied forces reorganize themselves after four days of hard fighting, and any advance would necessarily require the reduction of the French border fortresses. Thus, for the 12th, the two days immediately after the battle were spent resting at Nivelles before moving to Malplaquet on the 21st and then to Pommenal the day after, where there was another halt. Only on 25 June did the advance begin in earnest, but after that there was only a single day of rest until the allies entered Paris. This delay allowed the 12th time to recover their strength, so that although the end of the day at Waterloo had seen fewer than a hundred men still in the saddle, the monthly return completed on the day that they left Pommenal showed 20 officers, 31 serjeants, 3 trumpeters, 6 farriers and 215 effective rank and file, with 240 troop horses.[51]

Although the 12th saw no sign of the enemy as they rode southwards, the march on Paris was not without its problems. A higher-than-normal incidence of indiscipline in the weeks prior to Waterloo has already been noted, and this seems to have continued in the aftermath of the battle. It is possible that this may, in part, have been down to the poor performance of Bridger in his first days as commanding officer, with Hay insinuating that the major was drinking heavily during this time.[52] If true – and, as we have seen, Hay's gossipy memoirs cannot always been relied upon – this must surely have been a reaction to the shock of combat rather than a long-term problem, for it receives no further mention and indeed Bridger was praised in the regiment's next inspection and would receive a brevet to lieutenant colonel as a reward for his services at Waterloo. If the case against the new commanding officer must therefore rest as unproven, the same cannot be said for those under his command. Records indicate nine courts martial during the six weeks following Waterloo, with drunkenness at the root of most of them, and this continued to be a problem after the peace, although it was then attributed to the regiment being in dispersed quarters and away from the supervision of its officers.[53]

If the British troops were at times indisciplined, however, their Prussian allies were far worse, and – as in the south of France the previous year – the British troops were generally well received. It was still felt that another battle would be needed before Napoleon was finally brought down – Lieutenant Vandeleur, writing on 1 July, was expecting an assault on Montmartre and Saint-Denis the next morning, once the infantry were up[54] – but in fact military operations were now being swiftly overtaken by political considerations. With Wellington's army to the north of Paris and Blücher's moving round to take the city from the south, it was clear that the French capital could not be held. The French were still full of fight – especially against the hated Prussians, who were given a bloody nose at Versailles on 1 July – but by then Napoleon had already fled, and negotiations were under way for the return of the Bourbons. On 4 July a convention was concluded with the defenders, and two days later, after the French forces had evacuated Paris preparatory to withdrawing beyond the Loire, the first allied troops marched in. For the 12th, this initially meant duty in the Champs Elysées, followed by bivouacking in the Bois de Boulogne; on 24 July they were back on the Champs Elysées for a review by the Emperor of Russia, before at the end of the month marching north to take up cantonments in Normandy. This move marked an end to active campaigning, and the start of a three-year stint as part of the Army of Occupation that remained in France to secure the peace that had been won.[55]

Epilogue

ALTHOUGH THEY DID NOT RETURN to England until November 1818, the departure of the 12th Light Dragoons from Paris marked the end of their active campaigning service. Occupation duties, for which the regiment formed part of Major General Vivian's Second Cavalry Brigade along with the 18th Hussars,[1] were really more akin to peacetime service. There was, however, some difficulty in persuading the men of the regiment that their former enemies were now their friends, and that the old attitude that 'to hit or shoot a Frenchman was of little moment' no longer applied.[2] For the officers, duty was light and only socializing and shooting parties – the targets now quail rather than Frenchmen – served to alleviate the boredom. Boredom, too, may perhaps have contributed to the unsavoury gambling incident that brought the career of Lieutenant Stanhope to an ignominious end at this time.

The only distraction came from periodic reviews, intended for the most part not so much to assess the military qualities of the regiments in question as to show them off to visiting dignitaries, although an exception may be made for that of 29 April 1816, held on the field of Agincourt, in which all ranks who had taken part in the campaign of 1815 received their Waterloo Medals.[3] The first medal to be awarded to all participants in an action, the Waterloo Medal would be supplemented, though not until 1847, by the issue of the Military General Service Medal, covering the whole of the Napoleonic Wars, for which clasps were awarded for the regiment's Peninsular War battles.[4] 'Waterloo' also became one of the regiment's battle honours, to be added to 'Peninsula' and 'Egypt'. Notwithstanding its contribution to many of Wellington's Peninsula victories, the 12th did not receive any specific battle honours for these actions, although 'Salamanca' was rather belatedly awarded in 1951. Vitoria, strangely, has never been granted even though the 12th was more heavily engaged in that action than at Salamanca. Most controversially Villagarcia, surely more deserved than Salamanca or Vitoria, was rather controversially not deemed a significant enough fight to warrant a battle honour at all.[5] Officers and men who lived long enough to claim the Military General Service Medal were, however, entitled to claim clasps for both Salamanca and Vitoria as well as for the Nive and Nivelle and, for the real veterans, Egypt.

Frequent reviews of each other's forces, along with shared occupation duties, helped introduce the British Army more closely to the military ideas of other nations, which would soon be reflected in a change in the armament of the British cavalry that would have significant consequences for the 12th. After extremely limited use earlier in the eighteenth century, the lance had been reintroduced to Western Europe largely by the diaspora of Polish soldiers after the successive partitions of that country, becoming increasingly fashionable. Austria had *Uhlan* regiments composed of men from its own Polish territories, but it was in France where the concept truly established itself so that Napoleon ultimately fielded nine regiments of line lancers, and two more as part of his Imperial Guard. Other nations followed suit, and Britain was in fact rather behind the times in its adoption of the concept, which was eventually pushed forwards on the initiative of Major R. H. de Montmorency, who had been some years a prisoner in France and had there become acquainted with the drills and tactics employed by Napoleon's lancers. After some experimentation, the 9th, 12th, 16th, 19th and 23rd Light Dragoons were selected for conversion to lancers and notified by order of 28 September 1816. A party from each regiment was sent to the Cavalry Riding Establishment at Pimlico to receive instruction in the new drills, that from the 12th being under the command of Lieutenant Vandeleur, with the trained men then returning to help instruct the rest of the regiment. Initially the conversion was indicated by the cumbersome designation of 12th Light Dragoons (Lancers), but in March 1817 the regiment formally became the 12th (Prince of Wales's Royal) Lancers.[6]

Although the conversion was accompanied by an exotic new uniform, with Cossack-style trousers and a lance cap styled after the Polish *czapka*, and the facings changed from yellow to scarlet, it would take rather longer for the practical aspects of the transformation to take effect. The lances originally issued were long and unwieldy, and it would not be for be some years, and much experimentation, that a suitable pattern would be agreed upon.[7] In part, this problem may well be why Major General Vivian reported in April 1817 that at least a hundred of the regiment's troopers were lacking in sufficient size and strength to make proficient lancers. As with sword training, the lance exercises were practised on foot until the trooper was sufficiently competent to carry them out on horseback, and this lengthy process – made worse by the fact that the regiment was in dispersed cantonments – suggested to Vivian that it would be some time before the regiment would be fit to take the field. Occupation duties and lance training, he felt, were mutually incompatible.[8] Vivian's comments about the size and strength of the men raised an interesting point, for the lance was essentially a shock weapon optimized for use on the battlefield, so that conversion took light dragoons and made them into something more akin to medium cavalry. Although the lance was fashionable it already had its detractors as well, who pointed out that in anything other than the charge it had un-doubted weaknesses. Thus, its increasingly widespread adoption by the British Army through the nineteenth century represents a worrying fixation on that single aspect of the cavalry role, at the expense of the outpost, reconnaissance and skirmishing work that had been the mainstay of Peninsular War light cavalry service.

Such debates on cavalry doctrine and armament, which would continue in one form or another until the 1904 issue of infantry-pattern rifles merged all existing roles to create a true all-purpose cavalry, were for the most part still in the future when Sir Hussey Vivian raised his concerns over the 12th. Despite the general's worry that its presence in France obstructed the new training regime, the regiment remained overseas – albeit increasingly reduced in numbers as peacetime retrenchment kicked in – until the Army of Occupation was finally withdrawn. Thereafter, it settled into a largely uninterrupted run of peacetime service, broken only by the detachment of two squadrons to Portugal in 1826 as part of an ill-fated attempt to intervene in that country's looming civil war. Inevitably, as time went on and promotion, retirement and death took their toll, the figures who have peopled this history faded out of the regiment's story.

Sir James Steuart, of course, had already left, but he remained in harness as colonel of the 2nd Dragoons until his death in 1839, by which time he was the oldest and longest-serving soldier in the British Army.[9] Robert Browne, the first of the regiment's two Napoleonic commanding officers, did not rise quite so far, but nevertheless was a lieutenant general when he died in 1845. Having married the heiress Henrietta Clayton in 1803 he later adopted the surname Browne-Clayton, but his most significant contribution in later life seems to have been the erection of a monumental column to the Egyptian Campaign in the ground of his estate at Carrigadaggan Hill, County Wexford.[10] Frederick Ponsonby, meanwhile, took some time to recover from his Waterloo wounds, but eventually returned to regimental duty. He subsequently commanded troops in the Ionian Islands, and was promoted major general in 1825. Two years later he married Lady Emily Bathurst, with whom he would have six children, but remained on duty in the Mediterranean, moving on to be Governor of Malta from 1826 to 1835, during which time he received a knighthood. Having returned to England he died suddenly in January 1837, aged only fifty-three.[11]

Of the regiment's junior officers, James Bridger served as commanding officer whilst the 12th was on occupation duty, with Samson Stawell, who had been breveted major after Waterloo, as second-in-command. Stawell would later go on to command the regiment himself, as would Alexander Barton, who prior to receiving that appointment had commanded the two squadrons that went out to Portugal in 1826. John Vandeleur, meanwhile, rose only to major as a 12th Lancer, but would later, after a period on half-pay, go on to serve as commanding officer of the 10th Hussars from 1838 until his retirement in 1846. He married his widowed cousin Alice Stewart, née Vandeleur, with whom he had one son who was christened – perhaps inevitably as the Vandeleurs seem to have rivalled the Steuarts in lack of originality when it came to names – John Ormsby Vandeleur. John Vandeleur eventually died in 1864, with his collected letters being published by his family after his death.[12] His other namesake, the 12th's erstwhile brigadier, died in 1849 as a full general but saw no active service after Waterloo.

Whilst the fates of the regiment's officers are for the most part well-documented, those who served under them quickly fade from the historical record. Some, at least, were able to return to civilian life and make a success of themselves, as William Hay found when serving as Commissioner of the Metropolitan Police, a post to which he was appointed in 1840 some years after having left the Army as a captain. Inspecting the men of 'N' Division shortly after his appointment, Hay came across a familiar face in the ranks, and on asking the man's name confirmed that this was indeed the former Private Sackes who had served with him in the Peninsula. Sackes's appointment to the police had been on the recommendation of his old commanding officer, Frederick Ponsonby. By the time Hay penned his memoirs, Sackes had retired on a Police pension; Hay, for his part, remained in office until his death in 1855.[13]

As was stated in the Introduction, part of the genesis of this work was a desire to test, through the case study of a single regiment, the ideas about the regimental system that I had earlier presented in my first book, *Sickness, Suffering, and the Sword*. Inevitably, some of these themes fitted more closely than others to the story of the 12th Light Dragoons, but all the major points that I developed are reflected at least in part. Among these it is very apparent that varied results came about from the decentralization of administration from Horse Guards to the individual regiments and their colonels. Because Steuart was more diligent than most colonels, the 12th Light Dragoons was able to benefit from a well-organized system of recruiting and procurement of remount horses that kept it up to strength and in the field until the war's end. It was a near-run thing, to be certain, but in this the experience of the 12th was more or less typical of the British Army as a whole, which was stretched far too thin by the end of 1813, and which had arguably not fully recovered even by the time of Waterloo. However, the 12th was affected by delays and penny-pinching – the latter seen on Steuart's part as well as that of the Board of Claims that refused to reimburse him for his expenditure in making up the Egyptian short-falls – so far as their supply of accoutrements and clothing was concerned. Conflict also occurred, as we have seen, over officer appointments and pro-motions, although here the problem was in fact one of a colonel desiring less centralization and more independence. Steuart was not alone in thus attempting to recover lost privileges, but if he annoyed Horse Guards with his demands he at least did not go so far as the Duke of Northumberland, who in 1813 resigned the colonelcy of the Royal Horse Guards when he was refused sole control over commissions in his regiment.[14]

Following on from and directly linked to the issue of decentralization of administration, I also argued for the value of the tightly focused regimental identities that were forged as a result of the experiences of individual units. This, I suggested, could often serve to compensate for the problems caused for some units by decentralized administration, and although the 12th suffered comparatively little from this problem under Steuart's colonelcy the regiment certainly did acquire a reputation and identity of its own during the Napoleonic era, reflected in, amongst other things, its first nickname and the obvious pride that was taken by officers and men in its deeds and record. This built on existing successes in Egypt, and was in part deliberately shaped by Steuart's attempts to control the make-up of the regiment in terms of the origins and qualities of its officers and men. Primarily, however, it came as a result of the 12th's successes in the Peninsula, and these in turn stemmed in no small part from the effective leadership provided by Frederick Ponsonby. In my earlier book, I produced case studies of several unfortunate regiments and battalions whose effectiveness and reputation suffered under a bad commander, or in some extreme cases a succession of them. In the 12th, as the preceding narrative has demonstrated, we have an ideal study of the opposite in practice. A diligent, popular, and humane leader of men who was also possessed of no small ability as a soldier in battle, Ponsonby may rightly be considered as a model of unit-level leadership in the cavalry, to set alongside his well-known contemporaries in the infantry such as Sidney Beckwith, Henry Cadogan, Hugh Gough and George Napier.[15]

The importance of strong leadership was perhaps the most important argument that I put forward in my earlier book. The ability of an officer of character could mould a unit in his own image and, by example, help maintain it as an effective military organization even when the failings of the established system placed it under pressure. The 12th Light Dragoons were extremely fortunate – although they might not always have appreciated it at the time – to have the services of two such officers during their Napoleonic service in the shape of James Steuart and Frederick Ponsonby. Each, in different ways, gave devoted service to the regiment, and it is impossible to conceive of the 12th having performed as effectively as it did without the combined efforts of these two officers. The two men, however, were in many ways greatly opposed in style and ethos, to the extent that I have already suggested – in highlighting the two attributes for which Wellington praised the regiment in the quote that provides the title for this book – that Ponsonby could well stand as the personification of gallantry and Steuart of discipline. I further suggest, and believe that this is most strongly borne out by the story of the regiment's service under Wellington's command, that when things went well it was because the right balance was being maintained between the two qualities. Too much discipline, seen in particular with Steuart's insistence on pursuing the methods of peacetime bureaucracy and economy in the midst of a global war, and effectiveness could suffer. Equally, though, a surfeit of gallantry, as Ponsonby had the grace to admit had been exhibited at Waterloo, could risk everything in the heat of battle.

If the charge at Waterloo saw a momentary imbalance, with the 12th for a moment being swept up and carried away in the glory of an all-out mounted charge, discipline still quickly kicked in and enabled the surviving officers to restore order, extricate the regiment from its predicament and get it back into a fit state to continue the fight. The balance was still there, and equilibrium restored. But when we come to look at the legacies of the Napoleonic Wars – and, here again, we have a direct connection to the last of the arguments that I presented in *Sickness, Suffering, and the Sword* – the balance begins to shift and the lessons of that conflict can be seen to have been quickly obscured and even become lost in their entirety. In that earlier book, I argued that eventual success – no matter by how narrow a margin – served to hide the undoubted failings in

Britain's military system and prevent them being addressed by a post-war Army with new priorities and less money and manpower. For the same reason, attitudes that had prevailed throughout the Napoleonic Wars were confirmed and validated by eventual victory, whether or not they had in any way contributed to it. For the cavalry, this meant an increased preoccupation with the mounted charge and consequent neglect of the true role of light cavalry as outpost troops, of which the introduction of the lance was only one symptom.

In many ways, the 12th Royal Lancers were better placed than most to hang on to their Peninsula and Waterloo laurels, and to the skills that had earned them, for their time in Portugal during the 1820s gave them a renewed taste of active service, whilst their subsequent duties took them to the outposts of empire where classic light cavalry work was still required. Although the 12th did serve in the Crimea they were fortunate enough not to arrive until after the debacle of Balaklava had shown just how disastrous gallantry unchecked by discipline could be for light cavalry on the battlefield. But if Indian service kept the old skills alive it was also something to avoid if possible by officers with any pretension to fashion, and so the cavalry spirit retained its imbalance in favour of gallantry and forgot the grounding of discipline that was essential for that gallantry to serve as anything other than an empty gesture.

Today, Frederick Ponsonby is – and rightly so – a cherished figure in the story of what is still, as I write, the 9th/12th Royal Lancers; one of the 'the pantheon of Regimental gods', as a senior member of the current regiment rather nicely phrased it. But the regiment that Ponsonby led was the regiment that Steuart had nurtured, and without Steuart's hard work – and that of other unsung heroes of the depot such as Joseph Philips, Abel Hammon and James Bridger – the inspired nature of Ponsonby's leadership would have had no chance to make itself apparent. Perhaps as today's regiment readies itself for another great change in its history as it prepares for amalgamation to become part of the new Royal Lancers, space might be found in the Pantheon of the new regiment for both members of the double act who led the 12th Light Dragoons to victory two centuries before.

Frederick Ponsonby and James Steuart: Gallantry and Discipline.

Ponsonby's Orders, 31 March 1815

No. 1

Officers Commanding Troops may select four married Women to accompany each Troop, any women who accompany the Six Troops in defiance of this Order will forfeit all Claim on the Regiment.

No. 2

The Officers are to be posted as follows until further Orders.

Captain Stawell's Troop:	Lieut. Chatterton & Cornet Lockhart
Captain Wallace's Troop:	Lieut. Dowbiggen
Captain Sandys' Troop:	Lieut. Vandeleur
Captain Andrews' Troop:	Lieut. Heydon and Calderwood
Captain Erskine's Troop:	Lieut. Hay
Capt Barton's Troop:	Lieut. Goldsmid and Cornet Reed

No. 3

The Regiment to parade at 7 o'Clock tomorrow. Sir Denis Pack will inspect it on its march from the parade. All Baggage &c which is to go in the Waggon must be sent this Evening or early in the morning, as the Baggage waggon will march Off with the Regiment and no Waggon will be allowed to wait for the Baggage of any person. It is probable the Regiment will embark on their arrival at Ramsgate.

Source: 'Regimental Orders by Colonel Ponsonby, Canterbury, 31 March 1815', 912L:2088/5, 'Order Book', pp. 1–2.

Recruiting Parties, 1808–1815

The table lists all recruiting stations where parties from the 12th Light Dragoons were stationed between May 1808 and December 1815, giving the total number of men recruited and the average monthly recruiting yield. Stations are ranked in the table in order of total men recruited for the regiment.

Location	Country	Month from	Month to	Total recruits	Recruits per month
Leicester	England	May 1808	Dec. 1815	120	1.3
Clones	Ireland	May 1808	Feb. 1813	92	1.6
Glasgow[1]	Scotland	Sept. 1812	Dec. 1815	63	1.6
Castle Cary	England	Mar. 1812	Jan. 1815	22	0.6
Hamilton	Scotland	June 1811	Aug. 1812	37	2.5
Lisburn	Ireland	Oct. 1808	Sept. 1810	18	0.8
Lisburn[2]	Ireland	May 1815	Dec. 1815	8	1.0
Edinburgh	Scotland	April 1815	Dec. 1815	5	0.6
Clones[3]	Ireland	May 1815	Dec. 1815	4	0.5
Ayr	Scotland	Jan. 1814	Mar. 1815	3	0.2
Paisley	Scotland	July 1813	Dec. 1813	2	0.3
Kidderminster	England	April 1814	Nov. 1814	2	0.3
Strabane	Ireland	Oct. 1810	June 1811	2	0.2
Retford	England	Mar. 1811	May 1811	1	0.3
Martock	England	May 1813	Aug. 1813	1	0.3
Kilmarnock	Scotland	May 1813	June 1813	0	0.0
Glastonbury[4]	England	Sept. 1813	Nov. 1813	0	0.0
Bolton	England	May 1808	Sept. 1808	0	0.0
Newark	England	May 1810	Feb. 1811	0	0.0

Parties at Lisburn and Clones were withdrawn in 1810 and 1813 respectively, and reinstated in 1815. Because of the lengthy gap, these parties have been counted separately. Adding the two together gives Lisburn a total of 26 recruits, or 0.8 per month, and Clones a total of 96 or 1.5 per month.

Data is from regimental monthly returns. It should be noted that this lists only the number of recruits present with a given party, not the number recruited that month. However, recruits were generally kept with a party and then sent on to the regiments in large batches, and it is relatively straightforward to keep track of when this has occurred and make a count accordingly – whilst this is not a foolproof methodology, it allows for a ready comparison between recruiting stations. Parties with a start date of May 1808 were in place when details of recruiting parties began to be listed; similarly, parties with an end date of December 1815 may well have continued beyond that date but the end of the year was taken as a cut-off point for data.

Notes to the table:
1. Glasgow party briefly withdrawn after February 1815, but reinstated April 1815 and has been treated as a single entity.
2. New party dispatched 1815, counted separately from original party.
3. New party dispatched 1815, counted separately from original party.
4. Given as 'Glassenborough' in the returns; this could be Glassenbury in Kent, but seems more likely to be a bad rendering of Glastonbury, Somerset, since the party seems to have been the same one previously stationed at Martock in that county.

Bibliography

Archival Sources

9th/12th Royal Lancers Regimental Museum, Derby
    912L:2088/5 '12th Lancers Order Book 1815-1872'
    912L:2088/18 '12th Lancers [*sic*] Standing Orders c.1795'
    912L:2088/30 '12th Lancers Registry of Services 1715–1876'
    912L:2088/31 '12th Royal Lancers Record of Services of NCOs and Men June 1809 to Oct. 1865'
    912L:2088/43 'Letterbook of Col. W. Bury [*sic*] and Col. W. Pitt 1767–1772'
    912L:2088/44 'Letterbook of Col. Stewart [*sic*] 1806–1818'

The National Archives, Kew
Series PROB11, Records of the Prerogative Court of Canterbury
    PROB11/1683/155: Will of Richard Sidley, Regimental Quarter Master of the 12th Regt. of Royal Lancers
Series WO17, Office of the Commander in Chief: Monthly Returns to the Adjutant General
    WO17/35: 12th Light Dragoons 1793–1812
    WO17/256: 3rd Dragoons–14th Light Dragoons 1813
    WO17/272: 10th–25th Light Dragoons, Brunswick Hussars, Wagon Train and Staff Corps 1814
    WO17/288: 11th–25th Light Dragoons, Brunswick Hussars, Wagon Train and Staff Corps 1815
    WO17/1757: Egypt, 1801
    WO17/2464-2478: Spain and Portugal, 1808–1814
Series WO25: War Office and Predecessors: Secretary-at-War, Secretary of State for War, and Related Bodies, Registers
    WO25/1437: Casualty Returns. 12 Dragoons
Series WO27: Office of the Commander-in-Chief and War Office: Adjutant General and Army Council: Inspection Returns
    Wo27/90: 1806
    Wo27/96: 1809 Second Half-Year to 90th Foot
    Wo27/98: 1810 First Half-Year to 90th Foot

WO27/100: 1810 Second Half-Year to 90th Foot
WO27/104: 1811 First Half-Year to 90th Foot
WO27/106: 1812 First Half-Year to 30th Foot
WO27/111: 1812 Second Half-Year to 30th Foot
WO27/116: 1813 First Half-Year to 40th Foot
WO27/121: 1813 Second Half-Year to 50th Foot
WO27/126: 1814 First Half-Year to 40th Foot
WO27/129: 1814 Second Half-Year to 59th Foot
WO27/134: 1815 Second Half-Year to 50th Foot

Printed Primary Sources

Adjutant General's Office, *General Regulations and Orders for the Army*, London, W. Clownes, 1811

Adjutant General's Office, *Rules and Regulations for the Cavalry*, London, J. Walter, 1795

Anon., *A Collection of Papers Relating to the Expedition to the Scheldt Presented to Parliament in 1810*, London, A. Strahan, 1811

Anon., *The Light Horse Drill*, London, March and Teape, 1803

Anon., *Memoir Annexed to an Atlas Containing Plans of the Principal Battles, Sieges, and Affairs in which the British Troops Were Engaged During the War in the Spanish Peninsula and the South of France, from 1808 to 1814*, London, James Wylde, 1841

Bartlet, J., *The Gentleman's Farriery; or a Practical Treatise on the Diseases of Horses*, London, J. Nourse, 1770

Bonar, James (ed.), 'The Disposition of Troops in London, March 1815', *English Historical Review*, Vol. 16, No. 62 (April 1901), pp. 348–54

Browne, Major General Robert, *Regulations and Orders Observed in His Majesty's 12th, or Prince of Wales's Regiment, of Light Dragoons*, London, W. Clownes & Co., 1813

Combermere, Viscountess, and Captain W. W. Knollys, *Memoirs and Correspondence of Field Marshal Viscount Combermere*, London, Hurst & Blackett, 1866

Dallas, Alexander R. C., *Felix Alvarez; or Manners in Spain*, London, Baldwin, Cradock & Joy, 1818

Freeman, Strickland, *The Art of Horsemanship*, London, W. Bulmer & Co., 1806

Gleig, George Robert (ed. Ian C. Robertson), *The Subaltern: A Chronicle of the Peninsular War*, Barnsley, Leo Cooper, 2001

Glover, Gareth (ed.), *The Waterloo Archive*, Barnsley, Frontline, 2010–13

Granville, Countess, *Lord Granville Leveson Gower (First Earl Granville) Private Correspondence 1781–1821*, London, John Murray, 1916

Gurwood, Lieut. Colonel (ed.), *The Dispatches of Field Marshal the Duke of Wellington, During his Various Campaigns in India, Denmark, Portugal, Spain, The Low Countries, and France*, London: John Murray, 1837–39

———, *The General Orders of Field Marshal the Duke of Wellington KG*, London, W. Clownes & Sons, 1838

———, *General Orders Spain and Portugal*, London, T. Egerton, 1811–13

Hay, Captain William, *Reminiscences 1808–1815 Under Wellington*, London, Simpkin, Marshal, Hamilton, Kent & Co., 1901

Hinde, Robert, *The Discipline of the Light Horse*, London, W. Owen, 1778

James, Charles, *The Regimental Companion, Containing the Pay, Allowances and Relative Duties of Every Officer in the British Service*, London, T. Egerton, 1811

James, C., *A Collection of the Charges, Opinions, and Sentences of General Courts Martial*, London, T. Egerton, 1820

Maurice, Major General Sir J. F. (ed.), *Diary of Sir John Moore*, London, Edward Arnold, 1904

Page, Julia (ed.), *Intelligence Officer in the Peninsula: Letters & Diaries of Major the Hon. Edward Charles Cocks 1786–1812*. Tunbridge Wells, Spellmount, 1986

Siborne, Major General H. T. (ed.), *Waterloo Letters*, London, Greenhill, 1993

Sinclair, Captain G., *Cudgel-playing, Modernised and Improved: Or, the Science of Defence, Exemplified in a Few Short and Easy Lessons, for the Practice of the Broad Sword Or Single Stick, on Foot*, London, J. Bailey, 1800

Tomkinson, Lt. Col. William, *Diary of a Cavalry Officer in the Peninsular and Waterloo Campaigns 1808–1815*, London, Swan Sonnenschein & Co., 1894

Urban, Silvanus, *The Gentleman's Magazine and Historical Chronicle for the Year 1809*, London, John Nichols, 1809

——, *The Gentleman's Magazine and Historical Chronicle, January–June 1831*, London, John Nichols, 1831

Vandeleur, John, *Letters of Colonel John Vandeleur 1810–1846*, London, Rivington, Percival & Co., 1894

Vandeleur, John Ormsby, *Duties of Officers Commanding Detachments in the Field*, London, T. Egerton, 1801

War Office, *Instructions and Regulations for the Formations and Movements of the Cavalry*, London, T. Egerton, 1799

War Office, *A Collection of Orders, Regulations, and Instructions for the Army; on Matters of Finance and Points of Discipline Immediately Concerned Therewith*, London, T. Egerton, 1807

Wellington, 2nd Duke of (ed.), *Supplementary Despatches, Correspondence, and Memoranda, of Field Marshal Arthur, Duke of Wellington*, London, John Murray, 1858–62

Secondary Sources

Anglesey, Marquess of, *One Leg: The Life and Letters of William Henry Paget, First Marquess of Anglesey, KG, 1768–1854*, London, Leo Cooper, 1996

Anon., *British Minor Expeditions 1746 to 1814*, London, HMSO, 1884

Bamford, Andrew, *Sickness, Suffering, and the Sword: The British Regiment on Campaign 1808–1815*, Norman, University of Oklahoma Press, 2013

Barbero, Alessandro, *The Battle: A History of the Battle of Waterloo*, London, Atlantic, 2005

Brett-James, Antony, *Life in Wellington's Army*, London, Tom Donovan, 1994

Burnham, Robert, *Charging Against Wellington: The French Cavalry in the Peninsular War*, Barnsley, Frontline Books, 2011

Cannon, Richard, *Historical Record of the Twelfth, or the Prince of Wales's Royal Regiment of Lancers: containing an account of the formation of the regiment in 1715, and of its subsequent services to 1842*, London, J. W. Parker, 1842

Charrington, Richard, *Spearmen: The History of the 9th/12th Royal Lancers (Prince of Wales's)*, 9th/12th Royal Lancers Charitable Association, 2010

Chichester, Henry Manners, 'Madden, George Allen', in *Dictionary of National Biography*, London, Smith, Elder & Co., 1885–1900, Vol. 35, pp.292–5

Clayton, Anthony, *The British Officer: Leading the Army from 1660 to the Present*, Harlow, Pearson, 2006

Cokayne, George E. (ed.), *Complete Baronetage*, Exeter, William Pollard & Co., 1904

Collins, Major R. M., 'Colonel the Hon . Frederick Cavendish Ponsonby, 12th Light Dragoons', *JSAHR*, Vol. XLVI, No. 185 (Spring 1968), pp. 1–5

Coss, Edward J., *All for the King's Shilling: The British Soldier Under Wellington, 1808–1814*, Norman, University of Oklahoma Press, 2010

———, 'The Misadventures of Wellington's Cavalry, from the Peninsula to Waterloo', *Journal of the Waterloo Committee* 10 (April 1988), pp. 18–28

Dalton, Charles, *The Waterloo Roll Call*, London, Eyre and Spottiwoode, 1904

Divall, Carole, *Inside the Regiment: The Officers and Men of the 30th Regiment During the Revolutionary and Napoleonic Wars*, Barnsley, Pen and Sword, 2011

———, *Wellington's Worst Scrape: The Burgos Campaign 1812*, Barnsley, Pen and Sword, 2012

Ede-Borrett, Stephen, 'The British Army in Egypt', *Wargames Illustrated*, No. 42, March 1991, pp. 38–42

Field, Andrew W., *Talavera: Wellington's First Victory in Spain*, Barnsley, Pen and Sword, 2006

Fletcher, Ian, *Galloping at Everything: The British Cavalry in the Peninsular War and at Waterloo 1808–15. A Reappraisal*, Staplehurst, Spelmount, 1999

———, *Vittoria 1813: Wellington Sweeps the French from Spain*, Oxford, Osprey, 1998

Fortescue, Hon. J. W., *A History of the British Army*, London, Macmillan, 1899–1930

Fosten, Brian, *Wellington's Light Cavalry*, Oxford, Osprey, 1982

Gerges, Mark, 'Command and Control in the Peninsula: the Role of British Cavalry 1808–1814', unpublished PhD thesis, Florida State University, 2005

Glover, Michael, *Wellington's Army in the Peninsula 1808–1814*, London, David & Charles, 1977

Guy, Alan J. (ed.), *The Road to Waterloo: The British Army and the Struggle Against Revolutionary and Napoleonic France*, London, Alan Sutton, 1990

Haythornthwaite, Philip J., *The Armies of Wellington*, London, Cassell, 1994

Hofschröer, Peter, *1815: The Waterloo Campaign*, London, Greenhill, 1999

Holmes, Richard, *Soldiers: Army Lives and Loyalties from Redcoats to Dusty Warriors*, London, Harper Collins, 2011

Houlding, J. A., *Fit for Service: The Training of the British Army 1715–1795*, Oxford, Clarendon, 1981

Howard, Dr Martin, *Wellington's Doctors: The British Army Medical Services in the Napoleonic Wars*, Staplehurst, Spellmount, 2002

Howarth, David, *A Near Run Thing*, London, Collins, 1968

Johnson, David, *The French Cavalry 1792–1815*, London, Belmont, 1989

Johnston, Colonel William, *Roll of Commissioned Offices in the Medical Service of the British Army*, Aberdeen, Aberdeen University Press, 1917

Linch, Kevin B., 'The Recruitment of the British Army 1807–1815', unpublished PhD thesis, University of Leeds, 2001

Longford, Elizabeth, *Wellington: The Years of the Sword*, London: Weidenfeld & Nicolson, 1969

MacArthur, Roderick, 'British Army Establishments During the Napoleonic Wars. Part I: Background and Infantry', *JSAHR*, No. 87 (2009), pp. 150–72

——,'British Army Establishments During the Napoleonic Wars. Part II: Cavalry, Artillery, and Supporting Units', *JSAHR*, No. 87 (2009), pp. 331–56

Mackesey, Piers, *British Victory in Egypt: The End of Napoleon's Conquest*, London, Routledge, 1995

Muir, Rory, *Britain and the Defeat of Napoleon 1807–1815*, New Haven, Yale University Press, 1996

——, *Salamanca 1812*, New Haven, Yale University Press, 2001

——, *Wellington. The Path to Victory 1796–1814*, New Haven, Yale University Press, 2013

——, et al., *Inside Wellington's Peninsular Army*, Barnsley, Pen and Sword, 2006

Oman, Sir Charles, *A History of the Peninsular War*, Oxford: Oxford University Press, 1902–30

——, *Wellington's Army 1809–1814*, London, Edward Arnold, 1913

Philippart, John, *The Royal Military Calendar or Army Service and Commission Book*, London, A. J. Valpy, 1820

Ponsonby, Major General Sir John, *The Ponsonby Family*, London, Medici Society, 1929

Redgrave, Toby Michael Ormsby, 'Wellington's Logistical Arrangements in the Peninsular War 1809–14', unpublished PhD thesis, King's College, London, 1979

Robertson, Ian C., *Wellington Invades France: The Final Phase of the Peninsular War 1813–1814*, London, Greenhill, 2003

Stewart, Capt. P. F., *The History of the XII Royal Lancers (Prince of Wales's)*, London: Oxford University Press, 1950

Thompson, Mark S., 'Cavalry Actions in the Peninsular War', *BCMH Spring 2012 Conference Report*, pp. 2–8

Thoumine, R. H., *Scientific Soldier: A Life of General Le Marchant 1766–1812*, Oxford, Oxford University Press, 1968

Tylden, Major G., *Horses and Saddlery*, London, J. A. Allen, 1965

Urban, Mark, *The Man Who Broke Napoleon's Codes: The Story of George Scovell*, London, Faber & Faber, 2001

Veve, Thomas Dwight, *The Duke of Wellington and the British Army of Occupation in France, 1815–1818*. Westport, Greenwood, 1992

Weller, Jac, *Wellington in the Peninsula*, London, Greenhill, 1999

Websites and Online Articles

Bamford, Andrew, 'British Army Unit Strengths: 1808-1815', at http://www.napoleon-series.org/military/organization/Britain/Strength/Bamford/c_BritishArmyStrengthStudyIntroduction.html

Bunbury, Turtle, 'Browne Clayton of Browne's Hill, Co. Carlow', at http://www.turtlebunbury.com/history/history_family/hist_family_b_clayton.html

Burnham, Robert (ed.), 'Lionel S. Challis' "Peninsula Roll Call"', at http://www.napoleon-series.org/research/biographies/GreatBritain/Challis/c_ChallisIntro.html

Burnham, Robert, 'The British Expeditionary Force to Walcheren: 1809', at http://www.napoleon-series.org/military/battles/c_walcheren.html

Burnham, Robert, and John Cook, 'Nicknames of British Units during the Napoleonic Wars', at http://www.napoleon-series.org/military/organization/c_nickname.html

Department of Environment, Food, and Rural Affairs, 'Glanders and Farcy', at http://www.defra.gov.uk/ahvla-en/disease-control/notifiable/glanders-farcy/

Henry, D. G., 'Steuart Denham, Sir James, 8th Bt. (1744–1839), of Coltness and Westshield, Lanark', *History of Parliament Online*, at www.historyofparliamentonline.org/volume/1790-1820/member/steuart-denham-sir-james-1744-1839

Jupp, P. J. 'Blunden, Overington (1767–1837), of Castle Blunden, co. Kilkenny', *History of Parliament Online*, at http://www.historyofparliamentonline.org/volume/1790-1820/member/blunden-overington-1767-1837

McGuigan, Ron, 'British Generals of the Napoleonic Wars 1793–1815', at http://www.napoleon-series.org/research/biographies/BritishGenerals/c_Britishgenerals1.html

Read, Martin, 'The British 1796 Pattern Light Cavalry Sword', at http://www.napoleon-series.org/military/organization/c_swordpoint1.html

——, 'Cavalry Combat and the Sword: Sword Design, Provision, and Use in the British Cavalry of the Napoleonic Era', at http://www.napoleon-series.org/military/organization/Britain/Cavalry/Swords/Swordpoint/c_swordpoint2.html

Salmon, Philip, 'Ponsonby, Hon. Frederick Cavendish (1783–1837)', History of Parliament Online, at http://www.historyofparliamentonline.org/volume/1820-1832/member/ponsonby-hon-frederick-1783-1837

The London Gazette, at http://www.london-gazette.co.uk

Notes

Introduction

1. Steuart to Gordon, 912L:2088/44, 'Letterbook of Col Stewart [*sic*] 1806–1818'.
2. Bamford, Andrew, *Sickness, Suffering, and the Sword: The British Regiment on Campaign 1808–1815*, Norman, University of Oklahoma Press, 2013.
3. Holmes, Richard, *Soldiers: Army Lives and Loyalties from Redcoats to Dusty Warriors*, London, Harper Collins, 2011, p. 69.

Chapter I: The Colonel and his Regiment

1. Unless cited otherwise, the early history of the regiment is summarized from Cannon, Richard, *Historical record of the Twelfth, or the Prince of Wales's Royal Regiment of Lancers: containing an account of the formation of the regiment in 1715, and of its subsequent services to 1842*, London, J. W. Parker, 1842, pp. 9–17; Charrington, Richard, *Spearmen: The History of the 9th/12th Royal Lancers (Prince of Wales's)*, 9th/12th Royal Lancers Charitable Association, 2010, pp. 11–18; Stewart, Capt. P. F., *The History of the XII Royal Lancers (Prince of Wales's)*, London, Oxford University Press, 1950, pp. 1–34.
2. Burton to Townshend, 27 January, 4 February and 12 June 1768, all in 912L:2088/44, 'Letterbook of Col. W. Bury [*sic*] and Col. W. Pitt 1767–1772'.
3. Stewart, *XII Royal Lancers*, pp. 25–6; see also Houlding, J. A., *Fit for Service: The Training of the British Army 1715–1795*, Oxford, Clarendon, 1981, pp. 45–57.
4. Longford, Elizabeth, *Wellington: The Years of the Sword*, London, Weidenfeld & Nicolson, 1969, pp. 51–8; Muir, Rory, *Wellington: The Path to Victory 1796–1814*, New Haven, Yale University Press, 2013, pp. 12–23.
5. 912L:2088/18, '12th Lancers [sic] Standing Orders c.1795', p. 1. An updated set of orders, dealing only with the duties of officers, was published in 1808 by the regiment's former commanding officer, and re-issued in 1813 with some revisions. See Browne, Major General Robert, *Regulations and Orders Observed in His Majesty's 12th, or Prince of Wales's Regiment, of Light Dragoons*, London, W. Clownes & Co., 1813. I am obliged to Paul L. Dawson for alerting me to this publication, and providing me with a copy of the 1813 impression.

6. Unless cited otherwise, Steuart's biographical details are taken from Cokayne, George E. (ed.), *Complete Baronetage*, Exeter, William Pollard & Co., 1904, Vol. IV, pp. 376–7; Henry, D. G., 'Steuart Denham, Sir James, 8th Bt. (1744–1839), of Coltness and Westshield, Lanark', *History of Parliament Online*, at www.historyofparliamentonline.org/volume/1790-1820/member/steuart-denham-sir-james-1744-1839; Philippart, John, *The Royal Military Calendar or Army Service and Commission Book*, London, A. J. Valpy, 1820, Vol. I, pp. 305–17.

7. Philippart, *Military Calendar*, Vol. I, p. 306.

8. Fletcher, Ian, *Galloping at Everything: The British Cavalry in the Peninsular War and at Waterloo 1808–15. A Reappraisal*, Staplehurst, Spellmount, 1999, p. 27.

9. The double-barrelled form was sometimes used in letters *to* Steuart, as for example Calvert to General Sir J. Steuart Denham, 24 July 1813. Cannon, *Twelfth Lancers*, p. 81, suggests that he initially used the double-barrelled form himself, and then reverted to plain Steuart.

10. Burke, William, *History of the Commoners of Great Britain and Ireland*, London, Henry Colburn, 1835, Vol. II, pp. 50–1.

11. Browne, *Regulations and Orders*, pp. 58–60; Charrington, *Spearmen*, p. 20; Stewart, *XII Royal Lancers*, pp. 35–7.

12. Disbanded at the peace of Amiens, Fencible regiments were regulars but enlisted for home defence service only; see Haythornthwaite, Philip J., *The Armies of Wellington*, London, Cassell, 1994, pp. 173–4.

13. Maurice, Major General Sir J. F. (ed.), *Diary of Sir John Moore*, London, Edward Arnold, 1904, Vol. I, pp. 293–4.

14. Ibid, pp. 275–6.

15. 'Circular to the General Officers in the Southern District of Ireland', 13 March 1798, Philippart, *Military Calendar*, Vol. I, pp. 310–12.

16. Steuart to Philippart, 27 November 1814, 912L:2088/44, 'Letterbook'.

17. Fraser to Dundas, 15 September 1800, Stewart, *XII Royal Lancers*, p. 44.

18. Charrington, *Spearmen*, pp. 21–2; Stewart, *XII Royal Lancers*, pp. 40–4.

19. Ede-Borrett, Stephen, 'The British Army in Egypt', *Wargames Illustrated*, No. 42, March 1991, pp. 38–42; Mackesey, Piers, *Victory in Egypt*, London, Routledge, 1995, p. 19.

20. Wellington to Hill, 18 June 1812, Gurwood, Lieut. Colonel (ed.), *The Dispatches of Field Marshal the Duke of Wellington, During his Various Campaigns in India, Denmark, Portugal, Spain, The Low Countries, and France*, London, John Murray, 1837–9, Vol. IX, p. 240.

21. Monthly Return, 1 November 1801, TNA, WO17/1757.

22. Confidential Report, 21 March 1806, TNA, Wo27/90.

23. MacArthur, Roderick, 'British Army Establishments During the Napoleonic Wars. Part I – Background and Infantry', *JSAHR*, No. 87 (2009), pp. 150–72; 'British Army Establishments During the Napoleonic Wars. Part II – Cavalry, Artillery, and Supporting Units', *JSAHR*, No. 87 (2009), pp. 331–56.

24. Adjutant General's Office, *Rules and Regulations for the Cavalry*, London, J. Walter, 1795, pp. 19–20.

25. Steuart to Officer Commanding 12th Light Dragoons, 21 July 1807; Steuart to

Calvert, 20 June 1808: 912L:2088/44, 'Letterbook'. See also Holmes, *Soldiers*, pp. 63–6.

26. 912L:2088/18, 'Standing Orders', p. 62.
27. Steuart to Calvert, 20 June 1808, 912L:2088/44, 'Letterbook'.
28. MacArthur, 'Establishments Part II', p. 333.
29. Adjutant General's Office, *Rules and Regulations*, p. 19.
30. Notes to Monthly Returns, September–November 1810, TNA, WO17/35.
31. MacArthur, 'Establishments Part II', p. 334.
32. 912L:2088/18, 'Standing Orders', p. 40.
33. MacArthur, 'Establishments Part II', p. 335.
34. 912L:2088/18, 'Standing Orders', pp. 114–17.
35. For more details, see Bamford, *Sickness, Suffering, and the Sword*, pp. 106–12.
36. 'Copy of Sir James Steuart's Farewell letter to the 12th Light Dragoons on his being called to the command of the Royal North British Dragoons', 18 January 1815; Steuart to Philips, 2 December 1811: 912L:2088/44, 'Letterbook'.
37. Steuart to Coles, 29 June 1813; Steuart to Calvert, 7 August 1814: 912L:2088/44, 'Letterbook'.
38. Steuart to Officer Commanding 12th Light Dragoons, 10 August 1814, 912L:2088/44, 'Letterbook'.
39. Steuart to Gordon, 28 April 1808, 912L:2088/44, 'Letterbook'.
40. Steuart to Cox & Greenwood, 1 March 1812, 912L:2088/44, 'Letterbook'.
41. Steuart to Brown, 13 September 1806; Steuart to Blunden, 24 December 1812, 912L:2088/44, 'Letterbook'. The snaffle is a form of bit, the mouthpiece by which the action of the reins is transmitted.
42. Steuart to Wyndham, 31 August 1811, 912L:2088/44, 'Letterbook'.
43. 'Copy of Sir James Steuart's Farewell letter to the 12th Light Dragoons on his being called to the command of the Royal North British Dragoons', 18 January 1815, 912L:2088/44, 'Letterbook'.
44. Steuart to Officer Commanding Depot, 22 July 1813, 912L:2088/44, 'Letterbook'.
45. Steuart to Officer Commanding 12th Light Dragoons, 10 December 1814, 912L:2088/44, 'Letterbook'.
46. Using the Retail Price Index converter at http://www.measuringworth.com/ppoweruk/.
47. Steuart to Greenwood & Cox, 12 May 1808. The figure of £4,000 – £246,000 in today's money – comes from Steuart to Ponsonby, 26 November 1811, 912L:2088/44, 'Letterbook'.
48. Steuart to Greenwood & Cox, 14 March 1812; Steuart to Barry, 5 April 1813: 912L:2088/44, 'Letterbook'.
49. Steuart to Gibson and Peat, 7 February 1811, 912L:2088/44, 'Letterbook'.
50. 912L:2088/18, 'Standing Orders', p. 64.
51. Steuart to Calvert, 11 May 1813, 912L:2088/44, 'Letterbook'.
52. Steuart to Bridger, 28 May 1812; Steuart to Officer Commanding Depot, 14 February 1813: 912L:2088/44, 'Letterbook'.
53. Steuart to Greenwood and Cox, 3 November 1806, 912L:2088/44, 'Letterbook'.

54. Steuart to Officer Commanding 12th Light Dragoons, 23 March 1808, 912L:2088/44, 'Letterbook'.

55. Steuart to Greenwood, 3 February 1813, 912L:2088/44, 'Letterbook'.

Chapter II: **Officers and Gentlemen**

1. Howarth, David, *A Near Run Thing*, London, Collins, 1968, p. 20.

2. Coss, Edward J., *All for the King's Shilling: The British Soldier Under Wellington, 1808–1814*, Norman, University of Oklahoma Press, 2010, pp. 123–5, 155–6.

3. 912L:2088/18, 'Standing Orders', p. 3.

4. Howard, Dr Martin, *Wellington's Doctors: The British Army Medical Services in the Napoleonic Wars*, Staplehurst, Spellmount, 2002, pp. 11–45.

5. War Office, *A Collection of Orders, Regulations, and Instructions for the Army; on Matters of Finance and Points of Discipline Immediately Concerned Therewith*, London, T. Egerton, 1807, pp. 116–22.

6. Field Return, 23 October 1809, TNA, WO27/96.

7. Officer promotions, appointments and service histories in this chapter – unless otherwise referenced – are taken from *The London Gazette*, at http://www. london-gazette.co.uk/, and Burnham, Robert (ed.), 'Lionel S. Challis' "Peninsula Roll Call"', at http://www.napoleon-series.org/research/biographies/ GreatBritain/Challis/c_ChallisIntro.html.

8. Adjutant General's Office, *Rules and Regulations*, p. 1.

9. Ibid, p. 2.

10. Steuart to Ponsonby, 26 November 1811; Steuart to Cox & Greenwood, 29 November 1811: 912L:2088/44, 'Letterbook'.

11. Biographical sketch from Collins, Major R. M., 'Colonel the Hon . Frederick Cavendish Ponsonby, 12th Light Dragoons', *JSAHR*, Vol. XLVI. No. 185 (Spring 1968), pp. 1–5; Ponsonby, Major General Sir John, *The Ponsonby Family*, London, Medici Society, 1929, pp. 115–25; Salmon, Philip, 'Ponsonby, Hon. Frederick Cavendish (1783–1837)', History of Parliament Online, at http://www.historyofparliamentonline.org/volume/1820-1832/member/ ponsonby-hon-frederick-1783-1837; Stewart, *XII Royal Lancers*, pp. 64–5.

12. Prince of Wales to Bessborough, 11 December 1799, in Ponsonby, *Ponsonby Family*, p. 224.

13. Field, Andrew W., *Talavera: Wellington's First Victory in Spain*, Barnsley, Pen and Sword, 2006, pp. 115–23.

14. Graham to Liverpool, 6 March 1811, in Delavoye, Alex. M., *Life of Thomas Graham, Lord Lynedoch*, London, Richardson, 1880, p. 470.

15. Granville, Countess, *Lord Granville Leveson Gower (First Earl Granville) Private Correspondence 1781–1821*, 2 vols, London, John Murray, 1916.

16. Steuart to Bridger, 4 April 1812, 912L:2088/44, 'Letterbook'.

17. Hay, Captain William, *Reminiscences 1808–1815 Under Wellington*, London, Simpkin, Marshal, Hamilton, Kent & Co., 1901, pp. 51–3, 109.

18. Steuart to Egremont, 2 April 1811, 912L:2088/44, 'Letterbook'.

19. Notes to Monthly Returns, February–May 1812, TNA, WO17/35.

20. Glover, Michael, *Wellington's Army in the Peninsula*, London, David and

274 Notes to pages 37–44

Charles, 1977, p. 76. The sale of his majority in the 78th would have netted Spicer a further £2,600.

21. Steuart to Torrens, 14 September 1811, 912L:2088/44, 'Letterbook'.
22. Steuart to Torrens, 15 September 1811 and 12 January 1812; Steuart to Blunden, 30 January 1812: 912L:2088/44, 'Letterbook'.
23. Confidential Report, 20 April 1813, TNA, WO27/116.
24. Jupp, P. J. 'Blunden, Overington (1767–1837), of Castle Blunden, co. Kilkenny', *History of Parliament Online*, at http://www.historyofparliament online.org/volume/1790-1820/member/blunden-overington-1767-1837.
25. Steuart to Ponsonby, 24 December 1812, 912L:2088/44, 'Letterbook'.
26. Adjutant General's Office, *Rules and Regulations*, p. 14.
27. 912L:2088/18, 'Standing Orders', p. 24.
28. Adjutant General's Office, *Rules and Regulations*, p. 14.
29. Ibid.
30. Steuart to Officer Commanding 12th Light Dragoons, 15 November 1808, 912L:2088/44, 'Letterbook'; on the double commission, see James, Charles, *The Regimental Companion, Containing the Pay, Allowances and Relative Duties of Every Officer in the British Service*, London, T. Egerton, 1811, pp. 80–1.
31. Confidential Report, 24 December 1812, TNA, WO27/111.
32. Steuart to Torrens, 5 April 1813, 912L:2088/44, 'Letterbook'.
33. Steuart to Greenwood, Cox & Co., 1 August 1813, 912L:2088/44, 'Letterbook'.
34. Steuart to Conolly, 11 December 1806 and 22 May 1807; Steuart to Greenwood, 5 October 1807: 912L:2088/44, 'Letterbook'.
35. Notes to Monthly Returns, May 1810 to March 1811, TNA, WO17/35.
36. Notes to Monthly Returns, November and December 1815, TNA, WO17/288.
37. Steuart to Greenwood, 9 June 1814; Steuart to Stepleton, 9 June 1814; Steuart to Greenwood, Cox & Co., 19 July 1814: 912L:2088/44, 'Letterbook'. Dowdall had obtained his lieutenancy without purchase, hence his only being able to sell his cornetcy.
38. James, *Regimental Companion*, Vol.I, p. 62.
39. Haythornthwaite, *Armies of Wellington*, pp. 22–4, 27–8, 31–2; Holmes, *Soldiers*, pp. 137–55.
40. Glover, *Wellington's Army*, pp. 82–3.
41. Coss, Edward J., 'The Misadventures of Wellington's Cavalry, from the Peninsula to Waterloo', *Journal of the Waterloo Committee*, 10 (April 1988), pp. 18–28.
42. Based on an electronic search of the online version of *The London Gazette*, at http://www.london-gazette.co.uk, discounting exchanges between officers of the same rank, appointments from half-pay, and medical and veterinary officers.
43. Steuart to Barton, 23 January 1814, 912L:2088/44, 'Letterbook'.
44. Haythornthwaite, *Armies of Wellington*, p. 41. Marlow was the Junior Branch in relation to the Senior Branch at High Wycombe for serving officers, which eventually became the Staff College.
45. Hay, *Reminiscences*, pp. 3–6.
46. Steuart to Conolly, 22 May 1807, 912L:2088/44, 'Letterbook'.

47. Adjutant General's Office, *General Regulations and Orders for the Army*, London, W. Clownes, 1811, pp. 85–6.
48. 912L:2088/18, 'Standing Orders', p. 7.
49. Confidential Report, 18 April 1811, TNA, WO27/104.
50. Confidential Report, 20 April 1813, TNA, WO27/116.
51. Steuart to Bridger, 31 August 1811, 912L:2088/44, 'Letterbook'.
52. Confidential Report, 20 April 1813, TNA, WO27/116.
53. Notes to Monthly Return, 25 June 1811, TNA, WO17/35; Regimental Orders by Colonel Ponsonby, Canterbury, 31 March 1815, in 912L: 2088/5, '12th Lancers order book 1815–1872', pp. 1–2.
54. Steuart to Coles, 10 March 1813, 912L:2088/44, 'Letterbook'.
55. Confidential Report, 20 April 1813, TNA, WO27/116.
56. Steuart to Torrens, 19 February 1814, 912L:2088/44, 'Letterbook'.
57. Steuart to Stanhope, 1 February 1813, 912L:2088/44, 'Letterbook'.
58. Steuart to Blunden, 2 February 1813, 912L:2088/44, 'Letterbook'.
59. Steuart to Stanhope, 24 March 1813, 912L:2088/44, 'Letterbook'.
60. Steuart to Greenwood, Cox & Co., 8 May 1809, 912L:2088/44, 'Letterbook'.
61. Steuart to Browne, 3 November 1806, 912L:2088/44, 'Letterbook'.
62. Steuart to Greenwood & Cox, 14 March 1812, 912L:2088/44, 'Letterbook'.
63. 'General Sir James Steuart's Standing Orders to his Regiment the 12th or Prince of Wales's Regt. 12th [*sic*] Lt Dragoons', 2 November 1807, 912L:2088/44, 'Letterbook': compare with Adjutant General's Office, *General Regulations*, p. 41
64. Steuart to Brown, 4 November 1810, 912L:2088/44, 'Letterbook'.
65. Steuart to Greenwood, 5 October 1807, 912L:2088/44, 'Letterbook'.
66. For example, Steuart to Brown, 17 October 1806, 912L:2088/44, 'Letterbook'.
67. Steuart to Brown, 16 May 1809; Steuart to Greenwood Cox & Co., 25 July 1809: 912L:2088/44, 'Letterbook'.
68. Chichester, Henry Manners, 'Madden, George Allen', in *Dictionary of National Biography*, London, Smith, Elder & Co., 1885–1900, Vol. 35, pp. 292–5.
69. Clayton, Anthony, *The British Officer: Leading the Army from 1660 to the Present*, Harlow, Pearson, 2006, pp. 66–7.
70. Browne to Steuart , 11 December 1810, quoted as an extract in Steuart to Barton, 15 December 1810, 912L:2088/44, 'Letterbook'.
71. Steuart to Browne, 30 December 1810, 912L:2088/44, 'Letterbook'.
72. Steuart to Browne, 11 January 1811, 912L:2088/44, 'Letterbook'.
73. Steuart to Brown, 15 June 1809, 912L:2088/44, 'Letterbook'.
74. Ibid.
75. Steuart to Calvert, 15 July 1809, 912L:2088/44, 'Letterbook'.
76. Steuart to Brown, 13 October 1809, Steuart to Calvert, 14 October 1809: 912L:2088/44, 'Letterbook'. Wardroper's service history from Johnston, Colonel William, *Roll of Commissioned Offices in the Medical Service of the British Army*, Aberdeen, Aberdeen University Press, 1917, p. 186, but even this encyclopaedic tome is unable to furnish him with a Christian name.
77. James, C., *A Collection of the Charges, Opinions, and Sentences of General Courts Martial*, London, T. Egerton, 1820, pp. 744–5.

78. *The Examiner*, London, 20 November 1825.

Chapter III: **Rank and File**

1. 912L:2088/18, 'Standing Orders', p. 44.
2. Steuart to Calvert, 14 March 1812, 912L:2088/44, 'Letterbook'.
3. Linch, Kevin B., 'The Recruitment of the British Army 1807–1815', unpublished PhD thesis, University of Leeds, 2001, pp. 98–115. This remains the best summary of the way the British Army was recruited during the Napoleonic era, but see also Haythorthwaite, *Armies of Wellington*, pp. 44–52.
4. Steuart to Brown, 17 October 1806, 912L:2088/44, 'Letterbook'.
5. Steuart to Browne, 19 December 1809, 912L:2088/44, 'Letterbook'.
6. Ibid.
7. 912L:2088/18, 'Standing Orders', p. 173.
8. Linch, 'Recruitment', p. 111
9. Haythornthwaite, *Armies of Wellington*, p. 44.
10. 912L:2088/18, 'Standing Orders', p. 172.
11. Ibid., p. 173.
12. Notes to Monthly Return, 25 December 1814, TNA, WO17/272.
13. Steuart to Officer Commanding Depot, 7 June 1813, 912L:2088/44, 'Letterbook'.
14. 912L:2088/18, 'Standing Orders', p. 172.
15. Ibid.
16. 912L:2088/18, 'Standing Orders', p. 59; on the case of the 10th Hussars, see Linch, 'Recruitment', p. 178.
17. Steuart to Blunden, 3 September 1813, 912L:2088/44, 'Letterbook'.
18. See Appendix II. Detailed information on recruiting parties is not available prior to May 1808.
19. Notes to Monthly Returns, June–December 1815, TNA, WO17/288.
20. Steuart to White, 5 April 1813, 912L:2088/44, 'Letterbook'.
21. Steuart to Coles, 14 June 1813, 912L:2088/44, 'Letterbook'.
22. Steuart to Coles, 29 June 1813, 912L:2088/44, 'Letterbook'.
23. Steuart to Officer Commanding Depot, 12 July 1813, 912L:2088/44, 'Letterbook'.
24. Steuart to Jones, 31 July 1813, 912L:2088/44, 'Letterbook'.
25. Ibid.
26. Monthly Returns, June-December 1815, TNA, WO17/288.
27. 912L:2088/5, 'Order Book'.
28. 912L:2088/31, '12th Royal Lancers Record of Services of NCOs and Men June 1809 to Oct. 1865'.
29. 912L:2088/5, 'Order Book'.
30. Coss, *King's Shilling*, pp. 53–4.
31. The Field Return of 23 October 1809, TNA, WO27/96, indicates 157 privates with three years of past service – i.e. who had enlisted in 1806.
32. Data taken from Field Returns of 23 October 1809; 8 October (Depot) and 12 December (Regiment) 1812; 26 October 1815, in TNA, WO27/96, 111,

134. Data is for all non-commissioned ranks from private to troop quartermaster inclusive. Note that whilst figures for 1812 are combined totals for the regiment in the field and the depot, 1815 figures are for the six active troops only.

33. Data from Field Return of 23 October 1809, TNA, WO27/96.

34. Inspection Returns for October 1809 in TNA, WO27/96 1809, and October 1815 in TNA, WO27/134. On the Lanarkshire men, see Steuart to Browne, 18 December 1809, 912L:2088/44, 'Letterbook'.

35. Data included with Monthly Returns after 1808, TNA, WO17/35, 256, 272, 288, sampled at six-monthly intervals June 1808–December 1815. For details of this scheme, see Linch, 'Recruitment', pp. 67–71.

36. Steuart to Barton, 31 January 1814, 912L:2088/44, 'Letterbook'.

37. 912L:2088/18, 'Standing Orders', p. 58.

38. 912L:2088/18, 'Standing Orders', p. 61.This fascinating aspect of military life was outlined by Dani Coombs in a paper entitled 'Soldiers, civilians and the black market trade in "Regimental Necessaries", 1740–1830', at 'War, Society, and Culture in Britain, *c.* 1688–1830', conference held at the University of Leeds, 4–5 July 2013.

39. Described in Stewart, *XII Royal Lancers*, pp. 472–3; Fosten, Brian, *Wellington's Light Cavalry*, Oxford, Osprey, 1982, pp. 29–33.

40. Steuart to Browne, 4 March 1807, 912L:2088/44, 'Letterbook'.

41. Steuart to Greenwood, 2 April 1811, 912L:2088/44, 'Letterbook', indicates the purchase of feathers for both helmets and caps.

42. 912L:2088/18, 'Standing Orders', p. 60.

43. See, for example, Steuart to Officer Commanding 12th Light Dragoons, 24 March 1810. Steuart to Davenport & Co., 7 February 1811, specifies 'Horsemen's Greatcoats': both in 912L:2088/44, 'Letterbook'.

44. Steuart to Ponsonby, 26 November 1811, 912L:2088/44, 'Letterbook'; Confidential Report, 13 May 1812, TNA, WO27/106.

45. Stewart, *XII Royal Lancers*, p. 473; Fosten, *Wellington's Light Cavalry*, pp. 35–6.

46. Steuart to Bridger, 29 January 1812, 912L:2088/44, 'Letterbook'.

47. Vandeleur to Mother, 25 December 1812, 25 January 1813 and 3 October 1813, Vandeleur, John, *Letters of Colonel John Vandeleur 1810–1846*, London, Rivington, Percival & Co., 1894, pp. 59–69, 125–9.

48. Confidential Report, 8 October 1812, TNA, WO27/111.

49. 912L:2088/18, 'Standing Orders', p. 44.

50. Steuart to Officer Commanding Depot, 12 July 1811, 912L:2088/44, 'Letterbook'.

51. 912L:2088/18, 'Standing Orders', p. 44.

52. 912L:2088/5, 'Order Book'.

53. Coss, *King's Shilling*, pp. 69–70.

54. 912L:2088/5, 'Order Book'.

55. Houlding, *Fit for Service*, p. 161.

56. Medical Board report to the Army's Deputy Inspector of Hospitals, 31 December 1811, quoted in Linch, 'Recruitment', p. 106.

57. Steuart to Browne, 13 September 1806; Steuart to Officer Commanding Depot,

12 July 1811; Steuart to Bridger, 29 January 1812: all in 912L:2088/44, 'Letterbook'.

58. Steuart to Coles, 14 June 1813, 912L:2088/44, 'Letterbook'.

59. Steuart to Coles, 29 June 1813, 912L:2088/44, 'Letterbook'. I am obliged to Alexandre Heroy and Ron McGuigan for their insights into the military applications of cudgel-play.

60. Sinclair, Captain G., *Cudgel-playing, Modernised and Improved: Or, the Science of Defence, Exemplified in a Few Short and Easy Lessons, for the Practice of the Broad Sword Or Single Stick, on Foot*, London, J. Bailey, 1800.

61. Burnham, Robert, and John Cook, 'Nicknames of British Units during the Napoleonic Wars', at http://www.napoleon-series.org/military/organization/c_nickname.html. It is interesting to note that this name, bestowed in an entirely complimentary fashion two centuries ago, has now gone so far out of favour as to be deemed rather insulting by today's 9th/12th Royal Lancers – connotations of yielding and bending not sitting comfortably with the ideals of modern soldiering – to the extent that the author was politely but firmly advised against proposing it as a title for this work.

62. Linch, 'Recruitment', p. 202.

63. Bamford, *Sickness, Suffering, and the Sword*, pp. 245–59, 307–8.

64. Figures from Monthly Returns, TNA, WO17/35, 256, 272, 288.

65. Linch, 'Recruitment', p. 202.

66. Notes to Monthly Return of September 25th 1809, TNA, WO17/35; Steuart to Officer Commanding 12th Light Dragoons, 1 October 1813, 912L:2088/44, 'Letterbook', emphasis as original.

67. Notes to Monthly Return, 25 January 1810, TNA, WO17/35.

68. Notes to Monthly Return, 25 January 1812, TNA, WO17/35, which make it explicit that Bywater was taken on to Portugal rather than being sent back – as one might have expected – to the regimental depot.

69. Returns of Courts Martial, TNA, WO27/106, 111, 116, 121, 126.

70. Return of Courts Martial, TNA, WO27/116.

71. Return of Courts Martial, TNA, WO27/106

72. Return of Courts Martial, TNA, WO27/126.

73. Return of Courts Martial, TNA, WO27/111.

74. 912L:2088/18, 'Standing Orders', p. 44.

75. Return of Courts Martial, TNA, WO27/106.

76. See also Bamford, *Sickness, Suffering, and the Sword*, pp. 52–4.

77. Steuart to Bridger, 4 April 1812, 912L:2088/44, 'Letterbook'.

78. Steuart to Blunden, 24 December 1812, 912L:2088/44, 'Letterbook'.

79. Confidential Reports, 15 June 1810 and December 1814, TNA, WO27/98, 129.

80. Return of Courts Martial, TNA, WO27/106.

81. Adjutant General's Office, *Rules and Regulations*, p. 14. The regimental justice system is discussed at length in Divall, Carole, *Inside the Regiment: The Officers and Men of the 30th Regiment During the Revolutionary and Napoleonic Wars*, Barnsley, Pen and Sword, 2011, pp. 130–62, and I am also grateful for the insights provided by Bryan Macmillan relating to his research into British military justice of the era.

82. Return of Courts Martial, TNA, WO27/116.
83. Confidential Report, 24 December 1812, TNA, WO27/111.
84. Confidential Report, 13 May 1812, TNA, WO27/106. Caruthers eventually got his cornetcy in 1815, filling one of the Waterloo vacancies.
85. 912L:2088/18, 'Standing Orders', p. 38.
86. Ibid., pp. 32–5.
87. Ibid., pp. 40–1.
88. Ibid.
89. Data from Field Return, 23 October 1809, TNA, WO27/96.
90. Data from Field Return, 26 October 1815, TNA, WO27/134.
91. Return of Courts Martial, TNA, WO27/121.
92. Return of Courts Martial, TNA, WO27/134.
93. 912L:2088/18, 'Standing Orders', p. 78.
94. Return of Courts Martial, TNA, WO27/111.
95. Return of Courts Martial, TNA, WO27/134.

Chapter IV: Horses and Riders

1. Confidential Report, 21 March 1806, TNA, WO27/90.
2. A necessarily brief summary of Tylden, Major G., *Horses and Saddlery*, London, J. A. Allen, 1965, pp. 4–20.
3. Tylden, *Horses and Saddlery*, pp. 12–15.
4. Steuart to Taylor, 17 January 1812, 912L:2088/44, 'Letterbook'; for clarity it should be noted that the hand is a measurement of four inches, and that the height is calculated from the bottom of the hoof to the top of the withers – see Tylden, *Horses and Saddlery*, p. 2.
5. Steuart to Taylor, 17 January 1812, 912L:2088/44, 'Letterbook'.
6. 'Remarks on Major Windham's Letter of 28th August 1811', 912L:2088/44, 'Letterbook'.
7. Wellington to Liverpool, 7 December 1810, TNA, WO1/246, pp. 481–5. For Steuart's developing preference for mares for the 12th, see Steuart to Taylor, 7 April 1812, 912L:2088/44, 'Letterbook'.
8. Field Return, 23 October 1809, TNA, WO27/96.
9. Steuart to Bridger, 31 August 1811, 912L:2088/44, 'Letterbook'.
10. Confidential Reports, 13 May 1812 and 20 April 1813, TNA, WO27/106 and 116.
11. Vandeleur to Mother, 2 May 1813, Vandeleur, *Letters*, pp. 72–7.
12. Adjutant General's Office, *Rules and Regulations*, pp. 17–18.
13. Steuart to Bridger, 31 August 1811, 912L:2088/44, 'Letterbook'.
14. Steuart to Lieut. Philips, 2 December 1811, 912L:2088/44, 'Letterbook'.
15. Steuart to Ponsonby, 26 November 1811; Steuart to Taylor, 17 January 1812; Steuart to Bridger, 29 January 1812: 912L:2088/44, 'Letterbook'.
16. Wellington to Bathurst, 14 April 1813, Gurwood, *Dispatches*, Vol. X, pp. 295–6; the figure for shipping costs is from Wellington to Vice Admiral Berkeley, 16 September 1811, ibid., Vol. VIII, pp. 282–3.
17. Steuart to Bridger, 29 January 1812; Steuart to Calvert, 9 February 1812,

Steuart to Robson, 9 February 1812: 912L:2088/44, 'Letterbook'. There seems to have been some confusion over the Yorkshire dealer's name – it may have been Robertson or even Robinson, but a series of inconsistently addressed letters and a memorandum in Steuart's own appalling hand make it impossible to be certain.

18. Memorandum in Steuart's own hand, 18 February 1812, 912L:2088/44, 'Letterbook'.
19. Steuart to Bridger, 23 February 1812, 912L:2088/44, 'Letterbook'.
20. Steuart to Greenwood, Cox & Co., 1 March 1812, 912L:2088/44, 'Letterbook'.
21. Steuart to Bridger, 17 May 1812, 912L:2088/44, 'Letterbook'.
22. Steuart to Bridger, 28 May 1812, 912L:2088/44, 'Letterbook'.
23. Steuart to Greenwood, Cox & Co., 17 May 1812; 912L:2088/44, 'Letterbook'. See also Steuart to Bridger, 28 May 1812, ibid.
24. Steuart to Bridger, 22 June 1812, 912L:2088/44, 'Letterbook'.
25. Steuart to Taylor, undated [late June 1812], 912L:2088/44, 'Letterbook'.
26. Steuart to Bridger, 2 July 1812, 912L:2088/44, 'Letterbook'.
27. Steuart to Taylor, 18 July 1812, 912L:2088/44, 'Letterbook'.
28. Steuart to Blunden, 2 February 1813, 912L:2088/44, 'Letterbook'.
29. Steuart to Olphert, 23 August 1812, 912L:2088/44, 'Letterbook'.
30. Steuart to Blunden, 2 February 1813, 912L:2088/44, 'Letterbook'.
31. Steuart to Greenwood, 3 February 1813, 912L:2088/44, 'Letterbook'.
32. Steuart to Philips, 13 February 1813, 912L:2088/44, 'Letterbook'.
33. Steuart to Harris, 19 September 1813; Steuart to Philips, 3 October 1813: 912L:2088/44, 'Letterbook'.
34. Steuart to Harris, 3 November 1813, 912L:2088/44, 'Letterbook'.
35. Steuart to Philips, 4 November 1813, 912L:2088/44, 'Letterbook'.
36. Steuart to Harris, 26 April 1814, 912L:2088/44, 'Letterbook'.
37. Confidential Report, 2 May 1814, TNA, WO27/126.
38. 'Remarks on Major Windham's Letter of 28th August 1811', 912L:2088/44, 'Letterbook'.
39. Field Return, 12 December 1812, TNA, WO27/111.
40. Field Return, 26 October 1815, TNA, WO27/134.
41. Field Return, 8 October 1812, TNA, WO27/111.
42. Houlding, *Fit for Service*, pp. 292–3; see also 912L:2088/18, 'Standing Orders', p. 160–2.
43. Steuart to Bridger, 3 March 1812, 912L:2088/44, 'Letterbook'.
44. Adjutant General's Office, *Rules and Regulations*, p. 17.
45. Adjutant General's Office, *Rules and Regulations*, pp. 29–30; Browne, *Regulations and Orders*, pp. 38–45; on the increase to two per troop, see Steuart to Calvert, 20 June 1808, 912L:2088/44, 'Letterbook'.
46. Adjutant General's Office, *Rules and Regulations*, p. 18.
47. Steuart to Calvert, 14 March 1812, 912L:2088/44, 'Letterbook', emphasis as original.
48. Hinde, Robert, *The Discipline of the Light Horse*, London, W. Owen, 1778, pp. 12–14.
49. Browne, *Regulations and Orders*, plate facing p. 45.

50. Hinde, *Discipline of the Light Horse*, pp. 12–14.
51. Anon., *The Light Horse Drill*, London, March and Teape, 1803, p. v.
52. Steuart to Browne, 13 September 1806, 912L:2088/44, 'Letterbook'.
53. Hinde, *Discipline of the Light Horse*, p. 16.
54. Steuart to Browne, 13 September 1806; Steuart to Bridger, 29 January 1812: 912L:2088/44, 'Letterbook'.
55. Freeman, Strickland, *The Art of Horsemanship*, London, W. Bulmer & Co., 1806, pp. 13–14.
56. Steuart to the Officer Commanding Depot, 12 July 1811, 912L:2088/44, 'Letterbook'.
57. Read, Martin, 'The British 1796 Pattern Light Cavalry Sword', at http://www.napoleon-series.org/military/organization/c_swordpoint1.html; Thoumine, R. H., *Scientific Soldier: A Life of General Le Marchant 1766–1812*, Oxford, Oxford University Press, 1968, pp. 41–4.
58. Vandeleur to Mother, 4 August 1813, Vandeleur, *Letters*, pp. 110–16. On cavalry swordsmanship more generally, see Read, Martin, 'Cavalry Combat and the Sword: Sword Design, Provision, and Use in the British Cavalry of the Napoleonic Era', at http://www.napoleon-series.org/military/organization/Britain/Cavalry/Swords/Swordpoint/c_swordpoint2.html.
59. Lady Bessborough to Leveson-Gower, 8 December 1811, Granville, *Private Correspondence*, Vol. II, pp. 420–1.
60. Steuart to Bridger, 29 January 1812, 912L:2088/44, 'Letterbook'.
61. Ibid. I should also express a debt to historian and horseman David Blackmore for his insights into mounted combat and to the 1796 Sword and its associated drills in particular.
62. 912L:2088/18, 'Standing Orders', pp. 98–101.
63. Houlding, *Fit for Service*, p. 264.
64. Steuart to Ponsonby, undated [January 1813], 912L:2088/44, 'Letterbook'.
65. Fletcher, *Galloping at Everything*, pp. 17–18; Wellington to Payne, 27 January 1810, Gurwood, *Dispatches*, Vol. V, pp. 459–60.
66. James, *Regimental Companion*, Vol. III, p. 300–6.
67. 912L:2088/18, 'Standing Orders', p. 8.
68. Bartlet, J., *The Gentleman's Farriery: or a Practical Treatise on the Diseases of Horses*, 2 vols, London, J. Nourse, 1770.
69. 912L:2088/18, 'Standing Orders', p. 114.
70. Ibid., pp. 114–17.
71. Confidential Reports, 15 October 1810 and 8 October 1812, TNA, WO27/100, 111.
72. 912L:2088/18, 'Standing Orders', p. 114; Adjutant General's Office, *Rules and Regulations*, pp. 111–12.
73. Brett-James, Antony, *Life in Wellington's Army*, London, Tom Donovan, 1994, pp. 185–8.
74. Steuart to Greenwood, Cox & Co., 25 July 1809, 912L:2088/44, 'Letterbook'; Field Return, 23 October 1809, TNA, WO27/96.
75. Confidential Report, 24 December 1812, TNA, WO27/111.
76. Confidential Report, 13 May 1812, TNA, WO27/106.

77. Bartlet, *Gentleman's Farriery*, Vol. II, pp. 143–4.
78. Ibid., pp. 246–52.
79. Ibid., pp. 115–23.
80. Department of Environment, Food, and Rural Affairs, 'Glanders and Farcy', at http://www.defra.gov.uk/ahvla-en/disease-control/notifiable/glanders-farcy.
81. 'Confidential Report of the 12th Regiment of Light Dragoons, Inspected by Major General Fane, at Dorchester December 1814', TNA, WO27/129, emphasis as original.
82. General Order of 17 November 1810, Gurwood, Lieut. Colonel (ed.), *General Orders Spain and Portugal*, London, T. Egerton, 1811–13, Vol. II, pp. 207–8; for French practice, see Johnson, David, *The French Cavalry 1792–1815*, London, Belmont, 1989, p. 78.

Chapter V: Service at Home and Abroad

1. Postings can be tracked from the successive Monthly Returns, TNA, WO17/35, 256, 272, 288.
2. Stewart, *XII Royal Lancers*, pp. 57–8. I entertain some doubts over the veracity of this anecdote, which is unsourced and which would – notwithstanding the Prince's nominal connection to the 12th – make more sense if told of a 10th Hussar.
3. Confidential Report, 21 March 1806, and 'Return of Horses, Clothing, appointments &c wanting to complete the 12th (or PW) Regt of Light Dragns. to 772 being their present Effective Strength in Men, Blatchington, 25th March 1806', TNA, WO27/90.
4. Confidential Report, 21 March 1806, TNA, Wo27/90. For Houlding's argument, see *Fit for Service*, pp. 1–98.
5. Notes to Monthly Return, 1 July 1807, TNA, WO17/35.
6. Notes to Monthly Return, 1 August 1807, TNA, WO17/35.
7. Notes to Monthly Return, 1 January 1809, TNA, WO17/35.
8. 912L:2088/18, 'Standing Orders', p. 148.
9. 912L:2088/18, 'Standing Orders', p. 149.
10. Notes to Monthly Return, 25 April 1813, TNA, WO17/256.
11. War Office, *Instructions and Regulations for the Formations and Movements of the Cavalry*, London, T. Egerton, 1799.
12. Steuart to Browne, 13 September 1806, 912L:2088/44, 'Letterbook'.
13. Tomkinson, Lt Col William, *Diary of a Cavalry Officer in the Peninsular and Waterloo Campaigns 1808–1815*, London, Swan Sonnenschein & Co., 1894, p. 135.
14. Vandeleur, John Ormsby, *Duties of Officers Commanding Detachments in the Field*, London, T. Egerton, 1801, pp. 1–59.
15. Hay, *Reminiscences*, p. 57; Steuart to Bridger, 4 April 1812, 912L:2088/44, 'Letterbook'.
16. Confidential Report, 8 October 1812, TNA, WO27/111.
17. Confidential Reports, 20 April 1813 and 2 May 1814, TNA, WO27/116, 126.
18. Confidential Report, 8 October 1812, TNA, WO27/111.

19. General political and military background from Muir, Rory, *Britain and the Defeat of Napoleon 1807–1815*, New Haven, Yale University Press, 1996, pp. 21–78; on the planned cavalry reinforcements for Moore, see McGuigan, Ron, 'The Origins of Wellington's Peninsular Army', in Muir, Rory, et al., *Inside Wellington's Peninsular Army*, Barnsley, Pen and Sword, 2006, p. 54.

20. Figures computed from theatre-level returns in the WO17 series, reproduced in Bamford, Andrew, 'British Army Unit Strengths: 1808–1815', at http://www.napoleon-series.org/military/organization/Britain/Strength/Bamford/c_BritishArmyStrengthStudyIntroduction.html.

21. 'Return of the Regiments now under Orders for Foreign Service', Anon., *A Collection of Papers Relating to the Expedition to the Scheldt Presented to Parliament in 1810*, London, A. Strahan, 1811, pp. 25–7; on the background to the expedition, see Muir, *Britain and the Defeat of Napoleon*, pp. 79–90.

22. Order of battle from Burnham, Robert, 'The British Expeditionary Force to Walcheren: 1809', at http://www.napoleon-series.org/military/battles/c_walcheren.html; on Linsingen, see McGuigan, Ron, 'British Generals of the Napoleonic Wars 1793–1815', at http://www.napoleon-series.org/research/biographies/BritishGenerals/ c_Britishgenerals1.html.

23. Notes to Monthly Returns, June–September 1809, in TNA, WO17/35.

24. Steuart to Browne, 6 July 1809, 912L:2088/44, 'Letterbook'.

25. Monthly Return, 25 July 1809, TNA, WO17/35.

26. Vandeleur, *Letters*, p. 44.

27. McGuigan, 'Origins of Wellington's Peninsular Army', p. 54.

28. Bamford, *Sickness, Suffering, and the Sword*, pp. 270–1; Fletcher, *Galloping at Everything*, p. 17.

29. Chatham to Castlereagh, 2 August 1809, Anon., *Expedition to the Scheldt*, pp. 69–73.

30. Anon., *British Minor Expeditions 1746 to 1814*, London, HMSO, 1884, pp. 57–79.

31. Monthly Return, 25 September 1809, TNA, WO17/35.

32. Urban, Silvanus, *The Gentleman's Magazine and Historical Chronicle for the Year 1809*, London, John Nichols, 1809, Vol. II, p. 987.

33. Bamford, *Sickness, Suffering, and the Sword*, pp. 230–1.

34. Confidential Report, 15 June 1810, TNA, WO27/98.

35. Confidential Report, 15 October 1810, TNA, WO27/100.

36. Oman, Sir Charles, *Wellington's Army*, London, Edward Arnold, 1913, p. 349.

37. Wellington to Liverpool, 7 December 1810, TNA, WO1/246, pp. 481–5.

38. Notes to Monthly Return, 25 April 1810, TNA, WO17/35.

39. Liverpool to Wellington, 7 May 1811, Wellington, 2nd Duke of (ed.), *Supplementary Despatches, Correspondence, and Memoranda, of Field Marshal Arthur, Duke of Wellington*, London, John Murray, 1858–62, Vol. VII, pp. 119–20.

40. The reinforcement situation, and plans for the 12th, are discussed in Gerges, Mark, 'Command and Control in the Peninsula: the Role of British Cavalry 1808–1814', unpublished PhD thesis, Florida State University, 2005, pp. 201–2.

41. Bamford, *Sickness, Suffering, and the Sword*, pp. 142–4, 150–6, 174–6.
42. Monthly Return, 25 May 1811, TNA, WO17/35.
43. Wellington to Cotton, 2 June 1811, Gurwood, *Dispatches*, Vol. VII, pp. 646–7; notes to Monthly Return, 25 May 1811, TNA, WO17/35.
44. Wellington to Cotton, 18 June 1811, Gurwood, *Dispatches*, Vol. VIII, p. 32. Note, therefore, that this predates the reappointment of York as Commander-in-Chief the following day, rather than being a product of it as the author initially assumed prior to cross-checking the dates.
45. Notes to Monthly Returns, May and June 1811, TNA, WO17/35.

Chapter VI: To War in the Peninsula

1. The date of landing from 912L:2088/30, 'Registry of Services', although Oman, *Wellington's Army*, p. 352, gives 1 July; that Oman is in error is reinforced by the existence of a Monthly Return dated Belhem [*sic*], 25 June 1811, in TNA, WO17/35.
2. A good first impression of Lisbon may be had from Vandeleur, *Letters*, pp. 5–10, relating the writer's arrival there in September 1810 as an ensign of the 71st Highland Light Infantry.
3. Notes to Monthly Returns, June 1811–March 1812, TNA, WO17/35.
4. Monthly Return, 25 June 1811, TNA, WO17/35.
5. Notes to Monthly Return, 25 July 1811, TNA, WO17/35.
6. Monthly Return, 25 July 1811, TNA, WO17/35.
7. Gurwood, Lieut. Colonel (ed.), *The General Orders of Field Marshal the Duke of Wellington KG*, London, W. Clownes & Sons, 1838, pp. 113–16; see also Fletcher, *Galloping at Everything*, pp. 18–20.
8. Monthly Returns, September 1811–February 1812, TNA, WO17/35; Burnham, 'Challis' "Peninsula Roll Call"'.
9. Monthly Returns, November 1811–May 1812, TNA, WO17/35.
10. Steuart to Wellington, 30 September 1811, 912L:2088/44, 'Letterbook'.
11. Steuart to Greenwood, Cox & Co., 17 February and 1 March 1812, 912L:2088/44, 'Letterbook'. The latter notes a reply from Wellington to Steuart dated 29 January 1812, but this is not included in *Dispatches* or *Supplementary Despatches*.
12. 'Remarks on Major Windham's Letter of 28th August 1811', 912L:2088/44, 'Letterbook'.
13. Steuart to Cox & Greenwood, 1 March 1812, 912L:2088/44, 'Letterbook'.
14. Steuart to Ponsonby ('in answer to his Letter of 8th Sept 1811'), 9 October 1811, 912L:2088/44, 'Letterbook'.
15. Bamford, *Sickness, Suffering, and the Sword*, pp. 234–5, 284–5, and with respect to the 1811 arrivals, Gerges, 'Command and Control', p. 215.
16. Hay, *Reminiscences*, pp. 1–45, quoting pp. 33, 44.
17. Hay, *Reminiscences*, pp. 33–43, 76–7, quoting pp. 37, 77.
18. Oman, *Wellington's Army*, p. 352.
19. Thompson, Mark S., 'Cavalry Actions in the Peninsular War', *BCMH Spring 2012 Conference Report*, pp. 2–8; Fletcher, *Galloping at Everything*, pp. 3–7.

Oman, *Wellington's Army*, pp. 36, 103–4, has a rather more critical view.

20. Gerges, 'Command and Control', pp. 40–53, 145–55, 166–78, 258–61, 351; Fletcher, *Galloping at Everything*, pp. 90–9; McGuigan, 'British Generals'; Oman, *Wellington's Army*, p. 344.

21. Oman, Sir Charles, *A History of the Peninsular War*, Oxford: Oxford University Press, 1902–30, Vol. IV, pp. 288–474.

22. Wellington to Liverpool, 29 September 1811, Gurwood, *Dispatches*, Vol. VIII, pp. 303–10; Gerges, 'Command and Control', pp. 216–23, Oman, *Peninsular War*, Vol. IV, pp. 542–82, quoting p. 578. For men taken prisoner, see notes to Monthly Return, 25 October 1811, TNA, WO17/35.

23. 912L:2088/30, 'Registry of Services'.

24. Tomkinson, *Diary*, p. 120.

25. Wellington to Liverpool, 2 October 1811, Gurwood, *Dispatches*, Vol. VIII, pp. 315–16.

26. Wellington to Cotton, 7 October 1811, Gurwood, *Dispatches*, Vol. VIII, pp. 326–7.

27. Wellington to Cotton, 9 October 1811, Gurwood, *Dispatches*, Vol. VIII, pp. 328–9.

28. Monthly Returns and notes, October–December 1811, TNA, WO17/35.

29. Oman, *Peninsular War*, Vol. V, pp. 157–216.

30. Oman, *Wellington's Army*, pp. 358–60; Bamford, *Sickness, Suffering, and the Sword*, pp. 195–6.

31. Compare Thompson, 'Cavalry Actions', p. 7, with Gerges, 'Command and Control', p. 375.

32. McGuigan, 'British Generals'.

33. Lady Bessborough to Leveson-Gower, 26 March 1812, Granville, *Private Correspondence*, Vol. II, p. 433.

34. Notes to Monthly Returns, January–September 1812, TNA, WO17/35.

35. 912L:2088/30, 'Registry of Services'; Tomkinson, *Diary*, p. 128.

36. Monthly Return, 25 February 1812, TNA, WO17/2469.

37. Tomkinson, *Diary*, p. 128.

38. 912L:2088/30, 'Registry of Services'.

39. Tomkinson, *Diary*, p. 130.

40. General Order, 28 April 1812, Gurwood, *General Orders*, Vol. IV, p. 28.

41. Oman, *Peninsular War*, Vol. V, pp. 217–34.

42. Tomkinson, *Diary*, pp. 134–8.

43. Gerges, 'Command and Control', pp. 242–3; on the duties of such officers, see Burnham, Robert, 'British Observing Officers of the Peninsular War', in Muir, *Inside Wellington's Peninsular Army*, pp. 71–83.

44. Oman, *Peninsular War*, Vol. V, p. 265–73.

45. Wellington to Liverpool, 7 April 1812, Gurwood, *Dispatches*, Vol. IX, pp. 40–8; see Oman, *Peninsular War*, Vol. V, pp. 234–64.

46. Graham to Cotton, 10 April 1812, Combermere, Viscountess, and Captain W. W. Knollys, *Memoirs and Correspondence of Field Marshal Viscount Combermere*, London, Hurst & Blackett, 1866, Vol. I, p. 245.

47. I am obliged to José Luis Arcon for confirming the order of battle of the cavalry

component of d'Erlon's force from the 'Etat de Situation' of 1 May, 1812. See also Burnham, Robert, *Charging Against Wellington: The French Cavalry in the Peninsular War*, Barnsley, Frontline Books, 2011, pp. 65–70, 163–4; 204–5.

48. This narrative of the Battle of Villagarcia is compiled, unless otherwise cited, from Combermere and Knollys, *Memoirs and Correspondence*, Vol. I, pp. 246–56 (which includes Cotton's dispatch); Fletcher, *Galloping at Everything*, pp. 159–65; Fortescue, Hon. J. W., *A History of the British Army*, London, Macmillan, 1899–1930, Vol. VIII, pp. 412–15; Gerges, 'Command and Control', pp. 242–9; Oman, *Peninsular War*, Vol. V, pp. 277–9; Stewart, *XII Royal Lancers*, pp. 69–72; Thoumine, *Scientific Soldier*, pp. 160–74; Tomkinson, *Diary*, pp. 149–52.

49. Cotton to Ponsonby, 10 April 1810, Tomkinson, *Diary*, p. 152. Berlanga is some eleven miles east of Llerena.

50. Cocks to Mother, 15 April 1812, Page, Julia (ed.), *Intelligence Officer in the Peninsula: Letters & Diaries of Major the Hon. Edward Charles Cocks 1786–1812*, Tunbridge Wells, Spellmount, 1986, p. 174.

51. Tomkinson, *Diary*, p. 150.

52. Monthly Return, 25 March 1812, TNA, WO17/2469.

53. Tomkinson, *Diary*, p. 150; Cotton to Graham, 11 April, Combermere and Knollys, *Memoirs and Correspondence*, Vol. I, pp. 253–6.

54. Burnham, *Charging Against Wellington*, pp. 70–2; the 2eme Hussards had 308 men on 1 July.

55. The main source for Ponsonby being pressed is Thoumine, *Scientific Soldier*, pp. 169–70, but, as a biography of Le Marchant sourced from early eulogistic accounts of that officer's life, it suits the narrative to paint a picture of disaster redeemed by the intervention of Le Marchant's heavies.

56. Tomkinson, *Diary*, p. 150.

57. Fortescue, *British Army*, Vol. VIII, pp. 414–15.

58. Cotton to Graham, 11 April, Combermere and Knollys, *Memoirs and Correspondence*, Vol. I, pp. 253–6; Tomkinson, *Diary*, p. 151.

59. Tomkinson, *Diary*, p. 151.

60. 'Return of Killed, Wounded, and Missing, of the First Cavalry Division of the Army under the command of General the Earl of Wellington KB, in an affair with the Enemy's rear guard, near Llerena, on the 11th of April, 1812', Gurwood, *Dispatches*, Vol. IX, p. 67; fatalities in the 12th from Monthly Return and notes, 25 April 1812, TNA, WO17/35, and 912L:2088/30, 'Registry of Services'. The assertion that the bulk of the losses fell to the 5th Dragoon Guards is from Thoumine, *Scientific Soldier*, p. 171, but is backed up by a comparison of losses in Monthly Return, 25 April 1812, TNA, WO17/2469.

61. Burnham, *Charging Against Wellington*, pp. 163–5; Fletcher, *Galloping at Everything*, pp. 166–78.

Chapter VII: **To Burgos and Back Again**

1. Wellington to Liverpool, 26 May 1812, Gurwood, *Dispatches*, Vol. IX, pp. 172–8.

2. Oman, *Peninsular War*, Vol. V, pp. 315–34.

3. 912L:2088/30, 'Registry of Services'; Tomkinson, *Diary*, pp. 153–9.
4. Monthly Returns and notes, May–June 1812, TNA. WO17/35; Stawell's appointment from General Order of 23 April 1812, Gurwood, *General Orders*, Vol. IV, p. 67.
5. Wellington to Liverpool, 26 May 1812, Gurwood, *Dispatches*, Vol. IX, pp. 172–8; French strength figures from Muir, Rory, *Salamanca 1812*, New Haven, Yale University Press, 2001, pp. 263–4.
6. Muir, *Salamanca*, pp. 5–9; Oman, *Peninsular War*, Vol. V, pp. 334–82; Tomkinson, *Diary*, pp. 159–74.
7. 912L:2088/30, 'Registry of Services'; Tomkinson, *Diary*, pp. 163–9.
8. Ponsonby to Lady Bessborough, 6 July 1812, Granville, *Private Correspondence*, Vol. II, pp. 436–7; see also Tomkinson, *Diary*, pp. 174–6.
9. Ponsonby to Lady Bessborough, 6 July 1812, Granville, *Private Correspondence*, Vol. II, pp. 436–7.
10. General Order of 1 July 1812, Gurwood, *General Orders*, Vol. IV, p. 118; Tomkinson, Diary, p. 174.
11. Muir, *Salamanca*, pp. 9–11.
12. Tomkinson, *Diary*, p. 181.
13. 912L:2088/30, 'Registry of Services'.
14. Ponsonby to Lady Bessborough, 25 July 1812, Granville, *Private Correspondence*, Vol. II, pp. 449–51; Gerges, 'Command and Control', pp. 274–6.
15. Muir, *Salamanca*, pp. 19, 238.
16. Tomkinson, *Diary*, p. 181.
17. Gerges, 'Command and Control', p. 275. See also Muir, *Salamanca*, pp. 12–13, 19–20; Oman, *Peninsular War*, Vol. V, pp. 402–3.
18. Muir, *Salamanca*, pp. 16–18, Oman, *Peninsular War*, Vol. V, pp. 408–17.
19. Muir, *Salamanca, passim.*
20. Muir, *Salamanca*, pp. 62, 76; the earlier position is indicated in Gerges, 'Command and Control', p. 282.
21. Ponsonby to Lady Bessborough, 25 July 1812, Granville, *Private Correspondence*, Vol. II, pp. 449–51.
22. Lady Bessborough to Leveson-Gower, 21 Augsust 1812, Granville, *Private Correspondence*, Vol. II, pp. 449–51.
23. Muir, *Salamanca*, pp. 196–8, 205.
24. Casualties from 912L:2088/30, 'Registry of Services'; Muir, *Salamanca*, p. 249. The Monthly Return, 25 July 1812, TNA, WO17/35, lists five rank and file dead and two taken prisoner but this also includes losses on 18 July.
25. Muir, *Salamanca*, pp. 194–5.
26. 912L:2088/30, 'Registry of Services'. This account simply refers to this as Andrews's squadron, but Andrews was too junior to have held a squadron command at the outset of the battle hence the inference that it was his troop and Dickens's that made up the squadron engaged with Ponsonby, and that Andrews took over after Dickens fell.
27. 912L:2088/30, 'Registry of Services'; see also Oman, *Peninsular War*, Vol. V, pp. 475–518.

28. Ponsonby to Lady Bessborough, 28 July 1812, Granville, *Private Correspondence*, Vol. II, pp. 451–2.
29. Ponsonby to Lady Bessborough, 2 August 1812, Granville, *Private Correspondence*, Vol. II, pp. 454–6.
30. Oman, *Peninsular War*, Vol. V, p. 491.
31. 912L:2088/30, 'Registry of Services'; Tomkinson, *Diary*, p. 195.
32. Monthly Return, 25 August 1812, TNA, WO17/35.
33. Ponsonby to Lady Bessborough, 2 August 1812, Granville, *Private Correspondence*, Vol. II, pp. 454–6; Monthly Return, 25 August 1812, TNA, WO17/35.
34. Oman, *Peninsular War*, Vol. V, pp. 576–82.
35. Hay, *Reminiscences*, pp. 57–8.
36. Vandeleur, *Letters*, pp. v–vi; Monthly Return, 25 April 1812, TNA, WO17/35.
37. Hay, *Reminiscences*, pp. 64–72.
38. Vandeleur to Mother, 13 October 1812, Vandeleur, *Letters*, pp. 48–54.
39. Ibid.
40. Hay, *Reminiscences*, p. 72.
41. Vandeleur to Mother, 25 November 1812, Vandeleur, *Letters*, pp. 54–9; an exact date is not given, but from context it predates Wellington's abandonment of the Duero line on 5 November by only a day or two.
42. Tomkinson, *Diary*, p. 203.
43. Divall, Carole, *Wellington's Worst Scrape: The Burgos Campaign 1812*, Barnsley, Pen and Sword, 2012, pp. 39–98; Oman, *Peninsular War*. Vol. VI, pp. 21–51.
44. Tomkinson, *Diary*, p. 208. Tomkinson relates the story under the diary heading of 3 October, but the notes to the 12th's Monthly Return, 25 October 1812, confirm that the action took place on the 2nd.
45. Tomkinson, *Diary*, pp. 208–9.
46. Wellington to Paget, 13 October 1812, Gurwood, *Dispatches*, Vol. IX, p. 482; Wellington to Bathurst, 26 October 1812, ibid., pp. 507–13.
47. William Ponsonby to Lord Bessborough, 18 October 1812, Ponsonby, *Ponsonby Family*, p. 117.
48. Ponsonby to sister-in-law, undated, Ponsonby, *Ponsonby Family*, p. 117.
49. Oman, *Peninsular War*, Vol. VI, p. 75; Monthly Return, 25 October 1812, TNA, WO17/35.
50. 912L:2088/30, 'Registry of Services'.
51. Combermere and Knollys, *Memoirs and Correspondence*, Vol. I, pp. 292–5; Divall, *Worst Scrape*, pp. 102–6; Fletcher, *Galloping at Everything*, pp. 190–3; Gerges, 'Command and Control', pp. 329–33.
52. Oman, *Peninsular War*, Vol. VI, p. 75.
53. Hay, *Reminiscences*, p. 78.
54. Oman, *Peninsular War*, Vol. VI, pp. 111–28.
55. Vandeleur to Mother, 25 November 1812, Vandeleur, *Letters*, pp. 54–9.
56. Oman, *Peninsular War*, Vol. VI, pp. 132–6
57. Hay, *Reminiscences*, pp. 72–6. I am much obliged to Raul Gomez, Ron McGuigan, and Oscar Lopez, for assisting me in establishing the identity of the depot commander, referred to by Hay only as 'Captain J_____', and for

confirming its location. See also Burnham, 'Challis' "Peninsula Roll Call"'; Redgrave, Toby Michael Ormsby, 'Wellington's Logistical Arrangements in the Peninsular War 1809–14', unpublished PhD thesis, King's College, London, 1979, p. 175.

58. Hay, *Reminiscences*, p. 77.
59. Vandeleur to Mother, 25 November 1812, Vandeleur, *Letters*, pp. 54–9.
60. Oman, *Peninsular War*, Vol. VI, pp. 136–66.
61. Vandeleur to Mother, 25 November 1812, Vandeleur, *Letters*, pp. 54–9.
62. Hay, *Reminiscences*, pp. 79–91.
63. Oman, *Peninsular War*, Vol. VI, pp. 745–6, the retreat being calculated as beginning on 23 October and ending on 19 November.
64. Monthly Return and notes, 25 November 1812, TNA, WO17/35.

Chapter VIII: The Hard Road to Vitoria

1. Confidential Report, 24 December 1812, TNA, WO27/111.
2. General Order of 4 December 1812, Gurwood, *General Orders*, Vol. IV, pp. 227–8; Hay, *Reminiscences*, p. 119; Burnham, 'Challis' "Peninsula Roll Call"'.
3. Confidential Report, 24 December 1812, TNA, WO27/111.
4. Ibid. See also Return of Courts Martial, TNA, WO27/111.
5. Hay, *Reminiscences*, p. 92
6. Confidential Report, 24 December 1812, TNA, WO27/111.
7. Steuart to Torrens, 1 and 5 April 1813, 912L:2088/44, 'Letterbook'.
8. Steuart to Calvert, 9 June 1813, 912L:2088/44, 'Letterbook'.
9. Ibid.
10. Steuart to Cox & Greenwood, 1 March 1812, 912L:2088/44, 'Letterbook'.
11. Steuart to Greenwood, 11 June 1813, 912L:2088/44, 'Letterbook'.
12. Ibid.
13. Oman, *Peninsular War*, Vol. VI, pp. 156–8; for Steuart's opinion, see Steuart to Ponsonby, 3 April 1813, 912L:2088/44, 'Letterbook'.
14. Gerges, 'Command and Control', pp. 349–52.
15. Oman, *Peninsular War*, Vol. VI, pp. 750–1. Later in the year the 7th Hussars would also deploy to the Peninsula, and there were also four regiments of Portuguese cavalry still with the field army.
16. Steuart to Greenwood, Cox & Co., 1 August 1813, 912L:2088/44, 'Letterbook'.
17. Steuart to Gibson & Peat, 2 June 1813, 912L:2088/44, 'Letterbook'.
18. On the Staff Corps of Cavalry, see the biography of their commander: Urban, Mark, *The Man Who Broke Napoleon's Codes: The Story of George Scovell*, London, Faber & Faber, 2001, pp. 256–60.
19. 'Remarks on Major Windham's Letter of 28th August 1811', 912L:2088/44, 'Letterbook'.
20. Steuart to Torrens, 12 March 1812, 912L:2088/44, 'Letterbook'. 'Old', in this sense, meant experienced and not aged.
21. Steuart to Bridger, 4 April 1812, 912L:2088/44, 'Letterbook'.

22. Steuart to Ponsonby, undated [January 1813]; Steuart to Torrens, 11 October 1812: 912L:2088/44, 'Letterbook'.
23. Steuart to Torrens, 9 and 14 March 1813, 912L:2088/44, 'Letterbook'.
24. Steuart to Hammon, 24 March 1813, 912L:2088/44, 'Letterbook'.
25. Steuart to Ponsonby, 3 April 1813, 912L:2088/44, 'Letterbook'.
26. Steuart to Officer Commanding Depot, 2 April 1813; Steuart to Coles, 2 June 1813: both in 912L:2088/44, 'Letterbook'.
27. Steuart to Torrens, 1 April 1813, 912L:2088/44, 'Letterbook'.
28. Steuart to Greenwood, Cox & Co., 2 June 1813, 912L:2088/44, 'Letterbook'.
29. Burnham, 'Challis' "Peninsula Roll Call"'.
30. Hay, *Reminiscences*, p. 124.
31. Vandeleur to Mother, 20 May 1813, Vandeleur, *Letters*, pp. 78–88.
32. Monthly Return and notes, 25 May 1813, TNA, WO17/256. On the return of prisoners and stragglers, see also Bamford, *Sickness, Suffering*, pp. 250–2, and, in the specific context of the Burgos retreat, Divall, *Worst Scrape*, pp. 216–20.
33. 912L:2088/30. 'Registry of Services'; Hay, *Reminiscences*, p. 99.
34. Oman, *Peninsular War*, Vol. VI, pp. 238–51, 305–7, 311.
35. Vandeleur to Mother, 2 May 1813, Vandeleur, *Letters*, pp. 72–7.
36. Oman, *Peninsular War*, Vol. VI, pp. 303–4, 314–33.
37. Vandeleur to Mother, 20 May 1813, Vandeleur, *Letters*, pp. 78–88.
38. Vandeleur to Mother, 19 June 1813, Vandeleur, *Letters*, pp. 88–98.
39. Ibid.
40. Oman, *Peninsular War*, Vol. VI, pp. 353–74.
41. Vandeleur to Mother, 12 July 1813, Vandeleur, *Letters*, pp. 100–10.
42. Hay, *Reminiscences*, p. 102.
43. Oman, *Peninsular War*, Vol. VI, pp. 750–7.
44. This brief description is taken from the schematic in Weller, Jac, *Wellington in the Peninsula*, London, Greenhill, 1999, pp. 256–7, which conveys the basic layout of the battlefield without any pretence to exact detail. A more detailed map may be found in Oman, *Peninsular War*, Vol. VI, between pp. 435–6.
45. Fletcher, Ian, *Vittoria 1813: Wellington Sweeps the French from Spain*, Oxford, Osprey, 1998; Oman, *Peninsular War*, Vol. VI, pp. 384–450. It is to be regretted that the former, whilst one of Osprey's better offerings, is the only English-language treatment of the battle to have emerged in recent years.
46. Tomkinson, *Diary*, p. 245.
47. Hay, *Reminiscences*, p. 109.
48. Tomkinson, *Diary*, pp. 245–6.
49. Oman, *Peninsular War*, Vol. VI, pp. 424–8.
50. Ibid., pp. 433–8.
51. Tomkinson, *Diary*, pp. 250–1.
52. Hay, *Reminiscences*, pp. 113–14.
53. Vandeleur to Mother, 12 July 1813, Vandeleur, *Letters*, pp. 100–10; an earlier note, dashed off immediately after the battle, confirms the circumstances of Hammon's death; see Vandeleur to Mother, 22 June, ibid., pp. 98–100.
54. Dallas, Alexander R. C., *Felix Alvarez; or Manners in Spain*, London, Baldwin, Cradock and Joy, 1818, vol. III, p. 199. See also note on p. 298, which stresses

that 'the particular part of the battle of Vitoria here described is the progress and charge of Major General Sir G. Anson's brigade of cavalry, *being that with which the author is more acquainted from his own observation*' [emphasis added].

55. Hay, *Reminiscences*, p. 114.
56. Fatalities from casualty returns, June–July 1813, TNA, WO25/1437; wounded from Oman, *Peninsular War*, Vol. VI, p. 759, although there is some discrepancy here since this listing gives three rank and file deaths for the 12th, which does not match the regimental return.
57. Steuart to York, 7 July 1813, 912L:2088/44, 'Letterbook'.
58. Steuart to Officer Commanding Depot, 31 July 1813, 912L:2088/44, 'Letterbook'.
59. Steuart to Barton, 31 January 1814, 912L:2088/44, 'Letterbook'.
60. TNA, PROB11/1683/155: Will of Richard Sidley, Regimental Quarter Master of the 12th Regt. of Royal Lancers.
61. Oman, *Peninsular War*, Vol. VI, pp. 757–62.

Chapter IX: **Over the Pyrenees**

1. Hay, *Reminiscences*, pp. 114–15; Tomkinson, *Diary*, p. 253.
2. Oman, *Peninsular War*, Vol. VI, pp. 456–8; Tomkinson, *Diary*, pp. 256–9.
3. Tomkinson, *Diary*, p. 257.
4. Vandeleur to Mother, 12 July 1813, Vandeleur, *Letters*, pp. 100–10.
5. Ibid.
6. Tomkinson, *Diary*, pp. 261–3.
7. Gerges, 'Command and Control', pp. 371–6; Oman, *Wellington's Army*, p. 367.
8. Wellington to Anson, Wellington to Vandeleur, 2 July 1813, Gurwood, *Dispatches*, Vol. X, p. 489.
9. Vandeleur to Mother, 12 July 1813, Vandeleur, *Letters*, pp. 100–10.
10. Vandeleur to Mother, 18 August 1813, Vandeleur, *Letters*, pp. 116–21.
11. Oman, *Peninsular War*, Vol. VI, pp. 587–740, 765–8; Robertson, Ian C., *Wellington Invades France: The Final Phase of the Peninsular War 1813–1814*, London, Greenhill, 2003, pp. 56–98.
12. 912L:2088/30, 'Registry of Services'.
13. Oman, *Peninsular War*, Vol. VI, pp. 557–86, Vol. VII, pp. 1–62; Robertson, *Wellington Invades France*, pp. 47–55, 99–111.
14. Tomkinson, *Diary*, p. 267.
15. Oman, *Peninsular War*, Vol. VII, pp. 110–36; 912L:2088/30, 'Registry of Services'.
16. Vandeleur to Mother, 17 October 1813, Vandeleur, *Letters*, pp. 129–33.
17. Lady Bessborough to Leveson-Gower, undated [October/November 1813], Granville, *Private Correspondence*, Vol. II, pp. 486–7.
18. Quoted in Lady Bessborough to Leveson-Gower, undated [October 1813], Granville, *Private Correspondence*, Vol. II, pp. 479–80.
19. Monthly Return and Notes, 25 September 1813, TNA, WO17/256; Vandeleur to Mother, 4 August 1813, Vandeleur, *Letters*, pp. 110–16; Burnham, 'Challis' "Peninsula Roll Call"'.

20. Oman, *Peninsular War*, Vol. VII, pp. 159–208; Robertson, *Wellington Invades France*, pp. 137–57.

21. Hay, *Reminiscences*, pp. 125–6. Hay refers to his superior as 'Colonel' Bridger throughout this passage, but Bridger did not obtain his lieutenant colonelcy until two years later, and that by brevet only.

22. Gleig, George Robert (ed. Ian C. Robertson), *The Subaltern: A Chronicle of the Peninsular War*, Barnsley, Leo Cooper, 2001, p. 71.

23. 912L:2088/30, 'Registry of Services'.

24. Hay, *Reminiscences*, p. 126.

25. 912L:2088/30, 'Registry of Services'.

26. Hay, *Reminiscences*, p. 127.

27. Oman, *Peninsular War*, Vol. VII, pp. 209–81; Robertson, *Wellington Invades France*, pp. 158–86.

28. Vandeleur to Mother, 12 December 1813, Vandeleur, *Letters*, pp. 134–8.

29. Ibid.

30. Vandeleur to Mother, 19 December 1813, Vandeleur, *Letters*, pp. 138–43.

31. Ibid.

32. 912L:2088/30, 'Registry of Services'.

33. Monthly Returns and Notes, December 1813–February 1814, TNA, WO17/256, 272; see also Gerges, 'Command and Control', pp. 384–5.

34. Burnham, 'Challis' "Peninsula Roll Call"'.

35. Vandeleur to Mother, 6 March 1814, Vandeleur, *Letters*, pp. 143–8. Vandeleur's account is rather ambiguous and could be read to imply that he was on the north bank during the French attack on the bridgehead. If he was, it was not as a regimental officer, for the first men of the 12th did not cross until the following day. See also 912L:2088/30, 'Registry of Services'; Oman, *Peninsular War*, Vol. VII, pp. 330–40, Robertson, *Wellington Invades France*, pp. 194–200.

36. Hay, *Reminiscences*, pp. 130–131.

37. 912L:2088/30, 'Registry of Services'; Gerges, 'Command and Control', p. 393.

38. Hope to Wellington, 10 March 1814, Wellington, *Supplementary Dispatches*, Vol. VIII, p. 636.

39. Robertson, *Wellington Invades France*, pp. 215–16. Major General Richard Hussey Vivian had newly taken over the brigade previously under Alten.

40. Hay, *Reminiscences*, pp. 131–4. A good description of Bordeaux may be found in Vandeleur to Mother, 8 April 1814, Vandeleur, *Letters*, pp. 148–52, but Vandeleur was only in the city briefly, remaining otherwise with his cousin's staff at Dax.

41. Murray to Hope, 17 March 1814, Anon., *Memoir Annexed to an Atlas Containing Plans of the Principal Battles, Sieges, and Affairs in which the British Troops Were Engaged During the War in the Spanish Peninsula and the South of France, from 1808 to 1814*, London, James Wylde, 1841, p. 168.

42. 912L:2088/30, 'Registry of Services'.

43. Oman, *Peninsular War*, Vol. VII, pp. 400–2.

44. Hay, *Reminiscences*, pp. 133–7.

45. 912L:2088/30, 'Registry of Services'.

46. Hay, *Reminiscences*, pp. 138–41. For an outline of this operation as a whole, see

Oman, *Peninsular War*, Vol. VII, pp. 402–4.

47. Oman, *Peninsular War*, Vol. VII, p. 403.
48. Hay, *Reminiscences*, p. 142.
49. Oman, *Peninsular War*, Vol. VII, pp. 404–5.
50. Muir, *Path to Victory*, pp. 583–4.
51. Hay, *Reminiscences*, p. 143.
52. Fletcher, *Galloping at Everything*, pp. 217–19.
53. 912L:2088/30, 'Registry of Services'.
54. Hay, *Reminiscences*, pp. 154–155.
55. Notes to Monthly Return, 25 June 1814, TNA, WO17/272.
56. Oman, *Wellington's Army*, p. 276.
57. Vandeleur to Mother, 19 December 1813, Vandeleur, *Letters*, pp. 138–43.
58. Monthly Returns, TNA, WO17/35, 256, 272. Casualties include the two officers killed in action, but not Myler the commissary who was only attached to the regiment; figures for horses do not include officers' mounts.
59. 912L:2088/30 'Registry of Services'; see also Steuart to Calvert, 28 July 1814, 912L:2088/44, 'Letterbook'.
60. Steuart to Gordon, 9 June 1814, 912L:2088/44, 'Letterbook'.
61. Monthly Return and Notes, 25 August 1814, TNA, WO17/272.
62. See *London Gazette* of 7 April 1815, p. 651, in which these officers were all restored to regimental duty and full pay.
63. Monthly Returns and Notes, August 1814 to March 1815, TNA, WO17/272.
64. Steuart to Officer Commanding, 10 August 1814, 912L:2088/44, 'Letterbook'.
65. Confidential Report, December 1814, TNA, WO27/129.
66. Salmon, 'Ponsonby'.
67. Steuart to Ponsonby, 30 November 1814, 912L:2088/44, 'Letterbook'.
68. 'Copy of Sir James Steuart's Farewell letter to the 12th Light Dragoons on his being called to the command of the Royal North British Dragoons', 18 January 1815, 912L:2088/44, 'Letterbook'.
69. Career summarized from obituary in Urban, Silvanus, *The Gentleman's Magazine and Historical Chronicle, January–June 1831*, London, John Nichols, 1831, p. 466; see also Oman, *Wellington's Army*, pp. 344–6.

Chapter X: Waterloo

1. Hay, *Reminiscences*, p. 157.
2. Ibid.
3. Notes to Monthly Return, 25 March 1815, TNA, WO17/288. On the military response to the riots, see also Bonar, James (ed.), 'The Disposition of Troops in London, March 1815', *English Historical Review*, Vol. 16, No. 62 (April 1901), pp. 348–54.
4. Hay, *Reminiscences*, p. 158; Calvert to Officer Commanding 12th Light Dragoons, 23 March 1815, 912L:2088/5, 'Order Book', p. 1.
5. Calvert to Officer Commanding 12th Light Dragoons, 24 March 1815, 912L:2088/5, 'Order Book', p. 1.
6. Hay, *Reminiscences*, p. 158; 912L:2088/30, 'Registry of Services'.

7. Dalton, Charles, *The Waterloo Roll Call*, London, Eyre and Spottiwoode, 1904, pp. 75–6.

8. Monthly Return and Notes, 25 April 1815, TNA, WO17/288. For a full list of officers embarked with the regiment, see Appendix I.

9. 912L:2088/30, 'Registry of Services'.

10. Regimental Orders, 20 April 1815, 912L:2088/5, 'Order Book', p. 3.

11. Fletcher, *Galloping at Everything*, pp. 221–6.

12. Tomkinson, *Diary*, p. 279. On Uxbridge generally, see Anglesey, Marquess of, *One Leg: The Life and Letters of William Henry Paget, First Marquess of Anglesey, KG, 1768–1854*, London, Leo Cooper, 1996.

13. 912L:2088/30, 'Registry of Services'. Until the final organization was implemented, Vandeleur's command was the Second Brigade.

14. Vandeleur to Mother, 17 May 1815, *Vandeleur*, Letters, pp. 153–8.

15. General Cavalry Orders, 3 May 1815, 912L:2088/5, 'Order Book', p. 5.

16. Regimental Orders, 12 April 1815, 912L:2088/5, 'Order Book', pp. 2–3; see also Brigade Standing Orders, 3 May 1815, Brigade Orders, 5 May 1815: ibid., pp. 3–4.

17. Hay, *Reminiscences*, p. 159.

18. Vandeleur to Mother, 17 May 1815, Vandeleur, *Letters*, pp. 153–8.

19. Hay, *Reminiscences*, pp. 191–3.

20. Return of Courts Martial, TNA, WO27/134.

21. Unless otherwise cited, background on the campaign and battle from Barbero, Alessandro, *The Battle: A History of the Battle of Waterloo*, London, Atlantic, 2005; Fortescue, *British Army*, Vol. X, pp. 256–438; Hofschröer, Peter, *1815: The Waterloo Campaign*, London, Greenhill, 1999.

22. Ponsonby, *Ponsonby Family*, p. 119; this confirms that the account given in Hay, *Reminiscences*, pp. 159–161, is, at best, an embroidered version.

23. Hay, *Reminiscences*, p. 163. See also Tomkinson, *Diary*, pp. 278–9; Vandeleur to Mother, 23 June 1815, Vandeleur, *Letters*, pp. 160–5.

24. Hay, *Reminiscences*, p. 165; Tomkinson, *Diary*, pp. 280–1.

25. Anglesey, *One Leg*, p. 132.

26. Hay, *Reminiscences*, pp. 170–1.

27. See notes in Siborne, Major General H. T. (ed.), *Waterloo Letters*, London, Greenhill, 1993, p. 103, also J. O. Vandeleur to Siborne, 1 November 1845, Vivian to Siborne, 3 June 1839, ibid., pp. 106–7, 150–8.

28. Hay, *Reminiscences*, pp. 173–4.

29. Anglesey, *One Leg*, p. 133.

30. Fletcher, *Galloping at Everything*, pp. 237–66; see p. 257 re. Müffling.

31. Accounts by Ponsonby in Glover, Gareth (ed.), *The Waterloo Archive*, Barnsley, Frontline, 2010–13, Vol. IV, pp. 57–60, and Ponsonby, *Ponsonby Family*, pp. 119–22; letters from officers of the Fourth and Sixth Cavalry Brigades in Siborne, *Waterloo Letters*, pp. 102–22, 145–84; Hay, *Reminiscences*, pp. 176–84; Tomkinson, *Diary*, pp. 300–1; Vandeleur to Mother, 20 and 23 June, Vandeleur, *Letters*, pp. 158–65. I am particularly grateful to Paul L. Dawson for sharing his reinterpretation of this phase of the fighting at Waterloo, based on an extensive study of French as well as British accounts of the fighting. This has

helped reconcile a number of eyewitness accounts that are, on the face of it, at odds with the conventional course of events but which make perfect sense when taken in the context of Paul's reinterpretation. Paul's account is shortly to see publication by Black Tent Publications under the title *Charge the Guns! The Allied Cavalry in the Waterloo Campaign.*

32. J. O. Vandeleur to Siborne, undated, Siborne, *Waterloo Letters*, pp. 105–6; Fletcher, *Galloping at Everything*, p. 257.
33. Account by Ponsonby in Glover, *The Waterloo Archive*, Vol. IV, pp. 57–60; Barton to Siborne, 3 November 1834, Siborne, *Waterloo Letters*, p. 114–17.
34. Hay, *Reminiscences*, p. 178.
35. Fletcher, *Galloping at Everything*, pp. 258–9.
36. Ponsonby to Siborne 29 July 1836, Siborne, *Waterloo Letters*, pp. 112–14.
37. Ponsonby, *Ponsonby Family*, p. 120.
38. Tomkinson, *Diary*, p. 301.
39. Ponsonby to Siborne, 29 July 1836, Siborne, *Waterloo Letters*, pp. 112–14.
40. Tomkinson, *Diary*, p. 303.
41. Stewart, *XII Royal Lancers*, p. 96.
42. Hay, *Reminiscences*, p. 184.
43. Monthly return and Notes, 25 June 1815, TNA, WO17/288. See also Vandeleur to Mother, 20 June 1815, Vandeleur, *Letters*, pp. 158–60; Dalton, *Waterloo Roll Call*, pp. 75–6; 912L:2088/30, 'Registry of Services'.
44. Hay, *Reminiscences*, pp. 182–3.
45. Ibid,, pp. 188–9.
46. Barton to Siborne, 3 November 1834, Siborne, *Waterloo Letters*, pp. 114–17.
47. Sleigh to Siborne, 11 November 1841, Siborne, *Waterloo Letters*, pp. 107–8; Memorandum by Sir Richard Hussey Vivian, 18 January 1830, ibid., pp. 158–60; Hay, *Reminiscences*, p. 191.
48. Vandeleur to Mother, 20 June 1815, Vandeleur, *Letters*, pp. 158–60.
49. Ponsonby, *Ponsonby Family*, pp. 120–2; medical report by Surgeon Hume, ibid., pp. 225–6.
50. Hay, *Reminiscences*, pp. 208–9.
51. Monthly Return, 25 June 1815, TNA, WO17/288.
52. Hay, *Reminiscences*, pp. 198–9.
53. Confidential Report, 30 October 1815; Return of Courts Martial, TNA, WO27/134.
54. Vandeleur to Mother, 1 July 1815, Vandeleur, *Letters*, pp. 165–7
55. Hofschröer, *1815*, Vol. II, pp. 238–78; 912L:2088/30, 'Registry of Services'.

Epilogue

1. Veve, Thomas Dwight, *The Duke of Wellington and the British Army of Occupation in France, 1815–1818*, Westport, Greenwood, 1992, p. 34.
2. Hay, *Reminiscences*, p. 250.
3. 912L:2088/30, 'Registry of Services'.
4. Smurthwaite, Lesley, 'Glory is Priceless: Awards to the British Army during the French Revolutionary and Napoleonic Wars', in Guy, Alan J. (ed.), *The Road to*

Waterloo: The British Army and the Struggle Against Revolutionary and Napoleonic France, London, Alan Sutton, 1990, pp. 164–83.

5. Fletcher, *Galloping at Everything*, pp. 163–4.
6. Stewart, *XII Royal Lancers*, pp. 100–2; 912L:2088/30, 'Registry of Services'.
7. Stewart, *XII Royal Lancers*, pp. 101–2.
8. Veve, *Army of Occupation*, pp. 40–1.
9. Henry, 'Steuart Denham'.
10. Bunbury, Turtle, 'Browne Clayton of Browne's Hill, Co. Carlow', at http://www.turtlebunbury.com/history/history_family/hist_family_b_clayton.html.
11. Ponsonby, *Ponsonby Family*, pp. 122–5.
12. Vandeleur, *Letters*, pp. vi–vii.
13. Hay, *Reminiscences*, pp. 105–6.
14. Haythornthwaite, *Armies of Wellington*, pp. 18–19.
15. Bamford, *Sickness, Suffering, and the Sword*, pp. 44–85.

Index